Advanced Techniques
for Java™ Developers

Revised Edition

Daniel J. Berg

J. Steven Fritzinger

Wiley Computer Publishing

John Wiley & Sons, Inc.

NEW YORK · CHICHESTER · WEINHEIM · BRISBANE · SINGAPORE · TORONTO

Publisher: Robert Ipsen
Editor: Robert M. Elliott
Assistant Editor: Pam Sobotka
Managing Editor: Brian Snapp
Electronic Products, Associate Editor: Mike Sosa
Text Design & Composition: North Market Street Graphics, Lancaster, PA

Library of Congress Cataloging-in-Publication Data:

Berg, Daniel J.
    Advanced techniques for Java developers / Daniel J. Berg, J.
   Steven Fritzinger. — Rev. ed.
       p.   cm.
   Includes index.
    ISBN 0-471-32718-2 (pbk./CD-ROM : alk. paper)
    1. Java (Computer program language)   I. Fritzinger, J. Steven,
  1962– . II. Title.
  QA76.73.J38B48 1999
  005.13'3—dc21
                                 98-41506
                                      CIP

Printed in the United States of America.

10 9 8 7 6 5 4 3 2 1

Contents

Acknowledgments   xi

Reader's Guide to the Book   xiii

Chapter 1   The Java™ Industry   1

Introduction   1

The Java Platforms   4

ISO and Java   9

HotJava Browser   9

HotJava Views   9

JavaOS   10

JavaServer   10

Java Electronic Commerce   10

JavaSpaces   10

Jini   11

Java Naming and Directory Interface   11

Summary   11

Chapter 2   Understanding the Java Foundation Classes   13

Introduction   13

Delegation Event Model   15

Desktop Colors   24

Printing   27

ScrollPane Container   30

Popup Menu   32

Mouseless Operation   33

Data Transfer   36

Lightweight Component Framework   43

The Swing Set   46

Drag and Drop   50

Java 2D   51

Summary   51

Chapter 3   **Using Java Media**   **53**

Introduction   53

Welcome to Java City!   53

Design: Reaching Java City by Bridge from the Old World
to the New   54

Java Media API Overview   57

Java City Implementation   63

A Recipe for a Multimedia Web Using the JMF, Java 2D,
and Java Sound   66

Using Java 2D in Java City   70

Using Java 3D to Implement a Virtual Reality Experience
of Java City   71

Chapter 4   **Mastering Networking and I/O Techniques**   **73**

Introduction   73

Basic Networking Principles   74

Java Networking Principles   76

Networking and Java Input and Output   87

Summary   97

Chapter 5   **Using JavaBeans**   **99**

Introduction   99

JavaBeans Design Goal   99

Bean Events   103

Bean Properties   103

Bean Reflection and Introspection   105

Bean Customization   111

The Glasgow Additions   113

Summary   114

Chapter 6   **Designing Distributed Applications**   **115**

Introduction   115

Application Architectures   116

The Three-Tiered Advantage   123

Deploying Three-Tiered Applications   128

Limits of the Three-Tiered Architecture   130

Making the Move   133

Integrating Legacy Systems   136

Using the Java Platform in the Enterprise   139

Summary   143

Chapter 7   **Mastering Java Remote Method Invocation Techniques**   **145**

Introduction   145

Building on Past Experiences   146

Back to the Drawing Board   148

Distributed Systems Contrasted   149

RMI Design Goals   151

RMI System Architecture   152

Distributed Programming with RMI   154

A Simple RMI Client/Server Example   155

Callbacks from Server to Client   164

Passing Objects as Method Arguments   168

Remote Polymorphism at Last   171

RMI and the Java Servlet API   176

	Object Serialization Examples	179
	The Future of Java RMI	183
	Summary	184
Chapter 8	**Mastering JDBC Techniques**	**185**
	Introduction	185
	JDBC Architecture	187
	Using JDBC	189
	Anatomy of a JDBC Application	191
	Callable Statements	204
	Handling Large Data Fields	205
	Adding Value to an RDBMS	207
	JDBC 2.0	216
	Summary	220
Chapter 9	**Servlets and the Java Web Server**	**221**
	Introduction	221
	The Java Web Server Platform	222
	Advantages of Servlets	222
	A Simple Servlet	224
	Anatomy of an HTTP Servlet	225
	Installing the Servlet	228
	Some Considerations with Java Web Server	233
	Core Servlets	236
	User Input	236
	Using Init Parameters	242
	Servlet Beans	244
	Page Compilation	248
	Templates	250
	Session Tracking	256
	Servlets and the Java Enterprise APIs	259
	Summary	266

Chapter 10 Enterprise JavaBeans   **267**

Introduction   267

Enterprise JavaBeans   268

Example Session Bean   271

Choosing a Container   277

Under the Hood of EJBs   277

Example Entity Bean   279

EJB Architectures   287

Summary   290

Chapter 11 Using Java Threads   **291**

Introduction   291

What Are Threads?   291

Using Java Threads   294

Scheduling   304

Synchronization   313

Java on Multiprocessor Systems   327

Thread-Safe Classes   328

Java Threads versus POSIX   328

Summary   329

Chapter 12 Java Security   **331**

Introduction   331

Java Security Fundamentals   334

Security, Applets, and Web Browsers   346

Security, Applications, and the Enterprise   351

Extending the Security Model   352

Protection Domains and Java Applications   367

The Java Cryptography Extension   368

Security-Related Bugs   374

Summary   376

Chapter 13   Using the Java Native Method Interface   379

Introduction   379

The JNI   380

Method Naming   384

Parameter Naming   385

Referencing Data from a Native Method   387

Accessing Java Fields and Methods   389

Error Handling from Native Methods   391

Invoking Java from Native Code   391

Summary   394

Chapter 14   Understanding Network Computers   395

Introduction   395

What Is a Network Computer?   396

Is a PC an NC?   399

Network Computer Advantages   401

The Network Computer Market   404

Network Computer Competitors   408

Designing Applications for Network Computers   410

When Is My Client Too Big?   415

Deploying and Managing Network Computers   417

A Fallacy of Cost and Benefits   422

Summary   424

Chapter 15   Understanding JavaOS and JavaStation Details 425

Introduction   425

Overview of Sun's JavaStation Family   425

Summary   441

JavaOS   442

The "Main" Application (HotJava?)   457

JavaStation Software Bundle (Netra j)   463

Future Directions 464

Summary 466

Chapter 16 The Future of Java   **469**

Introduction 469

The Java Revolution 470

Vertical Market APIs 472

Maintaining Simplicity 474

Hegemony of the Java Platform 475

New Application Architectures 478

Jini 483

Summary 484

Appendix A   Further Reading   **485**

Appendix B   Authors on the Net   **487**

Index   **491**

Acknowledgments

Since this book is a multiperson effort, each one of us has some special people to thank. But first some acknowledgments from all of us:

Many thanks to all the people at Wiley for the effort in producing this book. Special thanks go to Bob Elliott, our editor, Emilie Herman, our point person, and Brian Snapp, our production manager.

A very special acknowledgment goes to James Gosling and Scott McNealy. James, a Senior Vice President and Fellow at Sun Microsystems, gave birth to the Java language environment and brought new life to the Internet, and Scott, Chief Executive Officer at Sun Microsystems, runs a cool company where we all can explore new technologies and work with the best people in the industry!

From Daniel:

I would first like to thank all the authors who have contributed to this book. Without you guys this book would have never happened! Thanks, guys! I would also like to thank my management at Sun, Matt Delcambre and Enis Konuk, for providing an environment where I could learn, design, develop, and understand Java technologies, as well as for their continued support of my publications. I would also like to thank the National Java Team and the Java ACES (a group of Java experts) for the exchange of ideas, problems, and solutions. And last, but not least, I would like to thank my wife Elaine for putting up with all the late nights and weekends when we could have been spending time together. I promise this is the last one! (At least until another great book idea comes along . . . just kidding.) Oh, and thanks to Samson and Barkley (my German Shepherds) for diligently waiting by my side while I was writing. Woof Woof!

From Steven:

Many thanks to Maurice Balick, Marianne Mueller, and Li Gong for their help in providing such great information. To my wife Claire, whose support made this revision possible. Oh, and my Golden Retriever, Hank, also made many invaluable contributions.

From David:

To my gorgeous bride, Julia, who has added more to my life than I could ever say. And to my "little buddy," Randy, for whom I do almost everything now. Even at 10 mph, I have time for you both.

From Doug:

Special thanks to Ann Wollrath, Jim Waldo, and Ken Arnold, who were the key creators of the Java RMI system, and who have been very helpful in sharing their knowledge and expertise. Also special thanks to Daniel Hiltgen, a student intern at JavaSoft during the time of this writing, who provided programming examples for the RMI chapter (Daniel has a bright future in software engineering).

From Geordie (aka Goose):

My involvement with this book would not have been possible without the assistance of numerous people. I would like to thank Mike Peck for bringing me into Sun, and giving me the opportunity to work with the finest group of individuals I've ever been involved with. Matt Delcambre assumed "ownership" of me some time later, and has been extraordinarily supportive of my various endeavors. Vic Bahl was the first person to suggest that I publish some of the material I've learned about JavaOS; he convinced me that I might actually be capable of writing. Of course, none of this would have been possible without the help of Dan Berg. Dan gave me the opportunity to try my hand at being an author, and his confidence in my abilities was an incredible motivational influence.

Finally, I'd like to thank the folks that read my initial drafts and provided feedback: Jill Debord, Chris Pane, and Bill Hoagland.

You all rule! I'm not worthy . . . I'm not worthy . . .

From Barton:

To my wife, Suzanne, for her never-ending patience, and to C.O. Fiske.

Reader's Guide to the Book

This is just what the world needs, another book on the Java™ language. Nothing in the computer industry has taken off faster than Java. With this rise in popularity, a plethora of books have been written covering Java. Well, we hope that this book will be a benefit to developers who want a better understanding of Java's advanced technologies as well as the techniques used to develop real-world Java applications. We did not focus solely on the Java language or APIs. Instead, we wanted to bring real added value, and share our knowledge and experiences in working with Java. We focus on the concepts, technology, and design principals needed to build most of today's large-scale applications. The book also contains the latest features that were added to Java™ 2 (formerly code-named JDK™ 1.2, the latest update to the Java Development Kit). Many of the ideas and examples that are presented are based on work we have done on real applications with some of the earliest corporate users of Java. All of these users of Java have helped in shaping online Java systems which are doing business today or are soon to be released. We hope that you find this book useful in your own developments, not only by explaining some of the new Java technologies, but also by sharing our experiences and techniques. Enjoy!

The following is a quick overview of the contents of each chapter. Although there is no real step-by-step flow between the chapters, we have tried to lay out the book in a logical reading and learning pattern. However, feel free to jump ahead to any chapter and go right to the topic that interests you.

Chapter 1 covers what's new in the Java industry and which APIs and packages are available: the new Java 2 (formerly JDK 1.2), Java Media, JECF, JNDI, JavaServer, JavaOS, HotJava, and much more. Some of the topics discussed are covered in more detail in following chapters. Other topics are simply introduced.

Chapter 2 covers the new Java foundation classes (JFCs). The JFC encompasses the abstract windowing toolkit (AWT), the Swing set of lightweight components, and other new graphical features. There are many new features that have been added to the AWT and in the JFC; this chapter describes the details of these new features.

Chapter 3 focuses on using Java Media, which is a set of new Java APIs and packages that add to Java's multimedia capabilities. The Java Media packages include: Java 2D, Java 3D, Java Media Framework, Java Sound, JavaShare, Java Animation, Java Telephony, Java Speech, and Java Advanced Imaging. This chapter describes the pieces of Java Media and how to use its features.

Chapter 4 covers mastering networking and input/output (I/O) techniques. This chapter covers Java's networking and I/O capabilities and how to use them in your applications. It does not go through all the basics, but covers the features used in most common applications. The chapter also shows some networking and I/O techniques used in developing Java applications. (Almost every application will involve some sort of networking and I/O functions.)

Chapter 5 deals with JavaBeans components. What are JavaBeans? This chapter introduces JavaBeans, the framework used in developing and using them, and the techniques involved in developing your own beans. It also discusses the benefit of JavaBeans and their use in any component architecture.

Chapter 6 covers some of the concepts used in designing and developing today's network applications. It shows how applications can be designed in a multitier environment and how such applications can utilize the resources on a network. Many of the concepts and techniques discussed in this chapter can be applied to the application technologies discussed in the rest of this book.

Chapter 7 covers Java's remote method invocation (RMI) packages, object serialization, and Java's use in the CORBA world. All of these technologies can be used to invoke and execute objects running in different address spaces. Distributed object processing is one focus, as well as how these objects can be used in the Java environment. All of the technologies and techniques discussed in this chapter can be used to develop and deploy distributed network-based applications.

Chapter 8 covers the mastering of JDBC techniques. The Java database connection (JDBC) packages allow Java programs to communicate with databases. Databases are used in almost every application handled. This chapter discusses the features and benefits of JDBC packages as well as their use in Java applications. Even if you don't know all there is to know about databases, this chapter shows the techniques needed to easily access most databases on the market.

Chapter 9 covers the JavaServer packages. The JavaServer is a new HTTP-based, all-Java Web server and a set of application APIs that can interact with the server. Since the JavaServer is written in Java, it can run on any of the Java platforms. This chapter also introduces the concept and use of servlets.

Chapter 10 covers the Enterprise JavaBeans specification and the new generation of application servers which are being implemented in transaction processors, database engines, and Web servers. Systems which implement the Enterprise JavaBeans specification enable scalable, manageable, highly distributed enterprise applications while preserving the Java platform's core value proposition of Write Once, Run Anywhere applications.

Chapter 11 covers the basic and advanced topics used in creating Java programs that use threads. Threads are part of the Java language and can be used quite easily in any Java program. This chapter will cover the use of threads in Java programs as well as the benefits and pitfalls that thread use may bring to your applications.

Chapter 12 focuses on understanding Java security. Security must be one of the most discussed topics when talking about Java. This chapter covers, in depth, the Java security model. It covers the applet security sandbox and the new protected domain model as well. The concepts discussed in this chapter can been used to design and develop some of the most secure applications in the market today.

Chapter 13 covers the Java native method interface (JNI). The JNI can be used to call programs that exist outside of the Java virtual machine as well as native programs calling into Java. The JNI can also be used to extend or replace some of the capabilities of Java. The concepts in this chapter will show the use of the JNI functions as well as when and why they should be used.

Chapter 14 focuses on understanding network computers. Network computers seem to be the hot topic in the computer industry. This chapter discusses what a network computer is and its reference platform. The chapter shows the real use of network computers without all the hype that surrounds them. It also details some of the design and development constraints that must be applied when developing applications for network computers.

Chapter 15 expands on Chapter 13 by detailing an implementation of a network computer as well as its operating environment. It goes into the internals and details of JavaOS and the JavaStation. It also details some of the benefits and pitfalls of network computers and their software operations.

Chapter 16 goes past the topics that we have discussed in the book to look at the possible future of Java. It also discusses what future application products may look like. Since Java is a quickly moving environment, this chapter should give you some insight to Java's upcoming directions.

For further information and updates, please see the companion Web site at www.wiley.com/compbooks/berg/.

CHAPTER 1

The Java™ Industry

Introduction

How did the Java language go from being a language to being an industry? Java has moved faster into acceptance than any other modern technology. It is no longer just a language, it has become much more.

The first alpha version of Java was published on the Internet in May of 1995 and it received one of the most enthusiastic responses of any language in the history of computing. Much of this enthusiasm existed because Java arrived at a time when the then-emerging World Wide Web faced a great problem: How do you publish complex, active data on the Web without maintaining many different versions of a custom helper application (one for each interesting hardware platform and operating system combination on the Web), and without forcing visitors to a site to find, fetch, and install the proper version of that helper before actually seeing any of the information on that site? By allowing Web publishers to publish both information and the application needed to make that information usable, and by delivering the application automatically to the site's visitor regardless of what platform the visitor was using, Java solved the helper application problem and became known as "the programming language for the Internet." This Write Once, Run Anywhere (hardware agnostic) capability would prove to be one of the biggest strengths of Java.

The Java platform's reputation was enhanced by its elegant and powerful language. The Java language combined a pure object-oriented programming model with a C-like syntax and notation which was familiar to two generations of programmers. In this way, while Java avoided the drawbacks of a hybrid object model, like that found in C++, it was still easily accessible to programmers working in C and C++. Especially for those developers already familiar with the concepts of the object-oriented methodology, the move to Java was almost painless.

Many of the important ideas incorporated into Java were not new; by 1995, object-oriented programming was already 30 years old. Architecturally neutral interpreters who could run the same executable on any supported platform had been familiar since the Berkeley P-System in the early '80s and the idea of small, network-distributable applets could be found in the Network extensible Window System (NeWS—James Gosling's mid-'80s, PostScript-based language and windowing system that in many ways was the intellectual forebear to Java). There was also an element of timing and good luck in the success of Java. The rise of the Web provided not only a compelling problem for Java to solve, it also provided a legion of developers eager to use the new platform and a way to distribute the results of their labors. The Web's ethic that all software used in support of the Web should be freely and widely available ensured that Java would be widely accepted.

The roots of Java as a programming environment for embedded systems shaped its design goals. From the beginning, Java was designed to be small, simple, safe, and secure. Small, because the handheld devices and settop boxes for which Java was designed did not have the 10s or 100s of megabytes of memory expected in a desktop machine. Simple, because popular operating systems and programming environments had grown so complex that few, if any, developers could fully understand and effectively use the systems. Safe, because users expected much higher levels of reliability and robustness from consumer devices than they expected from desktop computers; a desktop computer that failed to compute three times a week was considered normal while a toaster which failed to make toast once a year would result in angry letters to the manufacturer. And secure, because Sun's vision that "The Network is the Computer" demanded that these embedded devices be able to share executables over a network without compromising security.

These goals, while not intended for a Web-like environment, turned out to be critical to the acceptance of Java on the Web. Small, because Java applets would have to travel over thin pipes, like 28.8 modems, to get to the users. Simple, because the Web's Internet time–driven development cycle, many times shorter than traditional cycles, wouldn't slow down Web developers by the bulk and complexity of most 3GLs. Safe, because it is fundamentally harder to write buggy code in Java than in other system level languages; 30 years of experience with 3GLs have proven that programmers were simply not very good at the tedious bookkeeping tasks of memory management, pointer manipulation, and other rote functions forced on them by most languages. Secure, because users of the Web needed to be able to visit an unfamiliar site and have executable content thrust on them without fear of Trojan horses, viruses, and other coding nasties.

Java Goes to Work

Although the initial hype surrounding Java concentrated on the World Wide Web, the last 18 months have shown that Java will have an even greater impact behind firewalls on corporate intranets. This move to corporate computing has been driven by the realization that Internet technologies work just as well in-house as they do for communicating with customers and suppliers.

By moving to Internet standards like TCP/IP, Web browsers, and IMAP4, these corporations have found that they could modernize their IT systems using inexpensive, off-the-shelf products; build more flexible and adaptive applications; and reduce operating costs by replacing aging proprietary networking schemes.

Once a corporation had installed TCP/IP and a Web browser on every desktop, it could easily share data among its employees and, for fairly static information like employee handbooks and policy manuals, move from traditional paper publishing to much less costly Web publishing. After getting its feet wet with this purely informational use of the intranet, the next logical step was to develop transactional, business systems for the intranet. While Web browsers were becoming more capable of handling non-HTML information like e-mail, audio, and video, no browser manufacturer was including a travel authorization or expense accounting helper application with their off-the-shelf browser.

This is where Java comes in. Write Once, Run Anywhere clients are just as important on a heterogeneous intranet as on the Internet. With the extreme time pressure on most corporate development efforts, a simple, safe language that makes programmers more productive by keeping them in the editor and out of the debugger is a great boon. Finally, the idea of treating Java not as a programming language for a particular platform like a Windows PC or UNIX workstation, but as the fundamental computing platform, has proven to be a valuable conceptual shift. Programming to the pure Java platform protects the Write Once, Run Anywhere attribute by avoiding hidden OS-specific hooks found in some Java implementations and development tools. The Java Platform also allows applications written for traditional platforms, like PCs, to move to very nontraditional devices. SmartCards, telephones and telephone switches, networks peripherals, and Network Computers can now run Java applications. Instead of needing high-level and assembler languages and operating systems in order to exploit these nontraditional platforms, the Java platform covers all these devices with a single language, programming model, and OS. Java has even breathed new life into the handheld and settop-box markets for which it was originally designed.

Unfinished Work

As in any revolution, the initial release of Java left much work to be done. These unfinished tasks include Internationalization support, which was simply missing from the 1.0 version of the Java Developer's Kit (JDK). Many of these omissions have been corrected in the JDK 1.1 and Java™ 2 (formerly code-named JDK 1.2). Some of the unfinished tasks, though, stemmed not from recognized deficiencies in JDK 1.0, but from the recognition of Java as a true platform (not just a language) and from the growing sophistication of Java developers. Security restrictions placed on applets began to chafe. Business developers demanded more powerful networking tools and protocols along with access to legacy systems like databases and transaction processors. Corporate IT shops also demanded more powerful development tools for individual developers (editors, debuggers, visual GUI builders, etc.) and large development teams (application design tools, documentation and source code control systems, componentware and object repositories).

These needs have influenced both the development of Java 2 and many parallel efforts, both inside Sun and in the industry as whole, intended to round out the Java platform and spread it into new environments.

The Java Platforms

What exactly are the Java platforms? In order to answer this question, we must first find out what types of Java environments are available. There are four major types of Java environments available or under development: the general workstation platform, the Personal Java platform, the embedded Java platform, and the JavaCard platform. Each of these platforms provides Java capabilities to a particular class of hardware environments, including PCs, consumer electronics, smart cards, computer chips, and computer profiles. These Java environments are capable of running on a multitude of hardware platforms which make the number of Java-supported platforms enormous.

The Workstation Java Platform

The general Java platform was typically known as the JDK, usually referred to as the developer's kit for computer workstations or PCs. The current release, Java 2 (previously JDK 1.2), added several enhancements and bug fixes to the Java platform. The following is a short review of the changes.

Collections

A new set of APIs was added to Java 2 to support collections of objects. The Collection API provides a simple framework to organize and store multiple objects in a single container, making it easier for different APIs to communicate and pass data. Instead of passing a list of data, an API can pass a single collection which can contain multiple objects.

The Collection API provides a simple set of objects that can be used to store other objects, including Collection objects that can store a group of objects that may or may not be ordered, duplicated, or mutable. All of these objects can be used to store objects in different ways. For example, a set object may be used to store nonduplicate objects, and a table object may be used to store simple key and value mappings for objects in the collection.

Versioning

Versioned software is nothing new; as software systems change, a way of tracking such changes is needed. Java is no different; a way of tracking and discovering different versions of a piece of software is needed. Java 2 added some new methods that make it easy for a developer to discover the version of a particular piece of code. It is not enough to know what version a piece of code is in Java; we must also have a way to find the version of the Java Virtual Machine and the Java runtime. All of this is provided with a few new methods, some of which have been added to the System class to return information about the JavaVM and the runtime. For example, java.lang.Package class was added to gain information about a particular Java package, and a getPackage() method was added to the Class class. All of these methods can be used to gain information about Java and any of its packages; using a Package object, we can determine a package's name, version number, vendor or package supplier, package specification title, and the specification version. All of this information can be very useful to developers who need to know which particular package version is desired.

Serialization Enhancements

Several changes were made to Java serialization capabilities. The serialization process now includes the ability to access individual fields in a serialized class. This ability does not affect how serialization takes place but simply adds a way to access serialized fields in any given class. Before this addition, it was not possible to access a single field in a given serialized class. A Replaceable interface was also added to serialization, allowing a developer to replace a value before a field is serialized or just after it has been deserialized. This capability permits a current value to be substituted for a serialized value. Chapter 5 discusses and uses some of the new changes made to Java serialization capabilities.

Audio

Several changes were made to Java sound capabilities in Java 2. Most of the changes did not involve API changes; rather, the entire sound engine was replaced, providing enhanced capabilities such as the ability to play MIDI, .wav, aiff, and .au files. The sound engine also has a much better audio quality. None of these changes should affect how you use the audio capabilities of Java today.

One new API change that was made was the addition of a static method to retrieve an audio clip. The getNewAudioClip() method was added to the java.Applet class to provide developers with a way to gain access to an audio clip without having to use an AppletContext.

JavaBeans

JavaBeans provides a standard environment for developing software components. Although JavaBeans were added to the JDK 1.1, many enhancements have been made. Chapter 5 covers JavaBeans as well as the new enhancements.

JFC

The Java Foundation Class (JFC) have enhanced the AWT by adding a new set of lightweight components. The key to the JFC is in providing a portable cross-platform graphical environment that looks and behaves the same on all platforms. This functionality answers many of the problems that arise when you are developing graphical user interfaces (GUIs) for multiple environments. The JFC is covered in detail in Chapter 2.

Security

Java 2 added a new Java security API that provides developers with easy-to-use and secure functionality for all Java programs. Some of the new functionality includes digital signatures, encryption, authentication, and the protected domain concept, all of which are covered in Chapter 12.

Performance Improvements

There are several performance improvements that have been made to Java 2, one of which involves how constant strings are used in classes. String constants are now stored in a common location in the virtual machine and are shared across different classes, permitting the strings to be shared among classes that use the same constants, which reduces the amount of memory needed to store the strings.

Another enhancement has to do with how a program's heap is stored. The heap used to be common among all threads in a Java program; now a thread local heap is used, aiding in performance because the virtual machine no longer has to lock the entire heap when performing certain operations. One operation that has improved due to this change is garbage collection—the garbage collector can now lock a single thread's heap to perform the memory collection. This aids in how much time the garbage collector has a hold of the virtual machine's stack. As well, Java monitors have benefited from this change, reducing the time it takes to synchronize threads.

Java 2 also uses the JNI libraries to access native code that is used in the virtual machine. For example, the AWT peers are now accessed via the JNI functions.

There are also several other technologies that have been added to Java, such as Java 2D, Servlets, database connectivity, and RMI. All of these subjects are covered in detail in later chapters in this book.

Java Runtime Environment

The Java runtime environment (JRE) is simply Java 2 minus the development tools needed to create Java programs. The JRE is ideal for shipping with an application or installing on a computer, and provides the JavaVM and all the classes needed to run Java programs. Once you develop a Java application using Java 2 or other development tool, all you need on the computer on which you would like to run the application is the JRE. Table 1.1 shows a list of current JDKs and JREs for many different computer platforms.

Personal Java

Personal Java, a Java application environment designed for use on personal consumer devices where the requirements for a Java environment are quite different from a typical desktop computer system, consists of a set of core and extension APIs that have been designed for use on resource-limited environments. However, since Personal Java is a feature subset of the normal Java environment, any Personal Java applications written will run on a full-blown Java environment.

Personal Java is really just a small Java environment that can easily be ported to many different devices, in this case typically limited in memory, storage, and price. Personal Java makes it easy for consumer electronic software developers by providing them with a common platform on which to develop.

Embedded Java

Not much can be said about Embedded Java since it was still under development at the writing of this book. What we can say is that the Embedded Java

Table 1.1   The Java Platforms

PLATFORM OR OPERATING ENVIRONMENT	WHERE TO GET IT
AIX	http://www.ibm.com/Java
Amiga	http://www.finale-dev.com/java.html
BeOS	http://www.cyberclip.com/Be/coffeeBEan.html
Digital UNIX	http://www.unix.digital.com/products/internet/java.html
FreeBSD	http://www.csi.uottawa.ca/~kwhite/javaport.html
HP 3000	http://jazz.external.hp.com/src/java/index.html
HP-UX	http://hpcc997.external.hp.com/gsyinternet/hpjdk
IRIX	http://www.sgi.com/Fun/Free_webtools.html
Linux	http://www.blackdown.org/java-linux.html
MacOS	http://applejava.apple.com/index.html
Netware 4.1	http://java.novell.com
OpenServer 5	http://www.sco.com/developer/SCO Developer's Place
OS/2 Warp	http://www.ibm.com/Java
OS/390, OS/400	http://www.ibm.com/Java
Psion Series 3	http://www.inet.alsutton.com
RiscOS, RiscBSD	http://www.cs.waikato.ac.nz/~pnaulls/java
Solaris	http://www.sun.com/solaris/new/java
SunOS-4.X	http://www.csi.uottawa.ca/~kwhite/javaport.html
Unix Ware	http://www.sco.com/developer
Windows 95/NT	http://java.sun.com/products/jdk
Kaffe	http://www.kaffe.org

platform is designed for use in high-volume embedded devices, including network routers, switches, pages, phones, peripherals, control devices, etc. Embedded Java applications will be able to take advantage of existing real-time operating environments in order to take advantage of a particular device's capabilities. The Embedded Java platform has also been customized for use in constrained environments such as those provided in embedded electronics.

JavaCard

The JavaCard API is a specialized application interface that enables a new generation of smart card technology. This technology will allow smart cards to be used in electronic commerce, authentication, network access, gaming application, and much more. The key as always with Java is that the applications can be written using the JavaCard API and then will be able to run on any smart card device. The JavaCard API is tuned for the limited environment that exists in smart cards and is the only industry standard language and API for ISO 7816-4–compliant smart cards.

ISO and Java

Sun's goal is to make Java a standard. In many ways Java is already a standard, but Sun would like to make it a formal ISO standard. Standardization of Java is key for companies and governments that require certain standard levels; as well, it would help in assuring a user's investment in Java. Sun has submitted Java to become both a publicly available standard and a submitter to the standard through ISO's joint technical committee (JTC) which is ISO's information technology body. If passed, Sun will have the right to submit Java specification to the JTC for consideration.

HotJava Browser

The HotJava browser, sold by JavaSoft, is an HTML browser written entirely in Java; the browser is scalable, extensible, and customizable. Not only that, but this browser can run on any Java platform without any application code changes.

HotJava Views

HotJava Views is a pure Java-based desktop environment that can be used on network computers as well as regular desktop computers to provide a common-look-and-feel environment to Web users. This environment includes HTML browsing capabilities and some utilities such as an e-mail tool, a calendar tool, and a rolodex tool. HotJava Views can be used in place of a desktop and browser since it provides common desktop tools and browsing capabilities.

JavaOS

JavaOS, a tuned environment for the hardware platform on which it runs, provides a new Java platform for a variety of hardware environments. You can think of JavaOS as an environment that provides all the services of a normal JavaVM without requiring an operating system on which to run. This means that JavaOS can run in place of common operating systems on most hardware platforms. JavaOS is discussed in more detail in Chapters 13 and 14.

JavaServer

The JavaServer provides an Internet server written entirely in Java. This makes the HTTP server portable to all Java platforms and makes it easier for Java applications to communicate with the server. JavaServer is discussed in more detail in Chapter 9.

Java Electronic Commerce

The Java Electronic Commerce Framework (JECF) provides a secure and extensible framework for conducting business on the Internet as well as regular corporate networks. This framework will provide several levels of electronic commerce support, including the user interaction, currency transfers, and supplier integration. The ubiquity of Java will make JECF an easy choice for applications that need to do network-based commerce.

JavaSpaces

JavaSpaces provides a distributed persistence and data-exchange mechanism for Java-based applications. Distributed applications can take advantage of JavaSpaces to write data in a typed environment which groups and stores data in a safe manner. This data can then be read or updated in the space in which it was stored. This type of data persistence makes it easy for distributed object-based application to communicate and exchange data.

Jini

The Jini system is a Java-centric distributed computing system designed around the goals of simplicity, flexibility, and federation. The Jini system allows a group of machines to be federated together, allowing users of these machines to share resources in a simple, uniform way. The design of the system exploits the ability to move Java code from machine to machine.

Java Naming and Directory Interface

The Java Naming and Directory Interface (JNDI) provides an industry-standard way of connecting Java applications to other non-Java naming and directory services. This allows enterprisewide services to coordinate and communicate with other services in a uniform manner.

Summary

As you can see, there are more changes in the Java world than just Java 2. Many of the packages and capabilities will soon be available if they are not already. We are also sure that by the time you read this book many more features and capabilities will be added to the Java industry mix. If you are anything like us, you will look forward to learning about all the new technologies that make their way into Java. Take a seat and buckle up; it is going to be a fun ride!

Understanding the Java Foundation Classes

Introduction

Since the release of the JDK 1.1, the abstract windowing toolkit (AWT) has come a long way from where it started in 1995. There have been a vast number of changes and additions to the AWT, all of which make it a stronger windowing toolkit. If you have used the original AWT, then you may have run into some of its limiting factors. Instead of spending time talking about the old AWT and the problems it had, we will focus on the JDK 1.1 AWT and the new Java foundation classes (JFC). The JFC is not really an addition to the AWT; it is more of an umbrella that covers the AWT and the new lightweight components. The AWT still exists; it is now just part of the JFC. The role of the AWT has changed quite dramatically since the release of the JDK 1.1. It is no longer a cute little toolkit for producing platform-independent applications. It is now a full-featured toolkit that permits developers to deliver quality, full-featured user interfaces for Java applets and applications.

This chapter will cover the following AWT changes:

- **Delegation event model:** This is the event model that was added to the AWT to provide a flexible and scalable event mechanism. This is the same event mechanism that can be used throughout the Java classes as well as JavaBeans and the JFC.

- **Desktop color:** Desktop color provides the integration of common desktop color models with Java applications. This ability makes it easy for end users to choose the color scheme used when running Java applications.

- **Printing:** It may sound odd, but before the JDK 1.1 you could not print from Java programs. This new feature provides a simple interface from which you can print the contents of Java applications.

- **ScrollPane:** The addition of the ScrollPane class provides the ability to scroll AWT components.

- **Popup menus:** Popup menus were added to the list of widgets available to developers. We will show you how easy it can be to add these widgets to your programs.

- **Mouseless operation:** Do you think using a mouse is too slow? Well the JDK 1.1 added the ability to control graphical interfaces without using a mouse.

- **Data transfer and clipboard:** This is also known as cut and paste. You can now cut and paste information between Java programs as well as non-Java programs.

With the recent release of the JFC, we will cover many of its new features, including:

- **Lightweight component framework:** We will discuss the addition of lightweight components to the AWT as well as their use in the JFC.

- **JFC components:** There are a number of new high-level comments that have been added to the JFC. This set of components is also known as the swing set.

- **JavaBeans integration:** We will discuss how the new JFC components can act as JavaBeans as well as how they can interoperate with other JavaBeans.

- **Pluggable look and feel:** There has always been a heated debate over how graphical interface should look and feel. Well, now you can chose the look and feel of your interface or design your own.

- **Drag and Drop:** Drag and drop provides the ability to move data in a graphical manner between applications. The drag-and-drop capabilities that were added to the JFC will permit you to move data between Java applications as well as other native non-Java applications.

- **Java 2D:** The Java 2D API extends the capabilities of the standard AWT graphics by added high-quality graphical rendering libraries. This will permit developers to further extend the graphical abilities of Java programs.

There are enough changes and additions to the AWT that an entire book could be written just to cover the intricacies. We will give you a taste of the new features and their use, but in most cases we will not cover all of the minute details of the feature. If you have a need to understand all the ins and outs of the new AWT, we would refer you to a book that solely covers the AWT.

Since the JFC depends on features that were added to the AWT in the JDK 1.1, we will start with those features; then we will discuss the additions of the JFC.

Delegation Event Model

The event mechanism in Java is essential to building interactive event-driven applications. Events in Java provide the means for one object to communicate with another object by sending a message from the sender to the receiver. For example, a button may want to notify the program that it has been pressed by the user. This notification is given in the form of a Java event.

Event Objects

Events are the messages that are passed from one object to another. These messages are passed from the event source to one or more event listeners (see Figure 2.1). When the event is passed it causes a method to be invoked in the target listener object. The event itself is an object and can contain certain information or state about the particular event. The event object also acts as the only argument that is passed to the event listener.

Every event object in Java must extend the java.util.EventObject class. The convention for naming these events is to add the "Event" word to the end of the name of the event object. For example, if we wanted to create a new event called "Keyboard" we would define the event as:

```
public class KeyboardEvent extends java.util.EventObject {
  private char key;
  KeyboardEvent(java.awt.Component source, char key) {
    super(source);
    this.key = key;
  }
}
```

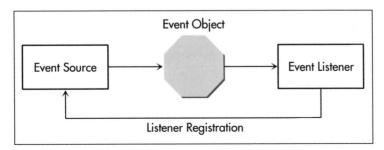

Figure 2.1 Event mechanism.

This example defines a new event called KeyboardEvent. In some cases you may want to create a new event object that just renames a particular event which would allow you to create a new type for the event. Similar techniques are used in creating new types of exceptions in Java.

Since events are objects, you can define methods and variables just like any other Java object. However, event objects should really be considered immutable. This means that the event objects data should not be visible outside of the object. You can create methods for the event object that are visible outside of the object. These methods can then be used to modify the internal state of the object. In the case of bean event objects you will want to define these methods following certain design patterns that allow other JavaBeans and other non-beans components to determine the proper data flow to and from the event object.

Event Listeners

Event listeners can be expressed as a method in a given class. Each of these methods is invoked when a particular type of event is triggered. These methods can then be logically grouped together into Java interfaces. Grouping event methods together allows us to define a common set of events all of which share the same related event type. So, in our example we might group together all keyboard events such as KeyPressed, KeyReleased, and so forth. The grouping of event methods is expressed using a Java interface. These event interfaces are commonly given a name ending in "Listener" and must extend the java.util.Event-Listener class.

To extend on the previous KeyboardEvent, we can now define a listener interface that defines what methods are called when an event of this type is thrown:

```
interface KeyboardListener extends java.util.EventListener {
 void keyPressed(KeyboardEvent ke);
 void keyReleased(KeyboardEvent ke);
 }
```

We now have an interface that defines what methods must be implemented if a particular object is to listen for a particular event. Let's now define an object that acts as a listener for keyboard events. In this case, an instance of myClass acts as a listener object for Keyboard events:

```
class myClass implements KeyboardListener {
 public void keyPressed(KeyboardEvent ke) {
  //implementation goes here
  }
  public void keyReleased(KeyboardEvent ke) {
  //implementation goes here
  }
 }
```

The methods that are defined in the EventListener interfaces should be named after a common design pattern. This design pattern allows other tools and objects to understand how the event system you have defined works. It also helps self-documenting the event structures that you create. The design pattern should follow the following rule for naming event methods:

```
void<What_event_occurred>(<Event_Object>e);
```

Event_Object in this case is the event object that has extended the java.util .EventObject class.

In some cases you may need to deviate from this design rule. Such a deviation may be required in order to support existing environments which would force you to create event methods that may require more than one parameter type. Although a deviation from the rule is allowed, it is discouraged in order to keep the general form and readability of your application common with others.

Event Listener Registration

Now that we know about event objects and event listeners, we need a way for the event listeners to register themselves with one or more event sources. This connection between event source and event listener is called event registration. Event registration permits the flow of events from the source to the requesting listener. Every object that is considered an event source must provide two methods for registering and unregistering event listeners.

Like other rules used in naming event methods, the registration and unregistration methods in an event source object must conform to a particular set of design patterns. The design pattern for EventListener objects is as follows:

```
public void add<ListenerType>(<ListenerType>listener);
public void remove<ListenerType>(<ListenerType>listener);
```

This design pattern identifies the containing object as having a standard multicast event source for the given ListenerType. The add<ListenerType> method adds the given listener to the list of objects that will receive the event associated with the ListenerType and the remove<ListenerType> removes the listener from the same list. It is a good idea to also define both of these methods as synchronized. This will prevent software race conditions from occurring when multiple objects are requesting service from these methods simultaneously.

The event specification does not define any behavior associated on the order on which listeners are added or removed from the event source. This tells us that we should not care in which order the listener objects have requested registration or deregistration from an event source. The specification also does not provide any default behavior if a listener is removed or added more than once on the same event source. However, as the implementor of a class that acts as an event source, it is your responsibility to maintain a list of event listeners. Each of the listeners on this list must be sent the event that the source generates.

Putting It All Together

Now let's put the whole thing together. The following example creates an event object, an event listener, an event source, and a test class to exercise the event model. Specifically this example creates a Counter class and a CounterEvent class. The Counter class simply increments a counter at random intervals. When the counter is incremented, a CounterEvent object is passed to all interested listeners.

First we create an EventListener interface for objects that wish to listen for CounterEvent events. The CounterChange Listener interface extends the EventListener class and defines a counterChange() method. The counterChange() method is called when the Counter object dispatches the CounterEvent.

Source Code: `CounterChangeListener.java`
```
public interface CounterChangeListener extends java.util.EventListener {
  void counterChange(CounterEvent e);
  }
```

Next we create the Counter class. This class is responsible for incrementing the counter as well as being the source of the CounterEvent. The count variable is incremented in a thread at random intervals. This class also contains three other interesting methods. The addCounterChangeListener() and remove-CounterChangeListener() methods must be in this class if any listener objects are to register with the Counter object event source. These two methods are called from potential CounterChangeListener objects.

The other method of interest is the notifyCounterChange() method. This method is called when the class needs to issue the CounterEvent to all of its listeners. This method simply runs through its list of listeners and sends each of them the CounterEvent. Notice that a temporary list of listeners is created in a synchronized block to prevent the vector of listeners from being modified as the method is dispatching the events. Since events are typically asynchronous in nature, it is highly recommended that the event source objects use this method of copying the list of listeners before the list is used in any way. It is also recommended that the actual calling of the target listener methods should not be executed while the calling method is holding a lock. This is achieved by locking the copying of the list of listeners, then calling the target methods from unsynchronized code. This will prevent common software race and deadlock conditions that can occur quite easily in event-processing code.

Events that are delivered to the list of listeners are delivered in a synchronous manner. The event source object makes a call to each of the target listener methods which are executed synchronously using the event source's thread.

Source Code: Counter.java

```java
public class Counter extends Thread {
  private java.util.Vector listeners = new java.util.Vector();
  private int count = 0;

  public Counter(int count) {
    this.count = count;
    }

  public Counter() {
    this(0);
    }

  public void run() {
    while(true) {
      try {
        sleep((int)Math.round(Math.random()*3000));
        }
      catch (InterruptedException e) {}

      count++;
      notifyCounterChange(count);
      }
    }

  public void startCounting() {
    this.start();
    }

  protected void notifyCounterChange(int count) {
    java.util.Vector tmpList;
    CounterEvent ce = new CounterEvent(this, count);

    synchronized(this) {
      tmpList = (java.util.Vector) listeners.clone();
      }

    for (int i=0; i<tmpList.size(); i++) {
      ((CounterChangeListener)tmpList.elementAt(i)).counterChange(ce);
      }
    }

  public synchronized void addCounterChangeListener(CounterChangeListener
                                                        ccl) {
    listeners.addElement(ccl);
    }

  public synchronized void
                  removeCounterChangeListener(CounterChangeListener ccl)
{
    listeners.removeElement(ccl);
    }
  }
```

Next we create the CounterEvent. The CounterEvent class extends the Event-Object class by adding a constructor and an accessor method to return the value of the count variable. The count variable is used as part of the event's private data. The class that implements the CounterEventListener can invoke the getCount( ) method on the CounterEvent when the event arrives.

Source Code: CounterEvent.java
```java
public class CounterEvent extends java.util.EventObject {
  private int count;

  CounterEvent(Object source, int count) {
    super(source);
    this.count = count;
    }

  public int getCount() {
    return(count);
    }
  }
```

Finally, we create a test class to see if our CounterEvent and CounterEventListener work correctly. The CountTest class implements the CounterChangeListener by adding the counterChange( ) method. This means that the CountTest class is capable of dealing with CounterChange events. The counterChange( ) method is called each time the Counter class dispatches a CounterEvent. The CountTest instantiates a Counter object, adds itself as a listener of CounterChange events, then tells the Counter object to start its counting. That's it. Now when the Counter object increments its counter, it dispatches a CounterEvent to all of its listeners. Since the CountTest class creates a Counter object and adds itself as a listener of CounterChange events, it will receive the events from the Counter object.

Source Code: CountTest.java
```java
import CounterChangeListener;
import CounterEvent;
import Counter;

public class CountTest implements CounterChangeListener  {

  public static void main(String args[]) {
    CountTest ct = new CountTest();
    }

  public CountTest() {
    Counter c = new Counter();
    c.addCounterChangeListener(this);
```

```
    c.startCounting();
    }

 public void counterChange(CounterEvent evt) {
    System.out.println("Counter value has changed: " + evt.getCount());
    }
 }
```

EVENT EXCEPTIONS

Listener methods, called by the event source objects, can throw exceptions. The exceptions that are thrown must be checked exceptions, not unchecked exceptions such as NullPointerException. The exception must be documented in the throws clause of the method. The event specification does not specify how the event source should handle an exception while calling a listener method. This could mean that one implementation of the event model could stop execution of an application on an exception from a listener method while another implementation may continue to deliver events. Keep this in mind as one implementation may work just fine with checked listener exceptions and another may not.

The registration type used in the previous example was considered a multicast event. This means that the event source, Counter class, can send events to any number of listeners. Multicast event sources are considered the default; however, you may want to create an event source that would only send events to a single listener. In this case the event source would be considered a unicast event source. The unicast registration methods are similar to the registration methods that are used with multicast registration. The design pattern used for unicast registration is as follows:

```
public void add<ListenerType> (<ListenerType>listener) throws
java.util.TooManyListenersException;

public void remove<ListenerType>(<ListenerType>listener);
```

Notice that the only difference in the design pattern between multicast and unicast event registration is the throws clause in the unicast's add method. The presence of the java.util.TooManyListenersException in the declaration of the add<ListenerType> method identifies that the source object is a unicast source. When more than one listener tries to add itself as a listener of a unicast source, the TooManyListenersException will be thrown. If you are designing the event source class, then you are responsible for throwing the TooManyListenersException.

Event Adapters

At this point we know about event sources, event listeners, and the event objects that are passed between the source and listener. We now introduce the concept of event adapters. An event adapter is simply an object that sits between an event source and an event listener. It interposes between the two by listening for events from the source and then may modify the event in some manner before delivering the event to the event listener. Figure 2.2 shows how an event adapter works.

Event adapters can be used in a number of different ways, such as a filter, demultiplexor, or acting as a queuing mechanism. Many GUI tools builders may use event adapters to control how events are passed between GUI components.

Let's take a look at how an event adapter can be used. Start with the same Counter example previously used, but we made a few changes to the CountTest .java file. First notice that CountTest no longer implements CounterChange-Listener and that we have added a new class called CountAdapter. The Count-Adapter class now implements the CounterChangeListener and is responsible for receiving and dispatching CounterChange events.

Source Code: adapter\CountTest.java

```
public class CountTest {

  public static void main(String args[]) {
    CountTest ct = new CountTest();
    }

  public CountTest() {
    Counter c = new Counter();
    CountAdapter ca = new CountAdapter(this);
    c.addCounterChangeListener(ca);
    c.startCounting();
    }

  public void evenCounterChange(int count) {
    System.out.println("Even: Counter value has changed: " + count);
    }

  public void oddCounterChange(int count) {
    System.out.println("Odd: Counter value has changed: " + count);
    }
}
```

The CountTest object creates a new Counter object but does not register itself as a listener. The CountTest object then creates a CountAdapter object and passes a reference of itself to the CountAdapter object. This permits the CountAdapter to deliver events to the CountTest object. Specifically, the Count-Adapter class calls the evenCounterChange() and oddCounterChange() meth-

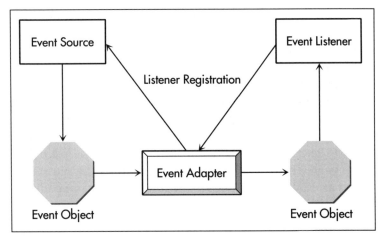

Figure 2.2   Event adapter.

ods in the CountTest object. Then a call is made to the Counter object to add the CountAdapter object as a listener. So the event source object, Counter, will send events to the CountAdapter object and the CountAdapter will call methods in the CountTest object when it receives the events. The CountTest class no longer has the counterChange() method as it no longer implements the CounterChangeListener interface.

Source Code: adapter\CountAdapter.java

```
class CountAdapter implements CounterChangeListener {
  private CountTest destination;

  public CountAdapter(CountTest destination) {
    this.destination = destination;
    }

  public void counterChange(CounterEvent ce) {
    int count = ce.getCount();
    if ((count % 2) == 0)
      destination.evenCounterChange(count);
    else
      destination.oddCounterChange(count);
    }
  }
```

The adapter in this example provides two services that were not available when the CountTest class implemented the CounterChangeListener itself. The first is the ability to call specific methods in the target class. This type of service can be quite handy when a class needs to listen for events of the same type from many different sources. For example an application may use many different button objects, all of which send button press events to its listener. The listener method in this case would need to determine what button has sent the event before it could perform the button's requested action. An adapter can be used to sit between multiple event sources and then determine what target method should be called based on what event source sent the event. The second service provided by the CountAdapter is a simple event filter. When the counter-Change( ) method is called by the event source, the adapter filters the count value into even and odd values. Then, depending on the value of the count, the adapter calls specific methods in its destination object. The event source in this case does not know that the events are being filtered and the CountTest object does not know that its events are being filtered. This is a simple example of how an adapter can be used as a filter, but it does show how useful event adapters can be.

Security

A word on security: Java code that is installed on a local disk is permitted to perform operations that can't be performed by code loaded from a network. Knowing this, it is important to realize that an event adapter may be installed on a local disk but the event source may have been loaded from a network. This will cause any operations called from the event source to conform to its security model, which in this case is quite limited. Keep this in mind when creating event adapters; you don't want the event adapter to perform operations that may be prohibited by the calling object. The event adapter must not look any more trustworthy or behave in a more secure manner than the event source that is calling it.

Desktop Colors

Most common applications being used these days leave the color scheme selection for a user interface up to the user. This is quite a convenience as different users prefer a different set of colors for use on their desktop. The color scheme used for most applications is usually set throughout by some sort of desktop color selector application. For example, in Windows95 it is possible to select and set colors for your desktop by using the display utility in the control panel folder. After you have selected the color scheme you wish to use, applications can then query the color manager to see what colors you have selected. Applications can then use your color scheme to set colors used in the application.

Java also has this ability. It is possible for Java programs to determine what color scheme has been selected on any platform and make these colors available to a Java program. This creates a consistency for component colors across Java applications as well as non-Java applications that use the same color scheme.

Java has a color object that can be used to store and represent any color you wish to create. This color object can then be used in methods that set colors for their respective components. In the same way that the Color object can store any type of color you want, the SystemColor class is provided to contain all the colors of the desktop color scheme. The SystemColor class will hold the colors that were selected using the native desktop color selector. It provides a standard set of colors that represent the colors used in the desktop color scheme. This class is automatically filled with the desktop colors when your Java application starts, so all you have to do is retrieve the colors from this class and set the appropriate colors in your Java application. All of the colors in the System-Color class are static, so you can't change them but you can use them. Table 2.1 lists all the colors that are defined in the SystemColor class.

Since you are not guaranteed that all desktop color schemes will contain all of the colors in the SystemColor class, Java will select appropriate non-null defaults for those colors. This gives you the benefit of using all of the colors in the SystemColor class without having to worry if a particular color is defined in the underlying system desktop. Also as a convenience, the AWT base components will automatically use the SystemColor class to set the color of the component to fit into the existing color scheme. You, of course, could change these color settings, but in most cases you can let the base component classes do the work for you.

Source Code: ColorView.java

```
import java.awt.*;
import java.awt.event.*;

public class ColorView extends Frame {

  private java.util.Hashtable getColors() {
    java.util.Hashtable colors = new java.util.Hashtable(26);
    colors.put("desktop", SystemColor.desktop);
    colors.put("activeCaption", SystemColor.activeCaption);
    colors.put("activeCaptionText", SystemColor.activeCaptionText);
    colors.put("activeCaptionBorder", SystemColor.activeCaptionBorder);
    colors.put("inactiveCaption", SystemColor.inactiveCaption);
    colors.put("inactiveCaptionText", SystemColor.inactiveCaptionText);
    colors.put("inactiveCaptionBorder", SystemColor.inactiveCaptionBorder);
    colors.put("window", SystemColor.window);
    colors.put("windowBorder", SystemColor.windowBorder);
    colors.put("windowText", SystemColor.windowText);
    colors.put("menu", SystemColor.menu);
    colors.put("menuText", SystemColor.menuText);
    colors.put("text", SystemColor.text);
    colors.put("textText", SystemColor.textText);
    colors.put("textHighlight", SystemColor.textHighlight);
    colors.put("textHighlightText", SystemColor.textHighlightText);
    colors.put("textInactiveText", SystemColor.textInactiveText);
```

Table 2.1   Desktop Colors

COLOR NAME	DESCRIPTION
desktop	Background color of desktop
activeCaption	Background color for active captions
activeCaptionText	Text color of the active captions
activeCaptionBorder	Border color of active caption
inactiveCaption	Background color of inactive caption
inactiveCaptionText	Text color of the inactive captions
inactiveCaptionBorder	Border color of inactive caption
window	Background color of desktop windows
windowBorder	Color of desktop window frames
windowText	Color of text inside of desktop windows
menu	Background color of menus
menuText	Color of text in menus
text	Background color of text
textText	Foreground color of text
textHighlight	Background color of highlighted text
textHighlightText	Foreground color of highlighted text
control	Background color of controls
controlText	Text color used in controls
controlLtHighlight	Light highlight color used in controls
controlHighlight	Highlight color used in controls
controlShadow	Shadow color used in controls
controlDkShadow	Dark shadow color used in controls
inactiveControlText	Text color used for inactive controls
scrollbar	Background color for scrollbars
info	Background color for spot help text
infoText	Text color for spot help text

```
      colors.put("control", SystemColor.control);
      colors.put("controlText", SystemColor.controlText);
      colors.put("controlLtHighlight", SystemColor.controlLtHighlight);
      colors.put("controlHighlight", SystemColor.controlHighlight);
      colors.put("controlShadow", SystemColor.controlShadow);
      colors.put("controlDkShadow", SystemColor.controlDkShadow);
      colors.put("scrollbar", SystemColor.scrollbar);
      colors.put("info", SystemColor.info);
      colors.put("infoText", SystemColor.infoText);
      return(colors);
      }

  public static void main(String args[]) {
    ColorView cv = new ColorView("Desktop Color Viewer");
    }

  public ColorView(String title) {
    super(title);
    setLayout(new GridLayout(6,5));
    java.util.Hashtable colors = getColors();
    for (java.util.Enumeration e = colors.keys() ; e.hasMoreElements() ;) {
      String type = (String) e.nextElement();
      Button b = new Button(type);
      Color c = (SystemColor) colors.get(type);
      b.setBackground(c);
      b.setForeground(new Color((c.getRed()<128)?(255):(0),
                                (c.getGreen()<128)?(255):(0),
                                (c.getBlue()<128)?(255):(0)));
      add(b);
      }
    pack();
    show();
    }
}
```

The ColorView.java example uses all the colors in the SystemColor class. This is a simple example that shows how to access the system colors. The example creates a set of buttons where the color of the button is set to the color representing the text description on the button.

Printing

It seams a bit odd that we would be talking about printing in an advanced Java book. Well, the simple fact is that before the JDK 1.1, printing in Java was impossible. There was no simple way to render AWT widgets and graphical elements to a print file. The good news is that this problem has been solved. There is now a platform-independent way to print Java applets and applications.

The JDK 1.1 added the ability for a Java frame to render its contents into a new type of graphics context. Printing from your Java program is really quite simple. The only major change in the AWT API that permits printing is the addition of the PrintJob class. The PrintJob class contains all the information needed to actually print the contents of a frame or component. In order to get a PrintJob object you need to call the getPrintJob( ) method which was added to the Toolkit class. The getPrintJob( ) method displays a dialog box asking the user for printing information, such as what printer to print to and how may copies should be printed. The print dialog that is used is native to the platform on which you are running which allows different platforms to handle printing in their own way.

Once you have the PrintJob object you need to get a graphics context for the print job. This is really no different than the graphics context that is used when you are rendering graphics on the screen. In this case, you call the get-Graphics( ) method on the PrintJob object to obtain the graphics context. Once you have the graphics context all you really need to do is call the printAll( ) method to send the job off to the printer. To demonstrate how printing works we will modify a previous example and add printing capability. For this we will use the ColorView.java example:

Source Code: ColorView2.java

```
import java.awt.*;
import java.awt.event.*;

public class ColorView extends Frame implements ActionListener {

  private java.util.Hashtable getColors() {
    java.util.Hashtable colors = new java.util.Hashtable(26);
    colors.put("desktop", SystemColor.desktop);
    colors.put("activeCaption", SystemColor.activeCaption);
    colors.put("activeCaptionText", SystemColor.activeCaptionText);
    colors.put("activeCaptionBorder", SystemColor.activeCaptionBorder);
    colors.put("inactiveCaption", SystemColor.inactiveCaption);
    colors.put("inactiveCaptionText", SystemColor.inactiveCaptionText);
    colors.put("inactiveCaptionBorder", SystemColor.inactiveCaptionBorder);
    colors.put("window", SystemColor.window);
    colors.put("windowBorder", SystemColor.windowBorder);
    colors.put("windowText", SystemColor.windowText);
    colors.put("menu", SystemColor.menu);
    colors.put("menuText", SystemColor.menuText);
    colors.put("text", SystemColor.text);
    colors.put("textText", SystemColor.textText);
    colors.put("textHighlight", SystemColor.textHighlight);
    colors.put("textHighlightText", SystemColor.textHighlightText);
    colors.put("textInactiveText", SystemColor.textInactiveText);
    colors.put("control", SystemColor.control);
    colors.put("controlText", SystemColor.controlText);
    colors.put("controlLtHighlight", SystemColor.controlLtHighlight);
```

```
      colors.put("controlHighlight", SystemColor.controlHighlight);
      colors.put("controlShadow", SystemColor.controlShadow);
      colors.put("controlDkShadow", SystemColor.controlDkShadow);
      colors.put("scrollbar", SystemColor.scrollbar);
      colors.put("info", SystemColor.info);
      colors.put("infoText", SystemColor.infoText);
      return(colors);
      }

  public void actionPerformed(ActionEvent ae) {
     PrintJob pj = getToolkit().getPrintJob(this, "Test Print", null);

     if (pj != null) {
       Graphics g = pj.getGraphics();

       if (g != null) {
         printAll(g);
         g.dispose();
         }
       }
     }

  public static void main(String args[]) {
     ColorView cv = new ColorView("Desktop Color Viewer");
     }

  public ColorView(String title) {
     super(title);
     setLayout(new GridLayout(6,5));
     java.util.Hashtable colors = getColors();
     for (java.util.Enumeration e = colors.keys() ; e.hasMoreElements() ;) {
       String type = (String) e.nextElement();
       Button b = new Button(type);
       Color c = (SystemColor) colors.get(type);
       b.setBackground(c);
       b.setForeground(new Color((c.getRed()<128)?(255):(0),
                   (c.getGreen()<128)?(255):(0),
                   (c.getBlue()<128)?(255):(0)));
       add(b);
       }
     Button print = new Button("Print");
     print.addActionListener(this);
     add(print);
     pack();
     show();
     }
  }
```

We have changed very little in this example. We added a new button, called print, that when pushed, would call the actionPerformed() method. Inside of the actionPerformed() method we added a few lines of code that perform the print operation. All we did was get the PrintJob object and a graphics context. Then we asked all of the widgets to render themselves into the graphics context by calling the printAll( ) method. The rendered graphics are then sent to the printer. It's that simple; give it a try.

ScrollPane Container

The JDK 1.1 added a new class called ScrollPane to solve the problem of scrolling widgets in Java. Before we had ScrollPane, scrolling an image, widgets, or containers was, in most cases, left to the developer. The process of scrolling was not efficient and usually did not produce visually acceptable results. This is all behind us now with the introduction of the ScrollPane. The ScrollPane class provides automatic scrolling of a single AWT component. It may seem restricting that the ScrollPane can only scroll one component, but remember that an AWT component can also be a container. This means that you could have a panel that contains may different widgets, all of which can be scrolled using the ScrollPane class.

The ScrollPane class is really simple to use. In fact, about the only thing you can modify on a ScrollPane object is how the scrollbars will appear and the adjustment of the scrollbars' scrolling increments. You can use the ScrollPane object like any other AWT component. Just add it to a container, then add a single container or component to the ScrollPane object. To demonstrate this we will again use the ColorView.java example to add scrolling to the set of widgets that are displayed:

```
Source Code: ColorView3.java
import java.awt.*;
import java.awt.event.*;

public class ColorView3 extends Frame implements ActionListener {

  private java.util.Hashtable getColors() {
    java.util.Hashtable colors = new java.util.Hashtable(26);
    colors.put("desktop", SystemColor.desktop);
    colors.put("activeCaption", SystemColor.activeCaption);
    colors.put("activeCaptionText", SystemColor.activeCaptionText);
    colors.put("activeCaptionBorder", SystemColor.activeCaptionBorder);
    colors.put("inactiveCaption", SystemColor.inactiveCaption);
    colors.put("inactiveCaptionText", SystemColor.inactiveCaptionText);
    colors.put("inactiveCaptionBorder", SystemColor.inactiveCaptionBorder);
    colors.put("window", SystemColor.window);
    colors.put("windowBorder", SystemColor.windowBorder);
    colors.put("windowText", SystemColor.windowText);
    colors.put("menu", SystemColor.menu);
    colors.put("menuText", SystemColor.menuText);
```

```
    colors.put("text", SystemColor.text);
    colors.put("textText", SystemColor.textText);
    colors.put("textHighlight", SystemColor.textHighlight);
    colors.put("textHighlightText", SystemColor.textHighlightText);
    colors.put("textInactiveText", SystemColor.textInactiveText);
    colors.put("control", SystemColor.control);
    colors.put("controlText", SystemColor.controlText);
    colors.put("controlLtHighlight", SystemColor.controlLtHighlight);
    colors.put("controlHighlight", SystemColor.controlHighlight);
    colors.put("controlShadow", SystemColor.controlShadow);
    colors.put("controlDkShadow", SystemColor.controlDkShadow);
    colors.put("scrollbar", SystemColor.scrollbar);
    colors.put("info", SystemColor.info);
    colors.put("infoText", SystemColor.infoText);
    return(colors);
    }

public void actionPerformed(ActionEvent ae) {
    PrintJob pj = getToolkit().getPrintJob(this, "Test Print", null);

    if (pj != null) {
      Graphics g = pj.getGraphics();

      if (g != null) {
        printAll(g);
        g.dispose();
        }
      }
    }

public static void main(String args[]) {
    ColorView3 cv = new ColorView3("Desktop Color Viewer");
    }

public ColorView3(String title) {
    super(title);
    ScrollPane scroll = new ScrollPane(ScrollPane.SCROLLBARS_AS_NEEDED);
    add(scroll);
    Panel p = new Panel();
    scroll.add(p);
    p.setLayout(new GridLayout(6,5));
    java.util.Hashtable colors = getColors();
    for (java.util.Enumeration e = colors.keys() ; e.hasMoreElements() ;) {
      String type = (String) e.nextElement();
      Button b = new Button(type);
      Color c = (SystemColor) colors.get(type);
      b.setBackground(c);
      b.setForeground(new Color((c.getRed()<128)?(255):(0),
                                (c.getGreen()<128)?(255):(0),
                                (c.getBlue()<128)?(255):(0)));
      p.add(b);
```

```
        }
      Button print = new Button("Print");
      print.addActionListener(this);
      p.add(print);
      pack();
      show();
      }
  }
```

Notice that all we did to this code was add a new ScrollPane object and added it to the frame. Then, we created a Panel object and added it to the Scroll-Pane object. Then all of the buttons were added to the Panel object. When you run this program, you will see that you can easily scroll the group of widgets.

Popup Menu

The 1.0 version of the AWT only supported pull-down menus that were part of a windows main menubar. In many cases, this level of menu support is suffi-cient; however, popup menus are being used more and more in today's graphi-cal applications. A popup menu is simply a menu that can be shown from anywhere within a GUI component. This makes it quite easy to create the menus that are context-sensitive: The menu items can change according to where the user requested the menu to be shown.

Using the new popup menus is similar to the way you would use normal menubar menus. The methods to add and remove menu items to and from the menu are the same. The only major difference between the two is that popup menus need to be exposed when a certain event occurs. In most cases, you will want to watch for a mouse popup trigger event:

Source Code: popUp.java
```
  import java.awt.*;
  import java.awt.event.*;

  public class popUp extends Frame implements ActionListener {
    class popPanel extends Panel {
      PopupMenu popUp;

    public popPanel(PopupMenu pm) {
      popUp = pm;
      add(pm);
      enableEvents(AWTEvent.MOUSE_EVENT_MASK);
      }

    public void processMouseEvent(MouseEvent me) {
      if (me.isPopupTrigger()) {
        popUp.show(me.getComponent(), me.getX(), me.getY());
```

```
        }
      super.processMouseEvent(me);
      }
   }

public popUp() {
   popPanel panels[] = new popPanel[4];
   PopupMenu pops[] = new PopupMenu[4];
   setLayout(new GridLayout(2,2));
   for (int i=0; i<4; i++) {
      pops[i] = new PopupMenu("Menu " + (i+1));
      for (int j=0; j<5; j++) {
         MenuItem mi = new MenuItem("Menu"+(i+1)+" Item"+(j+1));
         mi.addActionListener(this);
         pops[i].add(mi);
         }
      panels[i] = new popPanel(pops[i]);
      add(panels[i]);
      }

   panels[0].setBackground(Color.yellow);
   panels[1].setBackground(Color.red);
   panels[2].setBackground(Color.blue);
   panels[3].setBackground(Color.green);
   setSize(400,400);
   }

public void actionPerformed(ActionEvent ae) {
   }

public static void main(String args[]) {
   popUp pu = new popUp();
   pu.show();
   }
}
```

The popUp.java example demonstrates how the popup menu can be used as well as showing that different popup menus can be displayed when a popup request is made in different areas of the application.

Mouseless Operation

Why would an application that has a graphical user interface want to enable mouseless operation? Many GUIs that are developed today include a way to drive the application without the use of a mouse. There are many reasons for this, but one of the most common reasons is to provide expert users quicker access to application functions. When a user starts using a new application, it is common for the user to investigate and use the graphical menus contained in the application. Over time the user grows to understand what functions are needed and does not want to go through the menus to click on the desired action. It is much easier and quicker for a user to press a series of keys to perform an identical action that is contained in a menu. So the concept of mouseless operation in advanced graphical applications is not such an odd thing.

In previous versions of the AWT, the only type of mouseless operation that was supported was what the native widget peers provided. The peer operations did provide a way for the user to navigate through the application, but since this navigation depended on the peers' implementation, the navigation was not common across all platforms. In newer versions of the AWT, some basic mouseless navigation mechanisms were added. The basic navigation now supported may not be any more useful to you if the native peers on your platform already supported good navigation. However, now the navigation basics will be common across all platforms.

Focus Traversal

The basic technique of mouseless navigation is focus traversal. Focus traversal is the ability to cause a widget to have focus through the use of keyboard strokes. For example, if a GUI contains several text fields, it is common for the user to be able to tab through the fields. This means that as the user presses the tab key, the focus for text input is moved from text field to text field. The AWT uses the <tab> key to move the focus traversal forward though the components and the <shift-tab> key combination to move the focus in a reverse direction. Once a widget has focus, it is also common for another keyboard event to cause some sort of action with the widget. For example, if a text field has focus, then the keys that are pressed are entered into the text field; if a button has focus, then pressing the space bar or the return key may cause the button to fire its action. Focus traversal is quite simple to implement in Java. A new method has been added to the Component and ComponentPeer classes:

```
Public boolean isFocusTraversable();
```

This method simply returns a Boolean if the component being called supports focus traversal. You only need to worry about this method if you are extending a component, in which case you may want to override the new component's ability to handle focus traversal.

So how do you control the sequence of focus traversal in your application? It is quite simple: Focus traversal flows in the order in which components are added to their container. For example, using the following code, the focus traversal would move in sequence from tf1 to tf3 to tf2:

```
TextField tf1 = new TextField();
TextField tf2 = new TextField();
TextField tf3 = new TextField();
myContainer.add(tf1);
myContainer.add(tf3);
myContainer.add(tf2);
```

Keep in mind that the order in which components are added to a container may not be the order in which the components are displayed. This can cause some confusion when a rather complex layout is used to manage the look of an interface.

There is also another way in which you can force the order in which the focus traversal occurs. The add( ) method can also accept an integer that represents the position the component is to be in the traversal order. You can do this simply by adding this order to the add( ) method. For example, the following code would have the same traversal order as the previous code:

```
myContainer.add(tf1,1);
myContainer.add(tf2,3);
myContainer.add(tf3,2);
```

Menu Shortcuts

Another navigation aid that the new AWT provides is the ability to use menu shortcuts. Menu shortcuts are simply key sequences that perform the equivalent of selecting an item off a GUI menu. Menu shortcuts are also known as keyboard equivalents or menu accelerators. The AWT at this time only supports menu shortcuts and not any other type of menu navigation.

Menu shortcuts are usually displayed as a key sequence next to the menu item that the shortcut activates. This provides a simple visual indicator of a shortcut. As a user becomes more comfortable with a GUI menu interface, then he or she is able to see and use the shortcuts that are provided.

The implementation of menu shortcuts is quite simple. A few methods have been added to the AWT package that make it easy for your applications to support shortcuts. A new subclass of java.awt.event.KeyEvent was created called java.awt.MenuShortcut. This class is used by the new shortcut methods which are defined in java.awt.MenuItem and java.awt.MenuBar. Both the MenuItem and MenuBar classes contain methods that set and get menu shortcut key sequences. Shortcuts are not just a single keystroke, but are a sequence of keys, or a modifier and a key. Modifiers are used to signal that the key pressed could be considered a shortcut. For example, the modifier key on Windows and Motif is the <control> key and on Macintosh it's the <command> key. The modifier key used in conjunction with another key signals the GUI that a shortcut was requested. To find out what modifier key your system used, you can make a call to the java.awt.Toolkit.getMenuShortcutKeyMask( ). This method will return the integer representation of the systems modifier key.

Source Code: shortCut.java

```
import java.awt.*;

public class shortCut extends Frame {

  public static void main(String args[]) {
    shortCut sc = new shortCut();
    MenuBar mb = new MenuBar();
    Menu m1 = new Menu("File");
    Menu m2 = new Menu("Edit");
    mb.add(m1);
    mb.add(m2);
    m1.add(new MenuItem("New...", new MenuShortcut('n')));
    m1.add(new MenuItem("Open...", new MenuShortcut('o')));
    m1.add(new MenuItem("Save...", new MenuShortcut('s')));
    m1.add(new MenuItem("Save As...", new MenuShortcut('s', true)));
    m2.add(new MenuItem("Cut", new MenuShortcut('x')));
    m2.add(new MenuItem("Copy", new MenuShortcut('c')));
    m2.add(new MenuItem("Paste", new MenuShortcut('v')));
    sc.setMenuBar(mb);
    sc.setSize(200,200);
    sc.show();
    }


  }
```

Example shortCut.java demonstrates how menu shortcuts can be used in a GUI menu. Notice that any character can be used as a shortcut key as well as any key in combination with the shift key. It is also important to point out that there is no way to provide a menu shortcut that will show a particular menu. This is something that will have to be added to the AWT at a later date.

Data Transfer

Data transfer between applications or parts of applications is quite common in today's graphical applications. The ability to move a portion of text, a graphic, or just about any type of data from one place to another is the foundation of GUI data transfer. The transfer of data usually involves a virtual clipboard where the contents of the data being transferred can be temporarily stored. The action of transferring data is usually referred to as cut and paste or drag and drop. The Java AWT would be incomplete without these transfer capabilities. In earlier versions of the AWT the only type of data transfer permitted between GUI components was simple text and the text transfers could only take place between different text components in the same application.

The JDK 1.1 provides a simple clipboard API and the 1.2 version of the JDK provides the Drag-and-Drop API needed to support full intra- or inter-application data transfer. Not only does this new API permit data transfer between different Java applications, but it also permits data flow between Java and non-Java applications.

In order for an object to transfer data it must implement the Transferable interface defined in java.awt.datatrasfer.Tranferable. If an object is going to implement the Transferable interface, it must provide a series of data formats or data flavors for the data to be transferred. The list of data flavors given for any Transferable data should be provided from a highly descriptive format down to the least descriptive format. This is done to provide many different ways in which to represent the data. For example, if an object is created that represents a graph object and implements the Transferable interface, then that object may define several different representations or flavors of the graph. The richest or most descriptive flavor may simply return a reference to the graph object itself. A less descriptive flavor may return the JPEG (Joint Photographic Experts Group) graphic representation of the graph and an even less descriptive flavor may just return a series of values that represent the graph. Each of these flavors must provide the ability to return the data requested or throw some sort of exception. The exception thrown may inform the caller that the requested flavor is not supported by the object, the data is no longer available, or some other sort of error condition.

The AWT classes do provide some common data flavors that may be used as convenience classes for common data transfer, such as string transfers and numeric transfers.

Data Flavors

Data flavors provide a simple device for common data transfer between applications that may use different data formats. For example, using the previous graph object example, let's assume that the graph was created in a special charting and graphics application. Let's also assume that we would like to paste the graph inside of an HTML document. Now when the HTML editor requests the graph data, it will want it in a format that it can understand. The most descriptive representation of the graph was the graph object itself. Since the HTML editor can't use an object reference, a less descriptive flavor must be used. The HTML editor does understand JPEG files, so the JPEG data flavor can be used to access the graph. The JPEG data can then be transferred between the graph object and the HTML editor. This manner of representing data in different flavors permits applications to use many different types or formats of data. It also has the advantage that once a data flavor is defined, it can be used by any application that understands that flavor of data.

Each data flavor must provide three types of information. The first is a logical name for the flavor that uses the MIME (Multipurpose Internet Mail Extensions) type/subtype notation. (See RFC 1521 for more information on the MIME specification.) MIME supports registered data types as well as custom nonstandard data types. The nonstandard data types must be named with a preceding "x-" in front of their names. The second bit of information that a data flavor must provide is its common or human-readable name. This name could be used in an application to describe what type of data the object can present. Finally, the data flavor must provide a representation class used to actually permit the transfer of data.

The representation class defines what type of object is being passed between the data requestor and data provider. The Transferable interface defines the following method:

```
Object getTransferData(DataFlavor flavor)
```

Since the getTransferData( ) method returns an Object object a representation class is needed to take the ambiguity out of the returned data.

The DataFlavor class defines two different types of data flavors. The first type represents a Java class as the return type. This type of data flavor simply returns a Java class when the getTransferData( ) method is called. For example, a data flavor that represents the java.util.Data class may be defined as:

```
MIME-type="application/x-javaserializedobject; class=java.util.Date"
RepresentationClass=java.util.Date
```

This data flavor will return a Date object to the requesting application.

A MIME type represents the second type of data flavor that simply provides the ability for any MIME type to be accessed from the requesting application. For example, a data flavor that returns a simple text representation of a date could be defined as:

```
MIME-type="application/text"
RepresentationClass=java.io.InputStream
```

This data flavor would return an InputStream that the requesting class could read to get the text representation of the date. You can also define any type of RepresentationClass to return to the data requestor. Any particular flavor of data can also be represented by several different RepresentationClass classes.

You may ask why use a class to define a data flavor when a simple MIME sting could be used. Well, we had the same question. Rather than go through some long explanation of why we believe this was done, we will show what the specification says about why using a class is an advantage. From the 1.1 AWT specification:

1. *Usability.* These are attributes that should be associated with data formats, like the human-presentable name for the data format, that could only be associated with a logical string baroquely. With a DataFlavor object, these attributes are directly associated with the encapsulating DataFlavor object.

2. *Convenience.* Using DataFlavor objects gives us a convenient way of handling data format comparisons. An isMimeTypeEqual( ) method relieves the programmer of having to remember to convert his or her MIME types into a canonical form. (This is an issue because MIME type, subtype, and parameter names are case-insensitive and parameters can appear in any order.)

3. *Extensibility.* The abstraction will allow us to extend a flavor's attributes and methods over time if necessary.

4. *Performance.* Motif and Windows use atoms rather than strings to identify data formats. Using an object to identify each data format gives us a handy place to cache the atom corresponding to the MIME type name, reducing the number of atoms required. Similarly, the results of mapping MIME types like "text/plain" to platform-specific clipboard formats like CF_TEXT on Windows and TEXT on Macintosh can be cached.

There now, didn't that clear things up? Well if it didn't, we believe one of the main reasons for creating a class to define a data flavor is to provide the utmost flexibility. A great example of this flexibility is the case when multiple data items need to be transferred between applications. The data flavor class can be created to handle multiple data items and used to group together a set of data items, then provide methods in which to access each of the data items. You can see that this capability is not possible with simple MIME type strings.

Now let's take a look at an example that creates an object that implements the Transferable interface. The dateTrans.java program creates a dateTrans object that implements the Transferable interface. This class uses three different data flavors to represent a date. The date can be expressed as a real Date object, a String, or just plain text. This class can be used to transfer date data to and from Java programs. Notice that the class provides methods to allow another object to determine what data flavors are supported and to determine if a particular flavor is supported. The getTransferData( ) method is used to return the data, in a particular flavor, that has been requested.

Source Code: dateTrans.java
```
import java.util.*;
import java.awt.datatransfer.*;

public class dateTrans implements Transferable {

    private Date date;
```

```
        static final int DATE = 0;
        static final int STRING = 1;
        static final int TEXT = 2;

        DataFlavor myFlavors[] = {
          new DataFlavor(date.getClass(), "Date object"),
          DataFlavor.stringFlavor,
          DataFlavor.plainTextFlavor};

        public dateTrans(Date date) {
          this.date = date;
          }

        public DataFlavor[] getTransferDataFlavors() {
          return(myFlavors);
          }

        public boolean isDataFlavorSupported(DataFlavor flavor) {
          return(flavor.equals(myFlavors[DATE]) ||
                 flavor.equals(myFlavors[STRING]) ||
                 flavor.equals(myFlavors[TEXT]));
          }

        public Object getTransferData(DataFlavor flavor) throws
        UnsupportedFlavorException, java.io.IOException {
            if (flavor.equals(myFlavors[DATE]))
              return((Object)date);
            else if (flavor.equals(myFlavors[STRING]))
              return((Object)date.toString());
            else if (flavor.equals(myFlavors[TEXT]))
              return((java.io.InputStream) new java.io.ByteArrayInputStream
        (date.toString().getBytes()));
            else
              throw new UnsupportedFlavorException(flavor);
            }
          }
```

Clipboard

The clipboard is a common facility used to store data that has been cut or copied from an application. The storage place, the clipboard, can then be accessed from many different applications in order to paste or copy the data back to another application. We are sure that you understand how this process works since so many applications use this type of copy and paste mechanism. That same mechanism is available to Java programs. This allows data copied from a native non-Java program to be pasted into a Java program as well as data copied from a Java program to be pasted into a native program.

All of the clipboard capabilities in Java are contained in the java.awt .datatransfer.Clipboard class. The two main methods that you will need to use are the setContents() and getContents() methods. As you may guess, these methods set or get the contents of a clipboard. Using the Clipboard class you are able to create any number of clipboards, all of which can be used in an application. In addition to this capability, Java also has a special system-defined clipboard that can be accessed through the java.awt.Toolkit.getSystem-Clipboard() method. This system clipboard is the clipboard that will allow you to exchange data with native non-Java applications. It is set up for you automatically when you start a Java application.

Note that the system clipboard can only be accessed by Java applications and trusted applets. This is due to the fact that sensitive data may exist on the system clipboard when an untrusted applet tries to access it. Since this would be a security breach, access is only permitted by trusted applets and applications. This restriction may be lifted in the future when better mechanisms can be used to control the data flow between the system clipboard and an untrusted applet.

Source Code: clipTest.java

```java
import java.awt.*;
import java.awt.event.*;
import java.awt.datatransfer.*;

public class clipTest extends Frame implements ClipboardOwner,
                                                      ActionListener {

  TextField tf = new TextField(20);
  Label l = new Label();
  Button copy = new Button("copy");
  Button paste = new Button("paste");
  Clipboard sysBoard = getToolkit().getSystemClipboard();

  public static void main(String args[]) {
    clipTest ct = new clipTest("Clipboard Test Program");
    }

  public clipTest(String title) {
    super(title);
    setLayout(new GridLayout(4,1));
    add(copy);
    add(paste);
    add(tf);
    add(l);
    copy.addActionListener(this);
    paste.addActionListener(this);
    pack();
    show();
    }

  public void actionPerformed(ActionEvent ae) {
    if (ae.getSource().equals(copy)) {
      StringSelection data = new StringSelection(tf.getText());
```

```
        sysBoard.setContents(data, this);
        }
    if (ae.getSource().equals(paste)) {
      Transferable data = sysBoard.getContents(this);
      if (data != null)
        try {
          String incoming = (String)
                            data.getTransferData(DataFlavor.stringFlavor);
          l.setText(incoming);
          }
        catch (java.io.IOException ioc) {
          System.out.println("IO Error: " + ioc.getMessage());
          }
        catch (UnsupportedFlavorException usf) {
          System.out.println("Unsupport Data Flavor: " +
DataFlavor.stringFlavor.getHumanPresentableName());
          }
        }
      }
    }


  public void lostOwnership(Clipboard cb, Transferable data) {
    System.out.println("data changed");
    }
  }
```

Take a look at the clipTest.java example. This is a very simple example that
uses the system clipboard to copy and paste data. There are a couple of things
to note about this example before we walk through it. First, this example only
uses the system clipboard. Second, this example only tries to copy and paste
text data to and from the clipboard. If you remember from the previous data flavor section, you can create any type of data flavor, then use that data flavor to
copy and paste your data flavor to and from the clipboard. The clipTest example simply creates a couple of buttons used to start the copy- and paste-action.
A TextField is used as a place to copy text data from and a Label is used as a
place to paste the text data. So when you press the copy button, data is copied
from the TextField and placed on the system clipboard. When you press the
paste button, data is transferred from the system clipboard and pasted as the
Label text.

We created a clipboard called sysBoard that represents the system clipboard. The system clipboard was accessed by using the getSystemClipboard()
method. Notice also that our clipTest class implements ClipboardOwner. This
tells us that the clipTest class will be writing data to the clipboard.

In order to copy data onto the system clipboard we used the StringSelection
class to represent the transferable data we wished to copy. This data was then
used in the setContents() method to actually set the contents of the system
clipboard. The StringSelection class is a convenience class that can be used to
represent transferable data in the form of text strings. Keep in mind that we

could have defined our own type of transferable data which could then be used to set the contents of the clipboard.

We used the getContents( ) method to retrieve the data from the system clipboard. Notice that the data at this point is just represented in the form of Transferable data. We needed to convert the data into a String form that Java can understand. We did this by trying to get a stringFlavor for the data. If the Transferable data were presented in a form that could not be converted to a string flavor, then we would get an UnsupportedFlavorException.

That is it—pretty simple. Give it a try. Try copying data from the Java text field and pasting it in another program, say for example a word processor. Also try copying some data from some non-Java program, then pasting it in the test Java program. It works!

Lightweight Component Framework

Have you ever tried to create your own graphical control using the AWT? If you did, you probably extended the Canvas or Panel class. Although it is possible to create you own type of control extending from Canvas or Panel, it has its share of problems. One of the biggest problems is that the Canvas and Panel are both opaque windows that can make creating new GUI controls difficult. Canvases and Panels are also usually implemented using native window GUI components which can cause performance problems when a number of them are used in a component. Another issue is that the AWT uses native peers to represent the GUI component. This can be a good idea if you want your GUIs to have the native look and feel of the platform you are running on, but having peers also makes it difficult to synchronize state between the Java component and the native peer component. For example, when you create a checkbox component using the AWT, you also create a native implementation of the checkbox. The current state of the checkbox is stored in the native peer as well as the Java component. Keeping this state synchronized between the peer and the Java component requires several calls between the AWT and the peer. This can slow the performance of many AWT components.

To solve all of these problems the lightweight user interface framework was added to the JDK 1.1. JavaSoft added the capability for lightweight components to the JDK 1.1, but did not aggressively publicize its existence. The idea behind the lightweight UI framework is quite simple. It really just provides you with the ability to extend the Component and Container classes. This allows you to create your own components that do not have the problems that subclasses of Panel and Canvas have. Components that extend the Component or Container class are transparent, do not have native peers, and in all ways fit into the existing AWT and event model. This means that you can now render components that have transparent areas which allow you to paint any shape of component you like without destroying the image that exists behind the component. For example, you could create a round button. Since a lightweight component, one that extends Component or Container, does not have a native peer, the component does not require any communication between the Java representation of the component and its native peer. This, alone, makes the performance of many lightweight components far better than that of any heavy AWT components. Another advantage is that lightweight components are implemented all in Java, which permits the component to have the same look and feel across all Java platforms.

So, should you use heavyweight or lightweight components? Well, the good news is that it does not matter. You can mix lightweight and heavyweight components within any Java program. Lightweight components can contain heavyweight components and vice versa. The only thing to keep in mind is that heavyweight components will always be presented in the foreground over the top of any lightweight components; they are not transparent.

Source Code: texasButton.java

```java
import java.awt.*;
import java.awt.event.*;

public class texasButton extends Component {

  boolean inPoly = false;
  boolean mouseDown = false;
  ActionListener listener;
  Polygon poly = new Polygon(Texas.X, Texas.Y, Texas.X.length);

  public texasButton() {
    enableEvents(AWTEvent.MOUSE_EVENT_MASK |
AWTEvent.MOUSE_MOTION_EVENT_MASK);
    setBackground(Color.blue);
    }

  public synchronized void addActionListener(ActionListener l) {
    listener = AWTEventMulticaster.add(listener, l);
    }

  public synchronized void removeActionListener(ActionListener l) {
    listener = AWTEventMulticaster.remove(listener, l);
    }

  public void paint(Graphics g) {
    if (inPoly && mouseDown)
      g.setColor(getBackground().darker().darker());
    else
      g.setColor(getBackground());
    g.fillPolygon(poly);
    }
```

```
public void processMouseMotionEvent(MouseEvent e) {
  if (poly.contains(e.getPoint())) {
    if (!inPoly && mouseDown)
      repaint();
    inPoly = true;
    }
  else {
    if (inPoly && mouseDown)
      repaint();
    inPoly = false;
    }
  }

public void processMouseEvent(MouseEvent e) {
  switch (e.getID()) {

    case MouseEvent.MOUSE_PRESSED :
      if (inPoly) {
        mouseDown = true;
        repaint();
        }
      break;

    case MouseEvent.MOUSE_RELEASED :
      if (inPoly == true && mouseDown == true) {
        if (listener != null)
          listener.actionPerformed(new ActionEvent(this,
                                   ActionEvent.ACTION_PERFORMED, ""));
        repaint();
        }
      mouseDown = false;
      break;
    }
  super.processMouseEvent(e);
  }

public Dimension getPreferredSize() {
  return getMinimumSize();
  }

public Dimension getMinimumSize() {
  return new Dimension(160,150);
  }
}
```

Let's take a look at an example that creates a new lightweight component. The texasButton.java example creates a button that looks like the state of Texas. This component should work like a regular button. The button is formed using the Polygon object which represents the shape of Texas. The polygon is rendered either in the up position or down position from within the paint method. The state of the texasButton is changed in the processMouseEvent( ) method. This method sees the mouse events that are delivered to the component. When the mouse is released on the texasButton, an actionEvent is sent to the listeners of the event source. The texasTest.java program is the test program and adds a texasButton object to its frame. Notice that nothing special was done in the test program to add the texasButton. The texasButton was added and treated just like the regular Button class. You may also notice that we used a Texas class in the example. This class simply holds all the data points that form the shape of the texasButton. We did not include it in the source listings, but have put it in the accompanying CD for your reference.

Source Code: texasTest.java
```
import java.awt.*;
import java.awt.event.*;

public class texasTest extends Frame implements ActionListener {
  public static void main(String args[]) {
    test t = new test();
    }

  public void actionPerformed(ActionEvent ae) {
    System.out.println("Yee Haw");
    }

  public texasTest() {
    setBackground(Color.lightGray);
    texasButton cb = new texasButton();
    cb.addActionListener(this);
    add(cb);
    pack();
    show();
    }
}
```

That is about it. Hopefully, you can see how simple it can be to create your own lightweight components.

The Swing Set

No, this section is not about playground equipment. The Swing project at Java-Soft represents a new set of Java GUI components that use the new lightweight UI framework. The Swing set, as it is known, contains a number of basic components as well as some high-level components. All of the Swing set components are written in 100% Pure Java! This means that you can use these components on any Java platform, and they will all look and behave the same.

Since all the Swing set components use the lightweight UI framework, they all take advantage of the benefits of this new framework.

The Swing Components

Table 2.2 lists and describes all of the components that are contained in the Swing set.

So how do these components look? Figure 2.3 shows some of the new components. A majority of the Swing components extend from the JComponent class. The JComponent class is in many ways like its heavyweight counterpart, the Component class. However, the JComponent class provides more features to any class that extends from it than the Component class. These features include tooltips, keyboard accelerators, scrolling capability, borders, pluggable look and feel, and properties. Many of these features have been discussed in this chapter as new features of the JFC. The JComponent class includes all of these features by default, which means that any component that extends from it will also have access to the features.

Once you start using the new Swing components we believe that you will discover that they are easy to use, flexible, easily customizable, and faster than their heavyweight counterparts.

JavaBeans Integration

If you already know about JavaBeans, then you are probably wondering if the new Swing set components will work with existing JavaBeans. If you don't know what a JavaBean is yet, you may want jump ahead to Chapter 5, which discusses JavaBeans. In any case, you can be assured that all of the new Swing set components are JavaBeans-compliant. This means that any Swing component can be used in a Beans environment. This can be done by the simple fact that every Swing component is itself a JavaBean. Having Java GUI components that are JavaBeans will make it much easier for visual tool builders to integrate the Swing components into their environment. GUI components that are Beans will make it easy to visually manipulate any component in a graphical manner.

Pluggable Look and Feel

All of the Swing set components were designed using the model-view-controller concept. This concept permits the components to be broken up into three different parts. The model represents the state of the object. In this case the model would represent the state or data contained in the component object. The view represents the visual aspect of the component and its model data. A component view will use the state or data contained in the Model part of the component to visually represent the component. The controller is the part of the component

Table 2.2   The Swing Components

COMPONENT	DESCRIPTION
Tree View	A tree view component that displays hierarchical data
List View	A component that provides a list of strings and/or glyphs
Table View	A two-dimensional table for data
Toolbar	A component that implements toolbars
Internal Frames	Support for internal windows in an application
Borders	Generic border components to add border decorations
Pane Splitter	A component used to separate two containers
Tabbed Folder	A typical tab-based container organizer
Progress Bar	A progress bar that displays comments on the progress of a task
Slider	A slider widget used to represent continuous values
Styled Text	A component that supports HTML and rich text
Font Chooser	A font chooser dialog component
Color Chooser	A color chooser dialog component
File Chooser	A file chooser dialog component
Custom Cursors	Ability to replace default cursor with a custom glyph
Tool Tips	Ability to add tool tips to any component
Button	Generic button that supports text and check marks
Menu	Generic menu that supports text and check marks
Status Bar	A status bar component
SpinBox	Generic spin box component
ComboBox	General combo box component
Multimedia	Media controls for audio, video, and MIDI

that responds to user actions and changes the state of the component model. So when a user interacts with a component, the controller is responsible for receiving the interaction from the user, then setting the appropriate state in the Model.

It is not really important that you understand how the model-view-controller (MVC) design works. You do not need to know any of the MVC details in order to use the Swing components. However, if you do have a need to change any part of a Swing component, it is nice to know that the Swing architecture supports it.

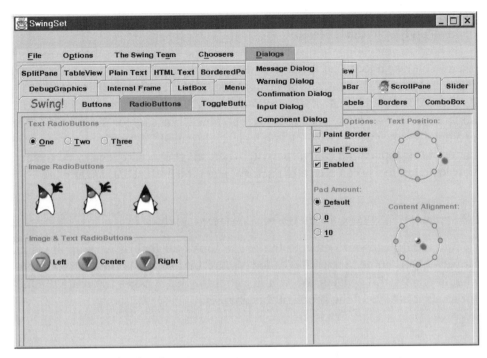

Figure 2.3   Example of Swing components.

Because of the MVC design of the Swing components, it is possible to use a pluggable look and feel for all of the components. This means that you can change how a component looks and works. It can be achieved by simply replacing the view and controller of any given component. Now any Swing component can have its own look and feel.

This is one way to get around the ever-present GUI wars. People have been fighting over how a particular GUI environment should look. Some people like the Windows look and feel, yet others like the Motif look, and still others like other looks and feels. The heavyweight AWT components skirted around this problem by making all components look like components that exist on the native platform. So, if you are using a Java program on Windows, then you would get a Windows look and feel. The Swing set went the other direction and said that all components look the same regardless of the platform. You can now end the wars because the pluggable look and feel ability of the JFC permits you or the user to choose the look and feel that you want to use.

The look and feel of a component can be changed dynamically so that users can try different choices and use the one that they like. You can also lock the look and feel so that an application will always look the same, regardless of the environment. The key here is that it does not matter; you can change the look and feel and avoid the GUI wars.

So how do you choose a look and feel? Well, the good news is that if you don't want to choose a look and feel, one will be selected for you. A default look and feel will always be present, so you do not need to concern yourself about this ability if you don't want to use it. If you do want to change the look and feel of your application, all you really need to do is set a new UIFactory for the program. For example, let's say we have a look and feel jar file called "MyLnF" and a main container of the application called "parent." Then, all you would need to do to set a new look and feel is call the setUIFactory() method in the UIManager class:

```
factoryName = "MyLnF";
UIManager.setUIFactory(factoryName,(Container)parent);
```

That is all it takes to change the entire look and feel of your application. However, you do need a jar file called MyLnF that contains the factory implementations for the widgets. We will not go into what it takes to create the factories, as it is beyond the scope of this chapter.

Drag and Drop

Drag and drop is a common graphical manipulation that is used in most of today's advanced GUIs. Drag and drop is basically the ability to graphically manipulate the transfer of data from one area or application to another. For example, you probably have used drag and drop when you have copied a file from one folder to another. You clicked on the target file and dragged the file to its new location, then released the mouse. The file was transferred from the source to the target. Of course, drag and drop can be used to perform other data manipulations.

The JDK 1.1 released the specification for drag and drop, but it did not get implemented until the Java 2 release. The difficulty in providing drag-and-drop capabilities in Java is due to the platform independence of Java. Many native platforms provide a way to perform drag and drop, but most platforms do this in a different way. JavaSoft wanted a way to perform drag-and-drop functions on all platforms so that developers could write to one API and know that it would work on all platforms.

Every drag-and-drop mechanism has the same basic elements that make up the drag-and-drop facilities. The Java drag-and-drop mechanism is no different. There must be some kind of drag source. This is the source item that represents the data to be copied or moved. There also must be one or more drop targets. The targets are graphical representations of areas where data from a drag source can be transferred. When a user clicks and drags in a drag source area, the drag-and-drop operation begins. While dragging, the user may pass the dragged icon or pointer over a drop target. When the icon passes over a suitable drop target, the targets graphical representation may change its appearance to notify the user that a legal drop can be made on that target. The user then may choose to drop the source on the target. If this happens, the data transfer will begin. In some cases, the data transfer can be transparent to the user or the data transfer may pop up a window to show the status of the transfer or ask more information from the user. At the writing of this book the implementation of drag and drop was not quite finished. If you need more information about drag and drop or its implementation, please see the JavaSoft Web page at java.sun.com.

Java 2D

The graphics capabilities that were provided in earlier releases of the JDK only provided the most basic of graphical rendering functions. Since these basic capabilities are not enough to fill the needs of some applications, Java 2D was added to the JFC to extend graphical capabilities. The new functions provided in Java 2D dramatically extend the graphics capabilities of Java. They include graphical rotation, scaling, alpha blending, and more.

We believe that these new capabilities are important enough that we have dedicated an entire chapter to the capabilities of Java 2D as well as other Java media capabilities. For more information about Java 2D and other Java Media functions refer to Chapter 3.

Summary

If you have used previous versions of the AWT, hopefully you can see that the new JFC goes far and above the original capabilities of the AWT. The JFC permits developers to create rich and full-featured graphics environments. With all the capabilities of the JFC and Java 2D you should be able to create any type of graphical interface you need. The JFC also goes a long way in solving some of the difficult problems that arise when designing a GUI application for a group of users.

Hopefully, this chapter gave you a better understanding of what capabilities the JFC has and how to use those capabilities in your own programs. Since the JFC is quite large and has many details, you may require more information than was presented here. If this is the case, we recommend that you find an advanced book that only covers the JFC and all of its details.

Using Java Media

Introduction

This chapter describes the overall structure and function of the most recently published Java Media API specifications. The focus is on the larger world view of the structure and organization of these various core and standard extension class libraries. We will use a real-world example to highlight the uses of Java Media in creating a rich and creative Web-based, time-critical media experience called Java City (see Figure 3.1). The body of this chapter is divided into three parts: design, implementation, and integration.

The Java Media API family currently consists of the following components (see Table 3.1).

Welcome to Java City!

Java City is a virtual city of today and was designed to be used as a storytelling device to promote the uses and applications of Java technology in the commercial enterprise computing world. This project makes use of several components of the Java platform including: JDK 1.1.3, Java Media Framework (JMF alpha),

Figure 3.1   Overhead picture of Java City.

Java 2D, and Java 3D. Throughout this chapter we will use Java City as the example reference implementation.

Design: Reaching Java City by Bridge from the Old World to the New

Perhaps the greatest challenge facing commercial multimedia developers and producers today is bringing forth an experience which the consumer can intuitively learn. So often, the navigation controls provided for a given application pose an arbitrary barrier to actually using the tool and benefiting from the intended experience—be it for work or leisure. The emergence of the Web browser in the 1990s can be compared to the emergence of the automotive dashboard in the 1930s, 1940s, and 1950s. It was quite enough for the novice or inexperienced motorist to keep one car on the road; imagine what it must have been like to attempt driving a car you had never seen and whose operation was vaguely similar but ultimately quite different from the one you knew.

The current fragmentation of computer users into the respective camps of Windows, Macintosh, UNIX, and others has benefited the owners of those interfaces much more than those they have sold to. The arrival of the Web browser brought with it the first real and measurable progress towards leveling this uneven playing field. Java is one of the fundamental underlying technologies

Table 3.1 Java Media API Components

JAVA MEDIA API CORE AND STANDARD EXTENSIONS (JAVA 2)
Java 2D*
Java 3D
Java Media Framework
Java Share
Java Sound*
Java Animation
Java Telephony
Java Speech
Java Advanced Imaging

*included in Java Core as of Java 2

driving this change. But with change comes the burden of having to deliver on the promises of streaming media, real-time video on the desktop, rich color, rich text, and 3D capabilities which are supposed to change the way we work, the way we play, and the way in which we think about the world around us. Sounds like pretty hefty baggage to be carrying into the new paradigm. So what does all this have to do with Java and the Java Media APIs? In a word, usability.

Design Criteria: Usability

The first target of any successful multimedia experience is almost always related to the usability of its interface, and more importantly the usability and reusability of the components of which it is made. Java and the Java Media APIs provide a layer of abstraction never previously available to multimedia developers. This abstraction means that Java Media–enabled applications will run on multiple platforms without platform-specific changes to your source code base. Before you start your first napkin sketch, before you write the first line of applet code, you know that you're working with a toolkit that is designed to be multiplatform from the very start. While it is quite true that a given implementation will have system-specific, lower-level components, the interface to those components is consistent across the Java Media API family and is guaranteed to be so. Since the Java language is licenseable, licensees must implement all core API components and these implementations must conform to the Java testing suite as well as with the language specification. As of this writing, the core Java 2 specification includes the Java 2D and the Java Sound APIs. This means that if a developer licenses the Java 2 to develop for its own uses and ultimately to resell to the world at large, its version of the runtime Java VM must support the functionality in those APIs. Of course, this doesn't make sense for someone who is licensing Java for use in embedded devices which have no display or audio. For these folks, it is possible to license a subset of the spec for use in these types of devices.

Design Criteria: Portability

As mentioned in the previous paragraph, portability is paramount to a successful multimedia experience. It is also one of the keys to the treasure chest of revenue for the smartest and most highly respected multimedia houses in the industry. Portability is everything when it comes to reaching the widest possible customer base. Without it, you are forced to market and sell to only those people who happen to have chosen the same operating environment to run in as you have to develop in, whether it is Windows, Macintosh, UNIX, or what have you. When it comes to multimedia applications, which are traditionally top heavy on user interface components, the discretization into implementations is even more strongly felt by the beleaguered end user. It is the rare multimedia application which runs on three or more platforms, but it is even rarer to find that it also runs in different implementations of a single environment, such as Windows from Microsoft, which has three separate camps to support, Win 3.1.x, Win 95, and Windows/NT. The UNIX world also suffers from this, with compatible binary formats, but proprietary chipsets and compilers. At best they can only agree to standardize at the source code level. Apple is perhaps the one example of a company that has implemented a cohesive and expansive multimedia-aware operating system, MacOS. While historically quite primitive when compared to other 32- and 64-bit, multitasking multiprocessing operating environments, it is fair to say that the majority of production print media and preproduction motion video are touched by a Macintosh in some form or other. Clearly, the more portable your application is, the better its chance for success in the real world, no matter how advanced the technology.

Design Criteria: Reusability

Also mentioned in the opening paragraphs on design criteria, the concept of code and content reusability is a powerful one with respect to multimedia systems development and deployment. When it comes to margin of return on investment in the Western world and increasingly in the Eastern world, media is king. No other form of commercial exchange has such a high rate of return for the initial raw materials. To put it simply, no one else makes more money than from the sale of creative ideas (except of course for the world's second oldest profession—one of the only industries that is massively profiting worldwide from the networked digital age). The natural resource of people's creative talent is a limitless resource which is highly prized and freely available. Traditional industries which rely on finite resources such as wood, paper, metal, and plastic will eventually exhaust themselves—perhaps in favor of new ones, but they are finite nonetheless. It is estimated that successful media houses of the twenty-first century will ultimately make the majority of their revenue streams from repurposed content. A less euphemistic way of putting it is reruns of reruns. Similar to this trend is the widespread availability of hardware and software systems that will enable this massive reordering of pre-existing multimedia content. In the same way that repurposed content will provide large rewards to the wise multimedia producer, so too will repurposed software provide substantial rewards to the savvy multimedia tools developer. A standard base of software APIs which comes from a single language and has been received with worldwide acceptance is hard to pass by.

Java Media API Overview

Before describing the process of implementing Java City using components of the Java Media API family, it makes the most sense to provide a quick overview of the APIs so we can provide the framework of understanding necessary to follow the implementation phase. To help with your understanding of translating from the general to the specific, you may wish to review the other areas of this book which refer to the overall Java computing platform, as we will refer to several component areas in this chapter which presume this knowledge.

The Java platform is the all-encompassing term used to refer to the entire array of Java technologies, most notably the critical components such as the runtime VM, the developer's kit, and the core Java APIs, such as Java.lang, Java.AWT, Java.net, Java.util, Java.io, and so forth. Within the Java platform is the notion of core APIs versus standard extensions. As mentioned previously, this distinction is most important to the licensees of the Java language, who by inference must develop and support conforming implementations of all core licensed APIs. At the current time, the Java 2D and Java Sound APIs are considered core and are of concern to all licensees. The remaining Java Media APIs, while not core components, must still be implemented by their respective licensees according to the publicly published specification wherever applicable. It is widely expected that all of the major computer software and hardware manufacturers will provide their own reference implementations. For example, Intel Corporation has released a beta developer's kit which includes the closest conforming implementation of the Java Animation API, pending its final release to the Java community by JavaSoft.

Table 3.1 lists the currently specified Java Media APIs, as of Java One, 1997. The following sections describe each area in varying detail, depending on the amount of publicly available information at publication.

Java 2D

The Java 2D API concerns itself with providing many of the basic and core services common to any 2D user interface, and text and image manipulation system. These include, but are not limited to: image copy, image display, compositing, scaling, rotation, translation, simple filtering, font handling, antialiasing, and so on. It provides methods for drawing lines and line styles, circles, splines, and other 2D geometric primitives. Color management is also addressed, allowing developers to plug into a consistent best-effort color management policy across multiple hardware and software systems.

Table 3.2 shows a quick reference of the top level class hierarchy of Java 2D as implemented in Java 2.

Java 3D

The Java 3D API is likely to be very unlike any other 3D API you will have encountered previously. This is because it is scene-graph based. This requires

Table 3.2   Java 2D Class Hierarchy

package java.javamedia.java2d	
Interface index:	
BufferedImageOp	Transform
Path	Transform2D
Class index:	
Affine Transform	GlyphMetrics
AffineTransformOp	GraphicsADV
BezierPath	GraphicsDevice
BufferedImage	HistogramClipOp
BufferedImageFilter	ICC_Profile
Color	ICC_ProfileData
ColorModel	ICC_ProfileGray
ColorTransform	ICC_ProfileRGB
ComponentLayout	IndexColorModelADV
Composite	Kernel
CompositeBase	LookupOp
CompositeOp	LookupTable
ConvolveOp	Paint
DirectColorModelADV	PointADV
FontADV	SharpenOp
FontDescriptor	ShowString
FontMetricsADV	StrikeSet
GlobalGraphicsEnvironment	Stroke
GlobalTextEnvironment	TextEncoder

the developers to think about the 3D objects which they want to model as living in a world which can change over the course of time. Most 3D APIs available to date, such as OpenGL, Direct3d, or XGL from Sun Microsystems, and Starbase from HP, only concern themselves with the objects the programmer wishes to model. This includes their placement in space and their static object properties, such as color, texture, and surface reflectance properties. This is fine if you are a mechanical engineer designing a crankshaft. However, if the programmer wishes to place these objects in a larger context, say within the context of the crankshaft in motion within the engine block designed by the folks down the hall, it's up to him or her to work out all the details of multiple objects in motion, and so forth. This motion is also referred to as a behavior.

The term applied to a collection of all objects in a given 3D space, their behaviors, and the ways in which they interact and change over time is called a scene graph. This is the first and most important thing to know about Java 3D. From there, if you have already worked with existing 3D APIs, it is not hard to understand the rest of what Java 3D provides. If you are completely unfamiliar with 3D techniques, all is not lost. Read on and we will discuss this in more detail towards the end of the chapter when we talk about Java City 3 in 3D.

Java Media Framework

The primary function of the Java Media Framework is to provide multimedia capabilities to Java applets and applications. The Java Media Framework, or JMF for short, is concerned with the reliable and content-neutral delivery of time-critical media in a variable bandwidth, distributed, networked environment. This is quite a mouthful, no? What it implies is that within the JMF class hierarchy, a developer should expect to find the following services:

- Time management services
- Event management services
- Synchronization sources and services

AWT HISTORY

It is interesting to AWT history that much of the original AWT functionality, as well as much of the missing functionality, is now present in Java 2D. This was an intended migration as Java gained prominence and was mandatory for widespread user interface. Originally, AWT was the "face" put on LiveOak, which until that time had almost no user interface API support. With the innovation of the Java foundation classes, it is believed that the majority of dispute between the division of responsibility of UI components and 2D components has been solved.

- Media player construction and control
- Media content factories and handlers

The Java Media Framework is key to overcoming one of the primary objections to using Java technologies in such demanding, time-critical, and unreliable computing environments. The first thing to realize about the JMF is that it does not necessarily implement the entire media-rendering pipeline as 100% Pure Java. Given the relative proliferation of streaming media players into most contemporary display-oriented computer systems, in the Java Media Framework these are thought of as any other component of the core operating system. That is, it is assumed that at least some pre-existing form of media player(s) will be present wherever Java Media Framework applets and applications are running. With this boundary established, what is left to do is to establish a powerful, consistent, and flexible native method interface which accommodates the superset of media object functionality. Extensibility is also designed in, so that new players can be easily added and, in most cases, loaded dynamically according to content type. Therefore, you only need to publish the content type and its player, rather than a complete reimplementation of the playback and authoring classes you've already built.

The JMF is also responsible for providing cross-platform synchronization of multiple instances of media objects. Players, recorders, transporters, encoders, decoders all communicate to deliver time-critical events in a consistent fashion.

Table 3.3 lists the top level class hierarchy of the media framework.

Java Sound

The Java Sound engine is a more evolved audio playback and control interface than in previous versions of the JDK. Providing high quality and full stereo 44-kHz digital audio, the Java Sound interface provides the ability to mix multiple sources and sinks of audio with support for popular formats and protocols such as WAV, AU, and MIDI. Other features include:

- Multichannel rendering
- Wave table synthesis
- Generalized audio synthesis interfaces

Java Share

As the information age moves forward into the twenty-first century, the promise of distributed computing is slowly finding its way into commercial software packages. However, one thing which remains relatively absent from these applications is the notion of distributed interaction. Leaving a significant portion of

Table 3.3 Java Media Framework Package Hierarchy

package java.media	
Interface index:	
CachingControl	GainChangeListener
Clock	GainControl
Control	MediaHandler
Controller	MediaProxy
ControllerListener	Player
Duration	TimeBase
Class Index:	
CachingControlEvent	PackageManager
ConnectionErrorEvent	PrefetchCompleteEvent
ControllerClosedEvent	RateChangeEvent
ControllerErrorEvent	RealizeCompleteEvent
ControllerEvent	ResourceUnavailableEvent
DataStarvedEvent	RestartingEvent
DeallocateEvent	StartEvent
DurationUpdateEvent	StopAtTimeEvent
EndOfMediaEvent	StopByRequestEvent
GainChangeEvent	StopEvent
InternalErrorEvent	StopTimeChangeEvent
Manager	Time
MediaLocator	TransitionEvent
MediaTimeSetEvent	
Exception Index:	
ClockStoppedException	MediaException
IncompatibleSourceException	NoDataSourceException
IncompatibleTimeBaseException	NoPlayerException
Error Index:	
ClockStartedError	NotRealizedError
MediaError	StopTimeSetError
NotPrefetchedError	

the power of telecommuting untapped, the lack of significant application data sharing and distributed interactive interfaces can get a much needed boost by incorporating Java Share technology.

The concept of application-aware data sharing is not entirely new; there are several packages available today which allow virtual workgroups to communicate. Many of the precursors to live application data sharing include the popular office productivity application suites such as Office97 from Microsoft or Lotus Notes from IBM Corp. What is new with Java Share is the ability to build application-unaware sharing of live and static data. What exactly does this mean?

Consider a popular business administration example. An employee has to submit her expenses on a regular basis and does so using an internally developed Java applet which allows her to tally and submit a month's expenses. During the review process, her manager spots an apparent discrepancy and wants to further review it. The approval form on the manager's version of the expenses applet has a button for clarification. Flagging the report for clarification also initiates the collaboration applet embedded in the expense report, launching a Java Share–enabled class to initiate a quick video conference with the employee if she is available. From there, the employee and the manager can both work on the same version of the expenses spreadsheet and solve the dilemma. While the expenses spreadsheet has been designed as a collaboration-aware applet, the manager's expense review was unaware of collaboration until it encountered a data type which enabled it.

Not surprisingly, the Java Share API is implemented using the Java RMI API, which stands for remote method invocation. Java RMI is also a key component of the JavaBeans architecture, which is likely to be the source of many Java Share applets. Software developers will simply decide whether their applet or application needs to share its data and, if so, how. Using Java Share–enabled Beans, they can quickly and easily build collaboration-aware and collaboration-unaware applets. Or at least that's how the story goes.

Java Animation

The Java Animation API was created to support the most common forms of 2D sprite animations. Support for motion paths, alpha blending, collision detection, and other behaviors which change over time are also provided.

Java Telephony

The Java Telephony API concerns itself with providing folks in the telco industry with a standard set of phone switch call and control interfaces. Because of Java's inherent applicability to contemporary phone switch hardware architectures, the Java Telephony API was created. The vast array of proprietary phone switches and terminal equipment currently manufactured have at least come to rely on the availability of mass-produced, cheap, and off-the-shelf microprocessors, such as Motorola, Mitsubishi, and others. Since Java already runs on several of these chipsets, using one common language to implement control software on these multiple platforms is a very attractive and cost-effective alternative.

Java Speech

The field of computer speech recognition and synthesis has come a long, long way since its first appearances in the 1960s research literature. Several manufacturers now comprise a sizable software and hardware industry, each with its own speech processing engine, most often designed to handle a certain aspect or subset of speech processing requirements. Until the 1990s, however, most speech recognition algorithms only recognized a very limited vocabulary of sounds which had to be spoken identically from utterance to utterance. Speech synthesis was even worse, forever producing endless variations on the deadpan and lifeless computer voice sounds we have all heard at one time or another. Perhaps the best examples of this (or worst if you take our meaning), were the talking cars of the mid- to late-1980s. This feature had a very short lifetime in modern automotive history.

The promise of speech recognition is to help remove our dependence on one of the most harmful input and control devices ever created. The combination of mouse and keyboard is debilitating tens of thousands of users a year. In addition, the rigid adherence to these devices has nearly eliminated any hope of physically challenged users to use a computer system as competently as the next person.

The Java Speech API, much like the Java Media Framework and the Java 3D API, will provide a high-level common interface to many of the contemporary native speech engines available today, opening up access to new computing platforms.

Java Advanced Imaging

The Java Advanced Imaging API is where developers should look for the more complete and more sophisticated image-processing functions than Java 2D. These include morphological image filters such as convolves, image smoothing, and image blending, and high quality image scaling, such as bilinear and trilinear approximations. It also has an advanced notion of operating on regions of interest, boundary conditions, and image tiling as well.

Java City Implementation

The original concept for Java City was to create a CD-ROM-based 3D virtual world as the basis for a demo which could be used over and over again to represent the applicability of Java in the commercial networked enterprise computing industry. Unfortunately for us, at that time the majority of Java Media was still in the specification phase with no existing Java classes written with which to build. The Java 3D specification wasn't even in alpha and the Java Media Framework was barely far enough along to use.

The driving principle behind the design and creation of Java City as a multimedia experience was to experiment with new forms of interactive infotainment. As many of you may already have experienced, every demo author and multimedia artist has his or her own ideas about user interface conventions, sequencing, and delivery of critical timed media and the navigation of multimedia environments. As a result, the majority of interactive CD-ROMs are vastly different—so different that we are forced to learn the interface and usability conventions of each new CD-ROM or Web site we visit. With the dawning of the Web browser age the average computer user has embraced a model of usability which is defined largely by the features offered by his or her browser of choice. Since most Web browsers now provide relatively similar features and functions, it is reasonable to migrate demo experiences to a Web-based format. By doing this, we have greatly reduced many of the usability barriers from which previous non-Web friendly demo interfaces suffered. The user is free to focus on the experience and the content instead of struggling with how to get to it. This is another reason why Java Media was chosen as the framework to implement with; it provided seamless access to the Java Virtual Machine to organize and implement all the higher level interaction constructs while allowing the development team to rely on the tried and true performance and reliability of native method content players.

Java City Was Not Built in a Day

Since we could not implement a Java 3D version of Java City, we decided to investigate the use of precomputer-generated digital video sequences (MPEG) to navigate through the city. Then, these sequences would be embedded into a local Web of HTML, Java applets, and imagery to create an interactive multimedia experience. In the evaluation process, we had to weigh the relative benefits and costs of using precomputed digital sequences over "live" 3D graphics. The primary benefit of the precomputed MPEG sequences was that we retained complete control over the synchronization of audio and video, since we were guaranteed a constant 30-frame-per-second playback rate. This kind of guarantee is rare or unheard of when navigating complex 3D geometric worlds. We also retained control over where the user went in the city, thereby ensuring that the visual cues, messages, and interactions that were intended for the user would have to occur. However, what we lost was the ability to freely move about in space according to the user's wishes, as well as risking the loss of immersion in the experience. As a rule, people seem to respond to immersion more readily in a highly interactive 3D experience over a comparable 2D experience. The exception to this is photo-realistic 2D image-warping virtual worlds, such as those created with QuickTime VR. Fortunately, the Java Media Framework itself does not restrict the content author to using only precomputed MPEG sequences; rather, this was a constraint imposed by the available tools at the time.

Before we begin talking about how we actually implemented Java City with applets, HTML, and MPEG players, it is worthwhile to describe the Java City tour in more detail, so that you can follow the tool development and integration phases. See Figure 3.2 for a Venn diagram of the Java City Website.

The first thing users see when they start Java City is the HotJava browser which displays a Sun logo as the splash screen. To keep the interface as minimalistic as possible, we only used a single forward "Next" link in the browser window itself, relying on all the other navigational interface support provided by the HotJava browser. The only function of this button was to move the user from start to finish through Java City.

Clicking on the next button of the splash screen was the cue to the player applet to load an MPEG1 movie from local hard drive and begin playback in the browser window. This 30-second movie features the opening shot which is a fly-through of a deep river canyon, revealing a panorama of Java City. Users are flown through a prerendered and predetermined camera path until they arrive at their first destination in the city, the James Gosling Auditorium. At this point, the video stops playing and control is returned to the user to initiate the next action. By clicking on the next button again, the player applet is restarted, but this time loads a different movie and teleports the user from standing outside of the auditorium to an example Java applet, such as the Cat Band from NaSoft.

At this point, the video screen is wiped completely and replaced with a traditional Java applet. From here, the users are free to explore the workings of the applet. When complete, clicking on the next button restarts the player applet and begins another video clip which transports them from the auditorium to a strip mall ending with a tight shot of a guitar store. Clicking again, the user is

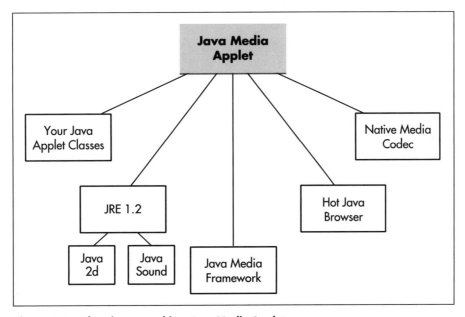

Figure 3.2   The pieces used in a Java Media Applet.

transported into the guitar store whereupon a new applet is loaded which allows the user to play back a selection of blues riffs from an interactive guitar applet.

To complete the tour of Java City, the users are transported to two more applets, then flown out of the city, ultimately docking with the Java City blimp and the fade-out to Sun logo, and then black screen. At the completion of this video clip, the next button returns the user to the opening splash screen. With this as the thumbnail sketch of what the Java City tour is all about, now let's talk about how to build it.

A Recipe for a Multimedia Web Using the JMF, Java 2D, and Java Sound

Since there are no Java Media–enabled multimedia authoring environments yet in existence, we had to build our own. Most or all of Java City was hand-assembled. In the near future, it is fully expected that many of these components will be encapsulated as JavaBeans and be capable of assembly using a visual multimedia authoring tool. In the absence of this kind of sophisticated power tools, we submit a quick recipe for building Java City:

9 parts precomputed MPEG1 sequences (using a commercial digital rendering package)

4 parts cool Java applets

1 part HotJava 1.x Web browser

1 part Java Virtual Machine, Java 2

1 part Java Media Framework class libraries

1 part Java 2D class libraries

1 part Java Sound class libraries

20 parts HTML Web pages

1 part native method MPEG1 decoder

Start by creating and linking all HTML pages together using a standard Web page authoring tool, substituting blank placeholders where the video playback applets and *cool applets* should be. Once the HTML Web has gelled and is firm to the touch of the browser, go back and begin inserting applet tags wherever links to video applets or cool applets are meant to go. Fold all required background images into the Web, as well as the nine MPEG1 sequences, compiled applet class files, the Java Virtual Machine, and the Java Media class libraries into one manageable directory structure. When you have assembled all the components, the content may be served to your guests by inviting them to launch the HotJava browser from their desktop.

Creating the HTML

Figure 3.3 provides an example HTML file with the more familiar HTML layout tags and background information, but also includes an applet tag that describes the location of the MPEG1 movie and the default background image to play it on. Inside the applet, we deal with any hotspot video regions to be processed. The last part of the HTML file includes a link to the next Web page to load.

The Player Applet

To create the player applet, most of the work has already been done for you between the Java Media Framework classes and the example player classes, and HTML examples that are part of the distribution. For the majority of cases, the *player applet* example will be sufficient, as it was in this case. To add features or functionality to the existing player classes, we recommend that you review the *Java Media Framework API* and the *Java Media Framework User's Guide*, both available in a variety of formats from the www.javasoft.com Website. Following is the pseudocode for a typical player applet which imports the media framework classes and instantiates a basic player.

```
import java.applet.Applet;
import java.awt.;
import java.lang.String;
import java.net.URL;
```

```
<HTML>
<HEAD>
<TITLE>JavaCity 2 - Welcome to JavaCity ! </TITLE>
</HEAD>

<BODY BACKGROUND="images/bckgd.fig" BGCOLOR-"#88888888"
TEXT="#000000" LINK="#000000" VLINK="#01424a">
<P>
<CENTER>
<APPLET code-JavaCity2.class width=1024 height=768>
<PARAM name=IMAGE value="images/JavaCityBack.gif">
<PARAM name=MOVIE value="JavaCity2.mpg">
</APPLET>
</CENTER>
<P>
<P><CENTER><A HREF="clip2.html">Next</A></CENTER>
</BODY>
</HTML>
```

Figure 3.3   Example HTML file.

```
import java.media.;
import sun.media.;

public class GenericPlayerApplet extends Applet implements
ControllerListener {

// media Player
Player player = null;

// component in which video is playing
Component visualComponent = null;

// Main panel which video is rendered to
Panel panel = null;

public void init() {

// Set up the default layout

// Strip applet tags from call that started us running

// Locate movie file and create media player object

// Add a controller listener object to connect to the
// player

}

public void start() {
// Call player.start() to prefetch and start the player.
}

public void stop() {
// Stop the player, player.stop()
// Deallocate the player
}

public void destroy() {
// Dispose of the current media player
}

}
```

Setting Up the Runtime Environment

To execute and run an applet such as Java City, the users will need to have the core JRE (Java runtime environment) files installed on their machine, as well as compatible versions of the Java 2D and JMF class libraries. The Java Sound libraries are included by default in the release of JRE/Java 2. This all presumes the existence of the HotJava 1.x Web browser or a suitable Java-enabled Web browser that implements Java 2 and does not have a customized security manager which prohibits the use of native method applications, such as the MPEG1 decoder. Lastly, you will need to have a media player resident on the machine you are running which has been integrated into the existing Java Media Framework classes. If you are unable to find such a player, it is quite possible that you will need to extend the player classes to provide support for your player, if no one else has done it for you. For details on exactly which players and which formats are supported on which platforms, we strongly suggest that you refer to the Java Media Web pages at www.javasoft.com.

Note, all that is minimally required is the JRE, a Java-enabled browser, and a set of Java classes written and supplied by you which can detect which pieces are resident on the machine and which ones are not. Based on this, it is possible to locate the missing pieces, and have them acquired and loaded onto the machine dynamically at runtime using the concept of a content handler. However, this capability is not provided by default in the JDK or Java Media releases. Details on how to create such a handler are beyond the scope of this book. See Figure 3.2 for a graphic depiction of the pieces required and their relationships.

Launching the Browser and Running the Applet

With the runtime environment now in place on your machine, here's a quickie tour of what actually happens behind the scenes of Java City.

HotJava Browser Is Launched

When the browser is launched by the user, the Java Virtual Machine is loaded into system memory and the HotJava application begins executing. This includes allocation of heap memory space, instantiation of the class loader, initialization of the garbage collector and thread scheduler, as well as connections to the native window system and security manager. Following this, the first page of HTML content is read and parsed by the HotJava browser and displayed for the user as the welcoming splash screen.

The Player Applet Is Initiated

When the user clicks "Next" to go to the first video sequence, the HotJava browser reads the next HTML file and parses it, encountering the first applet tag for the media player. This tag tells the browser to look for the Java Media class libraries compiled into the media player applet files and load them into the VM. Once these class files have been read into memory, the applet has now created and instantiated a virtual digital VCR. The applet includes a primitive control interface on the front panel of the browser window which includes buttons for play, stop, and pause. The media player applet then proceeds through the applet life cycle of start, stop, init, and run. In the main run loop, the media player applet initializes the native method interfaces to the native MPEG1 decoder and connects to it using a predefined control interface. This interface is the same for all media players and is part of the JMF control interface which must be implemented when adding new media players to the JMF player family. Once the connection to the native decoder has been established, the name and local file path of the MPEG1 movie is passed to the player, and decode and playback to the browser screen commences.

It is important to note at this point that not all media players in the JMF are or must be native methods. In future versions of the JRE and the Java Media Framework, it will be feasible to implement 100% Pure Java media decoders and encoders, possibly running on a 100% Java network computer (NC) or even on the average desktop PC, depending on the complexity of the media stream decode and encode requirements.

How the Player Applet Controls Playback and Response

Once the digital movie playback begins, the media framework classes assist the player applet in sampling mouse and keyboard inputs, and relaying those back to the player applet. At this stage, the player applet has loaded the media framework control classes and is controlling the media player events, such as start, pre-fetch, stop, pause, and so on.

Using Java 2D in Java City

At the time that Java City was being created, the Java 2D libraries were not available. However, this does not preclude us from talking about where the right places in such a multimedia production as Java City are for using Java 2D.

For each of the applets which appear between the video segments, it would have been desirable to include some professionally produced 2D graphics which would help to document the use and purpose of these applets. In fact, a future version of Java City will be using Java 2D to provide high-resolution professionally rendered and anti-aliased text to support the use of Java City. Prior to Java 2, the only fonts you had available were the ones supported by the JDK on your particular platform, short of writing your own font handler and renderer.

Java 2D provides the following features to the Java programmer:

Anti-aliased and internationalized font handling

2D primitive arbitrary shape support: lines, curves, 2D polygons

Geometric transformations: scale, rotate, translate

Spline paths

Using Java 3D to Implement a Virtual Reality Experience of Java City

While the existing version of Java City which uses prerendered digital video streams to accomplish the task of moving throughout the city makes good use of the Java Media Framework technologies, it could just as easily have been implemented with Java 3D.

When most people think of 3D and the Web, inevitably the term VRML enters the discussion. VRML stands for virtual reality modeling language, although to be exact, neither VRML 1.0 or VRML 2.0 are really formal languages in the same way we think of Java as a computer language. Unfortunately, there has been a good deal of misunderstanding among netizens who are interested in using Java 3D for their Web site content. What are the differences between Java 3D and VRML? Why is one better than the other? How do I use these tools and what do I use them for?

Most often, the distinction made between Java 3D and VRML is that Java 3D is an API for implementing and manipulating scene-graph-based 3D graphics, whereas VRML defines what is in a scene graph, or the format, placement, and appearance of the given objects and behaviors in a scene graph. For those not familiar with the concept of a scene graph, think of a tree-like, object-oriented diagram which describes the components of a 3D world from the most general objects at the top of the tree and the most detailed at the leaf nodes of the tree.

The design and creation of 3D graphics software systems has been evolving for the last 25 years. Most recently, in the mid to late 1990s the field of interactive 3D computer graphics software has agreed on the use of a single 3D graphics API, namely OpenGL from Silicon Graphics, Inc. (SGI). While very useful for constructing a description of 3D objects and their appearances in a highly compact and portable manner, all these objects and object properties are static. Obviously, this is not very useful for creating highly interactive virtual worlds. Just as people demanded more from their static HTML Web pages, so, too, does the world clamor for interactive 3D graphics.

At or about the time that Java first gained worldwide popularity, the VRML 1.0 wave of popularity was also spreading across the Web. Unfortunately, VRML 1.0 suffered from the same lack of dynamism which affected HTML and Open GL. In order for 3D to grow and proliferate on the World Wide Web, it must first be possible to construct complex and entertaining worlds in which netizens can interact.

CHAPTER

4

Mastering Networking and I/O Techniques

Introduction

A chapter on networking, in a book on Java, seems almost redundant. After all, Java was developed specifically with networking, and with network communications, in mind. The base packages of Java, from Sun Microsystems, include several networking interfaces for both Web-based network communications (opening, reading, and closing of URLs, and so forth) and lower-level, more basic network communications (creation and manipulation of network sockets). In addition, Java provides an entire set of libraries and objects for accessing databases over the network. These classes, included in JDBC, are becoming increasingly important in the networked age of online business and transaction-based computing over the World Wide Web, and are discussed in Chapter 8.

The basic packages, which include network communication capabilities, are those in the java.net hierarchy (of course!) and the java.io hierarchy. From here, you can easily begin programming fully network-capable Java programs. Since Java networking is based on the open standards of the Internet, those who already have experience with Internet network programming will feel right at home with Java (better, actually, since Java networking packages make things so much easier. But we're getting ahead of ourselves). If you know all about

TCP/IP network programming, feel free to skip the next few sections. Otherwise, hold on for a crash course in network software development!

Basic Networking Principles

Behind all the usefulness of the Internet is a vast array of complicated network programming. While we won't cover the serious complexities of network programming, since Java makes that unnecessary, we will cover enough basics so that you understand how the Internet works.

Overview

Before we begin talking about the specifics of Java network programming, it might be wise to spend just a few minutes on some of the basics of Internet networking in general. The Internet is generally based on the open networking standard protocols known as TCP/IP, or the Transport Control Protocol/Internet Protocol. These standard protocols, defined and maintained by the Internet Engineering Task Force (IETF), define how communications between computers over the Internet should take place. It is on top of the TCP/IP basics such as the HyperText Transfer Protocol (HTTP), the File Transfer Protocol (FTP), and many others that all Java network packages are layered. Since this is a higher-level view of network programming, we are not going to cover the specifics of data transmission through the TCP/IP stack or over the wire, but will focus on how to use these underlying protocols, through Java, to write network-capable applets and applications.

Clients and Servers

One of the first ideas to understand is the concept of clients and servers on a network; though a simple enough idea, understanding it is critical in order to write efficient, network-friendly applications (see Figure 4.1). Write an unfriendly network application and you could set off a storm of protest about your application.

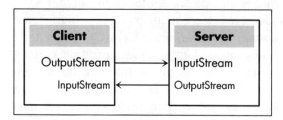

Figure 4.1   Client-server diagram.

Servers and Services

A server can provide *services* to network clients in a variety of ways. One of the most obvious, in today's world, is the Web server which provides documents, including graphics, sound, and Java applets to clients over the network. Other services commonly provided are e-mail (SMTP, or Simple Mail Transfer Protocol; IMAP4, or Internet Mail Access Protocol), network file access (NFS, for Network File Service; FTP, for File Transfer Protocol), naming services (DNS, for Domain Naming Service; NIS, for Network Information Services), and login services such as Telnet and rlogin. By writing your own Java-based services, you can provide whatever service you can dream up to offer over the network.

Clients and Services

Clients request services from the servers they find, or learn about, on the network. Again, knowing the server name, or address, port number, and protocol, a client can request any service it wants. Of course, the key is knowing the server name and port number so that the client can open a socket connection to the specified port.

Ports and Sockets

One last bit of explanation before we get to the Java part. The concept of ports and sockets, in the network and Java world, allows us to contact servers and request the services we need, at a known location. Much like a telephone call, we have to know the party we want to contact. In the network world, the party is the server and we contact it by name. In addition to this, we have to know the protocol we want to use, HTTP, for instance, and the port number to contact the server on for that protocol. In the example of HTTP, most Web servers can be contacted on port 80, though some also offer services over other ports. Most ports are assigned by the Internet Engineering Task Force and are adhered to by all manufacturers and networks. Port numbers are in the range of 1 to 9999, with the ports below 1024 being assigned and controlled by the IETF. So, once you know the name of the server you want, and the port number that the server offers that service over, you're ready to contact the server. You do this contact over a socket. A socket is simply a connection to a specific port number. Though the HTTP daemon *listens* for requests on port 80, it sets up multiple sockets on that port, so that it can talk to many clients at the same time.

Though all of this may seem a bit confusing now, once you begin using the Java networking packages, it will all become clear. So, let's move on to Java! In order for clients and servers to communicate, the concept of ports and sockets was developed so that programs would know where to look for one another over the network, and how to communicate with each other once they locate the service they want. All network services are offered on a numbered port and clients contact the server on that port to request service. A process will use a particular socket on that port in order to identify the specific process with which it is communicating, since multiple clients could open several channels of communication to a server listening on a port. In order to request services over the network, a program needs to know at least two things: the name, or address, of the machine which will provide the service and the port number on that machine on which the service is offered. The client may also need to know the protocol, or language, to speak, but we'll get to that.

Java Networking Principles

Now that we have a basic understanding of the general principles of network programming—the underpinnings of the Internet—let's dive into the specifics of how to implement those principles in Java.

Overview

Unlike many other programming languages, Java was designed with the network in mind, so networking support is built into the language, and rich support for much of the nitty-gritty details of network communication is taken care of by the underlying virtual machine implementation, class libraries, and networking APIs. The majority of the networking support in Java is contained in the java.net and java.io hierarchies, though the JDBC (Java Database Access Classes) also contain a fair amount of network support, as you might imagine. The RMI libraries, which handle Remote Method Invocation, also contain a significant amount of network support, since remotely invoking an object would obviously require some sort of network connectivity. However, with Java, you don't have to write all the low-level network code, as you did before. You can, if you'd like, but it's all supplied for you in the basic and extended Java class libraries.

Clients and Servers

The Java java.net class hierarchy provides the basic tools for developing both client and server applications for the Internet. With the java.net.socket class, you can create a network socket to a server, and begin sending data back and forth. With the java.net.ServerSocket class, you can implement a network server application that will listen on the network for incoming client requests, set up the necessary network connections, and begin communicating. What you do with these incoming requests—how you handle them—is up to your application. In order to handle such network communications, you might like to define your own network protocol, or network language, so that your server knows what your clients will say and how to answer them effectively.

Protocols and Protocol Handlers

With Java, you can support, and communicate in, a wide variety of network protocols or you can define your own and implement that. Support for basic HTTP, FTP, and other standard Web-services protocols are fully supported by Java. Should you want to *speak* something else between your clients and servers, you'll have to design and write that protocol yourself. You do this by writing what is called a *protocol handler*, a Java object which, when used by an applet or application, imparts the necessary understanding to communicate using the defined protocol. Once you have this protocol available, any of your Java applications or applets can then use this protocol handler to understand, and speak, the protocol. In addition to simply defining your own protocol, you can extend or implement protocols which are supplied by the Java APIs in order to add functionality.

For example, the java.io package provides an interface for serializing objects so that they can easily be written over the network. If your application needs to write serialized objects over the network, you may wish to implement this interface and define its behavior for your application. The following code example is the beginning of a new protocol we'll call NewProtocol, which, when finished, will implement the serializable interface:

```
Source Code: NewProtocol.java
// we'll need the basic I/O libraries here.
import java.io.*;
/**
 * Class that defines a basic serializable protocol handler
 **/

public class NewProtocol implements Serializable{
  // some data to send, as Strings
  private String[] sendData;
  private int numStrings = 0;

  /**
   * initialize a NewProtocol object and its strings
   * to be as many as dataLength
   * @param dataLength The number of strings to initialize
   **/
  public void initialize( int dataLength ) {
    sendData = new String[dataLength];
    numStrings = dataLength;
    for( int x=0; x<dataLength; x++ ) {
      sendData[x] = new String( "Data String: " + x );
      }
    }
```

```
/**
 * implement the write portion of the protocol handler
 **/
public void writeProtocol( ObjectOutputStream output ) throws IOException
                                                                        {

  // write out number of strings
  output.writeInt( sendData.length );

  // write out each string as bytes with a newline
  for( int x=0; x<sendData.length; x++ ) {
    output.writeBytes( sendData[x] + "\n" );
    }
  }

/**
 * Implement the read portion of the protocol
 **/
public void readProtocol( ObjectInputStream input ) throws IOException {
  // first get the number of strings to expect
  int dataLen = input.readInt();
  // convert input stream into a reader stream
  BufferedReader br = new BufferedReader(new InputStreamReader(input));

  System.out.println( "Reading: " + numStrings + " Strings.");
  // allocate a sufficient array
  sendData = new String[ numStrings ];

  // read in the strings one at a time
  for( int x=0; x<numStrings; x++ ) {
    sendData[x] = br.readLine();
    }
  }
}
```

This protocol definition does little other than define some basic read and write behavior of the object, so that other objects which use this protocol will be able to communicate with one another easily. Now that you have this protocol implemented, all you have to do is include it in any Java projects that wish to use it. Future applets will simply need to instantiate one of these objects, then use their readProtocol() and writeProtocol() methods to communicate with each other over the network.

The Server

Since we have this new protocol defined, we will need to write some basic code to implement a server process, which can run on a machine to listen for connections from prospective clients and carry on communications with them. As previously stated, the java.net.ServerSocket libraries provide a rich set of tools with which to implement a basic server process.

Source Code: BasicServer.java

```java
// we will need the basic networking and I/O packages for this
import java.net.*;
import java.io.*;

/**
 * Class that introduces Sockets and exercises the protocol object
 **/
public class BasicServer {

  public static void main( String args[] ) throws Exception {

    // create a server side socket
    ServerSocket server = new ServerSocket( 9999 );

    // create myself as a daemon thread on 9999
    while( true ) {

      // will block automatically and hand off socket
      Socket socket = server.accept();
      // once I have socket I can get the streams associated with it
      NewProtocol protocol = new NewProtocol();
      protocol.initialize(10);
      System.out.println( "Sending protocol" );

      ObjectOutputStream output = new ObjectOutputStream( socket
                                              .getOutputStream() );

      // write the Object
      output.writeObject( protocol );
      // close the network connection
      socket.close();
    }
  }
}
```

In the BasicServer.java example, we have set up a server process, or daemon, and started it listening on port 9999—a seldom-used port number—for client connections. When it receives a request for a connection, through the accept() method, it instantiates a new NewProtocol object, initializes that object, and writes the object out to the new client. It is very important for the server, once it has finished communicating with the client, to close the network connection. Once the network connection has been closed, the server can return to the top of the loop and begin listening for new connections all over again. You will notice, we trust, that this is not the most efficient way to service clients, as only one customer at a time can be connected to the server. So, in order to allow the server to handle multiple, simultaneous, network requests, we need to make the server multithreaded. By allowing the server to handle each connection in a separate, distinct thread, the server can continue to accept connections, and provide service, to new clients even while it is providing service to already connected clients.

```
Source Code: MultiThreadedServer.java
import java.net.*;
import java.io.*;
/**
 * Class that introduces Sockets and exercises the protocol object
 **/
public class MultiThreadedServer {

  public static void main( String args[] ) throws Exception {

    // create a server side socket - same as before
    ServerSocket server = new ServerSocket( 9999 );

    // create myself as a daemon thread on 9999
    while( true ) {

      // will block automatically and hand off socket
      Socket socket = server.accept();
      // pass socket along to the new thread
      new ThreadedSocket( socket ).start();
      // now go back to waiting while ThreadedSocket does the work
      }
    }
  }
class ThreadedSocket extends Thread {
// here is where all the real work is done.
  private Socket socket;

    ThreadedSocket( Socket socket ) {
    this.socket = socket;
  }

  public void run() {
    try{
      // once I have socket I can get its streams
      NewProtocol protocol = new NewProtocol();
      protocol.initialize(1000);
      System.out.println( "Sending protocol" );

      ObjectOutputStream output = new ObjectOutputStream( socket
                                              .getOutputStream() );

      output.writeObject( protocol );
      socket.close();
    }catch( Exception e ) {
      e.printStackTrace();
    }
  }
}
```

You may notice that the MultiThreadedServer.java example looks strikingly
similar to the previous, unthreaded, version. The difference is in the Threaded-
Socket class. By using a separate thread to handle the incoming connection, the

server can return immediately to listening for new requests for service. You will also notice that the run( ) method is almost exactly the same as the body of the previous server example. This is because it is the same! Only the fact that the ThreadedSocket example runs in its own thread, therefore allowing multiple connections, makes it different. Now is when your understanding of multiple sockets on the same port is important. While only one process can listen on any given port at any given time, that process can service multiple sockets on that port, thus allowing multiple, simultaneous connections.

Clients and Services

Now that we have a server to which we can connect, we should write a client to do the connection and put this all together. Again, referring to our basic lesson on clients, servers, ports, and sockets, we will need to know the name of the server we wish to contact and the port number on that server to connect to. Knowing just those two simple facts, in conjunction with implementing our common protocol, will allow us to communicate over the Internet.

Source Code: Client.java
```
// we will need the same networking and I/O Packages
import java.net.*;
import java.io.*;

/**
 * Class that shows connecting to a server and carrying on a protocol
 * @see network.Server
 **/
public class Client {

  public static void main( String args[] ) throws Exception {

    // open a socket to the host
    Socket socket = new Socket( "127.0.0.1", 9999 );
    // convention is that the host Address 127.0.0.1 refers to me

    ObjectInputStream input = new ObjectInputStream( socket
                                          .getInputStream() );

    // read using serialization
    NewProtocol protocol = (NewProtocol)(input.readObject() );

    socket.close();
    }
  }
```

As you can see, the client in the Client.java example is extremely simple. All it needs to do is locate the server, open a socket connection, thus getting input streams from the server, and read the server's output. Unlike the server example, which only had to know the port on which to listen, our client needs to know the name, or address, of the server as well as the port number. (You will notice the use of the address 127.0.0.1 in our example. By convention, any networked machine can refer to itself by the IP address 127.0.0.1. Had we wanted to connect to a remote machine, we would simply plug that machine's name, or IP address, into the address field, and connect.) By taking care of locating the server, managing the connection, and handling all of the low-level details of the communication process, Java makes writing networked applications simple and straightforward.

Uniform Resource Locators and Web Servers

A URL (uniform resource locator) is what tells your Web browser or Java program where to find resources on the World Wide Web. You can read configuration files from a server this way, read in account data for an accounting program, or write files back to the server using URLs. In addition, you can have your applet load specific Web pages for users by specifying the URL to load and loading it. In this section we will look at some ways of using URLs to handle data in an applet. We will look at how to construct a valid URL object, the first step, how to read data from a URL, and how to write data back to a URL—even how to do an HTML-style POST request via Java. Finally, we'll take a look at how to have your applet *send* a Web browser to a new page by loading a URL into the browser.

Constructing a Uniform Resource Locator in Java

Java provides three basic constructor methods for specifying a URL. Each one throws the MalformedURLException, which must be caught and dealt with before your applet can continue. Though you could ignore this exception, doing so now will only cause you problems later in the life of your application, so do it now. The three methods just mentioned for defining the URL object are:

1. `Public URL(String protocol, String host, int port, String file) throws MalformedURLException.`

2. `Public URL(String url) throws MalformedURLException.`

3. `Public URL(String host, String file) throws MalformedURLException.`

The first version requires you to provide the protocol (HTTP, FTP, JDBC, and so forth), the host to which you'd like to attempt a connection, the port on that host to which to connect, and the file to open. The constructor method will put all of these pieces together into a working URL for you.

```
try{
        URL myURL = new URL("http", "heaven.org", 8080, "members.html");
        System.out.println(myURL.toString());
}
catch(MalformedURLException exp) {
        // DEAL with this exception here!
}
```

These two constructs will produce http://heaven.org:8080/members.html as the output and would then allow you to connect to that URL (actually, it would most likely cause you grief later on, as heaven.org is not a true Web server, but that's another matter).

> **TIP** Note the following about valid versus invalid URLs: Even though the previous URL does not exist in the real world, the URL constructor method will not necessarily throw a MalformedURLException here. All the constructor method checks is that the URL looks valid; that it has all the right parts, in the right places, so that it could be a valid URL. Later in your code you will have to deal with the possibility that the URL constructed either does not exist or is somehow unreachable.

The second version assumes that you have already constructed a string that looks like a URL (http://stpeter.heaven.org/apply.html):

```
try{
        URL newURL = new URL("http://stpeter.heaven.org/apply.html");
        System.out.println(newURL.toString());
}
catch(MalformedURLException exp){
        //*DEAL* with your exception here!
}
```

Again Java does not verify that the specified URL exists, only that it looks right.

In the third version, all you provide is the host name and the file, and Java fills in the rest. If you are connecting via the HTTP protocol to the default HTTP port (80, by convention), then this is the simplest way to connect. Java will fill in the default values for you. Given the basic security restrictions for applets running inside of browsers, which require that an applet only be allowed to open a network connection back to the host from which it came, the most common way to use this constructor is to use the getDocumentBase() method to retrieve the host portion of the constructor.

```
try{
        URL newURL = new URL(getDocumentBase(), "/nextfile/index.html");
        System.out.println(newURL.toString());
}
```

EXCEPTION HANDLING

Here's a bit of preaching about exception handling in applications which we cannot resist: Simply handling the exception with a null handler, like catch(Exception exp) {} is not sufficient, as it may leave your program in an unstable state. Though it may not cause immediate difficulties, and will satisfy the compiler's requirement that the exception be caught, unintended consequences later on in your program can be very difficult to trace back to this type of exception handling. It is better programming practice, and it will save you hours of debugging down the road, if you figure out exactly how to recover from such an exception now, and do it, rather than waiting for that fatal error later! This type of exception handling is sometimes referred to as the *Novocain* method; it deadens the immediate pain of the exception, but that pain will most likely resurface again in the near future and be much harder to locate specifically.

```
catch(MalformedURLException exp) {
    //*DEAL* with the exception here!
}
```

With these three URL constructor methods, you are ready to begin writing Web-ready applications which can both read-from and write-to the World Wide Web. Though we wrote a specific protocol handler in the previous section, we are not using it here. Instead, we are using the built-in protocol handlers of Java and the Web browser to handle the communications. This will be very useful should we decide to switch our service from a standard Web server to, say, a secure Web server using the Secure Socket Layer (SSL) protocol. Rather than writing our own, we will again rely on the built-in protocol handler to manage the new protocol we are using. In the following sections, we'll see some examples of how to put these constructs to use in an application.

Reading from a URL

The simplest way to read data from a server—be it configuration files, variable lists, or whatever—is to store the configuration information as a file on the server and read it into the applet through a URL connection. For instance, if your applet has a Choice menu in it, and you would like the items in that menu to be dynamic, based on a configuration file, you would want to read in that file each time the applet was loaded. A simple method, such as the following one in the SetChoiceList.java example, will open the connection back to the server, read in the configuration file, and set the members of the Choice object accordingly.

Source Code: SetChoiceList.java

```
public Choice setChoiceList() {
  Choice ch = new Choice();
  URL furl = null;
  DataInputStream din = null;
  String buf;
  ch.addItem("Pick One");
  try {
     furl = new URL(getDocumentBase() + "resources.html");
     }
  catch (MalformedURLException e) {
    e.printStackTrace();
    ch.addItem("No Items Available");
    return ch;
    }

  String[] files = null;
  try {
    din = new DataInputStream(furl.openStream());
    }
  catch( IOException e) {
    e.printStackTrace();
    ch.addItem("No Items Available");
    return ch;
    }

  try {
    while((buf = din.readLine()) != null)
      ch.addItem(buf);
      din.close();
      }
    catch(IOException e) {
      e.printStackTrace();
      ch.addItem("No Items Available");
      return ch;
      }
  return ch;
  }
```

There are several things going on here and we will attempt to address them all. First, we create a URL object using the new URL() method, based on the server location and the file resources.html. Once this URL object is created (and notice that we deal specifically with the possibility that the URL is invalid, does not exist, or is unreadable at each stage, so as to avoid future problems), we open a DataInputStream to it using the URL's InputStream and begin reading the contents of the file. Each item is then added to the Choice list and finally the connection is closed by the client. All of this works because we are relying on the underlying HTTP protocol and the server's Web server process to administer the connection. All we need to do is read the file! Reading from a file on a

Web server can be an extremely useful tool and, as you can see, it is extremely easy to do, given by the built-in HTTP connectivity of Java.

Once you have the ability to read from a server, you can add cgi-like functionality to your Java applet—or connect it to legacy cgi- backend code—by having your applet both read-from and write-to the Web server as in code example WriteServer.java.

By adding the write capability, you make your applet capable of two-way communications with the Web server via the HTTP protocol.

Source Code: writeServer.java

```java
import java.net.*;
import java.io.*;
import java.applet.*;

public class writeServer extends Applet{

  public void init() {
    Object        content = null;
    URL           url     = null;
    String     tryURL = "http://heaven.org/cgi-bin/apply.cgi";

    try {
      url = new URL(tryURL);
      }
    catch (Exception e) {
      System.out.println("URL():"+e);
      }

    try {
      URLConnection urlcon  = url.openConnection();
      DataOutputStream don = new DataOutputStream(urlcon
                                          .getOutputStream());
      DataInputStream stream = new DataInputStream(urlcon
                                          .getInputStream());
      // write your data to the web server here
      // Read your data from the web server here
      }
    catch (Exception e) {
      System.out.println("openConnection():"+e);
      }
    }
  }
```

In the WriteServer.java example, we have used another new construct for reading and writing to and from a URL, the URLConnection object. This object, part of the java.net hierarchy, allows us to easily open read and write connections to the Web server and the specific URL. Once this URLConnection object has been made, we can get the input and output streams for it, and begin reading and writing those streams. While it would also be possible to simply open DataOutputStreams to the URL object, some restrictions in the security of Web servers prevent this (and you should be thankful that they do, as they prevent just anyone from rewriting your Web documents!).

Sending Your Applet to a URL

Saved until last, this is possibly the easiest thing for an applet to do with a URL. By enabling your applet to send the user's browser to another Web location, you open a whole realm of possibilities that you would not have on your own server. You can dynamically link to other documents, providing live content and up-to-date information. By adding these few lines to your applet, and adding the parameter "Goto" to your applet tag (see the following GoTo.java example), you can have your applet send the user to a designated URL at will!

Source Code: GoTo.java

```
...

String name = getParameter("Goto");
try {
  gotoURL = new URL(name);
  }
catch (MalformedURLException e) {
  // remember to handle errors!
  }


...

public boolean mouseDown(Event e, int x, int y) {
  getAppletContext().showDocument(gotoURL);
  return(true);
  }
```

It's that simple! By making the call to getAppletContext( ), you effectively get a reference to the browser itself. Once you have that reference, you can call the showDocument( ) method and the browser will load the referenced URL. This is one way to implement HyperLinks within a Java applet, as well as being able to *send* users to other sites on the Web.

Networking and Java Input and Output

That takes care of the networking portion of our chapter, but you will notice that many of the examples used methods from the java.io package, so we cannot leave this chapter until we cover those!

> **TIP** Whenever an exception occurs in your program that could possibly affect the continuation of the program, or the accuracy of the program, you should consider printing a message to the user's screen. Using the System.out.println() method is an easy way to let your users know that a potential problem has occurred. By combining this with the actual exception that has occurred, you can greatly help yourself in tracking down errors called in to you by users. Consider using error messages of the form:

```
try {
    // some code...
} catch (exception e) {
    System.out.printline("An error occurred:"+ e.getMessage());
    e.printStackTrace();
}
```

> I recommend adding the call to e.printStackTrace() to aid you in tracking down exactly where the error occurred, as this will print the entire trace of methods that were called up until the error occurred.

Java Input and Output

Reading input and writing output are basic to most applications. If we had no means to get data into or out of an application, it would be a pretty useless system! While most programming platforms require that you write all of the I/O functionality yourself, Java provides a rich set of libraries for making reading and writing data easy and almost foolproof.

Basic Input and Output

In order to make reading and writing easy, and platform-independent, the Java designers have added a layer of abstraction to remove the programmer from the complexities of low-level I/O. Java treats all I/O the same, whether you're reading from a file, from another Java program, or from the network. This convention allows you the flexibility to design your applications in a more generic fashion and postpone the decisions of where the data will come from until later—or leave it up to the end users as to whether they want to read their data from the Web or from a local file.

Data Streams

The basis of all I/O in Java is the data stream. A data stream is like a pipeline of data. Information can be put into the pipeline (written to the stream) or pulled out of the pipeline (read from the stream), as shown in Figure 4.2. Data streams

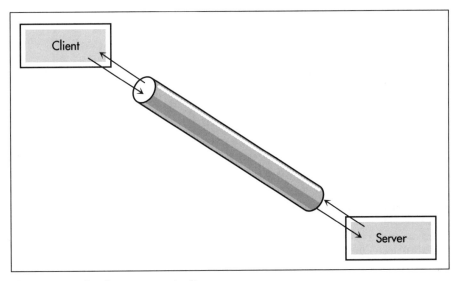

Figure 4.2   The data stream pipeline.

are set up between specific destinations for specific data so that applications can be assured that their data is being delivered successfully to its destination, or that it gets its data from the source reliably. In fact, the pipes analogy is so good that Java even implements an I/O type called a pipedInputStream and a pipedOutputStream.

The basic type of I/O for most programs is to simply write some output from the program to the user's screen, so that he or she can see that the program is actively doing something. In fact, you have seen examples of this throughout the book, as we have used the System.out.println( ) method to print status and error messages to the user.

File Objects

Java attempts to hide the differences between how different platforms handle files and directories by providing a fairly generic set of classes interfaces and methods for handling the creation, deletion, opening, closing, reading, and writing of files. The most obvious class is the File class. This class is used for creating, deleting, and getting the properties of files in a filesystem-independent way. Since different platforms use different methods of differentiating between simple files and directories, you should use the isDirectory( ) method to determine if a given file object is a plain file or a directory. Likewise, you should use the instance variable pathSeparator or pathSeparatorChar to determine how to specify an absolute path.

Source Code: FilePath.java

```java
import java.io.*;

public class FilePath {

  public static void main(String[] args) {

    File file1 = null;
    String[] files = null;

    if(args.length < 1) {
      System.out.println("Must specify a File.");
      System.exit(0);
      }

    file1 = new File(args[0]);
    if(!file1.exists()){
      System.out.println(args[0] + " does not exist on this system");
      System.exit(0);
      }

    System.out.println("System File Separator is: '" + file1.separatorChar
                                                      + "'");
    System.out.println("The absolute path of " + args[0] + " is: " +
                                          file1.getAbsolutePath());

    if(file1.canWrite())
      System.out.println("You have permission to write to " + args[0]);
    else
      System.out.println("You do not have permission to write to " +
                                                      args[0]);
    if(file1.canRead())
      System.out.println("You have permission to read from " + args[0]);
    else
      System.out.println("You do not have permission to read from " +
                                                      args[0]);
    if(file1.isDirectory()) {
      files = file1.list();
      System.out.println(args[0] + " is a directory containing:");
      for(int x = 0; x < files.length; x++)
        System.out.println(files[x]);
      }
    else
      System.out.println(args[0] + " is a file.");
      FileReader fred = new FileReader(file1);
      fred.ReadFile();
      FileWriter fwed = new FileWriter(file1);
      fwed.ReadWrite();
    }
  }
```

In the FilePath.java example, we create a new File object, determine its type (directory or plain file), then print out some of the properties of that file. It is important to notice that we first test to make sure that the file exists before looking at its properties. Why is this important? Well, it is also possible to create a file object even if the file referred to by that object does not yet exist! Now, why would you want to create a file object for a file that does not exist? Well, let's imagine that you want to create a new file. In order to ensure that you do not overwrite an existing file, you might create the file object, then test to see whether it exists already. If it does, you'll have to change your approach!

One other important thing to note in the FilePath.java example is that even though we create a file object, we have not yet opened the file; so, even though we can get a certain amount of information *about* the file, we still cannot get any information *out of* the file.

> **TIP** When attempting to do any type of file I/O it is highly advisable that you do some of the fundamental checks outlined in the FilePath.java example. Most notably, you should always check to make sure that you have the right permissions for a file before attempting to open the file for reading or writing. Skipping this step during programming can cause runtime errors which will be a constant source of aggravation for you and your users. The basic checks to perform are:
>
> 1. **Does the file already exist?**
>   - **Does it need to be there first?**
>   - **Can I create it?**
> 2. **If I need to read from the file, do I have permission?**
> 3. **If I need to write to the file, do I have permission?**
>
> If you perform these simple checks every time you attempt to access a file, you will save yourself a mountain of exception handling later.

Reading and Writing Files

Now that we've created a file object, and we know how to determine its type, and whether we have the right permissions to access it, we can start either putting data into, or getting data out of, the file. In the FileReader.java example, we actually open the file and read from it, writing the output to the screen. Put the two together, by creating a new FileReader object and calling its ReadFile() method in FilePath.java, and you have a way to print out the properties of a file, and, if it is not a directory and is readable, to then print out the contents of that file.

Source Code: FileReader.java
```
import java.io.*;

public class FileReader{

protected File fname;

  public FileReader(File fileName) {
    this.fname = fileName;
    }
```

```java
public void init(File fileName) {
  this.fname = fileName;
  }


public void ReadFile() {
  FileInputStream finstream = null;
  String[] files = null;

  if(!fname.exists()){
    System.out.println(fname.toString() + " does not exist on this
                                                   system");
    return;
    }


  if(!fname.canRead()) {
    System.out.println("You do not have permission to read from " +
                                            fname.toString());
    return;
    }


  if(fname.isDirectory()) {
    files = fname.list();
    System.out.println(fname.toString() + " is a directory containing:");
    for(int x = 0; x < files.length; x++)
      System.out.println(files[x]);
    }
  else
    System.out.println(fname.toString()+ " is a file.");
    System.out.println("The Contents of file " + fname.toString() + " is:
                                                   \n");
    try{
      finstream = new FileInputStream(fname);
      }
    catch (FileNotFoundException e) {
    // this should never happen, since we already checked it
      e.printStackTrace();
      return;
      }

    try{
      int c = 0;
      while((c = finstream.read()) != -1)
        System.out.print((char)c);
      finstream.close();
      }
    catch (IOException e) {
      System.out.println("IO Exception: " + e.getMessage());
      }
  }
}
```

Figure 4.3   Reading and writing a file.

Now that we can open and read files, we should look at writing back to files. Again, Java saves us a vast amount of time and energy by supporting, in a platform-independent manner, the writing of files. We can create a file, then write our data to it, no matter where our data comes from. In the FileWriter .java example, we see that all we need to do to write to a file, versus writing to the screen, is to get an OutputStream to the file. We then simply use the write( ) method associated with that OutputStream instead of using the System.out.print( ) method. In this example, the FileWriter object we create acts as a *middleman* for the data, transferring it from one stream to the other (see Figure 4.3).

Source Code: FileWriter.java

```java
import java.io.*;

public class FileWriter{

  protected File fname;
  protected File fnameout;

  public FileWriter(File fileName) {
    this.fname = fileName;
    String fout = new String(fname.toString() + ".out");
    fnameout = new File(fout);
    }

  public void init(File fileName) {
    this.fname = fileName;
    String fout = new String(fname.toString() + ".out");
    fnameout = new File(fout);
    }

  public void ReadWrite() {
    FileInputStream finstream = null;
    FileOutputStream foutstream = null;
    String[] files = null;

    if(!fname.exists()) {
      System.out.println(fname.toString() + " does not exist on this
                                                    system");

      return;
      }
```

```
   if(fnameout.exists()) {
     System.out.println(fnameout.toString() + "already exists!");
     return;
     }

   if(!fname.canRead()) {
     System.out.println("You do not have permission to read from " +
                                               fname.toString());
     return;
     }

   if(fname.isDirectory()) {
     files = fname.list();
     System.out.println(fname.toString() + " is a directory containing:");
     for(int x = 0; x < files.length; x++)
       System.out.println(files[x]);
     }
   else {
     try {
       foutstream = new FileOutputStream(fnameout);
       }
     catch(Exception e) {
       System.out.println("Cannot write because: " + e.getMessage());
       return;
       }

     try {
       finstream = new FileInputStream(fname);
       }
     catch (FileNotFoundException e) {
       // this should never happen, since we already checked it
       e.printStackTrace();
       return;
       }

     try{
       int c = 0;
       while((c = finstream.read()) != -1)
         foutstream.write(c);
       finstream.close();
       foutstream.close();
       }
     catch (IOException e) {
       System.out.println("IO Exception: " + e.getMessage());
       }
     }
   }
}
```

While in this example the FileWriter object transposes the contents of the
file exactly, making a perfect copy, you could use this object to look for

patterns in the original file and make changes, writing those changes to the new file.

As you get more sophisticated with I/O, you may wish to move towards Readers and Writers, which will allow you to read and write by lines, rather than by single characters. BufferedReaders and BufferedWriters will also help your programs become more efficient with I/O by buffering input and output until it is convenient to write a larger block of data.

More Advanced Uses for Streams

These examples have been pretty simplistic and pretty limited in their usefulness—especially as it relates to communicating over the Internet with Java. Given the rather stringent security restrictions on applets downloaded over the Internet—unless you digitally sign all your applets—the use of file I/O will be of limited value. At the other end of the spectrum from file I/O is the reading and writing of serialized objects. Serializing objects allows you the ability to add some persistence to Java objects so that data, and the state of objects, can be saved from one running of your program to another.

Writing an Object to a Stream

Almost any object in Java can now be created to implement the Serializable interface, thus allowing it to be written to, and read from, a stream. While the usefulness of this ability may not be immediately obvious, as your applications become more complex and the data they manage becomes larger and more cumbersome, the ability to save the state of an object from one invocation to the next becomes a real performance bonus.

INTERNET SHOPPING CART

A practical use for serializing an object and writing it to a disk is the Internet Shopping Cart. Let's say you are implementing an online shopping mall and you'd like to allow your customers to place items in their shopping baskets as they shop. This is easy enough to do, but let's also say that you'd like for those shoppers to be able to go away—exit your application or online mall—and when they return, still have their shopping cart full of the items they previously selected. By creating a shoppingCart object which implements the Serializable interface, you could, when the shopper exists your mall, simply write their shoppingCart object to disk. When they return, you simply reread their shoppingCart object and they can pick up shopping right where they left off. Wouldn't it be nice if real malls operated like that!

Figure 4.4 Reading and writing Java objects.

Object serialization is accomplished in exactly the same way as file I/O, in Java. We open an Object OutputStream and write our Serializable object to that stream. On the other end, we open an ObjectInputStream and read in that object. Additionally, on the server, we might wish to open a FileOutputStream and write that serialized object to a file for later use (see Figure 4.4).

All instance variables in the object, as well as any objects referred to by that object, are written out to the stream when you serialize the object. Static variables are not written (as they will be automatically restored). You can prevent any instance variable or referred-to object from being written to the stream by marking it with the keyword "transient." This keyword tells the object serializer to skip this value. You should, of course, be very careful to make arrangements to restore transient values somehow after reading a serialized object, otherwise you may encounter some unintended side effects down the road.

TIP You should always be careful when serializing objects—saving them to disk especially—as instance variables are saved in the serialized object. Saving sensitive account information on your online shoppers would be a bad idea, as a cracker who gained access to your system would then have access to your customers' account information.

In the end, serializing an object and writing it to a stream is exactly like writing to any other of Java's streams—and that's exactly the point! By removing many of the system dependencies from I/O, and by generalizing the I/O wherever possible, Java's architects have made a very flexible and extremely powerful system for managing I/O.

We already know how to create and write to a FileOutputStream, so chaining an ObjectOutputStream to that FileOutputStream object allows Java to handle the specifics of how to write the object, rather than characters, to the file:

```
File f = new File("ObjectFile.obj");
// remember to run your tests on this file first!
```

```
FileOutputStream foust = new FileOutputStream(f);
ObjectOutputStream objoust = new ObjectOutputStream(foust);
```

You could, if you wanted to make this code less readable, write it as:

```
ObjectOutputStream objoust = new ObjectOutputStream(new
FileOutputStream(new File("File.obj")));
```

But that would make doing the writability test on the file more difficult, so I don't advise it.

Likewise, reading the object back from the file is simply a matter of chaining an ObjectInputStream to a FileInputStream, and reading the stream:

```
File f = new File("ObjectFile.obj");
FileInputStream finst = new FileInputStream(f);
ObjectInputStream objinst = new ObjectInputStream(finst);
```

You can now read the object you wrote in the first example back in. The readObject( ) method, which does the actual reading of the object, simply returns an object. It is your responsibility to know what type of object you are reading in and to make the appropriate cast. Once you have done that, you have your original object back in its original form—minus any *transient* variables that may have existed in your original object, of course.

Summary

You now have the basics for performing network, as well as local, I/O. We have seen how to write both simple data—characters, numbers, and other textual data—as well as complex data such as Java Objects both to the network and to local files.

CHAPTER

5

Using JavaBeans™

Introduction

JavaBeans™ is a component model that provides a framework for software components to be developed, delivered, and deployed using Java. The components, *beans*, can vary in size from small building block components to complete applications such as a spreadsheet. These beans can be delivered in such a way that makes visual manipulation of the beans easy for software designers. The behavior of the bean can easily be modified through such visual manipulation. Beans can also be connected together to form new applications as well as other beans. All this can by done by simply plugging various beans together.

JavaBeans Design Goal

The JavaBeans environment is not intended to be a high-level document integration environment like OpenDoc. Instead, it is a rather low-level API similar to ActiveX and OLE, but unlike ActiveX and OLE it is portable between different software platforms. JavaBeans also have the advantage of interoperating with high-level document interfaces. The platform-independent architecture of JavaBeans permits several different component architectures to interoperate with beans. For example, JavaBeans will easily interoperate with other component environments like OpenDoc and Netscape ONE. In order to do this other component architectures will need to provide and imbed a core level of the beans architecture and APIs. The beans architecture will need to become part of the existing architecture to make beans behave like any other existing component. The bridge between existing component architecture and the beans API is left to developers to construct. As of the writing of this book several software companies have begun work on such bridges as well as JavaSoft's bridge between JavaBeans and Microsoft's ActiveX. Not all software environments will be able to support the entire beans API. However, in order for all environments to be beans-compliant, all platforms must support a reasonable default behavior for the entire API. In fact, this is the overall goal of JavaBeans: To deliver a reasonable default behavior for all components that would allow a developer to easily override this default behavior. For example, if a software environment does not support popup menus, then that environment must provide some reasonable default behavior in place of the popup menu. On top of this goal is JavaSoft's mantra: Keep it simple. The beans API is kept simple to make it easy for developers to get started and use JavaBeans. This means that you can easily start creating software components that will be compatible with JavaBeans.

JavaBeans Component Model

A component model can be described as a set of APIs and an architecture which allow developers to define and create software components. These components can range from small GUI widgets to large components such as a fully functional word processor. All of these components have the ability to be combined together dynamically. Some components, such as a GUI button, are visible while others may be invisible. Invisible components could include such things as sorting algorithms and filters. The key with any component is that it should have the ability to be dynamically connected together and interoperate with other components.

Most components cannot operate without containers in which to place the components. Containers are used to hold a set of components that have some sort of relation or context with each other. For example, a menu bar in a application could be a container while all the menu items are components. All the menu items share the context or state of the menu bar and can interact with each other. The menu bar is a container but can also be considered a component placed in the applications container. Components can be containers for other components while at the same time each can act as a component in another container.

Component models also provide many different services and mechanisms by which the components interoperate. These services include self-discovery, properties, customization, and event control. Each of these services and mechanisms is discussed in greater detail in the following paragraphs.

The self-discovery of a component permits the component to inform other components what interfaces and methods it supports. This allows the component to interact with other components in a dynamic behavior. For example, a text field component may have a setText( ) method that sets the value of its text field. The component would want to publish the fact that the setText( ) method is available for other components to call. The self-discovery mechanism makes it very easy for a component to publish its capabilities in a dynamic manner. JavaBeans uses introspection and reflection to provide information about a particular component.

All components have a set of properties that directly or indirectly affect the behavior, state, or appearance of the component. For example, a button component may have a label property, a foreground color property, and a font property all of which can be set or modified. The properties of a component can be modified from within a component or from an external mechanism which, in most cases, is another component. The JavaBeans component model makes it easy for component properties to be set or modified.

The customization of a component involves two things. The first is allowing a component to be modified in some way such as setting the component's properties. The second is to provide some way of storing the current state and properties of the component for later use. If a button component has its properties set to make the button appear in a certain manner, it would be nice to save that component with all the current properties. Then, the next time that component is needed it can be restored to look and behave the same as before the component was saved. This process of saving and restoring a component is commonly referred to as persistence. *Persistence* is the ability of an object to save and restore its current state.

Event control in JavaBeans provides the ability for any component to create an event or to respond to an event. Every component should be able to create an event and send that event to other components that have an interest in it. For example, when a button component is clicked, that component may need to send that event, the mouse click, to another component that wants to know when the button component has been clicked. In this case the component that is the target of the event is listening for the button click event.

Event types can also be created to make new definitions of an event. These custom events can be used to signal any type of condition in a component. There are no real distinctions between custom events and existing Java events. Any type of event can be raised and caught by any component.

Application Builders

Most of the previous services and mechanisms can easily be manipulated by a component application builder of some sort. Application builders allow the easy manipulation and customization of components. Such builders also allow components to be connected together in a common container environment. A builder can present all the properties, interfaces, methods, and events of a component in an easy-to-use format. This format is usually some sort of GUI that allows visual manipulation of the component.

Examples of such application builders include interactive development environments, Web page builders, and GUI builders. These tools can be used to assemble components that can range from simple GUI elements to complete applications. The visual manipulation of a bean can be quite simple from such a builder; however, a bean can also be manipulated through the use of normal APIs.

Since most development kits that use JavaBeans cost money, we will use what JavaSoft has provided, a simple implementation of an application builder. This simple builder is called the BeanBox and it provides some basic services that most application builders will provide (see Figure 5.1). The BeanBox is free from JavaSoft. We will use the BeanBox to demonstrate how JavaBeans can be used.

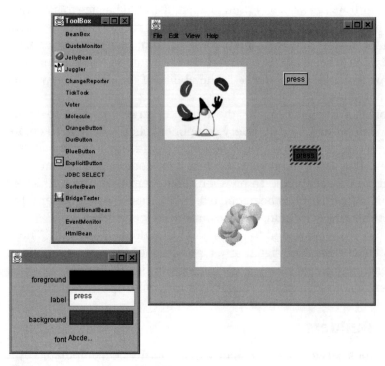

Figure 5.1   Snapshot of BeanBox.

Bean Events

The event mechanism used in JavaBeans is key in the communication and inter-operation of JavaBean components. An event model is needed to facilitate the transfer or notification of events between beans. The good news is that you don't need to learn event mechanism. The JavaBeans architecture uses the same event model that was added to the JFC and AWT. In fact, all event mechanisms in Java use this same model. We will assume that you are already familiar with the Java event model. If you are not familiar with it, Chapter 2 covers the event model and its operation. The event model and its workings will be used extensively in this chapter.

Bean Properties

Properties are used in many different facets of application programming. Properties can define how something looks, behaves, sounds, and so on. JavaBeans are no different. A bean property is a discrete named attribute of the bean that can affect how the bean looks, behaves, sounds, and so on. Properties can be of any type including native Java types as well as any class type. The properties of a bean can be set and changed (accessed and mutated) from many different sources. For example, the font used in a component may be a property and have a type of java.awt.Font. This property could be set and changed from a number of different mechanisms including a programming interface, a scripting language, or another bean.

Most of the properties that are used in a bean should remain persistent. This provides a mechanism for the bean to read and write a set of properties that remain with the bean even after the bean has been destroyed.

Access to a property is always provided through the use of methods in the object to which the property applies. This means that if a bean is to use a property it must provide methods in which to set or get the property. If a property is read only, then the owning class must define a getter method; if a property is write only, then the class must define a setter method. Both the setter and getter methods are regular Java methods which can contain program logic. These getter and setter methods should conform to a design pattern in order to make their use standard and to aid the documentation of such methods.

Properties should use the following design pattern:

```
public <PropertyType> get<PropertyName>();
public void set<PropertyName> (<PropertyType> pt);
```

For example, if a property of a bean is its foreground color, then the setter and getter methods for the bean may be defined as follows:

```
public java.awt.Color getFGColor();
public void setFGColor(java.awt.Color fgc);
```

Another design pattern can be used for properties that have simple Boolean types:

```
public boolean is<PropertyName>();
public void set<PropertyName> (boolean v);
```

This type of property is used to set and access Boolean-type property values. For example, a bean may have a property to identify if it is visible on the screen. In this case the property methods could be defined as:

```
public boolean is Visible();
public void setVisible(boolean vis);
```

Properties can also exist as an array of values. Properties of this type are referred to as indexed properties. In this case, the setter and getter of the property must have the ability to set and get the entire array or a particular element of the array. Again, a design pattern should be used when defining indexed properties.

This design pattern should be used when getting and setting a single element of the array:

```
public <PropertyElement> get<PropertyName> (int index);
public void set<PropertyName> (int index, <PropertyElement> e);
```

This design pattern should be used when getting or setting the entire array:

```
public <PropertyType>[] get<PropertyName>();
public void set<PropertyName> (<PropertyType>[] a);
```

A bean could, for example, use a set of float values that represents the values to be plotted on a graph. The values used in the array can be accessed using the following method declarations:

```
public float[] getGraph();
public void setGraph(float v[]);
public float getGraph(int index);
public void setGraph(int index, float v);
```

Any access method of a property may also throw any type of checked exception. This permits the setter or getter method to report exceptional conditions to the caller of the method. For example, an indexed property may want to throw an exception if the caller tries to access an unreachable value in the given array.

The beans specification also allows for bound and constrained properties. A bound property is a property that binds some sort of behavior to the change of the property. For example, when the color property of a component is changed, the component may want to bind the act of changing the color with another component that wishes to be informed when this event occurs. This would allow the other component to be notified when the color property has changed. Bound properties use the Java event model to deliver events from the property component to the particular component that wants to listen for the change.

Constrained properties are similar to bound properties, but in addition they support the validation of a property. For example, the change in the value of a property may need to be validated by another component. The validation can be performed by a component that is listening for the change in the property as did the bound properties. The component that is doing the validation may then either validate or invalidate the change in the property.

Further discussion and use of bound or constrained properties is beyond the scope of this chapter. For more information about this topic refer to the Java-Beans Specification (java.sun.com).

Bean Reflection and Introspection

Reflection and introspection provide a key resource that almost every Java bean or component architecture will require. Introspection is the process of one class inspecting another class to determine what properties, events, and methods it supports. The Java Core Reflection API provides a type safe and secure mechanism to support the introspection of classes and objects used in any Java program.

Reflection

Let's start by taking a look at the reflection classes. The JDK 1.1 added the java.lang.reflect package. This package contains several classes that permit the programmatic introspection of class and methods. We won't go into much detail about each of the classes and their methods; however, a general overview is required.

The reflection package added some new Java classes: Field, Method, Array, Modifier, and Constructor. The Field, Method, and Constructor classes are final and objects of these types can only be created by the Java Virtual Machine. The instantiated objects of these three classes are used to discover information about the objects to which they refer. Field objects are used to represent a field in a reflected object. The field can refer to a class variable or an instance variable. Constructor objects represent the constructors in a reflected class which can be used to create a new instance of the reflected class. The Method objects refer to abstract, class, and instance methods in the reflected object. Method objects can also be used to dynamically invoke a particular method in the given class. Since none of these classes have constructors, the Class class has been expanded to allow the instantiation of the objects. Methods have been added to Class that will return valid Method, Field, and Constructor objects. Class variables have also been added to other Java classes in order to represent the types for Java primitives. For example, the class type of the int primitive can now be represented by the class variable java.lang.Integer.TYPE.

Let's take a look at how these classes can be used. This example uses the getMethods() method in the Class class. getMethods() returns an array of Method objects that are contained in the underlying class on which the method was invoked. In this example the java.lang.Float class is used as the target class. Once we have the array of Method objects, we can print out the string representation of the methods. So this example simply prints all the methods that are defined by the java.lang.Float class. It will also print all of the methods in all of the superclasses of the Float class. Float extends java.lang.Number and Number extends java.lang.Object.

Source Code: reflectInfo.java
```
import java.lang.reflect.*;

public class reflectInfo {

 public static void main(String args[]) {

  Float b = new Float(1);
  Method mArray[] = b.getClass().getMethods();

  for (int i=0; i<mArray.length; i++)
   System.out.println(mArray[i]);
  }
}
```

Here is the output from running the example (note that there are quite a few methods found in the Float class and its superclasses):

```
public static java.lang.String java.lang.Float.toString(float)
public static java.lang.Float java.lang.Float.valueOf(java.lang.String)
public static boolean java.lang.Float.isNaN(float)
public static boolean java.lang.Float.isInfinite(float)
public static native int java.lang.Float.floatToIntBits(float)
public static native float java.lang.Float.intBitsToFloat(int)
public final native java.lang.Class java.lang.Object.getClass()
public int java.lang.Float.hashCode()
public boolean java.lang.Float.equals(java.lang.Object)
```

```
public java.lang.String java.lang.Float.toString()
public final native void java.lang.Object.notify()
public final native void java.lang.Object.notifyAll()
public final native void java.lang.Object.wait(long)
public final void java.lang.Object.wait(long,int)
public final void java.lang.Object.wait()
public int java.lang.Float.intValue()
public long java.lang.Float.longValue()
public float java.lang.Float.floatValue()
public double java.lang.Float.doubleValue()
public byte java.lang.Float.byteValue()
public short java.lang.Float.shortValue()
public boolean java.lang.Float.isNaN()
public boolean java.lang.Float.isInfinite()
```

The other two classes in the java.lang.reflect package are Array and Modifier. The Array class is final, and is used to create and access Java arrays. Since the Array class does not have a constructor, all of its methods are static. This class is used to create arrays of primitive or Java class types, and get and set values in the arrays. This capability is needed to work with arrays of parameters and fields in reflected objects. The Modifier class provides a set of utilities to identify language modifier information for a particular class or method. For example, the Modifier class can identify if a particular Field, Method, or Constructor is public, abstract, synchronized, and so forth.

Let's take a look at an example that we used previously. The adapter class example used an event adapter that called methods in a target class. Recall that the adapter class needed to know what type of class it was calling into, which forced us to create an adapter class that was specific to our target class. We can now write the adapter class as a generic adapter that can call into any class that supports its target methods. Here is the new code:

Source Code: CountAdapter.java
```
import java.lang.reflect.*;

public class CountAdaptor implements CounterChangeListener {
  private Object obj;
  private Method evenMethod = null;
  private Method oddMethod = null;

  public CountAdaptor(Object obj) {
    this.obj = obj;
    Class pt[] = {Integer.TYPE};
    try {
      evenMethod = obj.getClass().getDeclaredMethod("evenCounterChange",
                                                            pt);

    }
    catch (NoSuchMethodException nsme) { }
```

```
      catch (SecurityException se) { }

      try {
        oddMethod = obj.getClass().getDeclaredMethod("oddCounterChange", pt);
        }
      catch (NoSuchMethodException nsme) { }
      catch (SecurityException se) { }
      }

  public void counterChange(CounterEvent ce) {
    Object arg[] = {new Integer(ce.getCount())};
    try {
      if ((ce.getCount() % 2) == 0) {
        if (evenMethod != null)
          evenMethod.invoke(obj, arg);
        }
      else {
        if (oddMethod != null)
          oddMethod.invoke(obj, arg);
        }
      }
    catch (IllegalArgumentException iae) {
      System.out.println("Illegal argument: " + arg[0]);
      }
    catch (InvocationTargetException ite) {
      System.out.println("Illegal invocation: " + obj);
      }
    catch (IllegalAccessException ia) {
      System.out.println("Illegal access");
      }
    }
  }
```

Notice that the example uses reflection to determine if a particular method is supported in the calling class. The example no longer needs to know the object type that is being passed to it. It just needs to know if the class supports a needed method with a particular signature. If the method is found in the class, then that method can be dynamically invoked in other methods in the adapter class. This functionality makes it easy to build adapter classes that are generic where they are not tied to a particular class.

Security

Security can be a concern for the reflection classes. You may not want any object to inspect the contents of your class. The good news is that Java can control access to the information in a class by class basis. This means that you can control what methods, constructors, and fields are visible to reflection by performing some security checks on the class that is under reflection. First, a new method has been created in the java.lang.SecurityManager class. The method, checkMemberAccess( ), is called each time a reflection method is called. Since the Class class is the only class that contains methods that return valid instances of Methods, Constructors, or Fields, the security check is called from the methods in the Class class. If the checkMemberAccess( ) does not want to give access to a given object, then it throws a SecurityException and access is denied.

If the checkMemberAccess( ) method does allow access, then another level of security check is performed. Normal Java language access checks are used as the second level of security. These access checks are governed by modifiers such as protected and private. For example, if the security manager allows access to a method in a class, but the method is private, then access will be denied. Access, in this case, means that if a field is private, you can't set or get it; if a method is private, you can't invoke it; and if a constructor is private, you can't initialize new objects. If any of these checks violates Java's language access checks, then an IllegalAccessException is thrown.

Introspection

At its simplest, beans introspection is no different than Java reflection. Introspection provides a mechanism for an environment, which in most cases will be application builders, to discover what properties, methods, and events a bean supports. Java supports bean introspection using two mechanisms.

The first mechanism used to discover information about a bean is Java reflection. Reflection is used by default to discover what methods, fields, and constructors a bean supports. Once this information is obtained, design patterns are applied to deduce what properties, methods, and events are supported by the bean. This is the reason for all the design patterns that we have discussed. For example, let's see how introspection would discover a property of a bean. Say that we have a bean that has the following methods defined:

```
public Color getForegroundColor();
public void setForegroundColor(Color fg);
```

Introspection would use reflection to discover that the class contained the getForegroundColor( ) and setForegroundColor( ) methods. Then the property design patterns would be applied to these methods to determine that the bean supported a read/write foreground color property. Since we followed the design pattern for properties, introspection is able to determine that the two methods listed could read and write the bean's foreground color property. If we did not use the design patterns, then introspection would not be able to make a link between the given methods and a bean property. This example showed how introspection finds properties; however, the same mechanism is used to find methods and events. Here is a quick overview of the introspection mechanism:

1. Look at all public methods. All public methods are exposed as external methods of the bean.

2. Look for a property design pattern:

```
public <Property Type> get<Property Name>();
public void set<Property Name> (<Property Type> x);
public boolean is<Property Name>();
public <Property Element> get<PropertyName>(int x);
public <Property Element>[] get<PropertyName>();
public void set<Property Name>(int x, <PropertyElement> y);
public void set<Property Name>(<PropertyElement> x[]);
```

If any of the methods found in (step 1) match any of these patterns, then a property is identified for the bean as well as its accessors and mutators.

3. Look for an event design pattern:

```
public void add<EventListenerType>Listener
(<EventListenerType>Listener x);
public void remove<EventListenerType>Listener
(<EventListenerType>Listener x);
public void add<EventListenerType>Listener
(<EventListenerType>Listener x)
throws java.util.TooManyListenersException;
```

If any of the methods found in (step 1) match any of these patterns, then the bean is identified as an event source of the event type.

Unlike properties, both the add and remove methods must be present for event identification.

The second mechanism that is used to introspect a bean is a BeanInfo class (see Figure 5.2). You, as the implementor of a bean, can provide a BeanInfo class that is used to describe your bean. The BeanInfo class can programmatically describe anything about a given bean including behavior, properties, methods, events, and just about any other type of information you wish to provide. Let's take a look at how the BeanInfo class works:

Source Code: MyBeanBeanInfo.java
```java
import java.beans.*;

public class myBeanBeanInfo extends SimpleBeanInfo {

public java.awt.Image getIcon(int iconType) {
 if(iconType == java.beans.BeanInfo.ICON_COLOR_16×16) {
  java.awt.Image icon = loadImage("myBeanIcon.gif");
  return(icon);
  }
 if(iconType == java.beans.BeanInfo.ICON_MONO_16×16) {
  java.awt.Image icon = loadImage("myBeanIcon.gif");
```

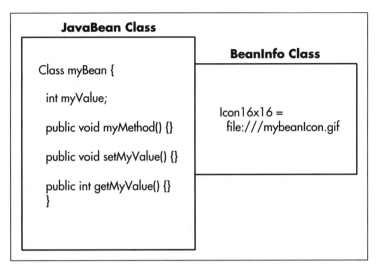

Figure 5.2   BeanInfo class.

```
return(icon);
  }
 else
  return null;
 }
}
```

Bean Customization

Customization of a Java bean permits a bean designer to provide a mechanism to customize a given bean. For example, a bean may have a complex set of properties that need to be set before the bean can be used. In this case, a customizer can be provided that could guide the user of the bean through some sort of setup. A customizer of this sort can act as a wizard and guide a user through the steps needed to customize the bean. The customization of a bean can be provided in two different ways: through the use of a property editor or through the use of a customizer class.

A property editor is a Java class that permits the graphical modification of a given property. For example, a property editor for a property with an integer type may display a simple text field where an integer value can be entered. Since a bean can have a property of any type, including complex data types, a specific property editor can be provided to permit the modification of the property. An editor can allow the reading and/or writing of any type of bean property. Since property editors can exist in many different forms, it is the responsibility of the tool that is using the property editors to use the best representation of a particular editor.

Property editors can be provided in the bean, in the tool using the bean, or in the JavaBeans runtime environment. The Java runtime does provide some common editors for built-in Java types. Many different types of editors can exist for a particular bean which can cause some confusion as to which editor should be used. However, the java.beans.PropertyEditorManager class provides a mechanism so that a particular editor can be registered as the editor for a given property type. This registry is loaded with all the built-in Java type property editors and new editors can be added to the registry as needed. When a property editor is needed for a particular type, the PropertyEditorManager is accessed to determine what editor should be used. This is done by first looking in the registry to determine if an editor has been registered explicitly for a given type. If the editor cannot be found in the registry, then the word "Editor" is added to the end of the name of the property type. For example, if the type name of a property is fgColor, then an editor with the name of fgColorEditor is loaded. If the editor is not found in the defining package, then a search begins in a specified list of packages. By default, the search list includes java.beans.editors.

If you are developing a bean that requires a special property editor, then you should create an editor named after the properties base type name and append the Editor keyword. When a property is changed using your editor, you should fire a PropertyChange event to notify the beans environment of the change in a property. This will permit the environment or tool to make any visible changes needed to the beans properties.

In most cases the use of property editors will be sufficient to modify a bean; however, a complex bean may require the use of a custom wizard. This wizard can aid the user in the customization of a bean. In this case a customizer class can be used to provide this level of interaction. Since a customizer class will interact with a user, it should extend the java.awt.Component class as well as implement the java.beans.Customizer interface. The customizer should display some sort of GUI that the user can interact with. This GUI is totally separate from the bean and may implement any type of behavior. The customizer can be as complex as needed to guide the user though the customization of the bean.

TIP Don't change the object used in the editor. Create a new instance of the object and change its value, then fire the propchanged event to notify the containing class to use the proper getter and setter methods to make the change in the property.

It is also recommended that after a property has been changed the editor should reread the beans properties because the change in one property may cause the change of another. This can be verified by doing an == and an Object.equals() to test to see if a property has changed.

In order to use a customizer class, you must provide a customizer class and a BeanInfo class for the bean. The customizer class must be added to the Bean-Info class so that the customizer can be found during introspection. The bean can find the customizer in the BeanInfo class by using the BeanInfo.get-CustomizerClass() method.

When using either a property editor or customizer you may want to preserve the changes made to the bean. To do this use the beans serialization methods to save the modified properties. This will prevent the user from having to edit the properties every time the bean is used.

The Glasgow Additions

JavaSoft has released a new JavaBeans specification—the Glasgow specification—that adds some new advanced features to the JavaBeans environment. The new features include a runtime containment and services protocol, an object aggregation and delegation model, a data-typing and object registry mechanism, and a Java activation framework.

The JavaBeans runtime containment and services protocol provides a way for a bean to discover what types of services may be available to it from its surrounding environment. It is quite easy for a bean to discover what services are delivered to it from the JavaVM, but it can be hard for a bean to know what services the native environment, where the JavaVM is running, may offer. This specification provides a standard mechanism for beans to extend their capabilities by utilizing the existing surrounding environment. It also aids in nesting a bean inside another bean by providing the nested bean with more information about its surroundings.

The object aggregation and delegation model will permit beans to act as aggregates of other objects. This permits beans to exhibit characteristics from multiple objects. It is of great benefit since Java can only extend a single class. The aggregation and delegation model allows a bean to take on the characteristics of multiple objects but still only have a single inheritance scheme.

The data-typing and object registry specification provides a framework where services can be applied to known data types. This will aid in determining what type a piece of data may be as well as encapsulating the access and operations that are available to the data. The Java activation framework will provide a common way for certain actions to take place on behalf of a certain piece of data. This will permit data to be transferred to a bean and the bean to determine how the data should be handled. For example, an audio stream may be passed to a bean and the bean could discover what type of data it was and call the appropriate audio player.

All of the Glasgow additions will expand the capabilities of JavaBeans, and will be added to the default JavaBeans environment as well as the JavaBeans development kit (BDK).

Summary

We hope that this chapter gave you a better understanding about what Java-Beans are and how they work. The key thing to keep in mind is that JavaBeans is a set of rules and procedures that can be followed to build universal components. Any class in Java can be a bean. If you follow the design guidelines specified by the JavaBeans architecture, even if you don't intend for a class to be a bean, you will go a long way in making your Java classes interoperable with almost any component architecture.

CHAPTER

6

Designing Distributed Applications

Introduction

The Java platform was originally designed as a language and environment for network-based, distributed applications. From the earliest days of the Green Project, the architects of the Java platform followed the motto that "The Network is the Computer."[1] As a result, JDK 1.0's support for network-based applications was built directly into the Java language. This support included raw sockets and the popular network protocol HTTP.

As the Java platform became more popular and systems designers began to use it in more sophisticated applications, the limits of JDK 1.0's low-level networking support became apparent. Few developers wished to write their own socket-based transport and RPC protocols. While HTTP worked well for passing textual and image data around the World Wide Web, it quickly became cumbersome when used for large client/server programs. To build large, distributed applications, programmers required the same kinds of sophisticated network tools available in other environments.

---

[1] "The Network is the Computer" is a trademark of Sun Microsystems, Inc.

Several solutions to this problem have been developed. These solutions included interfaces for communicating with relational databases and existing distributed applications, a lightweight Java-to-Java RPC, and a specification that allows business logic implemented as JavaBeans to run in off-the-shelf transaction processors, database engines, and application servers. The new Java APIs for the enterprise include:

- **Java Database Connectivity:** An interface to SQL-compliant relational databases based on the X/Open Call Level Interface (CLI) standard.

- **JavaIDL:** A mapping between the Object Management Group's (OMG) Interface Definition Language (IDL) and Java objects and a set of classes for interfacing a Java program to a CORBA-compliant Object Request Broker (ORB).

- **Java RMI:** A very lightweight, object-oriented Remote Method Invocation (RMI) mechanism which allows Java programs running in two different virtual machines, usually on two different machines, to share methods and data. Java RMI also contains the unique ability to distribute the behavior of the remote objects, not just the data, as is true of older distributed object mechanisms like CORBA and D/COM.

- **Enterprise JavaBeans:** A specification, implemented by major transaction processor and database vendors, which allows business logic implemented in Java to run in TPM and RDBMS. The EJB framework also provides basic services for transactional applications, such as threading, transaction control, life cycle management, and others.

Chapters 7 through 9 will examine the APIs in detail. This chapter focuses on network-based applications in general and compares the various Enterprise APIs to see where they best fit in a distributed architecture.

Application Architectures

Even though the truly monolithic application architecture has given way to two- and three-tiered client/server architectures and network computing, the monolithic view of applications continues to exert a strong influence on how we build distributed systems. As the Java platform completes the move to network computing it is important to recognize ideas and biases left over from the era of the monolith.

Monoliths

In the days of very large, very expensive machines the monolithic application, or IT stovepipe, was the most popular architecture (see Figure 6.1). These

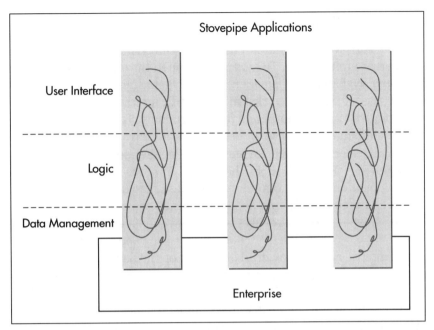

Figure 6.1 Monolithic programs, or stovepipes, contain all the code needed to manage the data, implement the rules of the application, and provide the user interface in a single intertwined mass.

monoliths consisted of a single chunk of code which controlled all aspects of the application, from data storage and retrieval to how the user interacted with the system. The rules by which the system operated were embedded in the implementation code. The system was intended as a single, complete, stand-alone application which neither required any other system to operate nor expected the results of its operation to be used by another system.

Stovepipes were popular for several reasons. The mainframes on which they ran were better able to manage a few large stand-alone jobs than a large number of communicating jobs. Also, few tools existed which could help automate the various subtasks which make up an application. Off-the-shelf databases and automated application development tools were not commercially available, forcing the individual programmer to implement this functionality by hand for each project. More importantly, the monolith is a very simple and easily understood architecture. For the business practices of the day, which before widespread automation were frequently monolithic themselves, the stovepipe was a natural way of implementing the application.

Unfortunately, stovepipes succeeded only in automating the existing business processes which had been developed to cope with the limits of hand processing data. They did nothing to exploit the new power made available by automated data processing.

Client/Server Architectures

Beginning in the early 1980s the monolithic architecture began to be replaced by the client/server architecture. This trend continued throughout the mid and late 1980s as the availability of smaller, cheaper departmental servers combined with the rise of desktop workstations and PCs made these devices an attractive alternative to mainframes and dumb terminals. The popularity of the client/server architecture was also increased by the introduction of off-the-shelf database managers designed for these new smaller servers and later by rapid application development tools that made it much easier to develop client/server applications using commercial database managers.

The client/server architecture split applications into two pieces in an attempt to leverage new inexpensive desktop machines. With client/server architectures, applications could employ sophisticated user interfaces and data visualization tools on the client side and use powerful databases on the backend. Distributing the processing load across many inexpensive clients allowed client/server applications to scale much more linearly than single host/single process applications could, and the use of off-the-shelf software components like an RDBMS greatly reduced application development time. The client/server architecture did, however, suffer from one major drawback. While the client could handle the user interface and data display tasks of the application, and the server could handle all the data management tasks, there was no independent place to store the logic which implemented the business processes the application was supposed to automate. Lacking a natural home for the business logic, programmers tended to include parts of the logic in the server and other parts in the client. As a result, the client and the server side of the application were totally dependent on each other. Neither could perform any useful work without the other. Even though they had been designed to run in a networked fashion, in a logical sense these applications were every bit as monolithic as their physically monolithic mainframe and super-mini predecessors (see Figure 6.2).

Because the application logic tended to be split between the client and the server, these logical monoliths were very tightly coupled. Rules for visualizing data became embedded inside the user interface and rules for how to integrate several different data sources became stored procedures inside the database. This distribution of logic made it very difficult to reuse the user interface code in another project with a different data source. It also made it difficult to use the database in another project which needed a different front-end, such as a different type of PC or workstation, an ATM, an automated response unit for touch-tone phone access, or another system which needed the data controlled by the application, but which did not wish to re-implement the business logic tucked away in the existing user interface.

The tendency to build tightly coupled logical monoliths was made worse by two factors. The early crop of client/server development tools did nothing to

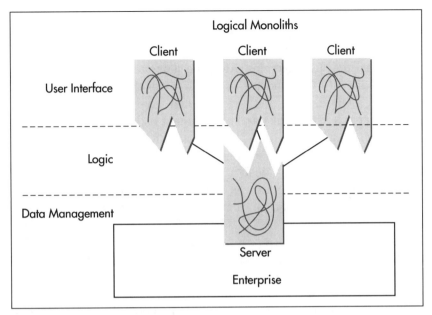

Figure 6.2 Many client/server applications are almost as monolithic as their true stovepipe counterparts.

help a developer compartmentalize the application's logic. In many cases, the tools actively prevented the compartmentalization of the logic by hardwiring the client-side code directly to the target database. The second, more subtle and more damaging factor, was that developers who grew up in the monolithic era were not accustomed to thinking of the logic as a separate part of the application, a part which should not be mixed with other layers of the application and which may have value to other parts of the organization. Neither was a new programmer being taught the importance of keeping the business separate. Despite years of talking about Model/View/Controller development, programmers still too often reverted to logically monolithic architectures.

The first-generation client/server application development tools were little more than intelligent screen painters which could build queries visually and display results in a graphical user interface. This was a great step forward in automated application development. Anyone who built database applications in the late 1980s will remember being very impressed the first time he or she saw a sales rep build a rolodex application without writing a single line of code. But for any application more complex than a rolodex the developer was still forced to handcraft all the application-specific code. Thus, the business rule which said, "It is meaningful to these analysts to compare the foo quantity with the bar quantity" was mixed in with the code which said, "Draw a bar chart here." Similarly, the business rule which said, "Foo can be calculated from these data from our accounts receivable system" ended up as part of the SQL which said, "Here's how you pull this column out of that database."

These limits of the first-generation tools were acceptable because developers did not consider that the business rules should be separate from the code which implemented the user interface and the DBMS. To a developer with 20 years of experience writing COBOL programs which manipulated flat files, implementing the business rules as part of the data management code made perfect sense. The idea of sequestering the business logic in its own self-contained modules simply did not fit within this style of application. Even in those systems that followed the principles of structured design, which did encourage separating the logic from the GUI and data, the focus was more often on making it easy to reuse code, usually with cut and paste, than on reusing executable modules in a running system.

These limits remained hidden for several years. The client/server revolution had promised IT shops a new generation of flexible systems which would reduce maintenance costs and allow the organization to adapt more rapidly to changing business needs. Over time, companies realized that these logical monoliths were, in many cases, every bit as brittle and complicated as the systems they were intended to replace.

The client/server architecture often failed because it did not recognize that business rules are as valuable or even more valuable than the code which implements them. This myopia led to the rules being buried deeply within applications where they could not be leveraged effectively across organizations. For example, a typical customer management system (CMS) would be written as a logical monolith which assumed a particular client system, such as a 3270 terminal, a PC, or workstation. At some point the company might decide that allowing customers to access their own account information through touchtone phones might be a valuable service to offer. But, because the various parts of the customer management application are tightly coupled, it is very difficult to give the telephony system access to the data and logic portions of the application. A custom adapter module, which probably re-implements a significant portion of the business rules and data manipulation routines, would have to be built to interface the legacy system with the telephony system (see Figure 6.3). If this adapter was written by developers with a monolithic view of applications, it would probably be as tightly coupled to the system to which it was being grafted as the components of the original system were. So, when the company later decides to make the same services available over the Internet, yet another custom adapter, which implements the same business rules a third time, will have to be developed.

Three-Tiered Applications

The three-tiered application architecture was developed to solve this problem. Three-tiered applications assume that the business rules which they imple-

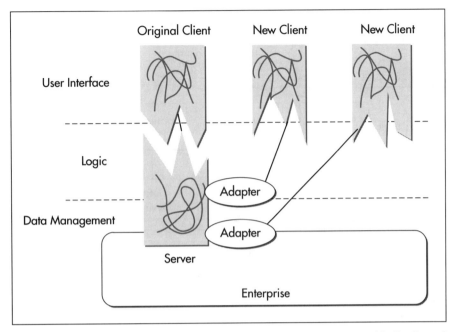

Figure 6.3 Ad hoc adapters are required to integrate new systems with distributed monoliths.

ment are of value and will eventually be required to interoperate with other systems. The three-tiered architecture does this by breaking the application into three distinct layers: data management, business logic, and user presentation, each with its own goals and design constraints (see Figure 6.4). The bottom tier handles data storage. Data should be stored in as raw a form as possible. No assumptions about how the data should be processed or what operations should be performed on the data should be made at this layer. The second tier, the logic layer, implements the business rules of the application. This layer makes no assumptions about how the data is stored. It simply expects the data layer to provide a generic way for it to access the raw data. The logic layer adds value to the raw data by applying business rules to it and by making it available to the third tier. The third tier implements the user interface. It knows how to format and display the cooked data coming from the logic layer in a way which is appropriate for the client device on which it resides. The interface layer also provides the user with access to services, such as update and query, provided by the logic layer. The user interface layer never talks directly to the data management layer and it never performs any value-added operations on the data. It depends wholly on the logic layer for both of these functions. Had our customer service application been originally written in a three-tiered manner, the addition of the telephony and Internet interfaces would have been much easier.

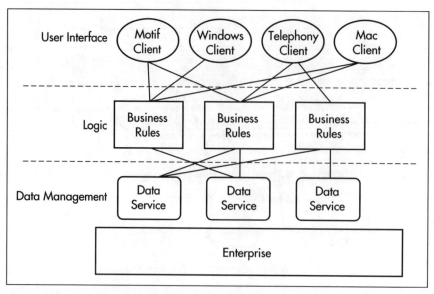

Figure 6.4   The three-tiered architecture, with distinct data, logic, and interface layers.

While the three-tiered architecture might seem like a minor extension to client/server, there is a subtle, critical difference. With the possible exception of GUI objects, the components which make up each tier do their jobs without assuming they are part of any application. Applications exist only as cooperating collections of components, and each component can simultaneously be part of many different applications (see Figure 6.5). The logic component which implements the rules for comparing foo to bar is a stand-alone, fine-grained service provider. It does not know when it is part of a market forecasting tool or part of an historical data analysis tool. It only knows that a member of another layer has requested its services.

The switch from seeing components as integral parts of applications to seeing components as stand-alone entities which can provide services for applications provides much of the power of the three-tiered architecture. The previous CMS example demonstrates this. Components of the data tier provide services to the logic tier without knowing if they are now part of the CMS application or part of a decision support tool or a market analysis tool. The logic components provide their services without knowing if the requests come from an 800-number operator inside of the company, a customer calling on a touch-tone phone, a customer coming over the Internet, or even a marketing team playing what-if scenarios to design a new service offering. Because the components have been designed as stand-alone service providers, not as embedded parts of an application, they can be part of all these applications simultaneously.

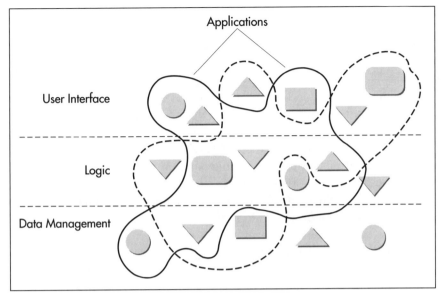

Figure 6.5   In the three-tiered architecture applications are made up of cooperating collections of networked components.

The three-tiered architecture first entered the IT world in the early 1990s. Since then there has been some debate as to whether there are actually only three tiers. Some authors argue that to isolate fully the various components of the data, logic, and presentation tiers there must be interface layers between the data and logic tiers and between the logic and presentation tiers. The addition of these two interface tiers results in the five-tiered architecture. Others argue that each tier can be divided into many subtiers, each of which provides a higher level of functionality than the subtier below it. This type of structure is called the N-tiered architecture. For the purposes of this chapter we can ignore these subtleties and treat these higher-order architectures as extensions of the basic three-tiered architecture.

The Three-Tiered Advantage

By explicitly recognizing business processes as a valuable asset and providing a separate place to store the logic which implements these processes, the three-tiered architecture solved many of the problems which the logical monoliths of the two-tiered client/server architecture failed to overcome. This gives three-tiered architecture many advantages over the simpler client/server architecture.

Agile Software

The CMS example showed that the three-tiered architecture could be used to create more flexible and easily modifiable systems. In a world where information technology is increasingly used as a strategic weapon in the fight to remain competitive, agile software is in great demand. The three-tiered architecture enables agile software in several ways. First, by treating software components as stand-alone data providers, service providers, and service consumers (the data, logic, and presentation tiers, respectively), the three-tiered architecture creates a software infrastructure of reusable parts. Much as a mechanical engineer working on a project is blessed with a large assortment of off-the-shelf motors, gears, and switches with which to work, a software engineer working in a three-tiered environment can build systems by assembling the pre-existing parts. This reuse not only speeds development by reducing the amount of new code which must be written for each new project, it increases overall system quality. Since the components have already been put into production in other applications, they are more thoroughly debugged than new code written for a single project.

By separating the idea of an application from the components used to implement an application, three-tiered applications are also easier to maintain and update. In the CMS example, suppose a bug is found in part of the logic running the system. In the monolithic version, the logic, and therefore the bug, is poten-

---

JAVA APPLICATION COMPONENTS

There is more to component-based software reuse than just building the components themselves. The components must also be available for the particular platform on which the project must be deployed as must the framework in which those components run. This has proven to be an almost insurmountable obstacle to reuse. If the components needed must be ported from one platform to another or if the database or other framework they run in doesn't exist on the new platform, then those pre-existing components are of little use to the developer.

The Java Platform helps solve this problem. Java components run on any underlying platform without porting or recompilation. The component interaction and container model, JavaBeans, is a standard part of the platform and is also guaranteed to be on the new target platform. Finally, enterprise services, like Enterprise JavaBeans and servlets, have been very widely implemented in off-the-shelf products, allowing the developer to take advantage of higher-level application frameworks without tying the application to a single vendor.

tially replicated in three separate systems. This replication triples the effort required to locate and fix the bug, and triples the testing effort required at the end of the cycle. This duplication also introduces the danger of version skew in the systems. If the bug is found and fixed in one system, but not the other two, a customer asking the same question of a CMS agent, over the automated touch-tone system and over the Internet, could get three different answers.

Worse yet, this duplication can slow the adoption of new business practices. Suppose the company's marketing department comes up with a new service offering. In an information-based service industry this offering might be little more than a new idea, an advertising campaign to promote the idea, and a software system which implements the idea. If the new system requires changes to all three versions of the CMS applications, then the new offering cannot be rolled out until all three systems have been updated. Given the chronic lateness of software development efforts, this can substantially delay the introduction of the new offering, reducing its profitability and increasing the risk that competitors can get a similar offering to market quicker.

A three-tiered architecture avoids both the maintenance and the update problem. Because each component in the architecture has a unique function which is not duplicated by any other component, bugs are more localized than they are in typical monolithic environments. This means that a bug needs to be fixed only once in a single component. This cuts down on the maintenance effort required to keep a system running and eliminates the danger of version skew throughout the system. It also means that new offerings can be created by modifying a small set of components once or adding new components to the system, rather than making the same modifications to duplicate modules throughout the system.

The Interconnection Problem

The three-tiered architecture also eliminates the need for the custom interconnections between pieces of a system which are often required in the monolithic world. The CMS example shows this in the three separate connection modules needed: the original code written for the customer service agent's application, the telephony interconnect, and the Internet connection. In this case, the single data source and the three applications result in the need for three connection modules. If the CMS needed information from two separate data sources and the logic for accessing those sources was duplicated in each application, the two sources and three applications would require six separate, custom interconnection modules.

In the worse case, each data source may require its own adapter for each application and each application may require an adapter for each data source. This $M \times N$ interconnect problem is barely manageable when M and N are small (in this example, 2 and 3 respectively). In a large organization, with many data sources and applications, the $M \times N$ problem can cripple its IT shop.

This problem is very similar to that encountered by hardware designers interfacing I/O devices to early computers. If a machine required a drum storage unit, a drum controller was built into the machine. The addition of another drum required another controller; if a card reader or tape was required, another separate controller was added. This multiplication of controllers quickly became unmanageable, forcing hardware designers to find a better way. They solved this interconnection problem by creating standardized buses which could be used by all I/O devices. The CPU was only required to know how to communicate with the bus. The I/O devices also talked to the bus without regard to what sort of CPU was at the other end. For CPU and I/O device designers the bus architecture replaced the $M \times N$ interconnection problem with the single task of interfacing their device to the bus.

The three-tiered architecture solves the $M \times N$ software interconnect problem by emulating the hardware bus architecture. Components, regardless of whether they reside in the data, logic, or presentation tier, interface to a standardized data bus. This data bus, built on an accepted network standard like CORBA, allows the various components to communicate with each other without the need for customized, single-purpose interconnects between each pair of components. This reduces the $M \times N$ problem to the $1 + 1$ problem of data sources talking to data consumers and service providers talking to service consumers.

Limited data availability was another aspect of the interconnection problem. As long as data was managed by a stovepipe-like application, that data was useful only to that application and could not easily be exploited by other parts of the organization. Moving to a three-tiered data bus architecture solves this problem by making the raw data sources available to any other application. So, not only can the business logic be used in many applications, each with a different interface, the data themselves can be used by many different sets of business rules, in many different applications. The data-processing stovepipe has been replaced by an architecture which makes data universally available.

Consider a typical stovepipe application, like an order entry system. This application would typically store its data in some application-specific manner which would be difficult to reuse. If that data were needed for a decision support system (DSS) a custom data conversion program would have to be written to pry the data out of its stovepipe. Then this conversion program would typically be run as a batch job, monthly, weekly, or even nightly, and the extracted data loaded from the data entry system into the DSS. This process is time-consuming, both in initial development of the custom programs and in periodic extractions. In a three-tiered environment with application-independent data sources, no additional extraction programs are needed in order to use data in several applications. The order entry system would store data into the data management layer, which the DSS would then use directly via the data management layer's interfaces. While, for performance or throughput reasons, the DSS will likely export the data to another database, it can do so without needing to write more code.

Distributed Systems Management

Two-tiered systems were also notoriously difficult to manage over time. Since substantial portions of the application's logic resided in the user interface, deploying bug fixes or enhancements to that logic required updating the copy of the code on each client machine. Especially in large organizations, which might have tens of thousands of clients, or in organizations with many small remote offices and no centralized systems management, this change could be extremely expensive. A large portion of the estimated $8,000 to $14,000 per PC per year management costs is caused by this problem.

The client update problem also slowed the rate at which organizations could change their business practices. If a new version of an application, which implemented some new product or service, became available, but deployment of that service required updating both the client and the server sides of the application, the organization faced a chicken and egg problem. If the server side was modified before the clients, the deployed clients would break. If the clients were updated before the server side changed, the new clients would be useless. Organizations caught in this dilemma will usually either underestimate the difficulty of making such a change and endure days or weeks of chaos as they try to change the entire installed base in a single effort, or undergo a long, expensive phase-in of the new software, during which IT is required to support multiple, incompatible versions of both the client- and the server-side code, and the new product offering is available to only a limited portion of the customer base.

Three-tiered applications, especially those implemented on the Java platform, can reduce the need for client updates and ease, but not necessarily eliminate, the pain of migration when the client must be updated. In a three-tiered application, most of the code resides in logic and data layers. Since these layers are typically deployed on centralized, backend machines which are surrounded by a professional support staff, bug fixes and enhancements to these layers are relatively painless. These changes can be made without touching the client machines and without introducing version skew into the application.

The client machines only need to be touched when the actual user interface code running on the client must be updated. In this case, the software-on-demand capability found in the Java platform allows these changes to be made without physically updating the disks of each client. Whether the application is distributed through HTTP and a Web browser or through an automatic application distribution system like Marimba's Castanet, the client-side software can be automatically updated without the expense of actually touching each PC.

Deploying Three-Tiered Applications

When implementing a three-tiered application, the question of where to put the pieces becomes critical. There are several opportunities to optimize the application by placing different parts in different locations on the network. The GUI will almost certainly run on the desktop. Given a network computer, which combines the local processing and display capabilities of a PC with the low cost of a character-based terminal, there is little need for an X or Windows terminal which would execute the GUI remotely and display it back to the client.

The data and logic are a different story. Here you must consider such factors as: How important is it that everyone in the enterprise, regardless of geographical location, sees the exact same data? How much bandwidth does the application require? How much latency can the user tolerate? Can either of these factors be optimized by judicious placement of parts of the application?

For example, suppose it was critical that every one in the enterprise saw a single consistent view of a database (see Figure 6.6). This could be a travel reservation system where a room in a hotel has been booked so that room must show up as unavailable whenever any other travel agent anywhere in the world tries to book it. Here the only real choice is to centralize the data in a single database so that it can be protected against simultaneous updates of the same resource by two different agents. While the application logic might be distributed to regional processing centers, or even deployed to the desktop itself, for scalability reasons, only a single copy of the data is maintained.

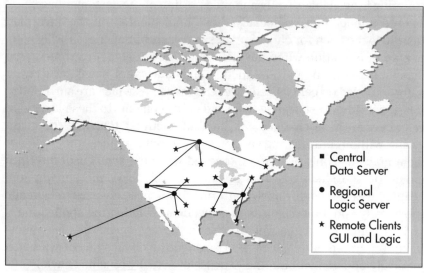

Figure 6.6   Critical, shared data are centralized for easy management.

In another case, global consistence of the data might not be that critical. For example, an order entry and forecasting system might deal only with data for a single region and feed new data back to the central database, but not to other regions. A region either doesn't need access to anyone's data but its own or it can afford to have the other regions' data be slightly out of date. In this case, the region's data may be stored in a regional machine and updates sent periodically to the central data store (see Figure 6.7). If needed, other regions' data could be updated nightly to give the local users a relatively fresh view of what is going on in the rest of the world. This scheme would greatly reduce the bandwidth needed by the application and reduce the latency experienced by the users.

A slight variation of this scenario might have a local copy of regional data which automatically updates the central copy, but has no local copy of another region's data. If, in a rare case, a user needs access to another region's data, the system can go to the central database to fetch the needed information. This scheme trades an increase in latency in a rare case for access to current information.

In yet another case, we might be trying to optimize computational efficiency against network bandwidth. Suppose that we have to perform a calculation whose results must then be shared among a large number of users. If this calculation is very expensive, say a very detailed weather simulation, it might make sense to do the calculation on a single, very fast machine (or split the job across a network of fast machines) and distribute the result to all the clients

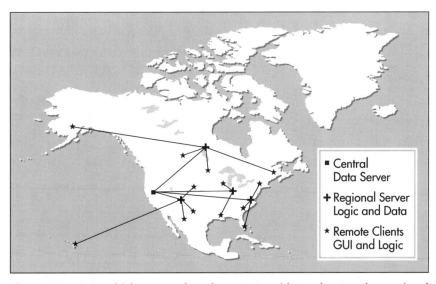

Figure 6.7 Data which are not shared corporate-wide can be stored on regional servers for faster access.

(see Figure 6.8). Once the results have been moved to the client machine, less expensive calculations like renormalizations and sorts can be run locally.

However, if the calculation is not particularly expensive, but the result set is quite large, network bandwidth might be a bigger concern than efficient use of the CPU. Here it would be beneficial to move the calculation to each client. While this split is wasteful in terms of computational cycles, with hundreds or thousands of processors calculating the same results from the same data, it reduces the demands for scarce network bandwidth to an acceptable load. In this case, we might eliminate the mid-tier servers entirely, implementing our well-designed three-tiered architecture on just two tiers of hardware (see Figure 6.9).

Limits of the Three-Tiered Architecture

Despite all of its advantages, there are several limits to the three-tiered architecture which may make it inappropriate for some applications. Two of the limits, size of the executable and speed of execution, are technical limits which result from the overhead of communicating between the various layers. The third limit is cultural; it involves the need to update legacy systems so they are useful in a three-tiered environment and to educate developers and manage-

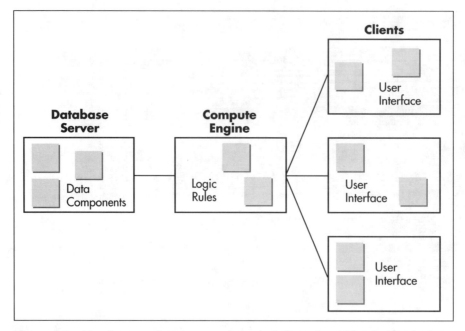

Figure 6.8   Very long-running or expensive calculations should be done once on a compute server and the results distributed over the network.

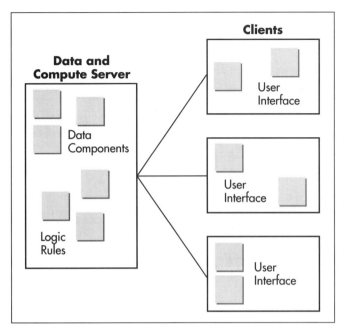

Figure 6.9   Three logical tiers can be implemented on two (or even one) physical tiers of machines.

ment about the practical considerations of three-tiered applications. Of the two limits, the cultural ones are often more difficult to overcome.

Size and Speed

Three-tiered architectures require a network-based data bus for communications between the tiers. Without this data bus, the application's developers are simply practicing good structured programming techniques which, while laudable, do not address the bigger issues of network distribution and scalability. This communications layer necessarily introduces some additional latency into the system. Also, the need for libraries or classes which interface to the data bus will typically increase the size of the application. For some systems, such as real-time data acquisition, high-volume online transaction processing, or embedded systems, the increase in executable size and the reduction in throughput is unacceptable.

Fortunately for companies wishing to adopt the three-tiered architecture, even systems for which the three-tiered architecture is an inappropriate implementation can be incorporated as part of a broader three-tiered application (see Figure 6.10). For example, a real-time data acquisition system embedded in a weather station could read in data from its instruments, buffer that data, then act as a data source for the rest of the enterprise.

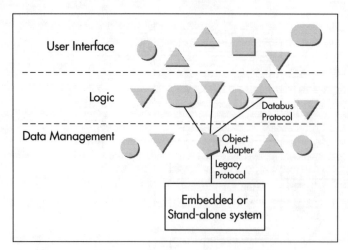

Figure 6.10 With an appropriate adapter, small stand-alone systems can be brought into the three-tiered world.

Legacy and Education Problems

Since the three-tiered architecture has been widely discussed only in the last several years, few if any organizations have the organizational infrastructure required to get the maximum benefits from three-tiered applications. Their data are imprisoned in flat files controlled by stovepipes or in databases tightly coupled with legacy applications. Their developers share a monolithic view of applications and they lack the cultural motivations and infrastructure needed to promote widespread reuse of components.

As an organization moves toward three-tiered applications, it must face each of these problems. These problems present great challenges which are made worse by a failure to recognize that they even exist. An organization which is attracted by the benefits of the three-tiered architecture should carefully plan how it will introduce this technology to its IT shop. What training is required, which applications can be moved first, how this will affect the organization's IT practices and people, and how long it will take for this technology investment to begin to pay dividends are all important questions which must be answered before the actual move is made.

The organization should also recognize that there are many more ways to fail at this move than there are to succeed. Despite the benefits of three-tiered applications and the often strong push from above to adopt this architecture, it is not possible for any established IT organization to move its legacy environments to three-tiered overnight. There will be conflicts for resources between ongoing maintenance and development efforts and the new three-tiered development. There will be awkward periods during which some systems have been moved to the new environment while other critical systems are still locked in legacy applications, and there will be mistakes and missteps in the initial implementation. Recognizing and planning for these difficulties can reduce, but not eliminate, these growing pains.

Making the Move

Early adapters of corporate-wide three-tiered architectures have found that it takes roughly three to five years to reorganize their business around the new infrastructures. Many of these organizations are just now getting past the growing pains and beginning to reap the promised benefits. While companies now contemplating making the move to the three-tiered architecture should plan on a similar duration for their efforts, they can benefit from the lessons learned by the pioneers.

Training

The three-tiered architecture introduces many new technologies to the typical IT shop: distributed applications, object technology, programming by interfaces, and new network protocols to name a few. A large amount of training and education will be required before many IT professionals will be able to use these technologies effectively. Time needed for this training and the associated unproductive period as developers learn, by trial and error, the intricacies of the methods must be accounted for when planning the move to three-tiered architectures.

While most IT shops today have extensive experience with SQL and relational database design, they probably are weak in distributed application design, object-oriented analysis and design, interface design, distributed application management, and the Java platform. Any training program must account for the organization's strengths and weaknesses in each of these areas and must build up the weak areas.

When designing the training program, the order in which these areas are addressed is just as important as the content of the courses. The world is full of programmers who write what are essentially FORTRAN programs in C because they learned the new language without first learning the concepts of structured programming, and of programmers who write perfect, procedural C code in C++ because they learned the syntax of C++ without first learning the intricacies of object-oriented analysis and design. If the underlying concepts and the new view of applications are not taught early in the program (preferably before the first Java language classes) and reinforced throughout the training, the organization risks raising a generation of developers who simply redevelop old, possibly distributed, monoliths in a new language. Organizations which fall into this trap will never gain the benefits promised by the three-tiered architecture.

People

With all the emphasis on the new architecture, the associated training, and new development groups, it is easy to create a new two-tiered class structure within the development organization. One class, consisting of young hotshots, receives an inordinate amount of attention from management, training dollars, and interesting new projects. The other class consists of the older developers who are relegated to maintaining the existing systems. Often there is an implicit assumption that as the new systems come online, these maintenance developers will die a natural death, along with the systems on which they work.

This class system is damaging and must be avoided for several reasons. First, the move to the new architecture will take several years. During this period the legacy systems will be the bread and butter of the IT organization. If the developers responsible for the upkeep of these systems feel that they will soon be out of a job and begin to leave the company, the IT shop will be unable to maintain and upgrade these critical systems. Second, the existing systems must be either integrated into the new architecture or replaced by functionally equivalent systems. The expertise in the legacy systems, including the "oral culture" of how they work and why they are implemented the way they are, will be invaluable to those developers working to bring the legacy systems into the new architecture. Also, some of these legacy systems may turn out to be "untouchable" and require years of ongoing maintenance. In these cases, the veteran developers will be an important part of the IT shop for years to come.

Managing the Change

In order to utilize the three-tiered architecture across a business, this architecture must be fully implemented across the entire organization. It does little good for the purchasing systems to be built in an open, interoperable manner if the accounts payable database is still controlled by a totally closed stovepipe. Also, one of the failings of many earlier systems was that they simply automated existing business processes without considering how the new information technology could be used to streamline these processes. The move to this new application environment gives the organization a chance to look at its current practices and possibly update them to reflect the advances of the recent wave of business process reengineering. Meeting both of these goals requires the support of and leadership from the highest level of IT management. In those companies that have successfully made the move to company-wide three-tiered architectures and data buses, the push for change came from the top down with the CIO supporting the rest of the organization during the often painful periods of transition.

Beyond the obvious tasks of setting the new technical direction for the organization and providing training time and budget, there are several subtle things which upper management can do to ease the adoption of the three-tiered architecture. One of the most important is to recognize that the initial efforts in creating the next-generation systems will be devoted to building infrastructure that may not be immediately useful to the organization. This period must be viewed as a long-term investment, and mid-tier managers and developers must be measured and rewarded appropriately. In a real-world environment, with deadlines to meet and pressure from outside the IT shop to produce results, making and protecting this investment is often a very difficult task.

One effective way to support this investment is to build a *culture of reuse.* Developers should be goaled on how often their components are used by others and, to prevent everyone from writing reusable code but no one actually reusing any of it, how often they reuse existing components. If the organization uses developer productivity metrics, these metrics may have to be changed. If the organization measures productivity in lines of code/day (still the most common way of rating programmers), a programmer who spends a day writing 300 lines of new code to accomplish a task will look more productive than a programmer who spends half of a day searching the corporate IT library for an existing component which accomplishes the needed task and writing 50 lines of code to integrate that component into the new system. Failure to modify productivity metrics to make the second developer rate much more highly than the first can sabotage any attempts to promote reuse.

Suitable productivity metrics become even more important for those developers producing the components which are to be reused. Experience has shown that it takes a significant additional effort to design, implement, and test high-quality components worthy of widespread reuse. One manufacturer of commercial component libraries estimates that it requires approximately seven times more effort to develop its components than it would to build a "one-shot" piece of code which performed the same function but could never be used outside of the program for which it was developed. The payoff for this seven-to-one investment does not come during the first project in which the component is used. The payoff comes after that component has been used over and over again in other projects, possibly years after the component was developed. For this reason, component designers who seem to spend all their time arguing about APIs and design trade-offs, instead of writing code, must (within limits, of course) be seen as performing useful, important work.

The culture of reuse also requires cooperation between development groups. Each group, regardless of on what individual system it is working, must be aware of what other groups are doing and of how what it is doing could affect those groups. Regular meetings between groups to discuss the overall architecture, ensure that it is adequate for the needs of all members to the IT organization, and evaluate how each group is fitting into the architecture are required. The organization may wish to host periodic inter-group code and design reviews, and to create a formal *component librarian* position responsible for ensuring that all new work fits seamlessly into the overall design for IT.

Integrating Legacy Systems

Since no organization can afford to throw away its existing systems and start from scratch with a new three-tiered architecture, the new systems must be phased in slowly and the legacy systems integrated with the new applications. There are two important considerations when dealing with legacy systems: how the legacy system should communicate with the data bus and what sort of interface the legacy system should present to the other components on the bus.

Interfacing with the Data Bus

The exact nature of the legacy system limits how it can be integrated with the three-tiered architecture. The structure of the existing system not only controls how it can best be attached to the data bus, but also what tier the resulting hybrid will occupy. For example, an existing client/server database application can be fairly easily interfaced to the bus using an adapter which speaks SQL on one side and the bus protocol on the other. Providing there are no conflicts between the operations of the legacy applications and the new system, this can be done without disturbing any existing two-tiered clients or applications (see Figure 6.11). The database becomes a new data source and the adapter a new component in the data management tier.

The worst part of this process is that inevitably some of the business logic will be too tightly wrapped up in the client and will have to be reimplemented in the new three-tiered system. This duplication of code makes maintenance more difficult and more error-prone, since each change must now be made twice. Because of these maintenance problems, this phased approach to wrapping a legacy system should be seen as only a short-term solution. The longer-term goal is to completely encapsulate the legacy system in three-tiered wrappers, so that it can then be dismantled without affecting critical applications. Tearing down the legacy systems will leave the IT shop with a much more rational infrastructure, where each piece of functionality is implemented only once, then leveraged throughout the organization.

Other types of legacy systems are harder to break apart. For 3270 applications, it may be next to impossible to untangle the data management code from the logic and the 3270 screens. The only choice may be to use a screen scraper as an adapter to the bus. In this case, the legacy application would encapsulate both the data management and the logic of the application, and the adapter would reside in the logic tier, providing services to other logic components and presentation components (see Figure 6.12).

Obviously, this is less desirable than separating the logic from the data. The data are still imprisoned by the application logic and cannot be easily used in other applications. This solution does nothing to address the maintenance problems and brittleness of monolithic applications. Unfortunately, this com-

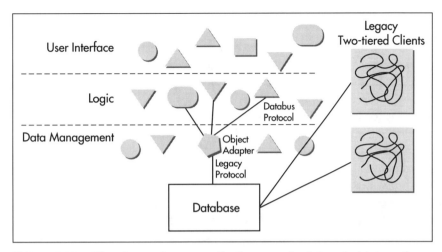

Figure 6.11 Client/server legacy applications can be integrated into a three-tiered structure without disrupting the existing application.

promise is often the only short-term solution to bringing a critical legacy system into the new architecture in the time available. As the three-tiered environment matures and as time allows, organizations which have been forced to make this trade-off should consider completely replacing the legacy system with a new, architecturally clean, three-tiered implementation. The facade used to interface the system to the three-tiered world will allow this older code to be ripped out and replaced without disturbing the other systems.

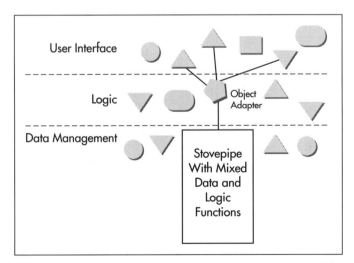

Figure 6.12 Truly monolithic systems may act as both data management and logic components in the new three-tiered model.

DESIGNING INTERFACES FOR LEGACY SYSTEMS

When integrating a legacy application to a three-tiered architecture, many developers will naively build an interface which exposes every possible operation preformed by the existing system. This can result in unwieldy and difficult-to-use components that add very little value to the architecture. For example, a legacy system which processes some data may be composed of several individual programs which act as filters on the data: one program sorting the data, one massaging the data in some way, and a third computing the needed output. Data are processed by sending them sequentially through the filters. If each of these filters has several flags which control its behavior, a naive interface would have to include a method call for each possible combination of flags. If each of the three filters in our example had two flags, each with two possible values, the resulting interface would have 64 separate methods, with names like:

```
sortAlphabetically()
sortReverseAlphabetically()
sortUniqueAlphabetically()
sortUniqueReverseAlphabetically()
```

   As the number of flags and possible values climbs, the number of methods provided by the interface quickly reaches the thousands or tens of thousands. One way to solve this problem would be to provide methods which set each flag individually and another method which performs the operation. If reasonable default values are chosen for flags which are not explicitly set, the resulting interface will be relatively clean and usable. If no reasonable default values can be assigned, though, the resulting stream of

```
setSortOrder(ALPHABETICAL)
setUnique(True)
sort()
```

method calls will quickly become unusable. Fortunately, most real-world systems, regardless of the number of flag permutations available, are only used in a few different ways. In the previous example, we might find that out of the 64 available permutations, only three are used by our business processes. These three combinations may then be modeled in the interface to the legacy system according to the business function they perform, not according to the values of the flags used. One method might be generateMailingList(); the second, getListByZipCode(); and the third, getListByAge(). These higher-level services would be very easy for another developer to understand and would make the component much easier to reuse.

In some cases a developer may be able to define a small number of business processes which are performed by the legacy system but still be left with a handful of oddball applications which require finer control over the operations of the system. In this case, the developer may wish to define two separate interfaces to the system: one which encapsulates the high-level business processes and one which uses the setFlag()/performOperation() syntax previously described. This will give developers using the legacy system an easy way to perform the simple tasks and still have access to the system's more complicated behavior. This philosophy of making the simple things easy, while providing a more complicated interface for the more difficult but less frequently used tasks, is very common in the Java platform.

Using the Java Platform in the Enterprise

The previous remarks apply to any distributed system, regardless of what language or languages are used to implement it. How does the Java platform fit into this architecture?

Interface Definition Language versus Remote Method Invocation

Both JavaIDL (Interface Definition Language) and Java RMI (Remote Method Invocation) are obvious candidates for building the data bus which connects the components of the various tiers. There is quite a bit of overlap between the functionality provided by JavaIDL and RMI, which can make it difficult to choose between the two.

JavaIDL is based on the OMG's CORBA. CORBA supports many different implementation languages, including C, C++, Java, and others. CORBA also specifies a wide range of backend support services, such as security, persistence, atomic transactions, and event queues. The CORBA specification has been available since 1991 and CORBA implementations are available from several vendors. Many application server vendors are also using IIOP as the backbone of their systems. These application servers often include Web servers, data access managers, and automatic relational-data-to-object-model mapping tools. These application servers provide an excellent way to integrate CORBA Services into Web applications.

Java RMI is used to communicate between two Java applications. Systems which use RMI must implement both the client and the server side of the application in the Java language. Since RMI is very new, it lacks the extensive backend services provided by CORBA and may require that the developer implement these services by hand. On the other hand, RMI is very lightweight; as a part of the Java Core APIs, developers can count on having RMI support in the client rather than having to download that code with the application. Also, other parts of the Java Enterprise platform, such as Enterprise JavaBeans, provide many of the services found in CORBA, making RMI a more attractive option.

RMI also allows the developer to describe each component's interface in Java. CORBA implementations require that the interface be described in the OMG's Interface Definition Language (IDL). The IDL descriptions are then compiled into the appropriate implementation language, be it Java, C++, or something else. This two-step process, which forces the developer to use at least two different languages, OMG-IDL and the real implementation language, complicates the development process and can result in a mismatch between the semantics of OMG-IDL and the native implementation language. In short, JavaIDL is the better choice for the data bus for systems which:

- Must interoperate with components not built in Java.

- Require sophisticated network services which are already specified by CORBA.

- Have some legacy components which already support CORBA interfaces.

- Wish to use some of the off-the-shelf functionality provided by companies like Netscape.

For new development which will use the Java language for both the client and server components and which does not require network services like those available in CORBA, Java RMI, with its straightforward extension of the Java object model to the network, would be the better choice. For legacy systems, using Java RMI combined with Java Native Interface calls to the existing system may be as easy to implement as adding a CORBA interface to the system would be.

Java RMI offers one major architectural advantage that has never been available to distributed application designers. Previously deployed distributed object mechanisms, such as CORBA and DCOM, only allow components of the application to talk to each other. They are merely object-oriented RPC mechanisms. In these systems, the name "distributed objects" is a misnomer. The objects merely talk to one another. They have no way to move across the network or to install themselves and execute on a remote machine. These limitations impose severe restraints on how an application can be designed. Since the implementation of each class (and all its subclasses) must be installed in advance on the remote machine, these systems cannot support such important features as late binding of classes to interfaces and automatic updating of system components.

Java RMI supports true distributed objects. In RMI, both an object's state and its implementation can be passed from one side of the network to the other. This allows the components of an RMI application to agree up front on the interfaces they will use and defer to runtime what classes will implement these interfaces. For example, one developer could create a generic compute engine that is deployed on a large multiprocessor machine. This engine uses RMI to import objects that implement a run( ) method. Clients can implement an algorithm or function they need and use the compute engine without having to install the code on the engine. This ability to support true object-oriented design techniques and late binding over the network has a profound effect on application design. Developers who have previously used only RPC mechanisms may need some time to understand this new ability and to figure out how best to use it in their applications.

The Java Database Connection

JDBC is an SQL-based API for interfacing Java programs to relational databases. While either JavaIDL or Java RMI can be used as the data bus, use of JDBC should be confined to data management components. In a three-tiered environment it is not appropriate for components in the logic or presentation tiers to talk directly to data sources. This would violate the encapsulation and abstraction maintained by each tier and result in the distributed monoliths common in the two-tiered client/server world. Instead of allowing logic and presentation objects to talk directly to the data sources, components of the data tier should interface with the actual data storage mechanism and present an abstract interface to the logic tier while hiding the implementation details of how and where the data are stored.

This architectural purity may make it difficult to implement some types of applications (see Figure 6.13). For example, an ad hoc query tool in a decision support system must be able to form and ask any imaginable query of the database. Since the developer cannot possibly produce a canned query or interface for every possible query, components in the logic tier may have to interface directly to the database. In these cases, the data tier should support an SQL mechanism for the logic tier. For other "normal" applications, the data tier should still implement an abstract interface. This will minimize the use of raw SQL and ease future maintenance.

This does not mean that JDBC code will never execute on a client machine. Although it is widely assumed that the three-tiered architecture is a *physical architecture* which must be implemented on at least three different machines communicating over a network, this is not true. The three-tiers are purely logical constructs. If an application is made of cooperating components which communicate over a network through well-defined interfaces and if those components clearly divided the roles of data management, business logic, and pre-

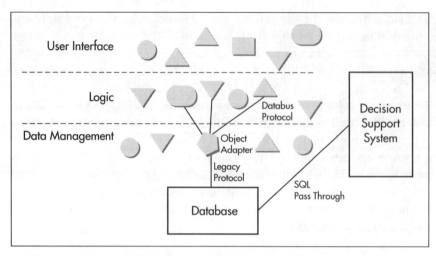

Figure 6.13   Some applications require direct access to data, violating architectural purity but increasing flexibility.

sentation among themselves, then this is a three-tiered application regardless of whether it is physically implemented on three separate machines, one machine, or 100 different machines. While a physically distributed implementation will be the most common architecture, there may be cases, especially given Java's automatic migration of code over the network, where components of the data tier actually execute on the client machine.

Enterprise JavaBeans

Distributed applications require an extensive infrastructure in which to operate. While Java RMI, IDL, and JDBC provide some of this infrastructure, their use is limited to defining how the components of the different tiers communicate among themselves. These APIs do nothing to ease the "grunt work" of service design: How do you activate the components on the different tiers, how do you handle server threading, how do you multiplex many user connections into a single database connection, how do you ensure that multipart transactions either finish completely or are completely rolled back, and other difficult issues. Traditionally, these issues have been solved by using a transaction process monitor (TPM) in the middle tier of the application. The TPM took care of component life cycle management, threading, performance issues such as connection multiplexing, and others. Using a TPM freed the designer to concentrate on the business logic that made the application valuable to the organization, not on the more mechanical tasks of how the pieces of the application were wired together.

Using a TPM does have some disadvantages, the most obvious being that all such systems are proprietary. Components written for one TPM are tightly wired to its specific APIs and are very difficult to port to different systems. This limits the organization's flexibility in how it deploys components. If the component should be deployed on a particular existing application server, but that server does not support the needed TPM, the organization is forced to purchase redundant hardware. Worse, the proprietary nature of TPMs limits the reusability of components. If a business component is written by one group using one combination of hardware, OS, and TPM, another group that needs to use the component on a different combination will be forced to either port the component or, more likely, write their own from scratch.

The use of Enterprise JavaBeans solves this problem. Enterprise JavaBeans allows business logic to be written as JavaBeans and used in any compliant TPM. The Enterprise JavaBeans framework allows the TPM to use and manage the Bean, and the Java platform's Write Once, Run Anywhere capability allows the Bean to be deployed on not only any combination of hardware and OS, but also on any TPM. Released in March of 1998, Enterprise JavaBeans is already supported by approximately a dozen major TPM and RDBMS vendors.

Summary

Previous application architectures, monoliths (both physical and logical), and truly distributed client/servers, have failed to deliver on the promised advantages of agile, easily maintained and modified software. The three-tiered architecture, by explicitly recognizing that business rules have value outside of the application which implements them and by recognizing that data are a valuable resource which should not be imprisoned by a single application, has gone a long way toward solving these problems. Organizations which began moving toward three-tiered systems three to five years ago are now reaping the benefits of this architecture in the form of reduced development time for new systems and easier access to their systems through new media like the Internet and automated response units.

The Java platform, with its Write Once, Run Anywhere capability and its simple yet powerful language, has proven itself to be an excellent implementation platform for presentation components and other components which execute on the client machine. The Java platform can now be used in the logic and data tiers, bringing the advantages of increased programmer productivity to these components. The new APIs fill a gap left in JDK 1.0 and allow developers to build complex and sophisticated network applications without forcing them to develop their own ad hoc communications mechanisms.

While organizations just beginning the move to truly distributed applications should plan for a long and sometimes painful move, they now have the advantages of using the Java platform in all layers of their development. They also can take advantage of the lessons learned by the early adopters of distributed environments to avoid some of the many pitfalls which lie in wait for the unwary IT shop. Organizations moving to three-tiered architectures can minimize their risk and maximize their return by following the lessons learned by the first wave of adopters:

- Define high-level interfaces to legacy systems. These interfaces should expose the business reason for these legacy systems, not their implementation details.

- Use Java APIs to build network-based implementations of these interfaces. JDBC can be used to interface to existing database systems. Either JavaIDL or Java RMI can be used to provide distributed object functionality to the system. Which is preferred will depend on a number of factors, including how the legacy systems are currently implemented, experience of the development team, and others.

- Use Enterprise JavaBeans to eliminate the "grunt work" of server design and allow the developers to concentrate on the valuable business logic.

- Make sure that each tier uses the functionality of the tier below it and provides value to the tier above it. Each tier should do its job while hiding the details of how that job is done from the tier above.

- When it makes sense, consider replacing the legacy systems with new backends. Once the legacy systems are buried under business-oriented interfaces, the organization can replace them at their leisure.

By following these guidelines, an IT shop can extend the life of its existing systems while simultaneously preparing for the future.

Mastering Java Remote Method Invocation Techniques

Introduction

Imagine for a moment that at every single node on the global Internet there was a Java Virtual Machine executing. This is the ultimate vision of *Java Space*, where objects live anywhere on the network, communicate seamlessly across the network, and move freely across the network whenever they are needed. Java RMI (Remote Method Invocation) finally makes the long-awaited vision of distributed objects a reality. This vision of distributed objects is not new, of course; there have been many attempts to capture the vision in the past. Although some may argue that the vision of distributed objects has already been demonstrated by other distributed technologies, traditional distributed object systems do not exhibit the true nature of object-orientation. Further, traditional approaches to distributed object-based architecture do not recognize and account for the intrinsic differences between local and distributed computing, resulting in problems in reliability and robustness as systems scale in size.

In the utopian view of a distributed object-based system, objects would demonstrate the traits that inherently define object-orientation, most importantly the familiar concepts of encapsulation, inheritance, and polymorphism.

Ideally, the system would be characterized by a unified model of encapsulation, inheritance, and polymorphism throughout the distribution, allowing the true nature of objects to be preserved. Further, the system would treat objects semantically the same in local programming as in remote (distributed) programming as much as possible, to simplify application development and maintenance. Finally, the system would recognize and account for the realities of how distributed processing differs from local processing, allowing the architecture to scale reliably and robustly. This utopian vision of distributed objects is precisely what Java RMI brings to the computing industry: a truly object-oriented distributed system, designed for large-scale, complex networking applications.

Java captured the attention of the world because it provided dynamic distribution of processing, actually sending code across the network and executing it in a remote location, and doing so in a secure manner. This capability promises great potential in easing the burden of software distribution, since the code is dynamically installed as needed and will execute on multiple platforms. These capabilities alone offer significant advantages over traditional approaches to software development and distribution. However, to leverage the power of inter-networking, Java objects need to be able to communicate seamlessly with one another across the network and between different virtual machines. The Java language environment provides standard classes for low-level remote communication via sockets (java.net), but for complex distributed processing we need to extend the Java object model and language environment across the network and among different virtual machines. This is the vision of *Java Space*, where objects can seamlessly invoke methods on other objects residing anywhere on the network, passing and returning actual objects as arguments during method invocation. Java RMI is the "distributed glue" that extends the Java object model beyond a single virtual machine address space, out onto the global network, dynamically interacting with other virtual machines.

Building on Past Experiences

The Java language environment is truly evolutionary, since it was designed based on researching other predecessor languages (notably C++, Objective C, Smalltalk, and Modula-3). The objective of the design was to adopt the best features from these predecessor languages while at the same time removing the complexities. The language design also introduced desirable features such as built-in networking, multithreading, garbage collection, and security for networked environments. Since you are reading an advanced Java programming book, you are likely familiar with the history of how Java developed as a special project under the guise of "First Person Inc." in the Silicon Valley. However, you may be surprised to hear that the technology now known as Java RMI (Remote Method Invocation) did not evolve out of the "First Person Inc." initiative; it evolved from research at Sun Microsystems Laboratories in Chelmsford, Massachusetts.

The researchers at Sun Labs took a close look at a number of distributed object-based systems and the principles upon which the architectures were based. Their findings were documented in a technical report entitled "A Note on Distributed Computing" (refer to Appendix A). They discovered that traditional approaches to object distribution (such as CORBA and others) were based on the assumption that there is essentially no difference between local and remote objects (from a programming perspective). The researchers proceeded to analyze differences between local and remote computing by examining many different distributed systems, and discovered that the traditional assumptions were false—we cannot ignore the intrinsic differences between local and remote objects. They concluded that distributed systems must treat local and remote objects as intrinsically different to account for differences in latency, partial failure, concurrency, and memory access in a distributed environment. Essentially, they were saying that we have to change our thinking about how objects interact in large-scale networked environments. If a distributed system is expected to be robust and reliable on a large scale, the system must recognize and account for the intrinsic differences between local and distributed computing. Further, developers of distributed applications must consider these differences at the application programming level, providing extra logic to deal with realities of unreliable network connections and partial failure of distributed processes. In order to scale a distributed application to a network the size of the Internet, logic is required to recover from partial failure. To put it most simply, if our systems don't provide logic to recover from partial failure, we can't scale anywhere reliably, and we certainly can't scale to the Internet.

It's interesting how these two research efforts came together. At the same time that James Gosling and company at First Person Inc. in Palo Alto were developing a new programming language called Oak (now known as Java), research engineers at Sun Laboratories in Chelmsford were analyzing various distributed object-based systems and looking for ways to resolve the differences between local and distributed computing. Both projects were based on researching past technologies and they shared the common goal of providing a simple yet powerful and safe environment for networked applications. It turned out that Java was the ideal delivery platform for what the Sun Labs engineers envisioned. The Java environment provided the infrastructure to deal effectively with the intrinsic differences between local and remote objects. The virtual machine provided architecture independence, so it was possible to extend the Java object model across the network. The homogeneous language environment facilitated true inheritance of object types. The Java bytecode was secure and downloadable, making it possible to transport objects across the network. All of these characteristics made it possible to dynamically bind objects anywhere on the network and to pass objects polymorphically.

Back to the Drawing Board

Java RMI is essentially an evolution of procedural RPC (Remote Procedure Call), adapted to an object-oriented paradigm. RPC allowed the programmer to execute remote function calls using the same semantics as local function calls, effectively making the remote procedure call look like a local procedure call. In an object-oriented system, however, it is a much more complicated scenario since objects are represented as graphs (hierarchies) of classes, where child subclasses inherit attributes from parent superclasses. Unlike procedural RPC, remote method invocations must be able to dynamically traverse the hierarchy of object graphs to be truly object-oriented. If we could ignore the intrinsic differences between local and remote computing, we would ideally create a distributed system that used the exact same object-oriented semantics for remote method invocation as for local method invocation, making the location of objects completely transparent to the programmer. This would be advantageous since the system designer could focus on a natural object model without worrying about object location. Unfortunately, history has shown that in reality there are obvious differences in latency, partial failure, concurrency, and memory access when we distribute processing between different machines. These differences may be less obvious in small-scale, tightly controlled, centrally administered systems. However, as applications and networks scale in complexity and size, these differences cannot be ignored and will eventually lead to serious problems. Since we are moving into a new network-centric paradigm, we can expect that distributed applications and the networks they rely on will grow in complexity and size.

If you've experienced the pleasure of sifting through mountains of procedural legacy code, you've likely arrived at the conclusion that we need object-orientation. The truth is that it's impossible to model reality without encapsulating data and behavior together, since they are inherently interrelated. The object-oriented approach facilitates not only good design, but also quick and easy modification because implementation details are encapsulated within objects. The implementation details may change over time but, because implementation details are hidden from other objects, there is no need to sift through mountains of code to analyze the impact of changes. The benefits of object-orientation have been clearly demonstrated in systems that operate locally on a single processor. However, extending this approach to complex network environments is a significant challenge, since there are conflicting realities. We want to remain purely object-oriented, yet we need to deal with the issues of latency, partial failure, concurrency, and remote memory management. The goal of the Java RMI system is to achieve balance between these conflicting realities. The RMI system attempts to preserve Java's object-oriented semantics as much as possible, while at the same time providing an infrastructure that deals with the realities of large-scale networking. Essentially, RMI is the fusion of object-orientation and internetworking technologies. We have experienced the power of each of these technologies independent of one another, but we haven't really been able to bring them together. With Java RMI, we leverage the potential of both technologies, unleashing powerful new capabilities.

Distributed Systems Contrasted

Before beginning to describe how and why the RMI system works, let's take a quick look at some other approaches to object-based RPC systems—for several reasons. Understanding the differences between RMI and other RPC systems leads to a better understanding and appreciation for what RMI offers. It also leads to a better understanding of where and when these technologies are best deployed, and hopefully helps to clarify some of the widespread misunderstanding about what these technologies are and are not. There is currently a great deal of confusion and competition between different distributed object-based systems. This is not surprising, since they share some common goals. When speaking about distributed object-based systems, most people immediately relate to the CORBA architecture. Although RMI and CORBA share the same objective of distributing objects among machines, each has some very different objectives. The CORBA model was designed for interoperability between different languages in a heterogeneous environment, while RMI was designed for distributed processing in the homogeneous pure Java environment. In a sense these two models are overlapping, but in another sense they are very different animals. Both of these systems have advantages within their domains and disadvantages outside of their domains. There have been many attempts to compare the two systems from a single perspective, but it is an apples-to-oranges comparison since they strive for different goals in different problem domains.

The CORBA architecture strives to glue together all of the different object models, regardless of implementation language or object location. CORBA is based on a unified vision that all objects should be treated equally whether they are C++, Smalltalk, Java, or even procedural modules written in COBOL. This unified vision also assumes that location of objects is an implementation detail that can be handled by the underlying system, essentially treating local objects the same as remote objects. This unified vision is important because it provides a wide scope of interoperability between systems. We all know that interoperability is important and necessary, but it also bears a cost. In order to glue dissimilar object models together, CORBA uses a common interface definition language (IDL) to map the object models together. Since IDL must be common between all languages, it cannot support the true object types of any given language. The net effect of this compromise is that the true types of objects are truncated as they pass through the CORBA system, compromising the object-oriented characteristics of any given language environment in the overall model. This type truncation is the net effect of translating from implementation languages (C++, Smalltalk, etc.) to the IDL model and vice versa. In contrast, RMI does not use the concept of mapping to an interface definition language. Because RMI remains within the Java language environment, no mapping between objects is required and true object types can be passed. Another significant difference between the two systems is that CORBA was designed to accommodate both binary compiled executable code and interpreted code for interoperability reasons. Java RMI only deals with bytecode; since bytecode is secure and downloadable, RMI has the capability of transporting objects, which means it can pass objects polymorphically. Another significant difference between the two systems is the distinction between local and remote objects. CORBA uses an object request broker (ORB) to locate objects; from the programmer's perspective there is essentially no difference between local and remote objects. While this may appear to be a useful feature, it ignores the reality of partial failure. RMI does not require the use of an object request broker (it uses a simple registry to locate objects). RMI makes a clear distinction between objects that can be invoked locally and remotely, and forces the programmer to provide exception-handling logic to recover from potential network failure.

As you can see, there are some significant differences between the CORBA and RMI models of distributed processing. CORBA provides a significant advantage in interoperability, but compromises object-orientation in the process. RMI provides significant advantages in the object-oriented domain, but is limited to the Java environment. There are many differing opinions about which technology should be used in actual practice. Some will argue that we need to move forward with the unified vision of CORBA and treat all objects equally. Others will argue that within the Java domain, it makes a lot of sense to leverage the new capabilities of RMI. Everyone knows that interoperability is important and that in the real world legacy system integration is fundamental. On the other hand, history has shown that too much diversity in platforms, languages, and tools creates a very complex environment that is very difficult and costly to manage and maintain.

The Java environment is all about reducing complexity and diversity. For the first time developers can seamlessly deliver applications across platforms. The Java environment has changed the rules of computing significantly. Because the virtual machine insulates the architecture from the programmer, a single language environment can span the entire spectrum. And, since the core language environment has a built-in transport system (RMI) to extend object-oriented programming between virtual machines, the rules have changed significantly.

Still, there are those who will continue to fight for a heterogeneous world where all objects are equal. Think of it this way: There is a dotted line somewhere between the old paradigm and the new paradigm. If you need to integrate Java applications with non-Java applications, CORBA is a useful tool. Another alternative is to create Java legacy wrappers using JNI (Java Native Interface) for integration and RMI for remote communications. If you are designing new applications that require Java-to-Java communications, RMI is the recommended alternative, fully object-oriented and network ready.

I have contrasted RMI and CORBA in detail because there has been a tremendous amount of discussion about these differences in many different forums. There are, of course, many other distributed object-based systems. A number of systems are similar to CORBA and therefore contrast similarly with RMI. The DCOM system, for example, is similar to CORBA and shares many of the limitations. Further, DCOM is less flexible than CORBA because it is more platform-dependent, resulting in a smaller scope of interoperability. These three systems (RMI, CORBA, and DCOM) are the major players in the distributed objects arena today, but there have been many interesting predecessors. The unified vision that CORBA strives for has a history in research systems like Arjuna, Clouds, and Emerald.

Another predecessor deserves special mention because Java RMI shares similar features. The Modula-3 Network Objects system is similar to Java RMI in that it is a homogeneous system that attempts to leverage the benefits of remaining in a single object model. Both Modula-3 and Java RMI are capable of transporting objects through the use of object serialization. Both systems also employ the concept of an abstract layer for the transport mechanism. However, Java RMI takes the concepts demonstrated in Modula-3 a few steps further. RMI provides another abstract layer that supports varying invocation semantics. RMI also leverages the Java language environment to provide exact matching and dynamic downloading of stubs at runtime.

RMI Design Goals

The RMI system was designed under the guiding principles that it must be as object-oriented as possible (by preserving the Java object model semantics) while at the same time recognizing the intrinsic differences between local and remote objects. The major goals of the RMI design are:

- Allow seamless remote method invocations between objects residing in different virtual machines
- Provide a distributed model which preserves the Java object semantics as much as possible
- Make the differences between local and remote objects apparent
- Allow callbacks from server to clients

- Preserve the safety provided by the Java runtime environment
- Make writing of distributed applications as simple as possible

In addition to these key goals, the RMI system was designed to be flexible and extensible. The design goals also included extensibility to provide:

- Varying remote invocation mechanisms such as unicast and multicast
- Varying remote reference semantics for activation, persistent, and non-persistent references
- Distributed garbage collection
- Capability of supporting multiple transports

RMI System Architecture

The RMI system is built in three layers: the stub/skeleton layer, the remote reference layer, and the transport layer. These layers are built using specific interfaces and defined by specific protocols in order to make each layer of the architecture independent of the other layers. This was done intentionally to make the system flexible, allowing modification of the implementation of any given layer without affecting the other layers. For example, the TCP-based transport could be modified to use a different transport protocol. As with most RPC-type systems, RMI uses stubs and skeletons to act as surrogate placeholders (proxies) for remote objects. The transport of objects between address spaces is accomplished through the use of object serialization, which converts object graphs to bytestreams for transport.

The Stub/Skeleton Layer

The stub/skeleton layer is the channel through which clients and servers communicate. When a server application is designed, stubs and skeletons are generated by a special compiler (rmic), which reads the server's bytecode and generates proxy classes to act as remote object placeholders. Client applications use stubs that correspond with server-side skeletons. Java RMI is capable of dynamically downloading stubs on demand, so if a necessary stub is not available on the client machine, it can be made accessible. The stub/skeleton layer of the RMI system is the interface between applications and the RMI system. This layer does not deal with transport issues or invocation semantics; it is only responsible for transmitting data to the remote reference layer of the RMI system. This transfer of data to the remote reference layer is done through the abstraction of marshal streams, which use object serialization to convert graphs of objects into bytestreams. A client-side stub is responsible for initiating remote calls, marshaling arguments to be sent, and unmarshaling return values. A server-side skeleton is responsible for unmarshaling incoming arguments from the client, calling the actual remote object implementation, and marshaling the return value (or exception) to the stream for transport back to the client.

The Remote Reference Layer

The remote reference layer is a middle ground between the stub/skeleton layer and the actual transport mechanism. The reason for having this middle ground is to provide the ability to support varying invocation protocols, independent of the client stubs and server skeletons. For example, a unicast protocol might provide point-to-point remote object references, while a multicast protocol might provide invocation to replicated groups of objects. Other protocols might deal with specific replication strategies, reconnection strategies, or persistent references (enabling activation of a remote object). The important thing is that the remote reference layer is independent of the other two layers. This means that the same stubs and skeletons can be used to implement differing invocation protocols transparently, and that the actual transport details are also transparently handled by the transport layer. Essentially, the remote reference layer transmits data between the stub/skeleton layer and the transport layer, providing support for different invocation protocols (unicast, multicast, and so forth). Note that the RMI system in the JDK 1.1 version does not yet support multicast invocation, replication strategies, or activation. These features will be added in a future release of the JDK.

The Transport Layer

The transport layer is a low-level communications layer that provides the actual shipment of marshal streams between different address spaces or virtual machines. The transport layer is responsible for setting up and managing connections, listening for incoming calls, and passing data to and from the remote reference layer. It also maintains a table of remote objects residing in particular address spaces. At the transport layer, remote objects are represented by object identifiers and endpoints. An object identifier is used to look up which objects should be the targets of remote calls. Endpoints represent particular address spaces or virtual machines. The transport layer creates channels between endpoints by establishing connections and physically transferring data through input/output. The RMI system uses a TCP-based transport, but the transport layer supports multiple transports per address space, so it is also capable of supporting a UDP-based transport or even TCP and UDP.

Distributed Garbage Collection

The RMI system provides a distributed garbage collector to automatically delete remote objects that are no longer referenced by any client. This is a nice feature to have because the programmer does not have to keep track of remote objects. RMI uses a reference-counting garbage collection algorithm that is similar to the garbage collector in Modula-3 Network Objects. The RMI system keeps track of all live references within each virtual machine. Reference counters are incremented whenever live remote references enter virtual machines. As live references become unreferenced by applications, the reference counter is decremented. When the reference counter reaches zero, this indicates that there are no longer any live references, so objects can be garbage collected. As long as a local reference to a remote object exists, it cannot be garbage collected, but can be passed in remote calls or passed to clients. Since RMI allows objects to be passed around, it must also keep track of virtual machine identifiers. The RMI garbage collector ensures that objects are only collected when there are no local or remote references.

Distributed Programming with RMI

The architectural overview in the previous section was very high-level and did not explain all of the inner workings of the RMI system. This was done intentionally. The beauty of the RMI system is that the system itself takes care of most of the work for you. Essentially, you don't need to worry about how the transport actually takes place or how the garbage collector works; these are transparent to the programmer. If you are interested in finding out how RMI works under the covers, you'll want to read the RMI specification and the Object Serialization specification (see Appendix A). Because the RMI system is truly object-oriented, distributed programming with RMI is natural. With RMI, you basically program distributed applications in the same way you would local applications, with a few exceptions. As long as you are aware of how local and remote Java object models differ, you can program RMI just like any other local Java application. To clarify the differences between local and remote objects, here are the rules. Remote objects are similar to local objects in the following ways:

1. Object references can be passed as arguments in any invocation.
2. Objects can be cast to interfaces using the built-in Java syntax for casting.
3. The instanceof operator can be used to test interfaces supported by an object.

Remote objects are different than local objects in the following ways:

1. Clients interact with remote interfaces, never with the implementation classes of the interfaces.

2. Local (non-remote) arguments are passed by copy rather than by reference (since references are only valid within a single virtual machine).

3. Remote objects are passed by reference, not by actual copy of implementation.

4. The semantics of some methods defined by class Object are specialized for remote objects (see the RMI specifications for details).

5. Clients must deal with additional exceptions that can occur during remote method calls due to network failure.

Unlike many other RPC systems, RMI requires no mapping to interface definition language (IDL), since RMI calls operate much like local calls. Remote methods do need to be defined in a remote interface, however, so that the compiler will know how to generate the necessary stubs and skeletons. To write an RMI application, you first define all remote methods in a remote interface, only specifying the method argument types and return types. The actual implementation of the methods is defined in another object that implements the remote interface. All remote objects must directly or indirectly implement the java.rmi.Remote interface. A convenient base class (Unicast-RemoteObject) for RMI servers is provided which makes development easy. To create an RMI server, you simply extend the UnicastRemoteObject class and implement the remote methods. Connections between clients and servers are established using a simple registry server. A server binds its name to the registry, then any client can look up the name of the server in the registry to establish a connection.

A Simple RMI Client/Server Example

Now that you've seen an overview of the Java RMI system, let's take a look at a simple programming example. We'll start with a basic client/server application, so you'll understand the fundamental RMI programming concepts, then move on to some more complex programming examples. This first example illustrates how to create a simple unicast (point-to-point) RMI client/server application. The application consists of a bank account server and bank teller clients that make deposits and withdrawals from remote locations. The objective of the first example is to show RMI connectivity in the context of the Java application. This simple framework can be easily extended to provide more complex processing.

Defining the Remote Interface

The first step in creating an RMI application is the definition of a remote interface between the client and server objects. The remote interface is simply a list of methods that clients can invoke remotely on the server. Only the method names, associated input arguments, and return types are defined in the remote interface. You'll program the actual implementation of the remote methods within the server object (which directly implements the remote interface). In this exercise, you need to define three remote methods that the bank teller clients can invoke on the server: Deposit, Withdrawal, and getBalance. The Deposit and Withdrawal methods accept transaction amount arguments and return the adjusted account balance. The getBalance method accepts no arguments and simply returns the current account balance.

Source Code: `accountRemote.java`

```
// define remote interface (accountRemote.java)

public interface accountRemote
  extends java.rmi.Remote {

  float Deposit(float amount)
    throws java.rmi.RemoteException;

  float Withdrawal(float amount)
    throws java.rmi.RemoteException;

  float getBalance()
    throws java.rmi.RemoteException;
}
```

You define the accountRemote interface by extending the java.rmi.Remote interface. This is the low-level RMI communications interface; any object intending to use RMI must implement this interface either directly or indirectly. Each remote method defined in the interface must throw the java.rmi.RemoteException. This exception will be thrown if errors occur during remote method invocation (due to network errors or server problems). Any methods defined in the remote interface are available for remote method invocation between the clients and server. The server directly implements the remote interface and clients indirectly implement the interface. The remote interface is the common communications channel between the client and server objects, simply defining all methods that are remotely invokable along with their input arguments and return types.

Creating the Remote Server

The bank account server is a simple unicast (point-to-point) remote server. You create the server by extending java.rmi.server.UnicastRemoteObject. This defines a nonreplicated remote object providing point-to-point object references between different virtual machine address spaces (residing locally or remotely). The server class (accountServer) directly implements the remote interface (accountRemote) defined earlier. The server uses the RMISecurity-Manager to protect its resources while engaging in remote communication with clients. The security manager restricts access to server resources by remote client stubs, providing the equivalent function of the applet security manager for RMI applications (preventing intrusion by rogue processes).

Source Code: accountServer.java

```
// create remote server (accountServer.java - part A)

import java.rmi.*;
import java.rmi.server.*;

public class accountServer
  extends UnicastRemoteObject
  implements accountRemote {

  float balance = 0;

  public accountServer()
    throws java.rmi.RemoteException {

    super();
  }
```

In order for remote clients to invoke methods on the server, the server must first bind its name to the registry (clients will look up the server name in the registry to establish remote references). You use the java.rmi.Naming class to bind the server name to the registry. In the main method of your server object, the RMI security manager is created and installed, the server object is instantiated, and the server name is bound to the registry for remote reference by clients. The server instantiation is placed within a try block, so that an exception will be caught if the server fails to bind to the registry.

Source Code: accountServer.java

```
// bind server to registry (accountServer.java - part B)

public static void main(String args[]) {

  System.setSecurityManager(new RMISecurityManager());

  try {
    accountServer name  = new accountServer();
    Naming.rebind("bankacct", name);
  }

  catch (Exception e) {
```

```
       System.out.println("Exception: " + e.getMessage());
       e.printStackTrace();
    }
}
```

The server now has all of the necessary programming to allow clients residing in different virtual machine address spaces to invoke its methods. This simple framework for remote connectivity is consistent for all RMI applications.
The server may now implement any number of additional remote interfaces and
methods seamlessly, since all remote communications are handled by referencing the registry. The server could also implement local methods that do not support remote invocation. To complete the bank account server, the only other
required programming is the actual implementation of the remote methods
Deposit, Withdrawal, and getBalance.

Source Code: accountServer.java
```
   // implement remote methods (accountServer.java - part C)

   public float Deposit(float amount)
     throws java.rmi.RemoteException {

     balance += amount;
     return balance;
   }

   public float Withdrawal(float amount)
     throws java.rmi.RemoteException {

     balance -= amount;
     return balance;
   }

   public float getBalance()
     throws java.rmi.RemoteException {

     return balance;
   }
}
```

Regardless of the number of remote interfaces and methods implemented in
the server, the same framework for establishing remote references with clients
is used (binding the server name to the registry). As long as the server is bound
to the registry, any client can look up the name, establish remote references,
and invoke methods on the server via the remote interface. The rmic compiler
is used to generate the necessary stub and skeleton surrogate classes for establishing remote references. The server source code is first compiled using javac,
then the rmic compiler is used to generate stub and skeleton classes:

javac accountServer.java

rmic accountServer

The rmic compiler reads the server's compiled bytecode (accountServer .class) and generates a client-side stub (accountServer_Stub.class) and a server-side skeleton (accountServer_Skel.class). Whenever the server source is recompiled using javac, the stub and skeleton classes should be regenerated using rmic to ensure that they reflect changes to the server source.

Creating the Remote Client

The remote bank teller client is a simple user interface for executing deposit and withdrawal transactions. When you program the client (accountClient .java), you need to import components from the rmi and net packages. The net components are required because the client must establish socket connections with the registry. The client object indirectly implements the remote interface (accountRemote) through declaration. Remote method calls in the client are prefixed with the remote interface name and suffixed with the usual method call syntax. For example, a remote call to the server's Deposit method would programmed as remote.Deposit(amount). In the main method of your client object, the RMI security manager is created and the client object is instantiated. The client instantiation is placed within a try block, so that an exception will be caught if the client fails to establish a socket connection with the registry.

Source Code: accountClient.java
```
// create remote client (accountClient.java - part A)

import java.awt.*;
import java.awt.event.*;
import java.rmi.*;
import java.rmi.server.*;
import java.net.*;

public class accountClient
  extends Frame {

  private accountRemote remote;
  private Button Deposit, Withdrawal;
  private Label Balance;
  private TextField Amount;
  private float OpenBalance;

  public accountClient() {

    super("Remote Bank Teller");
    connectServer();
    getOpenBalance();
```

```
      createPanel();
      this.addWindowListener(new windowHandler());
   }


   public static void main (String args[]) {

      System.setSecurityManager(new RMISecurityManager());

      try {
         Frame frame = new accountClient();
         frame.setBackground(Color.lightGray);
         frame.pack();
         frame.show();
         frame.setSize(220,150);
      }

      catch (Exception e) {
         System.out.println("Exception: " + e.getMessage());
         e.printStackTrace();
      }
   }
```

In order for the client object to invoke methods on the server, it must first look up the name of the server in the registry. You use the java.rmi.Naming class to look up the server name. The server name is specified as a URL in the format (rmi://host:port/name). The hostname that you specify must be the name of the machine that the registry resides on. If you choose not to specify a port number in the URL, the default RMI port number 1099 is implied. The name specified in the URL must exactly match the name that the server has bound to the registry (bankacct). The Naming lookup is placed within a try block so that an exception will be caught if the lookup fails.

Source Code: accountClient.java
```
// connect to server (accountClient.java - part B)

 public void connectServer() {

    try {
       remote = (accountRemote)Naming.lookup("rmi://hostname/bankacct");
    }

    catch (Exception e) {
       System.out.println("Exception: " + e.getMessage());
       e.printStackTrace();
    }
 }
```

The client now has all of the necessary programming to invoke methods on the server from remote locations. When the client object is initially constructed, you want it to retrieve the opening account balance from the server, so that the balance will display in the bank teller window. The getOpenBalance method invokes the getBalance method on the server, retrieving the account balance and storing it in the OpenBalance variable. The remote method invocation is programmed using the remote interface name (remote) as a prefix and the remote method name (getBalance) as a suffix, programmed as remote .getBalance( ). The remote method call is placed within a try block so that a remote exception will be caught if the invocation fails.

Source Code: accountClient.java
```
// invoke method on server (accountClient.java - part C)

public void getOpenBalance() {

  try {
    OpenBalance = remote.getBalance();
  }

  catch (RemoteException e) {
    System.out.println("RemoteException: " + e.getMessage());
    e.printStackTrace();
  }
}
```

The bank teller client requires a user interface for initiating the deposit and withdrawal transactions. The user interface is a simple window with a text field for amount entry, a label to display the balance, and buttons to execute deposits and withdrawals. The user will enter a transaction amount in the amount text field and select either the Deposit or Withdrawal button to execute the transaction. The buttons are associated with an actionListener to detect the button press. Upon detection of a button press, the actionListener instantiates an inner class (actionHandler) to invoke the appropriate remote method and return the new account balance. The updated balance will then be displayed in the balance label of the user interface.

Source Code: accountClient.java
```
// create user interface (accountClient.java - part D)

public  void createPanel() {

  setLayout(new BorderLayout());

  Panel amtpanel = new Panel();
  amtpanel.setLayout(new FlowLayout(FlowLayout.LEFT));
  amtpanel.add(new Label("Amount: "));

  Amount = new TextField(3);
```

```
   amtpanel.add(Amount);
   add("North", amtpanel);

   Balance = new Label(" Balance:   ");
   Balance.setText(" Balance:   $" + OpenBalance);
   add("Center", Balance);

   Panel buttonpanel = new Panel();

   Deposit = new Button("Deposit");
   Deposit.addActionListener(new actionHandler());
   buttonpanel.add(Deposit);

   Withdrawal = new Button("Withdrawal");
   Withdrawal.addActionListener(new actionHandler());

   buttonpanel.add(Withdrawal);
   add("South", buttonpanel);
}

class windowHandler
   extends WindowAdapter {

   public void windowClosing(WindowEvent event) {
     System.exit(0);
   }
}
```

The final step in creation of the bank teller client is programming the event handler that invokes the remote transactions. In this case, an inner class (actionHandler) is used for convenience sake. If the Deposit button is pressed by the user, the remote method Deposit is invoked via the remote interface, sending the deposit amount to the server and returning the updated balance. If the Withdrawal button is pressed, the remote method (Withdrawal) is invoked via the remote interface, sending the withdrawal amount to the server and returning the updated balance. The remote method calls are placed within a try block, so that remote exceptions will be caught if either invocation fails. In a real banking application, extra programming would be included to recover from remote exceptions.

Source Code: accountClient.java
```
   // process remote transaction (accountClient.java - part E)

   class actionHandler
     implements ActionListener {

     public void actionPerformed(ActionEvent event) {

       float balance, amount;
```

```
        try {
          amount = (new Float(Amount.getText()).floatValue());
        }

          catch (NumberFormatException e) {
          amount = 0;
        }

        Object source = event.getSource();

        try {

          if(source == Deposit) {
            balance = remote.Deposit(amount);
            Balance.setText(" Balance:  $" + balance);
            return;
          }
          else if(source == Withdrawal) {
            balance = remote.Withdrawal(amount);
            Balance.setText(" Balance:  $" + balance);
            return;
          }
        }

      catch (RemoteException e) {
        System.out.println("Remote Exception: " + e.getMessage());
        e.printStackTrace();
      }
    }
  }
}
```

Compiling and Executing the Example

To really appreciate the power of this simple client/server application, you need
to load it onto various network hosts and operating system platforms. Be sure
that you've specified the proper hostname in the client's connectServer method
(it must be the hostname of the machine running the server). Following is the
proper compilation and execution sequence:

javac accountRemote.java

javac accountServer.java

rmic accountServer

javac accountClient.java

rmiregistry

java accountServer

java accountClient

When copying the class files into directories, keep in mind that the client requires local access to the remote interface (accountRemote.class) and the stub (accountServer_Stub.class), while the server requires access to the remote interface (accountRemote.class) and the skeleton (accountServer_Skel .class). To test out Java's distributed capabilities, try executing multiple clients on a single machine and others on different machines. Then try executing clients on different operating systems. Even though this is a very simple example application, the power of Java's open architecture shines through, demonstrating seamless cross-platform remote method invocation.

Callbacks from Server to Client

If you actually try out the simple client/server example, you'll notice that there's a problem with the display of the new balance if multiple clients are executing transactions. When any of the clients initiates a deposit or withdrawal, the new balance is shown only on the client that initiated the transaction. For example, Client A starts up with a balance of $0 and deposits $10; the new balance of $10 appears in Client A's display. Client B starts up, reads, and displays the opening balance of $10. There is no problem so far, but if client B then deposits $10, the new balance of $20 only appears in Client B's display. Client A still displays a balance of $10, even though the actual balance is $20, since Client A has not been notified to refresh the balance. The actual transactions are working as expected; it's just the display that is problematic in this example. This can be easily resolved by adding a callback from the server to the clients. The callback is necessary any time the server needs to notify the clients that some event has occurred. To implement the callback, a new remote method setBalance is required, so you define it in a new remote interface (clientRemote.java).

Source Code: CB/clientRemote.java
```
// create remote interface (clientRemote.java)

public interface clientRemote
  extends java.rmi.Remote {

  void setBalance(float balance)
    throws java.rmi.RemoteException;
}
```

This remote interface will be implemented by the client and the setBalance method will be called by the server whenever a deposit or withdrawal transaction occurs, sending the new balance to the client. You add the implementation of the remote interface in the client (accountClient.java).

Source Code: CB/accountClient.java

```
// create remote client (accountClient.java)

public class accountClient extends Frame implements clientRemote {
  public void setBalance(float balance) {
    OpenBalance = balance;
    Balance.setText(" Balance:   $" + balance);
    }
  }
```

Unlike the server object, the client does not extend the UnicastRemoteObject; it can't because it extends Frame. But in order for the server to be able to invoke methods on the client during a callback, the client must make itself visible to the server. You do this by adding UnicastRemoteObject.exportObject(this) in the client's connectServer method. To issue callbacks to all active clients, the server will need to keep track of clients by registering them. So in the client's connect-Server method you also add a call to the server's register method, sending the client as an argument: remote.register(this).

Source Code: CB/accountClient.java

```
// connect to server (accountClient.java)

public void connectServer() {

  try {
    remote = (accountRemote)Naming.lookup("rmi://localhost/bankacct");
    UnicastRemoteObject.exportObject(this);
    remote.register(this);
  }

  catch (Exception e) {
    System.out.println("Exception: " + e.getMessage());
    e.printStackTrace();
  }
}
```

That takes care of the client side of the callback. The client now implements a new remote interface (clientRemote) and a new remote method (setBalance) to refresh the display whenever a transaction is invoked on the server. When any new client is instantiated, it will first look up the server in the registry as usual, required for invocation of the server's remote methods. Then the client will export itself, making it visible to the server (so the server can remotely invoke its new setBalance method). Finally, the client invokes a new remote method on the server to register itself for notification when the balance changes. To define the new remote method (register) you must first add it to the original accountRemote interface.

Source Code: CB/accountRemote.java

```
// create remote interface (accountRemote.java)

public interface accountRemote
  extends java.rmi.Remote {

  float register(clientRemote newClient)
    throws java.rmi.RemoteException;

  float Deposit(float amount)
    throws java.rmi.RemoteException;

  void Withdrawal(float amount)
    throws java.rmi.RemoteException;

  float getBalance()
    throws java.rmi.RemoteException;
}
```

On the server side (accountServer.java) a vector is needed to keep track of registered clients for notification. You declare and instantiate a vector, add the implementation of the register method, and add an update method (update-Clients) that loops through the vector of registered clients and executes the set-Balance method on each client, sending the balance as an argument. Synchronization is used on the register and updateClients methods to deal with the concurrency issues. To complete the callback, you add a call to the update-Clients method in the Deposit and Withdrawal methods.

Source Code: CB/accountServer.java

```
// create remote server (accountServer.java)

public class accountServer
  extends UnicastRemoteObject
  implements accountRemote {

  Vector clients;

  public accountServer()
    throws java.rmi.RemoteException {
    super();
    clients = new Vector();
  }

  // register client references

  public void register(clientRemote newClient)
    throws java.rmi.RemoteException {

      synchronized(clients) {
        clients.addElement(newClient);
```

```java
      }
    }

    // update client balances

    public void updateClients() {

      int count;
      clientRemote tmpClient;

      synchronized(clients) {

        if (clients.size() > 0){

          for (count = 0 ; count < clients.size() ; count ++) {
            tmpClient = (clientRemote)clients.elementAt(count);

            try {
              tmpClient.setBalance(balance);
            }

            catch (Exception e) {
              System.out.println("Failed to update client: "
                + tmpClient.toString());
            }
          }
        }
      }
    }

    // implement remote methods

    public void Deposit(float amount)

      throws java.rmi.RemoteException {
      balance += amount;
      updateClients();
    }

    public void Withdrawal(float amount)
      throws java.rmi.RemoteException {

      balance -= amount;
      updateClients();
    }

    public float getBalance()
      throws java.rmi.RemoteException {

      return balance;
    }
}
```

After making all of these changes, note that both remote interfaces (account-Remote and clientRemote) must be compiled with javac, the server (accountServer) must be recompiled with both javac and rmic, and the client (accountClient) must be recompiled with javac. With the new callback logic in place, all clients will automatically display the new balance when any of the clients invoke the Deposit or Withdrawal on the server. The usage of callbacks in this manner is obviously better than having the clients continually poll the server to see if the balance has changed. Since callback logic is defined in a remote interface, it is flexible enough to handle complex situations. In this scenario, the clients and server are demonstrating peer-to-peer behavior, since they are invoking methods on each other, each acting as both client and server.

Passing Objects as Method Arguments

In the simple client/server example, primitive float types (data only) are passed as arguments during remote method invocation. However, remote calls are not limited to passing only data as arguments; actual objects (data and behavior) may be passed as arguments. When an object is passed during a remote call, it is automatically packaged (serialized), sent across the network, and unpackaged (de-serialized) on the receiving end. The RMI system takes care of the serialization, ensuring that the entire object graph (hierarchy) is included to accurately reconstruct a replica of the object. The RMI system also ensures that any other objects that the serialized object refers to are also packaged up and sent. This makes remote method calls operate just like local calls, sending the true object types. The following example illustrates the passing of objects as arguments during remote method invocation. The object to be passed is defined in a simple class named Job. Job classes contain a string message (data) and a process method (behavior) which prints the string message. A remote interface (Distributor.java) defines a remote method getNewJob that returns a Job class. A remote server class (DistributorImpl.java) implements the getNewJob method, incrementing a counter and instantiating a new Job Class, passing the value of the counter as an argument to the Job's constructor. A client class (Client.java) invokes the getNewJob method on the server.

Source Code: Job.java
```
// define Job type (Job.java)

import java.io.*;

public class Job
  implements java.io.Serializable {

  String msg;
```

```java
  public Job() {
    msg = new String("(no string)");
  }

  public Job(String msg) {
    this.msg = msg;
  }

  public void process() {
    System.out.println("Processing Job " + msg);
  }
}
```

Source Code: Distributor.java
```java
// create remote interface (Distributor.java)

public interface Distributor
  extends java.rmi.Remote {

  Job getNewJob()
    throws java.rmi.RemoteException;
}
```

Source Code: DistributorImpl.java
```java
// create remote server (DistributorImpl.java)

import java.io.*;
import java.net.*;
import java.rmi.*;
import java.rmi.server.*;
import java.util.*;

public class DistributorImpl
  extends UnicastRemoteObject
  implements Distributor {

  int count;

  public DistributorImpl()
    throws RemoteException {

    count = 0;

    try {
      UnicastRemoteObject.exportObject(this);
      Naming.rebind("distributor",this);
    }
    catch (Exception e) {
      System.err.println("Failed to bind to RMI Registry");
      System.exit(1);
```

```
    }
  }

  public static final void main(String[] args) {

    try {
      DistributorImpl runner = new DistributorImpl();
    }
    catch (Exception e) {
      System.err.println("Failed to create DistributorImpl object"
        + e.getMessage());
    }
  }

  public Job getNewJob() {
    return new Job(" #"+count++);
  }
}
```

Source Code: Client.java
```
// create remote client (Client.java)

import java.net.*;
import java.rmi.*;
import java.io.*;

public class Client {
  Distributor server;

  public static final void main(String[] args) {
    Client runJob = new Client();
    runJob.process();
  }

  public Client() {

    try {
      server = (Distributor)Naming.lookup("rmi://hostname/distributor");
    }

    catch(Exception e) {
      System.out.println("Failed to find distributor"
        + e.getMessage());
    }
  }

  public void process() {

    try {
      Job myJob = server.getNewJob();
      myJob.process();
```

```
      }

    catch (Exception e) {
      System.out.println("Failed to receive job "
        + e.getMessage());
    }
  }
}
```

Here's the compilation and execution sequence for this example:

```
javac Job.java
javac Distributor.java
javac DistributorImpl.java
rmic DistributorImpl
javac Client.java
rmiregistry
java DistributorImpl
java Client
java Client
java Client
```

When a Client class is instantiated, it connects to the server and calls the get-NewJob method on the server. The server increments the counter, instantiates a new Job class (passing the incremented counter to the Job's constructor), and returns the new Job class to the client. Since the new Job class does not exist on the client machine, it must download the class. The RMI system automatically serializes the Job class on the server side, sends it across the network to the client, and reconstructs it on the client side. The client then invokes the process method on the Job class, *printing the value of the incremented counter.*

Processing Job 1

Processing Job 2

Processing Job 3

Remote Polymorphism at Last

One of the most powerful features of Java RMI is the ability to resolve remote method calls polymorphically. This means that different kinds of objects can respond to the same message, even if the required object kind is not available locally. Polymorphism is important because the implementations of objects change over time and we want changes to be transparent to other objects—this is one of the major benefits of object-orientation. Polymorphism is also fundamental if we want to design systems using powerful object-oriented (OO) design patterns. Think about it: If a system is not truly polymorphic, then we cannot implement most of the classic OO design patterns.

In a local (non-distributed) object-oriented system, polymorphism is relatively easy to achieve, since all object classes and interfaces are available locally (they all reside on a single machine). In a distributed system, however, polymorphism is not so straightforward; we cannot assume that all required classes and interfaces are available locally. In order to achieve true polymorphism, a distributed system must be able to dynamically access classes and interfaces that do not reside locally, and it must be able to do this at runtime during method resolution. When a method call is resolved, the system must be able to access classes and interfaces that may or may not reside on a different machine, so it must be capable of dynamically downloading classes and interfaces from other machines. The unique characteristics of the Java environment make it finally possible to achieve remote polymorphism. Java RMI is capable of demonstrating true remote polymorphism for the following reasons:

1. Object serialization allows the system to convert object graphs into streams for transport.

2. True object types are preserved during transport (object types are never truncated).

3. Secure bytecode allows the system to dynamically download classes, interfaces, and stubs.

4. Exact stub matching guarantees that the exact required object is available during method resolution.

As previously stated, a distributed system must be capable of dynamically downloading classes and interfaces in order to demonstrate true polymorphism. A common reaction to this statement is: "Why does a system need to download code to be polymorphic? I thought polymorphism was defined as the ability to dynamically resolve method invocations." The proof is in the implementation; the real tests are the ability to insulate implementation changes between objects (with no changes on the client side) and to implement polymorphic object-oriented design patterns that cross machine boundaries. Consider the following scenario that requires remote polymorphism.

Let's say we have a client and server that physically reside on two different machines. The client is aware of a remote method on the server that returns an object of type foo. Everything is working just fine. At a later date, developers modify the foo class on the server machine to implement some new behavior. They do this by extending the foo class, creating a new subclass bar that overrides some behavior in its superclass foo. Further, the developers modify the remote method on the server so it will polymorphically return the new subclass bar instead of class foo. After the changes have been implemented, the client application invokes the remote method on the server. Since the new class bar does not reside on the client machine, the client must download the class bar from the server at runtime to dynamically resolve the method call.

In the Java RMI system the scenario just described does not present a problem and does not require any changes to the client application. When the remote method is invoked, the RMI system will automatically serialize the new class bar on the server machine, ship it across the network, and reconstruct it on the client machine. With the Java RMI system, polymorphism works the same way remotely (crossing machine boundaries) as it works locally (on a single machine)—this is the real test of polymorphism in a distributed system. Ask yourself the following question: If a distributed system is unable to handle this scenario without requiring changes to the client application, is the system really object-oriented? Such a system is better described as being object-based, not object-oriented.

To demonstrate distributed polymorphism in action, let's take a look at a programming example. Recall the previous example, where we had a remote server (DistributorImpl.java) that generated Job classes and returned them to a client application (Client.java) by passing them through a remote interface (Distributor.java). In this example, the original Job class is extended (subclassed) to create two new specific subtypes (JobA and JobB). Note that both of these new subtypes override the original Job's process method. The original client application (Client.java) is used to process these new Job subtypes. The remote server (DistributorImpl.java) is modified to polymorphically return the two new specific types of Job classes (JobA and JobB).

Source Code: RP/JobA.java
```
// define JobA subtype (JobA.java)

import java.io.*;

public class JobA
  extends Job
  implements java.io.Serializable {

  public void process() {
    System.out.println("Processing Job A");
  }
}
```

Source Code: RP/JobB.java
```
// define JobB subtype (JobB.java)

import java.io.*;

public class JobA
  extends Job
  implements java.io.Serializable {
```

```
    public void process() {
      System.out.println("Processing Job B");
    }
}
```

Source Code: RP/DistributorImpl.java

```
// create remote server (DistributorImpl.java)

import java.io.*;
import java.net.*;
import java.rmi.*;
import java.rmi.server.*;
import java.util.*;

public class DistributorImpl
  extends UnicastRemoteObject
  implements Distributor {

  Vector jobs;
  int count;

  public DistributorImpl()
    throws RemoteException {

    jobs = new Vector();
    jobs.addElement(new JobA());
    jobs.addElement(new JobB());
    count = 0;

    try {
      Naming.rebind("distributor",this);
      UnicastRemoteObject.exportObject(this);
    }

    catch (Exception e) {
      System.err.println("Failed to bind to RMI Registry");
      System.exit(1);
    }
  }

  public static final void main(String[] args) {

    try {
      DistributorImpl runner = new DistributorImpl();
    }

    catch (Exception e) {
      System.err.println("Failed to create DistributorImpl object"
        + e.getMessage());
    }
  }
```

```
public Job getNewJob() {

  if( count < jobs.size()) {
    return (Job)jobs.elementAt(count++);
  }
  else {
    System.exit(0);
  }
  return null;
}
}
```

Here's the compilation and execution sequence for this example. Note that the original client application (Client.class) and the original remote interface (Distributor.class) have not changed, so they don't require compilation:

javac JobA.java

javac JobB.java

javac DistributorImpl.java

rmic DistributorImpl

rmiregistry

java DistributorImpl

java Client

java Client

When the client application is first executed, it connects to the server and calls the getNewJob method on the server. Instead of returning a class of type Job, the server polymorphically returns the JobA class. In this case, the RMI system will determine that the JobA class is a subtype of the Job class; therefore, both classes must be returned to the client. If these classes are not available on the client machine, the RMI system will automatically serialize them and send them across the network to the client. When the client executes the process method on the Job, it executes the overridden process method of the JobA class. When the client application is executed a second time, the server polymorphically returns the JobB class. The client executes the overridden process method of the JobB class.

This is a very simple example, but it demonstrates some very significant power. Remember, the Client class has not been modified; it expects a class of type Job to be returned from the server, and will invoke the process method on that returned Job class. The remote interface (Distributor.class) has not been modified either; it returns classes of type Job. But when the client executes the Job's process method, it is actually executing the overridden process method in the Job's subtype. In a nondistributed object-oriented system, this is the natural expected behavior of objects. But in a distributed system, this is only possible if the transport mechanism can send the morphed Job class across the network. Recall that RPC systems use stub classes which act as surrogate placeholders (external data representation) for remote objects. In this example, the stub has changed because the server was modified to polymorphically return JobA and JobB subtypes. This means that the system must also download the new stub to work properly. Java RMI is truly polymorphic because it does exact-matching of stubs during method resolution. The exact-matching of stubs makes it possible to preserve the true types of objects without truncation.

RMI and the Java Servlet API

Another interesting part of the Java platform is the servlet API. Most traditional Web servers were designed to serve files, not to provide dynamic processing capability. Dynamic processing on Web servers was introduced through the use of a common gateway interface (CGI), but this approach is inefficient and limited in functionality. To get beyond these limitations, Web server designers added server-side programming APIs such as NSAPI and ISAPI, but these are proprietary to particular servers. The Java servlet API provides a standard object-oriented server-side environment, allowing the programmer to use Java on both the client (applet) and server (servlet). A typical usage of this technology is to deliver GUI applets on the client side that communicate with a back-end process running as a servlet on the server. Communication between the applet and servlet can be programmed using standard HTTP requests, but another alternative is to use RMI as the communication channel between applets and servlets. The servlet can be programmed to operate as an RMI server, allowing the applet to execute methods on the servlet. This allows the programmer to use the simple method invocation syntax for applet-to-servlet communication. It also allows the passing of objects as method arguments and the implementation of object-oriented design patterns for Web-based applications. Another consideration is that the HTTP protocol was designed to serve files and is a stateless protocol. By using HTTP to dispatch servlets and applets which communicate via RMI, the state is preserved on the client and server sides.

The following example illustrates how RMI can be used for applet-servlet communication. The servlet (HelloServerImpl.java) implements a remote interface (HelloServer.java). This remote interface defines a remote method (message) that returns an object (Package). Note that in this example the servlet operates as an RMI server that returns objects to the applet (HelloClient.java). The servlet cannot extend the UnicastRemoteObject class, as in the other examples, because it extends the GenericServlet. Therefore, the servlet must export itself as a remote object using UnicastRemoteObject.exportObject(this) and bind its name to the RMI registry so the client can reference it. When the example is executed, the servlet is spawned via an HTTP request. The servlet exports itself as a remote object and binds to the RMI registry. The servlet then generates a Web page containing an applet tag and sends it to client's browser. The browser interprets the applet tag and downloads the applet. The applet looks up the servlet in the RMI registry, then invokes a remote method on the servlet. The servlet instantiates a new Package object and returns it to client as an argument in the remote method call. Finally, the client invokes the toString method on the returned Package object and prints the message contained in the Package.

Source Code: HelloServer.java

```
// define remote interface (HelloServer.java)

public interface HelloServer
  extends java.rmi.Remote {

  Package message()
    throws java.rmi.RemoteException;
}
```

Source Code: HelloServerImpl.java

```
// define rmi servlet (HelloServerImpl.java)

import java.io.*;
import java.rmi.*;
import java.rmi.server.*;
import java.servlet.*;

public class HelloServerImpl
  extends GenericServlet
  implements HelloServer {

  public void init() {

    try {
      UnicastRemoteObject.exportObject(this);
      Naming.rebind("hello",this);
    }

    catch (Exception e) {
      log("Failed to connect to RMI registry " + e.getMessage());
    }
  }

  public void service(ServletRequest req, ServletResponse res)
    throws ServletException, IOException {

    res.setContentType("text/html");
    PrintWriter out = new PrintWriter(res.getOutputStream());
```

```
        out.println("HTML>");
        out.println("<APPLET CODE=HelloClient CODEBASE=/ "
                      + "WIDTH=200 HEIGHT=100>");
        out.println("");
        out.flush();
    }

    public String getServletInfo() {
      return "Simple Hello world RMI servlet";
    }

    public Package message()
      throws java.rmi.RemoteException {

      return new Package("Hello World! (RMI Servlet)");
    }
}
```

Source Code: HelloClient.java

```
// define applet client (HelloClient.java)

import java.io.*;
import java.awt.*;
import java.applet.*;
import java.rmi.*;
import java.rmi.server.*;

public class HelloClient
  extends Applet {

  Label message;
  HelloServer server;

  public HelloClient() {

    message = new Label();

    try {
      server = (HelloServer)Naming.lookup("rmi://hostname/hello");
      Package tmp = server.message();
      message.setText(tmp.toString());
    }

    catch(Exception e) {
      message.setText("Error: " + e.getMessage());
    }

    this.add(message);
  }
}
```

Source Code: `Package.java`

```
// object to be passed (Package.java)

import java.io.*;

public class Package
  implements Serializable {

  String message;

  public Package(String msg)  {
    message = msg;          '
  }

  public String toString() {

    return message;
  }
}
```

Object Serialization Examples

Java RMI uses the Object Serialization API to pass and return objects during remote method invocation. The serialization classes convert graphs (hierarchies) of objects into bytestreams. Serialized objects may be written to a storage device for persistent retention of their state information or shipped across networks for reconstruction on the other side. Since the focus of this chapter has been on how to program distributed applications using RMI, there has been little detail about the serialization API. However, since RMI uses serialization while sending objects as arguments during invocation, it is useful to demonstrate how serialization works programmatically. The following examples show how object serialization can be used both for persistent storage and for transport across networks. If you want to delve deeper into the serialization API, you'll want to read the serialization specification (see Appendix A). The first example demonstrates persistent storage of objects (Serialize.java). The Serialize program accepts a filename as a command line argument. The write method creates a file output stream, associates it with an object output stream, and writes a String object to the stream. Then the read method creates a file input stream, associates it with an object input stream, and reads the String back in.

Source Code: `Serialize.java`

```
// persistent storage example (Serialize.java)

import java.io.*;
import java.util.*;
```

```java
public class Serialize {

  String fileName;

  public static final void main(String[] args) {

    Serialize example = new Serialize(args);
    example.write("Hello World!");
    System.out.println(example.read());
  }

  public Serialize(String[] args) {

    if(args.length < 1) {
      System.err.println("Usage: Serialize filename");
      System.exit(0);
    }
    else {
      fileName = args[0];
    }
  }

  public void write(String msg) {

    System.out.println("Writing message");

    try {
      FileOutputStream out = new FileOutputStream(fileName);
      ObjectOutputStream objOut = new ObjectOutputStream(out);
      objOut.writeObject(msg);
      objOut.flush();
      objOut.close();
    }

    catch(Exception e) {
      System.err.println("Failure while writing: " + e.getMessage());
      e.printStackTrace();
    }
  }

  public String read() {

    System.out.println("Reading message");

    try {
      FileInputStream in = new FileInputStream(fileName);
      ObjectInputStream objIn = new ObjectInputStream(in);
      String message = (String) objIn.readObject();
      objIn.close();
      return message;
```

```
    }

    catch(Exception e) {

      System.err.println("Failure reading: " + e.getMessage());
      e.printStackTrace();
      return null;
    }
  }
}
```

The next example illustrates how serialization can be used to transport objects and reconstruct them in different locations. The object to be serialized and transported is defined in the class Package. A server object (Server.java) creates a server socket that listens on a port, instantiates a new Package object and sends it to an object stream associated with the socket. The client application (Client.java) establishes a socket connection with the server and reads in the Package object from an object input stream. The client prints the message contained in the Package to demonstrate that the object's state information is shipped across the wire. Note that the Package class implements Serializable. Only objects that implement Serializable are allowed to be serialized for security reasons. If you want to ensure that any given object cannot be sent across the network, you can ensure that it is not a Serializable object.

Source Code: Package.java
```
// object to be sent (Package.java)

import java.io.*;

public class Package
  implements Serializable {

  String message;

  public Package(String msg) {
    message = msg;
  }

  public String toString() {
    return message;
  }
}
```

Source Code: Server.java
```
// server to send objects (Server.java)

import java.io.*;
import java.net.*;
```

```java
import java.util.*;

public class Server {

  public static final void main(String[] args) {

    Socket clientSocket = null;
    ServerSocket serverSocket = null;

    // establish server socket

    try {
      serverSocket = new ServerSocket(1234);
    }

    catch (IOException e) {
      System.out.println("Error establishing server port "
        +e.getMessage());
      System.exit(1);
    }

    // establish client socket

    try {
      clientSocket = serverSocket.accept();
    }

    catch (IOException e) {
      System.out.println("Accept failed: "+ e.getMessage());
      System.exit(1);
    }

    // write object to the stream

    try {
      ObjectOutputStream os = new ObjectOutputStream(
        clientSocket.getOutputStream());
      os.writeObject(new Package("Hello World"));
    }

    catch (Exception e) {
      System.out.println("Failed to write object: "
        +e.getMessage());
    }
  }
}
```

Source Code: SClient.java
```java
// read serialized object stream (SClient.java)

  import java.io.*;
```

```
import java.net.*;
import java.util.*;

public class SClient {

  public static final void main(String[] args){
    Socket clientSocket = null;

    // establish client socket
    try {
      clientSocket = new Socket("hostname", 1234);;
    }
  catch (IOException e){
    System.out.println("Accept failed: "+ e.getMessage());
    System.exit(1);
  }

    // read object from the stream
    try {
      ObjectInputStream is = new ObjectInputStream(
        clientSocket.getInputStream());
      Package msg = (Package)is.readObject();
      System.out.println(msg.toString());
    }
    catch (Exception e){
      System.out.println("Failed to read object: "
        +e.getMessage());
    }
  }
}
```

The Future of Java RMI

Java RMI was first included in the core language environment when JDK 1.1 was released. In this first version there are some limitations to the RMI system. In its first release, RMI only supports a protocol for unicast (point-to-point) method invocation. In a later release, multicast capabilities will be added to support server replication strategies. Also in the plans for RMI are support for persistent remote references and activation of remote objects.

Security will be added at the transport level, so that communications can be encrypted using SSL (secure socket layer) algorithms.

Another upcoming enhancement to Java RMI is integration with CORBA-Services via the IIOP wire protocol. This capability will be added to the RMI system due to feedback from Java developers who expressed desire to use both RMI and CORBA together. Since CORBA cannot leverage the power of having a single object model, a restricted subset of the Java object model will be created to integrate with CORBA. This will allow the programmer to use RMI-style semantics while accessing CORBAServices. However, the IIOP protocol does not provide all of the capabilities that the full RMI system requires (for example pass-by-value), so the IIOP communications channel will have limited capabilities compared to the full RMI API.

For example, non-remote objects passed as RMI calls over IIOP will need to be defined as public and final, all fields will need to be public, and classes will have constructors only, no methods. As a side effect of this restricted subsetting of the Java object model, it may also be possible in the future to use the same approach for integration with other RPC-type systems such as Sun RPC, DCE, and DCOM.

There is another Java API in development called JavaSpaces. This API is designed to make it easier to develop distributed applications by providing shared persistent object libraries.

The raw RMI API makes it possible to build large-scale distributed applications, but it's still too hard. JavaSpaces is a higher level of abstraction on top of RMI that allows the programmer to place objects into shared spaces or read objects from shared spaces. To find out more about the JavaSpaces API, check out the distributed systems home page at chatsubo.javasoft.com/javaspaces/. In the future, we can expect to see other new APIs emerge that build on the concepts of Java RMI, both from Sun Microsystems and other software vendors. The future certainly looks bright for distributed object-oriented programming.

Summary

Java RMI provides a framework for communication between Java programs running in different virtual machines. The RMI system is unique in that it preserves the full Java object model throughout the distribution, allowing true polymorphism of both remote and local objects. The syntax of a remote method call is exactly the same as the syntax of a local method call, making distributed programming easy and natural. Any Java object can be passed during remote method calls, including local objects, remote objects, and primitive types. The RMI system uses object serialization to convert object graphs into bytestreams for transport across the network and reconstruction on the other side. The RMI transport system is built to allow for varying invocation semantics, such as unicast, multicast, and specific replication strategies. The RMI system uses a TCP/IP-based transport mechanism to connect Java processes together across the network.

CHAPTER 8

Mastering JDBC Techniques

Introduction

Since the mid-1980s the lion's share of new business systems has been targeted toward commercial relational database management systems (RDBMS). Whether the RDBMS was used simply for data storage and retrieval in a larger, more complex system or was the focal point of the entire application, as in the current generation of two-tiered database applications, almost every system built in the last 10 years has an RDBMS hiding somewhere. Given the RDBMS's importance for both legacy systems and new development efforts, the need for a simple, powerful interface between the RDBMS world and the Java platform is obvious.

This interface should have several features. First, it should be consistent with the design and methodologies of the Java platform. It should share the same object interfaces and package structure, and should *feel* like an integral part of the platform. Java developers should feel at home with the RDBMS interface, just as they are with the networking and window system interfaces.

Just as important as it was for the interface to be acceptable to Java programmers, the interface must also be acceptable to database vendors. An elegant, simple set of APIs which matched seamlessly with the rest of the Java language would be of little use if it could not be implemented simply and effectively on top of existing databases. Finally, the architecture should be flexible enough to allow it to be implemented on top of existing middleware layers, across a variety of networking schemes, and on heterogeneous systems.

In the spring of 1996 JavaSoft (now Sun Microsystems' Java Software group) began work on a Java API to satisfy these requirements. The result was Java Database Connectivity (JDBC), version 1.0 of which was released in October of 1996. JDBC provides a set of APIs which allow Java programmers to incorporate database services into their applications. JDBC also includes specifications for database drivers, which hide the implementation details of a particular database from the API-level developers, a driver manager which allows a single application to access several different databases, through several different drivers simultaneously, and a mapping between standard database data types and Java classes and primitives.

The Java Language, SQL, and CLI

The JDBC is built around the Structured Query Language (SQL) and X/Open's Call Level Interface (CLI). The widely accepted SQL standard has already been in use for many years and in many ways defines the core of the relational database structure. CLI is widely known for its implementation in Microsoft's ODBC product. Using these two standards ensures that JDBC can be implemented on top of existing databases and that a large number of programmers are already familiar with the basic interface. While the designers of JDBC found a good starting place in ODBC, it could not be used directly in the Java platform and many of its features and design decisions made it undesirable to port the ODBC interfaces to the Java language. ODBC is a C interface, so use in JDBC would require native methods, which limit portability, raise important security concerns, and increase the maintenance burden on each individual client. ODBC's procedural methodology does not mate well with the Java object model. ODBC also makes extensive use of void pointers, which violate the type safety of the Java language, and multiple returns from functions, which are cumbersome to implement in the language.

Since a straight port of ODBC to the Java platform would not work, the JDBC designers went back to the CLI specification and to existing ODBC implementations to find the common elements which could be used in JDBC and to craft more and better solutions for those areas where no good fit could be found. The result is a set of database interface classes which can either be implemented on top of existing ODBC drivers, as was the case in most early implementations, or can be wired directly to the underlying database. While ODBC bridge solutions were the first JDBC drivers to market, they have largely been replaced by native drivers. This eliminates one level of abstraction and solves many performance and deployment problems found in the ODBC solutions.

JDBC can be implemented on top of most ANSI SQL92 Entry Level compliant databases. While SQL92 Entry Level conformance represents a least common denominator for today's databases, it is widely supported and provides most of the functionality needed for all simple and many more complex applications. JDBC also allows nonconforming queries and statements to be passed through to the underlying database. These statements do not even need to be in SQL. This allows developers to get access to any needed, specialized functionality provided by a database. Of course, by using these product-specific capabilities, applications lose the database independence normally provided by JDBC. For better or worse, this is a trade-off with which database designers have been familiar for years. Most organizations have developed coding practices, such as standardizing on a single RDBMS or specifying a minimum set of features a product must support, which minimize the impact of this trade-off.

JDBC Architecture

JDBC is implemented in several layers. These range from the top-level JDBC API, which will be used by most programmers, down to the individual JDBC driver, which is the interface between the application and a specific commercial database. The classes which implement these layers are found in the java.sql package. Figure 8.1 shows the major classes and structure of a typical JDBC implementation.

A typical JDBC application will instantiate one or more JDBC drivers under the control of the DriverManager class found in the java.sql package. The drivers are database-specific, so one is needed for each type of database the application needs to use. One driver could be a network-based driver which talks directly to a remote Oracle database. Another could be a bridge out to a locally installed ODBC driver which talks to an SQL server. When the application needs to connect to a particular database, it asks the DriverManager for a reference to the driver which can talk to that database. Using the reference returned by the DriverManager, the application can now ask the driver to open a connection to the database. The driver insulates the application from the database implementation, networking issues, and the actual location of the database. By encapsulating almost all the complexity associated with using a database, the driver makes JDBC programming much simpler and makes the resulting code much more portable across many databases.

After the driver has opened the connection to the database, it returns a reference to a Connection object. The Connection object is the porthole through which the application requests services from the database. It routes these requests through the driver, which formats them as needed and forwards them to the database. The Connection object also provides the application with a Statement object which is used to build the SQL statements which are executed in the database. After a Statement object executes the query, the selected rows are returned in a ResultSet object. The ResultSet gives the application access to

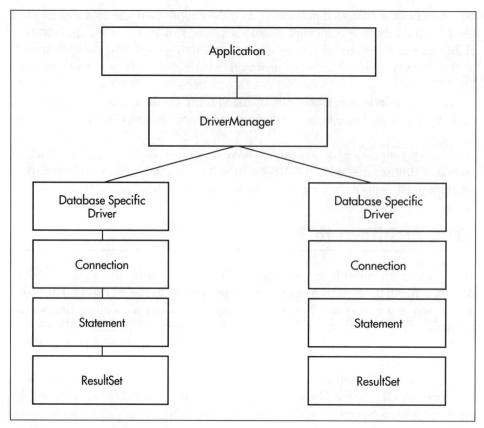

Figure 8.1   The JDBC architecture.

the returned rows and provides mappings between SQL data types and the appropriate Java classes and primitives.

Drivers and Driver Managers

The DriverManager is a class supplied by the java.sql package and instantiated by any applet or application which wishes to use JDBC. The Driver is actually an interface, not a class. Each database and middleware vendor provides an implementation of the Driver interface. This implementation knows how to handle all the details of communicating with its own database. Connection, Statement, and ResultSet are also interfaces, the implementation of which is provided by each vendor. Because the DriverManager and application only see the standard interface, not the implementation details, the use of interfaces provides database independence.

An implementation of the driver interface must deal with several issues. Is the database local or remote? If remote, does the database support a direct connection through some published protocol? Is there already an ODBC infrastructure in place which could be used? These choices lead to several implementation schemes (see Figure 8.2). Again the actual implementation details are hidden from the application by the encapsulating standard interfaces.

Using JDBC

By design, JDBC makes simple things simple. The most common database actions, like inserting rows into a table or extracting data from a table, require only one or two calls. Most JDBC applications will follow the simple structure of loading the needed database driver and opening a connection to that database. This requires less than five lines of code. After that the application can use the simple Statement object to communicate with the database. The following simple example should make these steps clear.

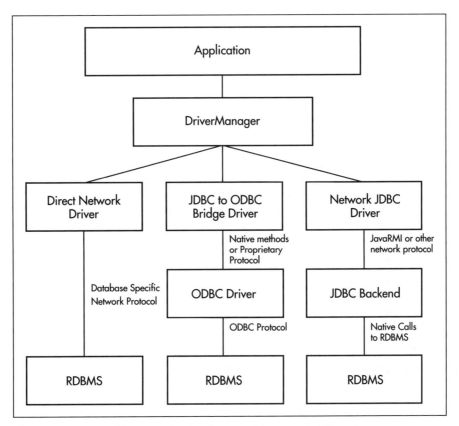

Figure 8.2   JDBC drivers can be implemented in several different ways.

Table 8.1 Scheme of Inventory Table

COLUMN NAME	DATA TYPE
Ingredient	char(40)
Quantity	real

Simple Example

This example uses JDBC to print the current inventory levels of various ingredients at the Pie à la Modem Baking company. The example uses the Structured Query Language to pull the needed rows from the database.

The inventory levels are stored in the Inventory table of the PieData database (see Table 8.1). Each row in the Inventory table contains the name of an ingredient and the quantity on hand. For simplicity the units in which an ingredient is measured are implicit in the type of the ingredient. So 100 flour means 100 cups and 300 apples means 300 medium apples. The rest of the system is assumed to know these units.

Source Code: SimpleJDBC\SimpleJDBC.java
```
import java.sql.*;

public class SimpleJDBC {

    public static void main(String args[]) {
        try {
            Class.forName("com.sybase.jdbc.SybDriver");
            String databaseName = "jdbc:sybase:Tds:piemachine:5001";
            Connection con = DriverManager.getConnection(databaseName,
                                                "pieguy", "BananaCream");
            Statement stmt = con.createStatement();
            ResultSet rs = stmt.executeQuery("select * from Inventory");
            while (rs.next()) {
                System.out.println(rs.getString(1) + ": " +
                                                rs.getFloat(2));
            }
        } catch( Exception e ) {
            e.printStackTrace();
        }
    }
}
```

Here is the output of this simple example:

```
flour: 300.0
mock apples: 600.0
sugar: 200.0
```

```
cinnamon: 50.0
apples: 2100.0
lemons: 250.0
peaches: 600.0
```

Anatomy of a JDBC Application

This small application shows all of the basic features of JDBC. It starts by importing the java.sql package. This package contains most of the interfaces and classes used by the JDBC. Some of the interfaces and abstract classes in java.sql are never actually implemented in that package. The implementation of these classes is left to the database-specific driver, the classes of which must also be available to the application.

Installing a Driver

Figures 8.1 and 8.2 show the relationship of the database-specific driver to the rest of the JDBC system. The first action a JDBC application usually takes is to load the database-specific driver into the DriverManager. This is done in the line:

```
Class.forName("com.sybase.jdbc.SybDriver");
```

When a JDBC driver is loaded in this manner, a static method in the driver's class instantiates a copy of the driver and registers it with the DriverManager. Once the new driver has been registered, the DriverManager is responsible for keeping track of it, the application developer does not need to keep a reference to it. The driver will avoid the garbage collector because it will always be referenced by the DriverManager.

JDBC allows an application to install multiple drivers. If an application needs to communicate simultaneously with databases from several different vendors, it will have to load a driver for each of those databases. Again, the Driver-Manager takes care of keeping track of the various drivers. Once the developer has loaded a driver, it can be safely forgotten.

JDBC can also automatically load drivers. At startup, the DriverManager looks for a system property called jdbc.drivers, which should contain a colon-separated list of drivers. If this property is found, the DriverManager will attempt to load each driver in the list. In general, this method is inappropriate for applets, since the developer cannot assume that the correct drivers are listed in the client's properties files. If not every JDBC application needs every driver in the list, then automatic loading at startup can lead to unnecessarily long load times and wasted memory. Also, if the properties file on thousands of client machines must be modified to load the proper drivers, this can lead to a needless maintenance problem each time the Driver class must be changed. Of course, anyone building an architecture which requires any modifications to the client side of a Java application has already missed a very important point.

Making a Connection

After the driver is loaded, we must connect through it to the database. This poses two problems. First, where is the database we need? Second, which of the possibly many Drivers installed is the right one for that database?

The first problem has many facets. Where on the whole of the Internet is the machine hosting the RDBMS? On which port is the RDBMS listening for connections? And finally, what type of RDBMS is it? The World Wide Web has already faced these problems and solved them with the uniform resource locator (URL). A URL of the form protocol//hostname:port/path specifies what protocol to use to access some information (HTTP versus FTP), the machine on which the information lives, and where on that machine to find the information.

This syntax is easily adapted to the needs of JDBC. A URL specifying a database would be of the form jdbc:<subprotocol>:<subname>://hostname:port/database. This provides the DriverManager and appropriate driver with all the information needed to locate the needed database. Optional parameters can be added to the end of the URL using the <attribute-name>=<attribute-value> syntax.

When making a connection, the database URL is passed to the Driver-Manager. We see this in these two lines:

```
String databaseName = "jdbc:sybase:Tds:piemachine:5001";
Connection con = DriverManager.getConnection(databaseName,"pieguy",
                                              "BananaCream");
```

where "pieguy" and "BananaCream" are the user and password for the database login.

While the URL lets the DriverManager know where to find the database, it leaves open the question of which of the drivers to use to make this connection. In order to resolve this question, the DriverManager traverses the list of loaded drivers and asks each in turn if it can connect to the database named in this URL. A Driver will usually only accept requests for a single sub-protocol. For example, an Oracle Driver would detect that the sub-protocol in this previous URL specifies a Sybase database and immediately reject the request. This allows the DriverManager to interrogate the loaded drivers with a minimum of overhead.

The Connection Interface

Once the DriverManager has found the needed driver, that driver returns a Connection object which is passed back to the calling application. In JDBC Connection is actually an interface that provides a network-independent way to pass statements to an RDBMS and get results back. The Connection interface provides methods which control the nature of the connection (automatic versus manual commits), get catalog and metadata regarding the database, close the connection, and handle warnings from the database.

The Statement Interface

The Connection interface contains the createStatement method which returns a Statement object. Again, Statement is actually an interface which provides RDBMS independent methods for executing queries. Each RDBMS vendor provides a class which implements the statement interface. In our example the line

```
Statement stmt = con.createStatement();
```

provides our application with this object.

The Statement interface provides methods for setting time-out defaults on queries, getting maximum field sizes and maximum number of rows returnable, setting cursors in the database, and other advanced features. The Statement interface also contains three very simple methods: executeQuery(String), executeUpdate(String), and the more general execute(String). In a typical 80/20 rule fashion, these three methods do most of the work required of the Statement interface. The remaining 20 percent or so of corner cases still require the more advanced methods, but in a beautiful example of Java APIs keeping the simple things simple, the three execute methods are all many programmers will ever need to use. In our example, we use the executeQuery(String) method to get all the rows in the Inventory table:

```
ResultSet rs = stmt.executeQuery("select * from Inventory");
```

Manipulating Results

ResultSet is another interface for which each vendor must provide an implementation. As with the Statement interface, the ResultSet interface contains a handful of methods which do most of the work and many methods which will most likely only be used by a few applications.

After executing a query, the returned ResultSet will have a cursor pointing to the returned rows. Contrary to expectations, this cursor does not initially point to the first row of the results. Instead the cursor points *above* the first row. This is actually very convenient, since it allows us to use a simple while loop to step through all the rows in the results by writing:

```
while (rs.next()) {
    System.out.println(rs.getString(1) + ": " + rs.getFloat(2));
}
```

This is very much like the Enumeration class's hasMoreElements() and nextElement() methods already familiar to most Java programmers. The one danger of this construct is that when executing a query which you absolutely know will only return a single row, it is very tempting to write:

```
ResultSet rs = stmt.executeQuery("Some query");
int i = rs.getInt(1);
```

While this seems natural when you are writing it, it will generate an SQLException at runtime because rs does not actually point to the returned row when we call rs.getInt( ). Even though we know there is only one row, we still must call rs.next( ) before rs.getInt( ) to advance the cursor to the first valid row.

> **TIP** Are you sure this query will really only ever return one row? If you're dealing with a value the database guarantees will be unique, like a key or declared unique value, this is a safe assumption. But in other cases, this assumption could lead to subtle bugs which only show up after the system has been in production long enough for everyone to forget that this assumption was ever made.

The first call to the next( ) method moves the cursor to the first row in the ResultSet. Each subsequent call to next( ) advances the cursor until the ultimate call exhausts the returned rows and returns false.

As we step through the ResultSet, we presumably wish to do something with the returned data. In order to do anything useful, we must be able to access the value of each column in a row. Also, since we are writing in the Java language, these accesses must be type safe. The ResultSet interface provides methods for returning a column's value and mapping that value to a Java primitive data type or class. These methods follow the naming convention of getXXX(int) and getXXX(String). In each of these two cases, the XXX is replaced by a Java primitive data type or Class. The method returns the type indicated by its name.

JDBC can index a ResultSet by either column number or name. The getXXX(int) version of the get methods returns the value of the given column in the database. The getXXX(String) version returns the value of the column named by the argument to the method. These two versions have been provided because some developers need the efficiency of numerical indexing and others prefer the flexibility and portability of symbolic indexing. Developers should be aware that, depending on the particular database in question, numerical indexing can be much more efficient.

In our example, we use numerical indexing to extract the Ingredient name and the Quantity on hand:

```
String str = rs.getString(1);
int q = rs.getInt(2);
```

We could have just as easily written:

```
String str = rs.getString("Ingredient");
int q = rs.getInt("Quantity");
```

Java to SQL Data Type Mappings

The ResultSet interface provides getXXX() methods which map between Java primitive data types and classes, and widely supported SQL data types. Table 8.2 lists the mapping between SQL and Java types and the associated getXXX() method.

The getXXX() methods can also be used to convert between one type in the

GOTCHAS

Despite its apparent simplicity, the ResultSet does have several gotchas. Most of these result from the need to ensure that JDBC can be implemented on any RDBMS. We've already seen one example of this in the getXXX(int) versus getXXX(String) methods. Because of underlying implementation issues, the getXXX(int) form of the method can be much faster. There are other, less obvious issues which a JDBC programmer must take into consideration.

For example, when reading columns the developer should be careful to read the columns in numerical order (with the left-most column being numbered 1) and to read each column only once. While some RDBMSs will allow out-of-order reading and rereading of columns, not all RDBMSs will. Applications which depend on being able to reread a column sacrifice portability.

For similar reasons, the ResultSet does not give an indication of how many rows were returned by a query. It would be very handy if one could know in advance how many rows were available, for loops could be used to process the ResultSet and arrays could be allocated to hold the processed data. Unfortunately, not all RDBMSs tell you how many rows were returned. So JDBC programmers are stuck with while loops and Vectors.

Perhaps the most confusing gotchas in JDBC is the wasNull() method. It is possible that a column in a returned row will contain no data. In this case the column will contain the special SQL value of NULL. A NULL is fundamentally different from an empty string or a 0, so it cannot be represented as one of the Java primitives without losing important information about the column. Nor would it make sense to throw an exception every time a NULL value was encountered. After all, this is not necessarily an error. In order to cope with the NULL value, the ResultSet interface contains the wasNull() method; it is called after a getXXX() method in order to check if the returned value is an SQL NULL. A typical use of wasNull() would be:

```
int i = rs.getInt(1);
if (rs.wasNull()) {
// Take appropriate action.
// Maybe assigning a default value or
// throwing an exception.
}
```

Table 8.2   SQL Type to Java Type Mapping

SQL TYPE	JAVA TYPE	METHOD
CHAR	String	getString
VARCHAR	String	getString
LONGVARCHAR	String	getString
NUMERIC	java.math.BigDecimal	getBigDecimal
DECIMAL	java.math.BigDecimal	getBigDecimal
BIT	boolean	getBoolean
TINYINT	byte	getByte
SMALLINT	short	getShort
INTEGER	int	getInt
BIGINT	long	getLong
REAL	float	getFloat
FLOAT	double	getDouble
DOUBLE	double	getDouble
BINARY	byte[]	getBytes
VARBINARY	byte[]	getBytes
LONGVARBINARY	byte[]	getBytes
DATE	java.sql.Date	getDate
TIME	java.sql.Time	getTime
TIMESTAMP	java.sql.Timestamp	getTimestamp

database and a Java type which may be more convenient for the application programmer. For example, getString() can be called on a column containing any SQL type. The resulting String will contain the appropriate stringified representation of that type.

To an object purist, this plethora of getXXX() methods may seem offensive. After all, every Java object extends Object, so a single getObject() method could be used to fetch the column's value and a cast could be used to narrow the result to the appropriate Java type. JDBC's designers actually considered this interface but soon decided that getObject() looked a lot better in javadoc than it did in Java code. As this example from the JDBC specification demonstrates,

```
int i = ((Integer)rs.getObject(1,java.sql.Types.INTEGER)).intValue();
```

is much less readable (and writable) than a simple:

```
int i = rs.getInt(1);
```

Generic getObject(int) and getObject(String) methods are provided. These allow great flexibility in how column values are manipulated by a Java program. Of course, this flexibility comes at the cost of greater complexity. The getObject method will probably be most frequently used inside of database application builders which will automatically generate the needed Java code and onerous casts. When combined with the DatabaseMetaData and ResultSetMetaData classes, which return information about what tables are in a database and what data is in each table, the generic getObject methods give the designers of database application builders everything they need to deploy 100% Pure Java builder tools.

TIP Having opened the connection to the database, executed our query, and processed the results, we must now clean up after ourselves by breaking the connection to the database. We could simply let the Connection and Statement objects go out of scope and trust that their finalize () methods will take care of any cleanup. While this may work, if the application won't be exiting soon simply throwing away these objects can lead to some problems. Remember that the Connection and Statement objects have encapsulated a lot of networking and RDBMS-specific complexity for you. This may include locking resources in the database or holding socket connections open. If you simply throw away your reference to these objects, you are trusting the garbage collector to come along and call their finalize() methods. But if the application is not in need of memory, the garbage collector may not be called for quite some time. So, if your application continues to run after disconnecting from the database, it is good practice to explicitly close the database connections to ensure that you are not inadvertently monopolizing valuable resources.

In our example, we have placed the close() calls in the finally clause of the enclosing try block:

```
try {
  // JDBC processing
}
catch (Exception e) {
  // Something happened
}
finally {
  stmt.close();
  con.close();
}
```

This is because with any networked application, as with any database application, there are several sources of errors. The network could go down. There could be a syntax error in your SQL or a new version of the RDBMS on the server could be incompatible with the JDBC Driver version in your client. Each of these cases would generate an Exception which would cause the try block to exit prematurely. If the close() methods were at the end of the try block, we would again be depending on the garbage collector to clean up after us. Even worse, if con and stmt were instance variables, they may never get garbage collected and would hold their server-side resources, unused, until the application exited. Placing the close() calls in the finally clause ensures that regardless of how the try block exits, we properly clean up after ourselves.

Building on the Example

Writing SQL code by hand can be difficult. In typical Java development tools, there is no debug or even a syntax checker for SQL. This means getting the SQL right requires many long trips through the edit/compile/debug cycle. There is also the danger that, if several programmers are writing SQL against the same database, subtle inconsistencies in how they treat the data could introduce bugs to the system. To avoid these problems, it is often a good idea to bury the raw SQL as deeply as possible in reusable database accessor classes. Writing the SQL once and having the rest of the system call these canned queries saves a lot of painful hand-coding. (Of course, if we really wanted to make things easier for the developers, we'd use any one of a dozen or so automated JDBC-SQL mapping tools. But that's a different subject.) It also isolates database-dependent parts of the application in a few packages, making it easier to switch databases.

Here is an example of how to isolate the SQL and database-dependent parts of an application in an accessor class. The InventoryManager encapsulates all the needed SQL code and presents a much higher level API for other developers to use. It contains several functions for common operations, like replenishing inventory levels and checking how much of an ingredient we have on hand.

Source Code: Inventory\InventoryManager.java

```
package pie.inventory;

import java.sql.*;
import java.util.Vector;
import java.util.Enumeration;

public class InventoryManager {
  Statement stmt;
  String databaseName = "jdbc:sybase:Tds:java-aces.east:5001";

  // Load mSQL driver when class is first loaded.
  public InventoryManager() {
```

```
  try {
    Class.forName("com.sybase.jdbc.SybDriver");
  }
  catch( Exception e ) {
    e.printStackTrace();
  }
}


public boolean checkInventory(String ingredient, float amount){
  try {
    Connection con =
            DriverManager.getConnection(databaseName, "fritz",
                                                      "jdbctst");
    stmt = con.createStatement();
    ResultSet rs = stmt.executeQuery(
      "SELECT Quantity FROM Inventory WHERE Ingredient = '"
      + ingredient +"'");
    rs.next();
    if (amount > rs.getFloat(1))
      return false;
    else
      return true;
  } catch (Exception e) {
    e.printStackTrace();
  }
  return false;
}


public boolean checkInventory(Vector ingredients) {
  try {
    Connection con =
            DriverManager.getConnection(databaseName, "fritz",
                                                      "jdbctst");
    stmt = con.createStatement();
    Enumeration e = ingredients.elements();
    while (e.hasMoreElements()) {
      InventoryItem i = (InventoryItem) e.nextElement();
      ResultSet rs = stmt.executeQuery(
      "SELECT Quantity FROM Inventory WHERE Ingredient = '"
        + i.item + "'");
      rs.next();
      if (rs.getFloat(1) < i.amount)
        return false;
    }
    return true;
  } catch (Exception e) {
    e.printStackTrace();
  }
  return false;
}
```

```
    public float quantityOnHand(String ingredient)
      throws SQLException {
        Connection con =
                DriverManager.getConnection(databaseName, "fritz",
                                                        "jdbctst");
        stmt = con.createStatement();
      ResultSet rs = stmt.executeQuery(
        "SELECT Quantity FROM Inventory WHERE Ingredient = '"
        + ingredient +"'");
      rs.next();
      return rs.getFloat(1);
    }

    public void replenish(String ingredient, float quantity)
      throws SQLException {
        Connection con =
                DriverManager.getConnection(databaseName, "fritz",
                                                        "jdbctst");
        stmt = con.createStatement();
      ResultSet rs = stmt.executeQuery(
        "SELECT Quantity FROM Inventory WHERE Ingredient = '"
        + ingredient +"'");
      rs.next();
      stmt.executeUpdate(
        "UPDATE Inventory SET Quantity = " +
        (rs.getFloat(1) + quantity) +
        " WHERE Ingredient = '" + ingredient +"'");
    }

    public void forecast(Vector v){
    }
}
```

Any program which needs to access the Inventory data can now do so by instantiating an InventoryManager and letting it do the dirty work. The following example does just that to check inventory levels and to restock some items.

Source Code: Inventory\InventoryMain.java

```
package pie.inventory;

import java.sql.*;

public class InventoryMain {
  public static void main(String args[]){
    InventoryManager im = new InventoryManager();

    try {
      System.out.println("Got lots of apples: " +
                                    im.checkInventory("apples", 90f));
      System.out.println("I've got " + im.quantityOnHand("apples") + "
                                        apples");
```

```
        im.replenish("apples", 100f);
        System.out.println("Now I've got " + im.quantityOnHand("apples") + "
                                                    apples");

        System.out.println("Got lots of lemons: " +
                                    im.checkInventory("lemons", 91f));

        Vector v = new Vector();
        v.addElement(new InventoryItem("apples", 6f));
        v.addElement(new InventoryItem("flour", 4.5f));
        System.out.println("I have enough apples and flour: "
                                            im.checkInventory(v));
    } catch (Exception e) {
        e.printStackTrace();
    }
  }
}
```

When run, InventoryMain produces the following output:

```
Got lots of apples: true
I've got 1900.0 apples
Now I've got 2000.0 apples
Got lots of lemons: true
I have enough apples and flour: true
```

Transactions

By default each command issued through a Statement or PreparedStatement object is contained in its own transaction and the results of that command are automatically committed to the database. Frequently applications designers will need explicit control over transactions and when database changes are committed. The application may be dealing with two or three databases at once and need to roll back earlier changes in one database if a later change to another database fails. The classic example is an ATM transaction which attempts to withdraw $100.00 from a savings account and deposit it in a checking account. If the deposit does not commit properly, the customer certainly doesn't want the withdraw to stand. JDBC provides this level of transaction control through options on the Connection object. Calling setAutoCommit(false) on a Connection object gives the programmer manual control over commits. Here is a simple example:

```
Connection con = DriverManager.getConnection(dbUrl,dbLogin,dbPass);
    con.setAutoCommit(false);
    Statement stmt = con.createStatement();
    PreparedStatement pStmt = con.prepareStatement
                    ("insert into transtable values (?, ?)");
```

```
    // Commit this transaction.
    pStmt.setInt(1, 1);
    pStmt.setString(2, "This transaction will be committed.");
    pStmt.executeUpdate();
    stmt.execute("commit work");

    // Roll back this transaction.
    pStmt.setInt(1, 2);
    pStmt.setString(2, "This transaction will be rolled back.");
    pStmt.executeUpdate();
    stmt.execute("rollback work");

    // Let this transaction fail automatically when we exit.
    pStmt.setInt(1, 3);
    pStmt.setString(2, "This transaction will fail when we exit.");
    pStmt.executeUpdate();
```

Prepared Statements

Often in a database application one will need to execute the same statement
multiple times. A method may be handed an array of information and have to
insert each element into a database or a method may receive many different
names or other identifiers and be expected to return the results of a query for
each element in the vector. Both of these cases could be handled with a for or
while loop which iterates over the array, building and executing a unique query
for each element. For example, in checkInventory above we are given a vector
of ingredients and amounts and have to make sure we have enough of each
ingredient on hand. We accomplish the task like this:

```
try {
    Statement stmt = con.createStatement();
    Enumeration e = ingredients.elements();
    while (e.hasMoreElements()) {
        InventoryItem i = (InventoryItem) e.nextElement();
        ResultSet rs = stmt.executeQuery(
            "SELECT Quantity FROM Inventory WHERE Ingredient = '" +
                                                     i.item +"'");
        rs.next();
        if (rs.getFloat(1) < i.amount)
            return false;
    }
    return true;
} catch (Exception e) {
    e.printStackTrace();
}
return false;
```

where ingredients is a vector of InventoryItems, each of which contains the
name of an ingredient and the amount needed in the recipe.

While this construct is fairly straightforward, it is also very inefficient. Each time a query is sent to the RDBMS, the database must parse and optimize the query. If the query is even moderately complex, this could take quite some time. When multiplied by the number of elements in the vector, this overhead could have a big impact on the application's performance.

Fortunately, most RDBMSs support prepared statements which can be created, parsed, and optimized once in the database, and used over and over again by the application. JDBC supports prepared statements with a subclass of the Statement class called the PreparedStatement. A PreparedStatement is created through a call to a Connection object, much as Statement is:

```
PreparedStatement pStmt = con.prepareStatement(
"SELECT Quantity FROM Inventory WHERE Ingredient = ?");
```

There are two big differences between a Statement and a PreparedStatement. The first is that the PreparedStatement's constructor takes an SQL statement as an argument. This allows the constructor to create the query in the database only once. The second difference is the ?s in the SQL statement. Unlike a regular Statement which is built up from scratch each time it is executed, a PreparedStatement is stored, unchanging, in the code. If there was no way to change the parameters to the PreparedStatement each time it was executed, the whole idea would be pretty useless. That's where the ?s come in. Each ? represents a parameter which can be set before executing the query. The underlying database substitutes these IN parameters into the precompiled statement before executing it. In our inventory database example, we could use a PreparedStatement instead of rebuilding a regular Statement each time through the loop:

```
try {
  PreparedStatement pStmt = con.prepareStatement(
    "SELECT Quantity FROM Inventory WHERE Ingredient = ?");
  Enumeration e = ingredients.elements();
  while (e.hasMoreElements()) {
    InventoryItem i = (InventoryItem) e.nextElement();
    pStmt.setString(1, i.item);
    ResultSet rs = pStmt.executeQuery();
    rs.next();
    if (rs.getFloat(1) < i.amount)
      return false;
  }
  return true;
} catch (Exception e) {
  e.printStackTrace();
}
return false;
```

PreparedStatement is not only implemented more efficiently in many databases, but it is much easier to use in a program. The tedious code:

```
"select Quantity from Inventory where Ingredient = '" + i.item +"'"
```

is very difficult to get right the first time, resulting in many trips through the edit/compile/debug cycle to track down the missing single quote which causes an SQLException every time you execute the query. It is much easier to use a PreparedStatement and the setXXX( ) methods.

Just as the getXXX( ) methods provide a mapping from SQL data types to Java types, the setXXX( ) methods map Java types to SQL types as shown in Table 8.3.

Neither setString( ) nor setBytes( ) provide a unique map to an SQL data type. This is because JDBC drivers may limit how many chars and bytes can be placed in a VARCHAR or VARBINARY. setString( ) and setBytes( ) will use a VARCHAR or VARBINARY when possible. But if the data overflows these structures, the methods will instead map to the longer LONGVARCHAR and LONG-VARBINARY.

Callable Statements

JDBC also supports stored procedures through the CallableStatement, a subclass of the PreparedStatement. Like the PreparedStatement, Callable-

Table 8.3 Java to SQL Type Map

JAVA TYPE	SQL TYPE	METHOD
String	VARCHAR or LONGVARCHAR	setString
java.math.BigDecimal	NUMERIC	setBigDecimal( )
boolean	BIT	setBoolean
byte	TINYINT	setByte
short	SMALLINT	setShort
int	INTEGER	setInt
long	BIGINT	setLong
float	REAL	setFloat
double	DOUBLE	setDouble
byte[]	VARBINARY or LONGVARBINARY	setBytes
java.sql.Date	DATE	setDate
java.sql.Time	TIME	setTime
java.sql.Timestamp	TIMESTAMP	setTIMESTAMP

Statement's constructor takes the statement it is to execute as a parameter, as shown in this example from the JDBC specification:

```
CallableStatement stmt = con.prepareCall(
"{call getTestDate(?, ?)}");
```

Here the ?s are used not to designate parameters to be passed into the query, but instead represent results returned by the call. These are known as OUT parameters. Before calling this statement, we must tell the CallableStatement what the type of each of the OUT parameters is:

```
stmt.registerOutParameter(1,java.sql.Types.TINYINT);
stmt.registerOutParameter(2,java.sql.Types.DECIMAL, 2);
```

Now, after executing the stored procedure, we can use the getXXX() methods to retrieve the OUT parameters:

```
rs = stmt.executeUpdate();
byte x = rs.getByte(1);
BigDecimal n = rs.getBigDecimal(2,2);
```

Handling Large Data Fields

Many RDBMSs support binary large objects (BLOBs). BLOBs are used to store large, variable-length chunks of data in a column in the database. These chunks could be large images, say an X-ray in a medical database or a photo of a mangled car in an insurance system, or a file containing reams of text and documentation for a loan approver's database. While this data could be placed in a LONGVARCHAR or LONGVARBINARY SQL type, when dealing with multi-megabytes of data, BLOBs are a more efficient and convenient implementation.

JDBC supports BLOBs in the PreparedStatement. While setting the values of the IN parameters to the statement, parameters which represent BLOBs can be set to a java.io.InputStream. When the statement is executed, the JDBC driver will read the contents of the InputStream and pass the data to the underlying RDBMS. We could use BLOBs to store photos of various pies. These photos could be retrieved and included in Web pages to tempt visitors to buy something or included in the page congratulating them on their fine purchase.

The following example shows how to read a datastream from a file, store it into a BLOB in the database and retrieve the BLOB.

Source Code: JDBCBlob.java
```
import java.sql.*;
import java.io.*;
```

```
public class JDBCBlob {
    public static void main(String args[]) {
    try {
            Class.forName("com.sybase.jdbc.SybDriver");
            Connection con = DriverManager.getConnection(
                            "jdbc:sybase:Tds:piemachine:5001",
                            "pieguy","BananaCream");
            PreparedStatement pStmt = con.prepareStatement(
                "INSERT INTO test (name, picture) values ('apple', ?)");

            File inFile = new File("/photos/apple.gif");
            int fileLength = (int) inFile.length();
            FileInputStream in = new FileInputStream(inFile);

            pStmt.setBinaryStream(1, in, fileLength);
            pStmt.executeUpdate();

            File outFile = new File("/photos/newapple.gif");
            FileOutputStream out = new FileOutputStream(outFile);

            Statement stmt = con.createStatement();
            ResultSet rs = stmt.executeQuery(
                "select picture from test where name = 'logo'");
            rs.next();

            InputStream inStream = rs.getBinaryStream(1);
            byte [] picData = new byte [inStream.available()];
            inStream.read(picData);

            out.write(picData);
            out.close();
        } catch (Exception e) {
            e.printStackTrace();
        }
    }
}
```

First we would have to create a PreparedStatement containing the needed insert and an InputStream:

```
PreparedStatement pStmt = con.prepareStatement(

        "INSERT INTO test (name, picture) values ('apple', ?)");

File inFile = new File("/photos/apple.gif");
int fileLength = (int) inFile.length();
FileInputStream in = new FileInputStream(inFile);
```

Then set the IN parameters and execute the statement:

```
pStmt.setBinaryStream(1, in, fileLength);
pStmt.executeUpdate();
```

When it comes time to read the BLOB back out of the database, use the ResultSet's getBinaryStream( ), getAsciiStream( ), or getUnicodeStream( ) methods. These methods take a column index and return an InputStream which can be read to use the data. getBinaryStream( ) is best suited for retrieving LONG-VARBINARY values; getAsciiStream( ) and getUnicodeStream( ) are used for retrieving LONGVARCHAR. The JDBC driver takes care of converting the incoming data to ASCII or Unicode if needed. When using the getXXXStream( ) methods, programmers must be careful to read all the data from the stream before trying to retrieve the value of another column retrieved by the query. The next call to a getXXX( ) method implicitly closes the InputStream, so any unread data will be lost.

In the above example we read the photo out of the database and write it to a new file here:

```
File outFile = new File("/photos/newapple.gif");

FileOutputStream out = new FileOutputStream(outFile);

Statement stmt = con.createStatement();

ResultSet rs = stmt.executeQuery(
    "select picture from test where name = 'logo'");
rs.next();
InputStream inStream = rs.getBinaryStream(1);
byte [] picData = new byte [inStream.available()];
inStream.read(picData);

out.write(picData);
out.close();
```

Adding Value to an RDBMS

In Chapter 6 we described the three-tiered architecture and how to partition applications into collections of cooperating objects. It seems obvious that relational databases would be the data layer, forming the base of a three-tiered design. Actually, the question of exactly where the database lives can be a little more complicated.

If a design contains an RDBMS, then something else in the design must know how to store and read data to and from that RDBMS. An obvious solution is to use JDBC in the objects of the logic tier to allow them to manage the data they need to get their job done (see Figure 8.3).

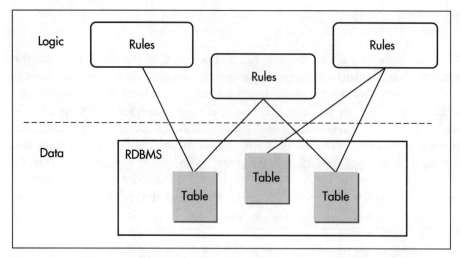

Figure 8.3   Elements of the logic tier can use JDBC to access data sources.

The problem with this design is that it ties the business logic directly to the data source and requires that the expert in the business rules also be proficient in database design. Remember that two of the most important goals for the three-tiered design are to isolate the logic from the data source, so that in time the database may be replaced without rewriting the logic or the logic replaced without having to rebuild the connection to the data, and to allow less technical, but possibly more business savvy, developers to reuse the work of more technical developers. These goals are better achieved by the design shown in Figure 8.4.

In this design a layer of data service objects sits between the business logic and the actual relational database. These objects encapsulate the database, hiding the complexities of the RDBMS from objects in the logic tier by providing higher-order business services which handle the mundane tasks of queries and inserts for the business objects.

In a true three-tiered fashion, each layer adds value to the layer below it, making it easier for developers working at the layer above it to use those services. The data manager layer handles the bookkeeping tasks of data storage and retrieval. The data service objects use those very low-level services to build a high order, easier to use (but usually less flexible) data layer for the rest of the system. The business objects use these data services to construct the heart of applications and make these applications available to any type of interface or GUI which may wish to use them.

Three, Five, or *N* Tiers

Some authors have argued that adding a data service layer actually creates another formal tier, resulting in a five-tiered architecture (the fifth tier comes

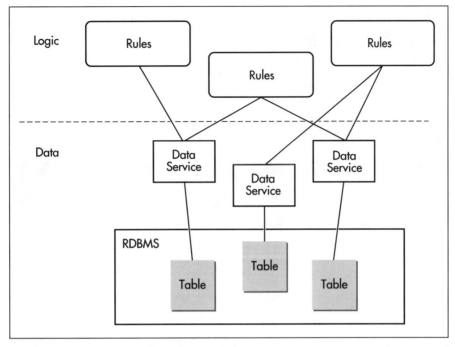

Figure 8.4 An intermediate layer of data access components solves several architectural problems.

from a similar interface between the business rules and the GUI components). Others have generalized this further to the *N*-tier architecture, with fine structure and splitting of each major class of objects into different subtiers. While these debates may be of academic interest, the question of whether the data service objects are a distinctly separate tier or simply peers of the RDBMS inside of a single data tier seems mostly philosophical. The important points are that the business logic is isolated from the RDBMS by a set of services and that these services add value to the flow of data; they are not simply middleware which pass raw SQL requests through to the RDBMS.

Example

We can demonstrate these principles by completing the Pie à la Modem Baking Company example previously used. We've already seen the InventoryManager class. Now we'll round out the accessor classes by providing managers for the Product, Order, and Recipe databases (see Tables 8.4, 8.5, 8.6, 8.7). Finally an OrderEntry class will use the layer of data manager classes to place orders for pies and other baked goods (we'll only show the ProductManager and Order-Entry classes here. Complete source code is on the CD-ROM).

Table 8.4 Inventory Table

FIELD	TYPE
Ingredient	CHAR
Quantity	REAL

Table 8.5 Recipes Table

FIELD	TYPE
ProductNumber	INT
Ingredient	CHAR
Quantity	REAL

Table 8.6 Products Table

FIELD	TYPE
Pie	CHAR
ProductNumber	INT

Table 8.7 Orders Table

FIELD	TYPE
Name	CHAR
Addr1	CHAR
Addr2	CHAR
City	CHAR
State	CHAR
ZipCode	CHAR
ProductNumber	INT
Quantity	INT
DeliveryType	INT

The four data managers are InventoryManager, RecipeManager, Product-Manager, and OrderManager. These classes are used by the OrderEntry class (see Figure 8.5).

ProductManager

The ProductManager is typical of the data managers. It provides five methods for looking up product numbers by name, product names by number, changing names and numbers, and creating new products:

```
int getProductNumber(String)
void setProductNumber(String,int)
String getProductName(int)
void setProductName(String, int)
void addProduct(String, int)
```

Each of these throws an SQLException if it encounters an unrecoverable error.

Source Code: product\ProductManager.java
```
package pie.products;
```

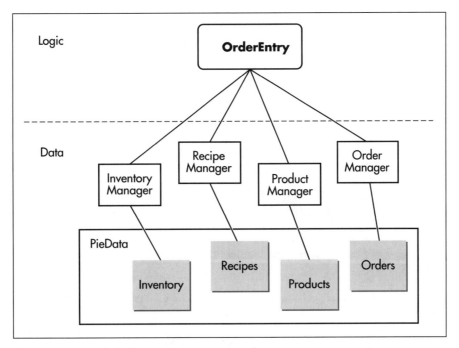

Figure 8.5   An OrderEntry component uses data access components.

```
import java.sql.*;
import java.util.Vector;
import java.util.Enumeration;

public class ProductManager {
  String databaseName = "jdbc:sybase:Tds:java-aces.east:5001";

// Load JDBC driver when class is first loaded.
  public ProductManager() {
    try {
      Class.forName("com.sybase.jdbc.SybDriver");
    }
    catch( Exception e ) {
      e.printStackTrace();
    }
  }

  public int getProductNumber(String name)
    throws SQLException {
      Connection con =
          DriverManager.getConnection(databaseName, "fritz", "jdbctst");
      Statement stmt = con.createStatement();
    ResultSet rs = stmt.executeQuery(
```

```
          "SELECT ProductNumber FROM Products WHERE Pie = '"
          + name +"'");
      rs.next();
      return rs.getInt(1);
  }


  public void setProductNumber (String name, int number)
    throws SQLException {
      Connection con =
          DriverManager.getConnection(databaseName, "fritz", "jdbctst");
      Statement stmt = con.createStatement();
    stmt.executeUpdate(
      "UPDATE Products SET ProductNumber = " + number +
        " WHERE Pie = '" + name +"'");
  }


  public String getProductName(int number)
    throws SQLException {
      Connection con =
          DriverManager.getConnection(databaseName, "fritz", "jdbctst");
      Statement stmt = con.createStatement();
    ResultSet rs = stmt.executeQuery(
      "SELECT Pie FROM Products WHERE ProductNumber = "
      + number);
    rs.next();
    return rs.getString(1);
  }


  public void setProductName (String name, int number)
    throws SQLException {
      Connection con =
          DriverManager.getConnection(databaseName, "fritz", "jdbctst");
      Statement stmt = con.createStatement();
    stmt.executeUpdate(
      "UPDATE Products SET Pie = '" + name +
        "' WHERE ProductNumber = " + number);
  }


  public void addProduct (String name, int number)
    throws SQLException {
      Connection con =
          DriverManager.getConnection(databaseName, "fritz", "jdbctst");
      Statement stmt = con.createStatement();
    stmt.executeUpdate(
      "INSERT INTO Products (Pie, ProductNumber) VALUES ('" +
        name + "', " + number + ")");
  }
}
```

The other data managers provide similar services.

OrderEntry

All of the application logic resides in the OrderEntry class. This class does not know anything about the database which resides at the lowest level. In fact it does not even import a single class from java.sql. It only knows about the services provided by the data managers.

OrderEntry only has one method, placeOrder. It takes nine arguments, corresponding to the nine fields in the Orders database and, following several rules along the way, uses the OrderManager to place the order. The business rules revolve around what kind of delivery is requested in the order. If the order is for standard four- to six-week delivery, OrderEntry simply calculates how much of each ingredient is needed to fill this order, updates the inventory forecast, and places the order.

Things get more complicated if the order requests overnight delivery. In this case, before placing the order, OrderEntry must first check the current time. No overnight delivery orders can be accepted after 2:00 P.M. EST since there will not be enough time to bake, cool, and package the pie before the last pick-up. After ensuring that there is enough time to prepare the pie, OrderEntry checks to make sure we have enough of each ingredient on hand to fulfill the order. Only after checking these two conditions is the order actually placed.

Source Code: orderentry\OrderEntry.java

```
package pie.orderentry;

import pie.inventory.*;
import pie.order.*;
import pie.products.*;
import pie.recipes.*;
import java.util.Vector;
import java.util.Calendar;
import java.util.Enumeration;

public class OrderEntry {
  OrderManager om;
  InventoryManager im;
  ProductManager pm;
  RecipeManager rm;

  public OrderEntry() {
    om = new OrderManager();
    im = new InventoryManager();
    pm = new ProductManager();
    rm = new RecipeManager();
  }

  public void placeOrder(String name, String addr1, String addr2,
                         String city, String state, String zip,
                 String productName, int quantity, int delivery)
```

```java
throws TooLate, LowInventory, CouldNotPlaceOrder, Exception {
 /*
  * We must follow several rules here.
  * First if order specifies overnight delivery, check current
  * time. If it is after 2:00 pm, we can't make and ship the pie
  * in time, so throw a TooLate exception.
  * Also, if it is an overnight order, check inventory levels for
  * all ingredients.  If we're short of anything throw a LowInventory
  * exception.
  * If this is not an overnight delivery, just enter the order in
  * the inventory forecast and place the order in the Orders table.
  */

try {
   // The order entry screens know about product names.
   // Map the name to a product number.
   int productNumber = pm.getProductNumber(productName);
   OrderItem oi = new OrderItem(name, addr1, addr2, city, state, zip,
                                productNumber, quantity, delivery);

   // Get the recipe needed for this type of pie, then multiply the
   // amounts of each ingredient in the recipe by the number of pies
   // in this order.
   Vector itemVector = rm.getRecipe(productNumber);;
   InventoryItem item = new InventoryItem();

   for (int i = 0; i < itemVector.size() ; i++) {
     item = (InventoryItem) itemVector.elementAt(i);
     item.setAmount(item.getAmount() * quantity);
     itemVector.setElementAt(item, i);
   }

   if (delivery == OrderItem.STANDARD) {

     // Here's the easy part. Just place a forecast saying that
     // we'll need this much of each ingredient needed to make this pie
     // then place the order.
     im.forecast(itemVector);
     om.placeOrder(oi);

   } else {

     // If it's after 2:00 we can't accept an over night order.
     Calendar c = Calendar.getInstance();
     if (c.getHours() > 13)
       throw new
             TooLate("Can't request overnight delivery after 2:00 pm
                                                      EST");

       // Nor can we accept an over night order if we're short on
                                                      inventory
```

```
            if (!im.checkInventory(itemVector))
               throw new
                    LowInventory("Can't make that many " + productName + "s
                                                                  now");

               om.placeOrder(oi);
            }
        } catch (Exception e) {
            e.printStackTrace();
            throw new CouldNotPlaceOrder("Unexpected error: " + e);
        }
    }
}
```

OrderEntry first instantiates one of each of the four data. This causes the
data managers to be created once and saves time on each call to placeOrder( ).
Each time placeOrder( ) is called OrderEntry uses the four data managers to
check the business conditions previously listed. If everything is okay, the order
is placed. If something is wrong, OrderEntry throws one of three exceptions to
signal the error: TooLate for overnight orders which come in after 2:00 P.M. EST,
LowInventory for overnight orders which can't be fulfilled, and CouldNot-
PlaceOrder for general errors.

Other Considerations

This example should be complete enough to give you a feel for how to build
good three-tiered applications using data managers and the JDBC. However, for
a real-world system, there are still several pieces which are missing. For example, what would happen in this example if two overnight orders came in at the
same time? Could a race condition allow both orders to be placed, even though
we don't have enough flour to fulfill both? How could we avoid this condition?
Would it be better to synchronize OrderEntry's placeOrder( ) method or should
we depend on database locking to prevent these errors? For that matter, the
placeOrder( ) method never decrements the amounts held in inventory and the
forecast( ) method is just at stub. There is also one really big performance issue
lurking in these examples. We create a new Connection and Statement in each
method of the various managers. This will seriously limit the scalability we can
expect from this system. These oversights are sure to cause trouble in a production system.

In a real production system, of course, the answers to these questions will
depend on exactly how the system is put together. If we could guarantee that
there would only ever be a single OrderEntry object, we could synchronize
the placeOrder( ) method. This may be appropriate for distributed object systems which would depend on a single system-wide instance of OrderEntry.
Systems which could have several OrderEntry objects simultaneously placing

orders would have to rely on synchronization in the data managers or locking in the database tables in order to protect data integrity. Also, the hardcoded database URLs and driver classes make it harder to deploy and manage the system and the fact we've duplicated this information in several modules is a bug waiting to happen. A real world system would have to deal with all these issues.

> **TIP** Don't spend too much time thinking about these problems now. These code examples are only intended to show you how to use the JDBC API and to get you thinking about how to architect database applications with Java. *It is not intended to solve the many hard deployment, performance, or maintenance problems which plague real world systems.* As we'll see in Chapter 11, the Java platform already provides a very good solution to these hurdles.

One thing that may look like a serious omission is the complete lack of pricing and payment systems. We have no idea how much it costs to make a pie or how much we charge for it. Even if we had a price, there is no way for the customer to pay us! While this may look like a big thing to miss during the requirements analysis phase of the project, it is actually by design. The Pie à la Modem Baking Company has seen how many companies have made it big by giving away their products for free on the Internet. Pie à la Modem thinks that this strategy could make them the de facto standard baked goods company. While giving away product has worked well for some (but certainly not all) of the software companies that have tried it, it remains to be seen if the same pricing scheme will work when real production and shipping costs are involved.

JDBC 2.0

By providing a standard way to access any SQL database, JDBC 1.0 fulfilled a great need in the Java platform. However, JDBC 1.0 was lacking several important and useful features found in most database access APIs. For example, JDBC 1.0 supported only unidirectional, forward scrolling cursors, there was no support for batch updates to a database, and other common operations were missing. These lacks have been corrected in JDBC 2.0, a new set of core Java APIs and standard extensions.

JDBC 2.0 was designed with several major goals in mind. First, JDBC 2.0 is backwards compatible with JDBC 1.0 applications and drivers. Existing JDBC code should run without modification in a new JDBC 2.0 system. Second, JDBC 2.0 supports new advanced database features such as SQL3 datatypes, arrays, and direct support for BLOBs and CLOBs. Third, JDBC 2.0 provides support for

JavaBeans with the new RowSet class. Other goals included maintaining JDBC 1.0's easy-to-use API structure, minimizing conceptual changes in the new APIs, and providing access to other new Java Enterprise APIs like Java Naming and Directory Interface, Java Transaction Service, and Enterprise JavaBeans. The major new features implemented in JDBC 2.0 are:

- ResultSet enhancements—JDBC 2.0 ResultSets support bi-directional scrolling cursors and the scroll-sensitive ResultSets which allow an application to see changes made to the data after the ResultSet has been returned.

- Batch updates—inserts, updates, and deletes can be batched in a single database request, providing a potentially large performance gain in some applications and finer control over transaction commit and rollback in others.

- New data types—JDBC 2.0 now support SQL3 data types, storing Java objects in an RDBMS, user defined datatypes, and customizable mappings between SQL3 structured types and Java classes.

- RowSets—a class which encapsulates a set of rows, allowing serialization of results from the database and limited disconnected operation on that data.

- JNDI naming—while the URL syntax used to locate database in JDBC 1.0 has worked well, the new JNDI service provides a much more manageable way to name network resources. JDBC 2.0 applications can use JNDI to insulate themselves from the JDBC driver and URL.

- Connection Pooling—a JDBC application can now "pool" many user sessions into a single database connection, saving the expensive server side resources needed to support each individual connection.

- Distributed Transactions—JDBC 2.0 also supports standard two-phase commit protocols (via the Java Transaction Service) to guarantee the integrity of transactions which span multiple databases.

New Packages

The JDBC 2.0 APIs have been divided into two packages: additions to the existing java.sql package and a new javax.sql package. Any new features which required additions or extensions to existing classes or interface were included in java.sql. Features which were fundamentally new, such as the interfaces to JTS and JNDI and the new Array, BLOB, and CLOB data types, reside in the new javax.sql package. The designers of JDBC 2.0 have been careful to avoid modifying any existing interface or class in a way which would break backwards compatibility.

Where Can You Use JDBC 2.0?

Since JDBC 2.0 is part of the new Java 2, your JDBC 2.0 application probably will not run on older Web browsers and other existent Java implementations. Your clients must support Java 2 to support JDBC 2.0. For stand-alone applications you always have to option of distributing the needed JRE version with your application. If your application must run in client Web browsers, you may want to consider using the Java Plug-in to bundle the needed JRE with your applet.

Using Scrolling ResultSets

The JDBC 1.0 ResultSet was forward-only and used read-only concurrency. That means that you could only read the results of a query from first to last, reading each row only once, and changes made to the underlying database can not be seen from the application. JDBC 2.0 continues to provide this simple ResultSet and adds two new types of ResultSets: the scroll-insensitive and the scroll-sensitive. A scroll-insensitive ResultSet can move both forwards and backwards through its rows and also supports absolute and relative positioning of the cursor (move to the fifth row, move backwards two rows). A scroll-insensitive ResultSet cannot see changes to the underlying database. A scroll-sensitive ResultSet, on the other hand, not only scrolls backwards and forwards through the returned rows, it will automatically update itself if any row it contains changes in the database.

You choose which type of ResultSet you want by providing two new parameters to the Connection.createStatement and Connection.prepareStatement methods. These two parameters specify the resultSetType and resultSetConcurrency. They are used as follows:

```
Statement stmt = con.createStatement(ResultSet.TYPE_SCROLL_SENSITIVE,
                        ResultSet.CONCUR_READ_ONLY);
```

This would create a scrollable, insensitive ResultSet. These parameters can also be used in the Connection.prepareStatement call. Calling createStatement without these two parameters will create a good old JDBC 1.0 style forward-only, insensitive ResultSet.

Once you have a ResultSet you can move through it by using the ResultSet.next method, just as you did in JDBC 1.0. If the ResultSet is scrollable, you can also use any of several new methods to navigate through the returned rows. For example, if rs is a scrollable ResultSet, `rs.first()` moves to the first row in the ResultSet. `rs.absolute(10)` moves to the tenth row. `rs.relative(3)` moves forward three rows.

One danger with scrollable a ResultSet is that you never know ahead of time how many rows will be returned by a query. Can your network, client PC, and application really handle a 10 million row ResultSet in one chunk? Probably not. Fortunately, there is a simple way to limit how many rows will actually be returned by a query at one time. The `stmt.setFetchSize` method allows you to limit the number of rows returned in one gulp to a reasonable number.

If the ResultSet is updatable (`ResultSet.CONCUR_UPDATABLE`) you can update the contents of a row by moving to that row and calling one of the updateXXX methods. For example,

```
rs.first();
rs.updateString("pie", "Banana Cream");
rs.updateRow();
```

will change the value of the "pie" column to "Banana Cream". Just as there are setXXX and getXXX methods for all the basic SQL datatypes, there is an update-XXX method for each type. No change is made to the database until the updateRow method is called. At any point up to the call to updateRow, you can cancel the changes by calling cancelRowUpdates.

You can insert a new row into a ResultSet by first moving to the special InsertRow in the ResultSet and then using the updateXXX methods to set the column values. The insertRow method is used to update the database. Similarly, the deleteRow method will remove a row from the database.

Batch Updates

For performance reasons, it is often desirable to send insert, update, and delete requests to a database as a single command. JDBC 2.0 now supports this capability with the Statement.addBatch method. If stmt is a Statement object the following code will insert several rows into the Inventory and Products tables:

```
stmt.addBatch(
    "INSERT INTO Products (Pie, ProductNumber) VALUES ('Banana Cream',
                                                        10)");
stmt.addBatch(
    "INSERT INTO Inventory (Ingredient, Quantity) VALUES ('Bananas', 50)");
int [] updateCounts = stmt.executeBatch();
```

The executeBatch method returns an array of integers. Each element of that array indicates how many rows of a table were affected by the update. The batch statements are executed in the order in which they were added to the batch. If any of the statements fails, a BatchUpdateException is thrown and the remaining updates are ignored. By catching the BatchUpdateException you can roll back the updates which did complete, providing some level of transactional integrity.

Batch updates can also be used with PreparedStatements. This provides a very convenient and efficient way to perform multiple updates against a table.

```
PreparedStatement pStmt = con.prepareStatement(
            "DELETE FROM Inventory WHERE NAME = ?");

Enumeration e = v.elements();
while (e.hasMoreElements()) {
    pStmt.setString(1, (String) e.nextElement());
    pStmt.addBatch();
}
int [] updateCounts = pStmt.executeBatch();
```

Summary

JDBC provides a simple and flexible way to use relational databases in Java applications. This enables both new Java applications which use the power of RDBMSs and gives Java systems access to use legacy data in existing databases. When combined with clean three-tiered design, JDBC enables data service managers which can be used by many applications and by developers who may not be skilled in SQL, database design, or administration.

CHAPTER

9

Servlets and the
Java Web Server

Introduction

The Web has undergone a rapid transformation from a simple publishing medium to a sophisticated application environment. More and more of the Web's content has moved from rarely changing HTML files to dynamically generated pages which are displayed once and thrown away. Many sites, especially large retail sites which must deal with constantly changing inventory and prices, consist entirely of dynamically generated pages, with no HTML files at all.

Dynamically generated content has many advantages: There is no version control of HTML files, pages can better reflect a changing environment, and content can be tailored to each visitor. There is, however, one drawback. Dynamically generated sites require much more sophisticated programming to create and deliver their content. While static HTML pages can be created by graphics artists, copy writers, and other non-technical staff, dynamically generated sites require tools like Perl, TCL, and CGI, and the people who know how to use them. The new Java Servlet API and the Java Web Server can help these technical content developers by giving them an easy-to-use, powerful, flexible Java platform for building Web pages on-the-fly.

The Java Web Server Platform

There are several reasons for the popularity of the Java platform in end-user applications and the client side of distributed applications. The Java language automates many of the more tedious programming tasks, like memory management, freeing the programmer to concentrate on the actual application, not on the details of language trivia. Java core classes contain many useful data manipulation and storage classes, further reducing the amount of non-application-specific code the programmer must write. Finally, Write Once, Run Anywhere puts an end to the many porting efforts required to support every possible client.

Developers of the server side of an application can also benefit from these features. They receive the same productivity benefits from the Java language and classes. And while server-side programmers must frequently handle details of file systems and OS-specific structures, like configuration files and port numbers, with a little caution and forethought, server applications written to the Java platform can also be made to run anywhere. Mid-tier components, which can use the Java Enterprise APIs to insulate themselves from OS details, can often be made as platform-independent as client-side applets are. For organizations which might be forced to develop on a different platform than the deployment platform—for example, a small development shop equipped with Windows NT PCs but which must deploy on UNIX machines managed by an ISP—Write Once, Run Anywhere server components are as important as Write Once, Run Anywhere client applets. OS-independent server components also allow the IT organization more flexibility in moving to new server systems, since critical business applications are no longer tied to a single hardware/OS combination.

This chapter discusses a new Java standard extension API for writing servlets, server components which can be used to generate HTML pages dynamically, act as front ends for databases, rendezvous points for distributed applications, and other mid-tier functions. The Servlet API is implemented by the Java Web Server, a Run Anywhere HTTP server written entirely in Java.

Advantages of Servlets

One of the first major innovations on the World Wide Web was the Common Gateway Interface (CGI). Before CGI the Web was a very static medium. Information was published in the form of unchanging pages of text and pictures. CGI gave Web masters the ability to generate HTML pages dynamically. Not only could Web content be customized for each user, but also users could send information back to the HTTP server. This two-way flow of data changed the Web from a simple publishing tool into an application delivery mechanism for electronic commerce, intranet applications, and other transactional tools.

Performance

Having been added to the existing set of Web protocols almost as an after-thought, CGI has several flaws, the most obvious of which is performance. The simplest way to implement CGI in existing HTTP servers was to have the server create a new process, hand the calling parameters into the CGI script running in that process, then read the resulting HTML page from the process and return it to the invoking Web browser. This sequence of forking a process, executing the script, reading back the results, and cleaning up the now unneeded process was very inefficient. Web servers which primarily serve up dynamic pages generated by CGI could spend as much time on operating system overhead as they did serving pages.

Several companies have developed extensions to the basic HTTP server intended to overcome CGI's performance problem. Netscape, Microsoft, and others have introduced systems based on shared libraries, DLLs, and socket protocols which replace the dynamically invoked CGI script. While these systems fixed CGI's performance problems, they did so at a price. Each system introduced proprietary APIs which tied the resulting code to a single platform. The new Java Servlet API also solves the performance problems associated with CGI, but without introducing the proprietary APIs which limited the usefulness of other systems. Tests on live, production servlet systems show servlet invocation can be up to 30 times faster than CGI. Servlets are an open Java API and are supported on many HTTP servers. This extends the basic Write Once, Run Anywhere to the backend of the Web.

In practice, a servlet works in much the same way as a CGI page generator. A servlet is a Java class which is loaded into a Web server and, in response to an HTTP request to its host Web server, uses local information, parameters passed in from the requesting browser, and other resources to build an HTML page or other recognizable type of response and returns that page to the server. Since the servlet runs in the same process and address space as its host Web server, there is very little interprocess overhead associated with calling a servlet. The HTTP server simply invokes the servlet in a separate thread and forwards the results to the requesting Web browser. This is much faster than the fork/exec/ clean-up sequence required by typical CGI.

Ease of Use

Ease of use was another drawback to traditional CGI scripts. User parameters were either appended, as name/value pairs, to the URL used to call the CGI script or included in HTML POST or GET requests. The CGI script then had to parse the parameters, do its processing, then write the resulting information, along with the type of the response, back to the HTTP server. Extensions found in some vendors' Web servers, like Perl subroutines for parsing parameters, solved the ease-of-use problem, but again at the cost of introducing proprietary interfaces. Non-platform-specific parsers have been written for some of the common CGI languages, like TCL, C, and various shell languages, but these often were unsupported shareware, not ported to every platform or not available for every language.

Servlets address this problem by providing parameters to the servlet in pre-parsed hash tables. These hash tables provide easy access to user information passed to the servlet.

Security

CGI also suffers from several widely reported security problems. Since CGI scripts are frequently written in languages which do not share the safety features of Java, it is often too easy to cause these scripts to fail by overrunning memory buffers or causing other internal errors. If these scripts can be made to fail in a predictable way, these failures can be used to attack the security of the HTTP site. Since servlets are written in the inherently safer Java language, these kinds of attacks are much less likely to succeed. Web servers which implement servlets and Java 2 can use protection domains to implement application-specific security policies.

A Simple Servlet

Here is a simple servlet that dynamically generates an HTML page which contains the current date and time along with a random phrase:

```
Source Code: PhraseServlet.java
import javax.servlet.*;
import javax.servlet.http.*;
import java.io.*;
import java.util.Date;
import java.lang.Math;

public class PhraseServlet extends HttpServlet {

    // Set up an array of adjectives to describe the state the
    // web server.
    String [] adjectives = {"happy",
                            "sad",
                            "thrilled",
                            "annoyed",
                            "pained"};

    // Set up an array of adverbs to modify the adjectives.
    String [] adverbs = {"very",
```

```
                                 "slightly",
                                 "a little",
                                 "totally"};

  // The doGet method is called whenever the Servlet is invoked via
  // an HTTP GET.
  public void doGet(HttpServletRequest req, HttpServletResponse res)
   throws ServletException, IOException {
    Date now = new Date();
    res.setContentType("text/html");

    PrintWriter out = res.getWriter();

    out.println("<HTML><HEAD><TITLE>Phrase Servlet</TITLE></HEAD>");
    out.println("<BODY BGCOLOR=#FFFFFF><CENTER><P>");
    out.println("At ");
    out.println(now.toString());
    out.println(" this web server is feeling ");
    out.println(adverbs[(int) (Math.random() * adverbs.length)] + " " );
    out.println(adjectives[(int) (Math.random() * adjectives.length)] +
                                                            ".");

    out.println("</P></CENTER></BODY></HTML>");

    out.flush();
    out.close();
    }
}
```

When this servlet is run, it returns a randomly generated HTML page, which looks something like this:

```
<HTML><HEAD><TITLE>Phrase Servlet</TITLE></HEAD>
<BODY BGCOLOR=#FFFFFF><CENTER><P>
At
Fri Jul 24 17:03:45 EDT 1998
 this web server is feeling
very
happy.
</P></CENTER></BODY></HTML>
```

Anatomy of an HTTP Servlet

This very simple example demonstrates the basic features common to all servlets. First, notice that we import two packages: javax.servlet.* and javax.servlet.http.*. The Java Server extension contained in the class javax.servlet is a generic framework for building servers and daemons. It contains APIs for processing service requests, plugging into management structures, dispatching worker threads, and other common server tasks. The javax.server.http package, which is the focus of this chapter, is an implementation of Java servlets specifically tailored for Web servers and HTML page generation.

The doXXX Methods

In order to do anything useful, a servlet will usually override the doGet method in HttpServlet. doGet is invoked by the Web server each time a client browser requests, via an HTTP GET request, access to a URL which maps to that servlet. HttpServlet defines doXXX methods which correspond to other HTTP requests, including doDelete, doOptions, doPost, doPut, and doTrace. Any or all of these can be overridden by a servlet to support different types of HTTP access.

The doXXX methods take two arguments: a ServletRequest, which by convention is called req and a ServletResponse, typically called res. These two classes contain methods and state variables which allow the servlet to communicate with its host Web server. Figure 9.1 shows how the ServletRequest and ServletResponse objects are used. The doXXX methods must be declared to throw two exceptions: ServletException and IOException. The following doGet method shows a typical method signature.

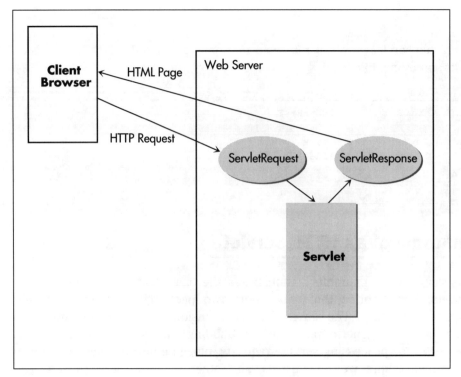

Figure 9.1 A Web server with embedded servlet.

```
public void doGet(HttpServletRequest req, HttpServletResponse res)
   throws ServletException, IOException {
```

The ServletRequest class contains all the information the servlet needs regarding the current request. This class has methods which return a dictionary of all parameters supplied to this request by the client Web browser. The class also contains methods for looking up a particular parameter, the identity of the remote host making the HTTP request, and other information useful to the servlet. While this extremely simple example does not use any of the services provided by the ServletRequest object, we will use this object in later examples.

The ServletResponse class allows the servlet to return its results to the Web server. The previous simple servlet example uses two of ServletResponse's methods. The setContentType(String) method is used to indicate the type of information the servlet is returning. Allowable types include text/html, text/plain, and other MIME types. Here we used text/html to return our dynamically generated HTML page.

```
res.setContentType("text/html");
```

The other important method in the ServletResponse is getWriter( ). This method returns a PrintWriter associated with an OutputStream, which the servlet uses to write its results back to the Web server. The servlet does whatever processing is needed to create an HTML page in response to the request, then writes the HTML code to the PrintWriter.

```
PrintWriter out = res.getWriter();
```

The ServletResponse object has another method, getOutputStream, which returns a raw ServletOutputStream. If your server generates textual information such as HTML pages or plain text, the PrintWriter returned by getWriter is usually more convenient. If your servlet generates images, datastreams, or other nontextual data, use the ServletOutputStream returned by getOutputStream.

TIP This output stream can be used to return just a part of a page at a time. This is useful when it might take a long time to build the entire page. For example, if the servlet uses several databases to build its response, it can write the header and beginning of the HTML page to the output stream before accessing the databases. This will improve the perception of performance by allowing the requesting Web browser to begin to render the page, giving the user some immediate feedback that something is happening.

Building HTML Pages

Servlets can return any type of information that they want to: images, data streams, whatever. In this case, we are generating a Web page, using standard

HTML. All we have to do in the body of the doGet method is generate a properly formed HTML page and write it to the output stream:

```
out.println("<HTML><HEAD><TITLE>Phrase Servlet</TITLE></HEAD>");
out.println("<BODY BGCOLOR=#FFFFFF><CENTER><P>");
out.println("At ");
out.println(now.toString());
out.println(" this web server is feeling ");
out.println(adverbs[(int) (Math.random() * adverbs.length)] + " " );
out.println(adjectives[(int) (Math.random() * adjectives.length)] + ".");
out.println("</P></CENTER></BODY></HTML>");
```

In this simple example, we write the HTML, with the results of some simple calculations, to the output, then flush the stream. In a more complicated application, we could implement an on-line shopping catalog, a new human resources system, or any other type of application.

Installing the Servlet

Before running our servlet, it must be installed in a servlet-capable Web server. Sun's Java Web Server is one Web Server that supports the servlet APIs. For the rest of this chapter, we will use the Java Web Server to deploy and run our servlets.

Servlets can be installed in the Java Web Server either at startup, as permanent features of the server, or dynamically, allowing for new servlets to be added to a system without the need to restart the server and allowing clients to load servlets into the Java Web Server over the network. We will first load PhraseServlet into the server for testing, then give it a name on the server and arrange for it to be loaded at startup.

We must make our servlet's class file or files available to the Web server. The Java Web Server can load a servlet class file from one of three sources: its CLASSPATH, a special directory called servlets, or from a URL. Servlets loaded from the CLASSPATH are equivalent to a class loaded into a Java application from the CLASSPATH. It has whatever permissions are associated with being loaded from the local file system and is loaded once, when first invoked. Servlets loaded from the servlets directory are loaded via a special Class-Loader; they can be dynamically reloaded while the server is running. Servlets loaded from a URL need not reside on the local machine and will be contained by the SecurityManager (under JDK 1.1) or protection domain (under Java 2) appropriate for their codebase and signatures.

We will want to load our servlet from the servlets directory. This directory is found in the Java Web Servers top-level directory; for example, on a Solaris machine it could be /opt/JavaWebServer1.1/servlets. Copy PhraseServlet.class into that directory.

The servlet can now be accessed through the URL <machine>:<port>/ servlet/PhraseServlet. When Java Web Server receives a request for this URL, it uses an internal servlet called invoker to load the PhraseServlet class, builds appropriate ServletRequest and ServletResponse objects, and uses them as arguments to PhraseServlet's service methods. Then, just as with CGI scripts, the servlet's output is returned, via HTTP, to the requesting Web browser (see Figure 9.2).

TIP Since servlet classes loaded from the servlets directory can be dynamically reloaded, you can use the invoker as a handy test harness for servlet debugging. Simply copy the servlet's classes to <serverhome>/servlets and reload the page in your Web browser. The invoker servlet will notice that a newer version of the servlet is available, reload the classes, and run your new code.

Permanently Installing a Servlet

Next we will permanently install the servlet in our Web server. Here we will do two things. We will have the servlet loaded when Web server starts, reducing latency, and assign an alias to servlet. This alias allows us to give another name to the servlet, possibly a name with an .html extension. This disguises

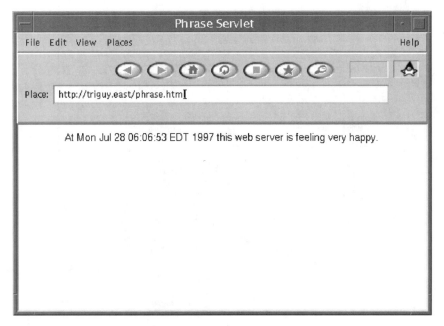

Figure 9.2 Output from the PhraseServlet.

the fact that a URL points to a servlet instead of a regular HTML page. More important, it allows us to hide the name of the classes which implement the servlet. What would happen if we were to publish the /server/PhraseServlet URL for our servlet, then three months later change the implementation class to HappyPhraseServlet? Updating all our cross-links and bookmarks is a headache most of us would like to avoid. By hiding the implementation classes, an alias allows us to sidestep this problem.

The Java Web Server includes a set of administrative applets which we will use to install our servlet. These applets are, by default, found at http://<machine>:9090/. If port 9090 is not available on your machine, the port number for the administrative applets can be changed. Accessing this URL brings up the admin applet's login screen, shown in Figure 9.3. When first installed, the user and password are set to admin and admin. These applets allow anyone who can

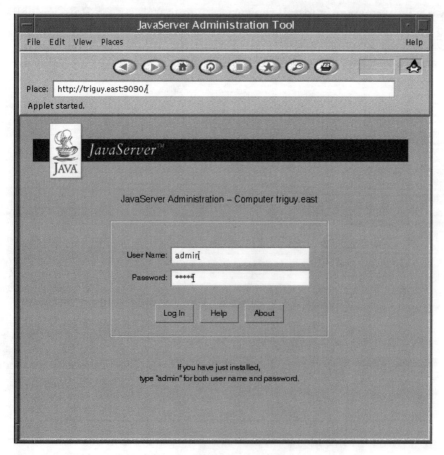

Figure 9.3   The Java Web Server administration login.

access port 9090 on your machine to administer your Web server, so you should change at least the admin password as soon as you install the Web server.

Once you've logged in, you'll see a table listing all the services managed by these applets. Note that the Java Web Server is actually a collection of possible services. In addition to the regular Web server, we could also start an SSL-enabled secure server and a proxy server. Select Web Service from the list and press the Manage button. This will bring up the popup shown in Figure 9.4.

Select the Servlets tool from the upper tool bar. This will bring up a list of all servlets known to the system. First, we will add the PhraseServlet to this list, then set some options on how it should be loaded. Select Add from the list and enter "phrase" as the Servlet Name and "PhraseServlet" as the Servlet Class. Pressing Add will then bring up the screen shown in Figure 9.5. On this screen, we can provide a short description of the servlet, like "Returns a random

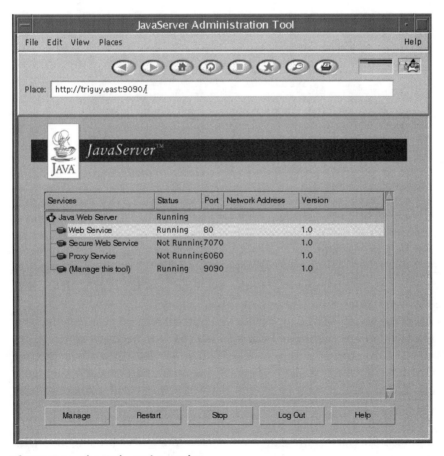

Figure 9.4 The Web service applet.

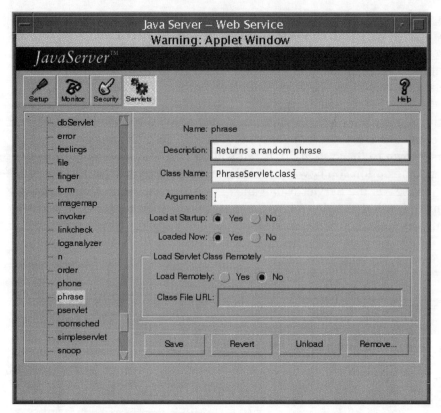

Figure 9.5   The Servlet administration applet.

phrase," and set any properties the servlet needs at startup. The last thing we'll do on this screen is tell the server to always load this servlet, using the Load at Startup radio button. After completing this screen, hit the Save button in the lower button bar. We can now access our servlet through the URL http:// <machine><:port>/servlet/phrase. By using this URL in all pages that reference this servlet, we isolate ourselves from the class name of the servlet. If we ever change the class name of our servlet, the alias "phrase" will remain valid.

Now that the servlet is configured into the Web server and given an alias, we may optionally define an alternate URL we want to use to access this servlet. To do this, select Setup from the upper tool bar, then Servlet Aliases from the tree view on the left side of the applet. This will bring up the screen shown in Figure 9.6. Select Add to create a new entry in the list of aliases. Under Alias enter an appropriate alias, like "/phrase.html," for this servlet. Under Servlet Invoked enter "phrase" (this is the name we gave PhraseServlet in the Servlet administration applet). Hit Save. We can now access our servlet using the URL http://<machine>:<port>/phrase.html.

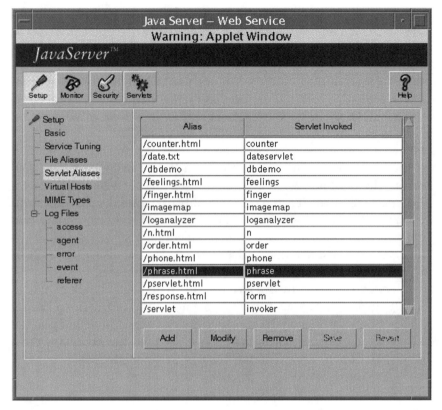

Figure 9.6   Servlet alias Administration.

Some Considerations with Java Web Server

Having a Web server written entirely in the Java language and extensible with Java servlets raises a couple of considerations which we should examine. Thread safety, overall site security, and performance are all important issues which are subtly different in the Java environment than they are in traditional CGI services.

Thread Safety

The Java Web Server is multithreaded and can simultaneously handle connections from many different clients. When Java Web Server first starts, it creates an acceptor thread and a working pool of handler threads. The acceptor thread sits in a tight loop listening for incoming connections. Upon receiving a request, the acceptor thread passes it to one of the handler threads in the pool. If no idle handler thread exists, the acceptor will create a new thread to handle the request. There is a tunable limit on the maximum number of handler threads that may exist. If there are no idle handlers and this maximum has already been reached, the server will block until a handler becomes available. Unused handler threads will expire if left idle for too long. Another tunable parameter limits the minimum number of handlers that will always be kept alive.

There is a chance that a servlet could be invoked by two separate handler threads at the same time. Since the servlet is a thread inside the Java Web Server, each servlet must be made thread safe. Calls to a servlet's doXXX methods are not synchronized, so it is the responsibility of the servlet's developer to ensure that any critical code sections or shared internal state is properly protected from concurrent access. Each thread executing a servlet gets its own copy of the ServletRequest and ServletResponse, so two simultaneous calls to a servlet will not trash each other's input and output parameters.

The javax.servlet package provides an easy way to implement a single thread servlet. Simply declare that your servlet implements the SingleThreadModel interface. This empty interface tells the servlet's container (in this case, the Java Web Server) that the servlet is not thread safe and the container must ensure that no two threads are executing the servlet simultaneously.

```
public class MyServlet extends HttpServlet
    implements SingleThreadModel {
```

Concurrency was usually not an issue with CGI. Because the Web server forked a separate process for each request, there were no concurrency problems. It is only because servlets exist as separate threads, all sharing the same address space, inside the Java Web Server that threads safety is required.

Security

Servlets can be dynamically downloaded from the Internet, just as applets can be loaded into a Web browser. The servlet administrative applet shown in Figure 9.5 includes an option to load a servlet from any URL, not just a local file. This mobile code, coming from a potentially untrusted source, raises the same security issues that applets do. How can an untrusted piece of code be allowed to execute on a server without compromising security? This question is even more important for servlets than it is for applets. A break-in to a server is usually far more dangerous than a break-in to a desktop, since servers usually contain greater quantities of more valuable data than desktops do.

Just as Web browsers use protection domains and the Sandbox policy to protect the client machine, the Java Web Server can use protection domains to isolate untrusted servlets from vulnerable server-side resources. All untrusted servlets are run in a separate thread group and are restricted by the site's security policy. Servlets can also be signed and JAR'ed, just like applets. The site can define separate policies for each supplier of signed servlets, perhaps allowing one customer free access to a directory or database reserved for that customer while blocking all access to resources devoted to other customers. See Chapter 12 for details on how to implement protection domains and other security considerations.

Performance

Can a Web server entirely written in Java keep up the demands of a heavily loaded Web site? Is Java fast enough to be a reasonable implementation platform for high-demand services? Recent testing with the Java Web Server indicates that for many sites performance is acceptable. The Java Web Server, running on a mid-range SPARC desktop, generated a SPECweb96 rating of 606 operations per second, a figure which translates to roughly 50 million hits per day. Even at the highest load, latency was below 10 milliseconds. While this figure is roughly half the performance found in competitive servers, 50 million hits per day is enough throughput for many sites. Also, remember that this is the first generation for this product. With advances in both Java execution technology, like HotSpot, and in the tuning of the Java Web Server itself, we can expect a large increase in Java Web Server's performance.

BUT I DON'T USE THE JAVA WEB SERVER

All this sounds great, but there is just one problem. What if you don't use the Java Web Server at your site? If your current Web server has been in place for years, has never caused any problems, and you have a large investment in backend CGI scripts or add-on software for this server, you are very unlikely to move to a new Web server just to get the benefit of servlets.

For those who do not wish to switch servers, servlet extensions are available for several popular Web servers, which allows those servers to host servlets including Netscape's Enterprise server, Microsoft's IIS, and the Apache Web server. These extensions allow you to take advantage of servlets without changing your current Web architecture.

Core Servlets

Parts of the Java Web Server are actually implemented by special servlets known as the core servlets. We already used the invoker when we were testing our first servlet. The ssinclude is another example of a core servlet. It is invoked whenever a page containing server-side includes (indicated by the page ending in a .shtml) is encountered. The ssinclude servlet takes care of processing the server-side includes and outputting the final page. Other core servlets include the file and image map servlets, which handle requests for static files and for server-side image maps.

User Input

One of the most common uses of dynamic page generation is to process input from HTML forms. In this case, simple forms, consisting of text fields, pull-down menus, and other GUI elements are used to collect information from the user. This information is then bundled into an HTTP GET or POST request which invokes the appropriate program on the Web server. The program uses this input to form database queries, look up files, place orders for goods, or to take other actions. The program returns the requested information or a confirmation that the order has been placed in an HTML page.

The servlet API facilitates this kind of user interaction by providing an easy mechanism for receiving and parsing input from HTML forms. Remember that when a servlet is invoked, it is handed a ServletRequest object which contains information about the request. The ServletRequest object contains several methods for reading input parameters passed to the servlet. The servlet can use ServletRequest's getParameterNames method to find out all the parameters available in the request and getParameterValues( ) to find out the value of a particular parameter.

Here is a simple servlet which takes input from an HTML form and uses it to construct a response:

```
Source Code: FormServlet.java
import java.io.*;
import java.util.*;
import javax.servlet.*;
import javax.servlet.http.*;

public class FormServlet extends HttpServlet
{

    public void doPost(HttpServletRequest req, HttpServletResponse res)
        throws ServletException
```

```
    {
        PrintWriter out = null;
        try {
            // first, set the "content type" header of the response
            res.setContentType("text/html");

            //Get the response's PrintWriter to return text to the client.
            out = res.getWriter();

            out.println(
                    "<HTML><HEAD><TITLE>FormServlet output</TITLE></HEAD>");
            out.println("<BODY BGCOLOR=#FFFFFF><P>");

            // Get the emotion parameter.  If it's null or if the
            // first String in the array has a length of 0, then
            // nothing was entered.
            String [] emot = req.getParameterValues("emotion");
            if (emot != null && emot[0].length() != 0) {
                out.println("Today you are feeling " + emot[0] + ".");
            } else {
                out.println("Nothing entered. Are you feeling quite
                                                        today?");

            }
            out.println("<BR><BR>");

            // Get the days parameter. If days is null, then
            // nothing was checked.
            String [] days = req.getParameterValues("days");
            if (days != null) {
                out.println("One these days you usually feel
                                                happy:<BR><UL>");
                for (int i = 0 ; i < days.length; i++) {
                out.println("<LI>" + days[i] + "</LI>");
                }
                out.println("</UL>");
            } else {
                out.println("No days checked. Aren't you ever happy?");
            }
        } catch(Exception e) {
            e.printStackTrace();
            out.println(e);
        }

        out.println("</BODY></HTML>");
        // Close the writer; the response is done.
        out.flush();
        out.close();
    }
}
```

And here is a simple HTML page which could be used to invoke the servlet:

Source Code: paramtst.html

```
<HTML>
<HEAD>
<TITLE>Survey</TITLE>
</HEAD>

  <BODY>
     <FORM ACTION=/servlet/ForServlet method=POST>

     <BR><BR>How do you feel today?<BR>
       <BR><input type=text name=emotion>

     <BRBR>On which days are you usually happy?<BR>
       <BR>Sunday<INPUT TYPE=checkbox NAME=days VALUE=Sunday>
       <BR>Monday<INPUT TYPE=checkbox NAME=days VALUE=Monday>
       <BR>Tuesday<INPUT TYPE=checkbox NAME=days VALUE=Tuesday>
       <BR>Wednesday<INPUT TYPE=checkbox NAME=days VALUE=Wednesday>
       <BR>Thursday<INPUT TYPE=checkbox NAME=days VALUE=Thursday>
       <BR>Friday<INPUT TYPE=checkbox NAME=days VALUE=Friday>
       <BR>Saturday<INPUT TYPE=checkbox NAME=days VALUE=Saturday>

     <BR><BR><INPUT TYPE=submit><INPUT TYPE=reset>
    </FORM>
  </BODY>
</HTML>
```

Using getParameterValues

getParameterValues takes a String, the name of the parameter, and returns an array of Strings containing the values set for that parameter. This means that even if you absolutely know the parameter will only have one value, you still have to pull that value out of the array:

```
String s = req.getParameterValues("test")[0];
```

You must do this because some HTML form elements work by assigning multiple values to a single parameter name, like the checkbox shown earlier. The getParameterValues method simply bundles up all the values associated with the parameter name and returns them in the String array. This simplifies the API by allowing one method to handle both single-valued and multi-valued parameters. It also makes parameters a bit more self-describing without having to define a Reflection API to tell you where the parameter came from or how many values it contains. This ability can be used in conjunction with the getParameterNames method to allow your servlet to discover parameters it might not be expecting in the request.

There is always the chance a user will leave a field blank. In this case, we must test to see not only that the parameter's name exists, but also that the parameter has a valid value. We do this by testing getParameterValues's returned String array. Typically, if the array is null or if the first String has zero length, the corresponding form field was left blank.

Why Use Servlets Instead of Applets?

If legacy systems have already been modified to accept network connections or other programmatic ways to use their services, why should you use a servlet to access those systems? Won't it be easier to use an applet to talk directly to the service, skipping the servlet entirely? Won't an applet allow you to give the user a better visual presentation than you could accomplish with HTML? Won't an applet move some of the processing load off your hardware and onto the user's machine, reducing your costs? The answer to all these questions is "Yes" and we expect that many applications will consist of an applet using CORBA, RMI, or an ad hoc protocol to connect to backend services. While this may be the typical use of Java in distributed applications, there are several reasons for using a servlet as middleware, instead of allowing an applet direct access to legacy systems.

Applet Security

When choosing between applets and servlets, security is always a primary concern. The application designer must be aware of both the end user's security issues and of server-side concerns which arise from giving outsiders access to our systems. These security issues also raise questions about ease of use and accessibility for the end user.

For the end user, the first question that must be asked is, "How much do I trust the publisher of this applet?" If you, as an application designer, use an applet to talk with several backend systems, you assume that the end user trusts you enough to accept your digital signature on these applets and exempt your applets from the "only phone home" policy. For many systems, like Internet catalogs and other e-commerce systems, assuming this level of trust may not be appropriate. An Internet catalog depends heavily on impulse buyers who stumble upon the site ready to buy. If you force these users to first look up a secure copy of your public key and configure it into their browser before making purchases, users may become frustrated with the process and move on to another site. For these impulse buyers, lowering the entry barriers to a site is critical.

The end-user security issue also brings up the question of how much access do you really need to a user's machine? In general, an application designer should request no more capabilities on the user's machine than are absolutely needed to accomplish the job at hand. Gratuitously forcing the end user to obtain and manage public keys, without a clear need in the application for that kind of access, not only weakens the user's security, it also annoys and alienates a large section of the user population. If you can accomplish your task without leaving the confines of the Sandbox policy, your application should not ask the user for any more rights or privileges.

Web application designers should keep in mind the security considerations of their end users and avoid burdening their applications with unneeded signatures. For many simple applications a servlet, which runs on the publisher's machine and adds no security burden to the end user, is the perfect solution to this problem. The servlet can either work in conjunction with an applet, acting as a proxy to backend service distributed across several machines, or it can generate HTML responses from information provided by those services.

Server Security

As business systems migrate onto the Internet, backend security becomes more and more difficult to manage. Internet security used to consist of one heavily armored firewall machine screening the intranet from the Internet and passing through only a few well-defined protocols, like HTTP and e-mail. As e-commerce has become more sophisticated, the simple firewall has become more and more cumbersome. New applications and protocols either require holes in the firewall to allow them to operate or piggyback on HTTP. Both of these solutions decrease the effectiveness of corporate security, one by opening more routines through the firewall and thus potentially more holes, the other by masquerading forbidden services as the more acceptable HTTP. Since these piggyback requests usually go to a proxy on the Web server, which is not as tightly controlled as the firewall, they carry the potential for abuse.

Many companies are solving these problems with a two-tiered firewall solution which provides a so-called demilitarized zone or DMZ. The idea is to have two firewalls between the Internet and intranet. Web servers and other systems which must be available to the outside world sit between the two firewalls. The first firewall only allows through acceptable protocols like IMAP-4 and HTTP, thus allowing typical Internet service like Web servers and e-mail. The second firewall is more restrictive. It blocks all access from Internet machines and strictly limits the ports, protocols, and machines which can be accessed by machines living in the DMZ. By providing two layers of protection, DMZs make it more difficult for electronic thieves and vandals to reach critical business systems while still providing (limited) bidirectional access to the Internet. DMZ firewalls can either be implemented by two separate firewalls routing between the Internet, DMZ, and intranet or by some of the newer sophisticated firewall products which can create a virtual DMZ with a single box.

If a company has adopted a DMZ firewall, it may be difficult to architect an applet-based electronic commerce system. An applet, having crossed the Internet firewall and attempting to connect to a server in the corporation, would be blocked by the second firewall. Its requests would be coming from an untrusted host on the Internet and would not be allowed onto the intranet.

Servlets fit very well into this kind of an environment. A servlet can act as a proxy for the applet, forwarding requests through the second firewall to the backends. Since the servlet can be more closely controlled and the types of services it offers limited, this is a more secure solution than simply opening holes in the second firewall.

Intellectual Property

Protecting intellectual property is another important security consideration. Any executable content passed on to an end user's machine is vulnerable to decompilation. This is true whether the executable content is written in the Java language, Visual Basic, or any other language. While there are some programs which make decompilation harder, no system exists, or indeed can exist, which would make decompilation impossible.

This raises an important concern for many types of applications. If anyone on the Internet can get access to your source code, do you risk losing control of your intellectual property when you publish it as executable content? For some systems, the answer is a qualified "No." There is little a competitor could gain by decompiling your GUI code, so for simple applications there is little risk. But for those applications which contain a significant amount of business logic, such as investment analysis and rating systems, the risk may be much greater. For these systems, a competitor may gain a great deal by decompiling your executable and learning what the application does and how it is put together.

Servlets provide a good place to hide this proprietary business logic. Since the servlet never leaves its host Web server, it is not vulnerable to decompilation. Only the servlet's output is visible to the client, never the process by which it computed that output.

Ease of Development

For those applications which generate only simple tabular data or text output, an applet interface is often overkill. For many applications, especially those which involve only simple report generation, HTML is all that is needed to display their results. In these cases, a servlet may be chosen over an applet, simply to reduce the development time needed for the application. If the application does not require the GUI and local processing benefits provided by an applet, servlets may be an attractive alternative.

Network Limitations

Web applications designers must also worry about download times. For a user at the end of a 28.8 modem, a simple HTML page which requires only a few thousand bytes is often more desirable than a graphics-intensive applet which consumes hundreds of thousands of bytes. If an application does not require or use the benefits provided by an applet, a servlet is often the better solution. If an applet does not add value to a page, servlet-generated HTML will arrive faster, display on any device, and often can present the needed information just as effectively as an applet.

Using Init Parameters

In addition to parameters passed in with HTTP POST requests, the servlet classes support init parameters that can be set when installing the servlet into the Java Web Server. These parameters can be used to set runtime variables that may only be known at install time; for example, the JDBC URL for a database or other information you don't want to hard-code into the servlet.

Init parameters are passed to the servlet's init method in the ServletConfig object. They can be accessed using ServletConfig's getInitParameter method. Like getParameterValues, getInitParameter takes as an argument a single String that contains the name of the desired parameter. Unlike getParameterValues, getInitParameter returns a String, not an array of Strings. This is because an init parameter only has a single String as its value.

In the code shown next, we have modified PhraseServlet to take advantage of init parameters. Instead of hard-coding the value of the adjectives array, we'll build it in the init method by reading the init parameters. When we install the servlet, we'll define an arbitrary number of adjectives. Each adjective will be stored in a parameter with a name of the form emotX, where X is an integer starting with 0. Our init method will look for emot0, emot1, emot2, and so on. It stops looking after the first time it fails to find an appropriately named parameter. We set the parameters using the Servlet pane of the servlet admin tool (see Figure 9.7). Here is the init method for the class PhraseServlet2 (the rest of the servlet is identical to PhraseServlet.java).

> **TIP** When using init parameters, you cannot access your servlet via the http://<machine>:<port>/servlet/ClassName URL. You must explicitly configure the servlet into the Java Web Server and access it via the /servlet/alias URL. If you don't use the alias form of the URL, the invoker servlet won't know to read the needed init properties and pass them to the servlet's init method.

```
Source Code: PhraseServlet2.java init()
String [] adjectives;

init(ServletConfig config)
  throws ServletException {
    boolean haveAdjectives = false;
    boolean moreAdjectives = true;
    Vector v = new Vector();
    int i = 0;
    String s;
```

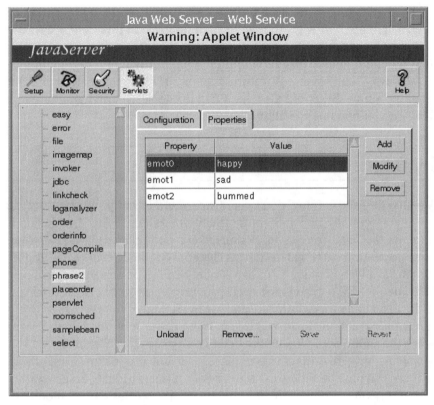

Figure 9.7   Phrase2 servlet.

```
while (moreAdjectives) {
  s = config.getInitParameter("emot" + i++);
  if (s != null) {
    v.addElement(s);
    haveAdjectives = true;
  } else {
    moreAdjectives = false;
  }
}

if (haveAdjectives) {
  adjectives = new String [v.size()];
  for (i = 0 ; i < v.size() ; i++) {
    adjectives[i] = (String) v.elementAt(i);
  }
} else {
  throw new UnavailableException(this, "No adjectives sets.");
}
}
```

There is a chance that something could go wrong during the initialization of our servlet. There are two ways to handle such failures. In this case, we throw an UnavailableException with a String argument that states why initialization failed. If someone requests this servlet after it has thrown an UnavailableException, the Java Web Server will return a simple HTML page containing the text of the exception. We could also set a flag in the servlet and generate our own HTML page explaining the failure.

Servlet Beans

I'll bet you see this one coming, don't you. Once you add init properties to your servlets, they essentially become configurable components that live inside a host container, the Java Web Server. Sounds like a job for JavaBeans, doesn't it. JavaBeans is a natural extension to the servlet concept, and JavaBeans support was added in Java Web Server 1.1. To use servlet beans, you simply define a pair of getXXX and setXXX methods for each property your servlet bean requires, package the bean in a proper JAR file, and set Bean Servlet to "Yes" when using the admin applet to add the bean to the Java Web Server. After loading the bean, you can use the admin applet to set the bean's properties (see Figure 9.8).

Servlet beans have two major advantages over init properties. First, while init properties can only be set during the servlet's initialization, bean properties can be set at any time. This means that the bean's properties can be modified, on-the-fly, while it is running. You don't need to unload and reload the servlet or restart the Web server to get it to reread the properties. The second major advantage is that, like all JavaBeans, servlet beans are self-describing. When someone installing your servlet bean presses the Properties tab, the properties list is automatically populated with every property used in your bean, along with the default value. This greatly reduces the chance of installation problems and cuts down the amount of documentation needed to support the bean.

Here is an example of a servlet bean that turns the contents of a database table into an HTML table. The bean uses five properties: dbDriver, dbUrl, dbLogin, dbPass, and dbTable. These properties store the class name of the JDBC driver, the URL of the desired database, the login and password used to access the data, and the table of interest. The needed getXXX and setXXX methods, such as getDbDriver( ) and setDbDriver(Strings), are defined at the end of the file.

Source Code: DatabaseBean.java

```
import javax.servlet.*;
import javax.servlet.http.*;
import javax.servlet.ServletOutputStream;
import java.io.IOException;
import java.sql.*;
import java.util.Enumeration;
```

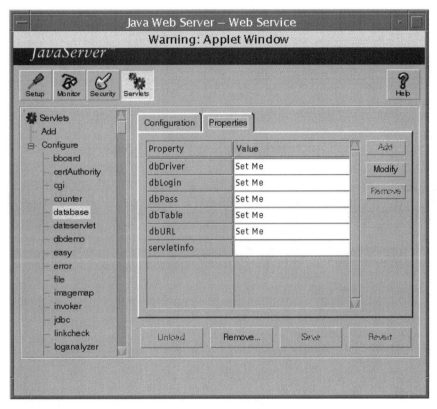

Figure 9.8   Setting a servlet bean's properties.

```
public class DatabaseBean extends HttpServlet {
  String dbDriver = "Set Me";
  String dbUrl = "Set Me";
  String dbLogin = "Set Me";
  String dbPass = "Set Me";
  String dbTable = "Set Me";
  Connection con = null;
  Statement stmt = null;

  public void doGet(HttpServletRequest req, HttpServletResponse res)
  throws IOException
  {
    res.setContentType("text/html");
    ServletOutputStream out = res.getOutputStream();

    out.println("<HTML>");
    out.println("<HEAD><TITLE>Database table output</TITLE></HEAD>");
    out.println("<BODY BGCOLOR=#FFFFFF>");
```

```java
    try {
      Class.forName(dbDriver);
      Connection con = DriverManager.getConnection(dbUrl, dbLogin, dbPass);
      stmt = con.createStatement();
      ResultSet rs = stmt.executeQuery("select * from " + dbTable);
      ResultSetMetaData rsMeta = rs.getMetaData();
      int colCount = rsMeta.getColumnCount();
      out.println("<P>"+dbTable+"</P>");
      out.println("<TABLE BORDER><TR>");
      for (int i = 1; i <= colCount; i++) {
    out.println("<TD>"+rsMeta.getColumnName(i)+"</TD>");
      }
      out.println("</TR>");

      while (rs.next()) {
        out.println("<TR>");
    for (int i = 1; i <= colCount; i++) {
      out.println("<TD>"+rs.getString(i)+"</TD>");
    }
    out.println("</TR>");
      }
      out.println("</TABLE>");
    } catch(Exception e) {
      out.println("Something went wrong: " + e);
      e.printStackTrace();
    } finally {
      out.println("</BODY></HTML>");
      out.close();
    }
  }

  public String getDbDriver() {
    return dbDriver;
  }

  public void setDbDriver(String s) {
    this.dbDriver = s;
  }

  public String getDbURL() {
    return dbUrl;
  }

  public void setDbURL(String s) {
    this.dbUrl = s;
  }

  public String getDbLogin() {
    return dbLogin;
  }
```

```
public void setDbLogin(String s) {
  this.dbLogin = s;
}

public String getDbPass() {
  return dbPass;
}

public void setDbPass(String s) {
  this.dbPass = s;
}

public String getDbTable() {
  return dbTable;
}

public void setDbTable(String s) {
  this.dbTable = s;
}
}
```

Once installed and properly configured, this bean can generate a report from
any database accessible on the network. Figure 9.9 shows a sample output.

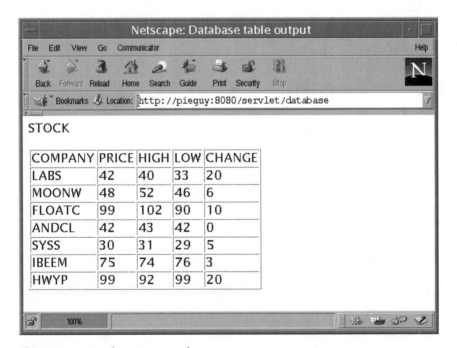

Figure 9.9   DatabaseBean servlet.

Page Compilation

Page compilation is another new feature added to Java Web Server 1.1. With page compilation you can use the Java language as a simple scripting language for Web pages. Using the <JAVA> and </JAVA> tags, Java code can be freely intermixed with the rest of the HTML in a page. This allows you to use Java code to generate all or part of the HTML for the page without writing a full-blown servlet. Here is our familiar phrase servlet, rewritten to use page compilation.

Source Code: phrase.jhtml

```
<HTML>

<HEAD>

<TITLE>

This is a test page.

</TITLE>
</HEAD>
<BODY>
<JAVA TYPE="import">
java.util.Date
java.lang.Math
</JAVA>
<UL>
<JAVA>
  // Set up an array of adjectives to describe the state of the
  // web server.
  String [] adjectives = {"happy",
                          "sad",
                          "thrilled",
                          "annoyed",
                          "pained"};

  // Set up an array of adverbs to modify the adjectives.
  String [] adverbs = {"very",
                       "slightly",
                       "a little",
                       "totally"};

  Date now = new Date();

  out.println("<HTML><HEAD><TITLE>Phrase Servlet</TITLE></HEAD>");
  out.println("<BODY BGCOLOR=#FFFFFF><CENTER><P>");
  out.println("At ");
  out.println(now.toString());
  out.println(" this web server is feeling ");
  out.println(adverbs[(int) (Math.random() * adverbs.length)] + " " );
```

```
    out.println(adjectives[(int) (Math.random() * adjectives.length)] + ".");
    out.println("</P></CENTER></BODY></HTML>");
</JAVA>
</UL>
</BODY>
</HTML>
```

The first interesting thing about this example is the name of the file. The extension .jhtml is the standard name by which the Java Web Server recognizes HTML pages with embedded Java code. The Java Web Server contains a servlet called pageCompile that reads the .jhtml file, uses the HTML and embedded Java code to generate a full-blown servlet source code file, compiles the servlet, and runs it to generate the final HTML for the page. If your Web server has not been configured to recognize .jhtml files, you'll have to create a servlet alias using the Java Web Server admin applet. Just create a new servlet alias that aliases *.jhtml to pageCompile.

The <JAVA> tag can include one of several optional parameters that tell pageCompile what sort of Java code block is being defined. In the preceding example, we include the block:

```
<JAVA TYPE="import">
java.util.Date
java.lang.Math
</JAVA>
```

The TYPE= "import" tag tells the pageCompile servlet that we will import Java packages in this block. The pageCompile servlet will place this section of code at the legal position in the resulting .java file and will generate the needed import statements.

The main <JAVA> block is where we do most of the work for the servlet. While this code is almost identical to the previous implementations of the phrase servlet, notice that here we don't have to define the PrintWriter out. The variable name "out" acts as a reserved word in the pageCompile servlet. It is automatically set to the PrintWriter associated with the output stream for the resulting servlet.

Page Compile Performance

The first time someone accesses your .jhtml file, there will be a noticeable delay before the page is returned. This is because the pageCompile servlet must generate the code for the needed servlet, compile that servlet, and run it before returning the needed HTML to the requestor. All this takes several seconds.

The second and subsequent request for that .jhtml file is another story. Having generated and compiled the servlet once, the pageCompile servlet simply invokes that class again with the proper HttpServletRequest and HttpServlet-

Response objects. This process is almost as fast as invoking a regular servlet and is many times faster than a typical CGI implementation.

Each time a .jhtml file is accessed, the pageCompile servlet checks to see if that file is newer than any servlet class pageCompile may have previously generated from that file. If the file is newer than the class, pageCompile will build and compile a new servlet from the page. This allows you to change the .jhtml file on the fly and have pageCompile take care of updating the classes in the Web server.

When to Use Page Compile

The page compile feature is very powerful. It allows you to build dynamic HTML pages without lots of rote coding, source management, and installation. It is excellent for including simple information, such as messages of the day and dates, or performing simple scripting, such as using one greeting for the morning and another for the afternoon. However, dynamically generated page compile servlets do have their drawbacks.

First, the class file from the pageCompile servlet is not loaded from the CLASSPATH. This means that it falls under the domain of the Web Server's SecurityManager in JDK 1.1 or a Protection Domain in Java 2. Java code generated from the .jhtml file cannot talk to other machines or access certain properties of the Java runtime and, in general, lives under the same restrictions under which applets live. This is an important security feature. You won't want a user on your site to write a .jhtml file that contains a call to System.exit and brings down your whole site the first time someone accesses the page.

There is another reason to limit your use of dynamically generated .jhtml files. Business logic embedded in a .jhtml file is almost impossible to reuse in other systems and access to it is severely limited. We know from Chapter 6 that reusability of logic and access to existing functionality by other systems are two very important goals for well-architected systems. If you write reams of JDBC code in a .jhtml file, you will probably find yourself rewriting this code in a true servlet or other form in the near future.

Templates

The Java Web Server contains another servlet that makes life easier for Web content developers. The template servlet takes an outline, called the template, of what an HTML page should look like and merges it with contents of a real HTML page to produce the finished page. This allows the site master to define a common look and feel for all of the site's Web pages. Content developers then need only create the body of each page; the site's look and feel is automatically applied by the template servlet. Here is an example of a default.template file:

Source Code: default.template

```
<HTML>
<HEAD>
<!-- The Head command is necessary for placing any page head content into
     the document for the time being -->
<subst data="HEAD"/>
</HEAD>
<BODY bgcolor=#ffffff>
<TABLE>
<TR>
<TD ALIGN=CENTER WIDTH=750 HEIGHT=213>
<IMG SRC="/images/pie-logo.gif" WIDTH=600 HEIGHT=213>
</TD>
</TR>
<TR>
<TD>
<TABLE>
<TR>
<TD ALIGN=LEFT VALIGN=TOP>
<FONT SIZE=-1>
<A HREF="http://pieguy/home.html">Home</A><BR>
<A HREF="http://pieguy/servlet/select">Place Orders</A><BR>
<A HREF="http://pieguy/map.html">Visit Us</A><BR>
<A HREF="http://pieguy/specials.html">Daily Specials</A><BR>
<A HREF="http://pieguy/related.html">Related Sites</A><BR>
</FONT>
</TD>
<TD>
<subst data="BODY"></subst>
</TD>
</TR>
</TABLE>
</TD
</TR>
<TR>
<TD ALIGN=CENTER>
<FONT SIZE=-1>
The Internet's finest baked goods.
</FONT>
</TD>
</TR>
</TABLE>
</BODY>
</HTML>
```

For the most part, the template file is just like any other HTML file. The only difference is the new <SUBST></SUBST> tags. When an HTML page is requested, the Java Web Server invokes the template servlet, which merges the HTML in a file with the template and returns the completed page to the requesting browser. The DATA parameter of the <SUBST> tags controls where parts of the requested HTML file are placed in the dynamically generated page. The preceding example is typical of how the <SUBST> tags are used. The template's header contains a pair of <SUBST DATA= "HEAD"></SUBST> tags and the template's body contains a pair of <SUBST DATA= "BODY"></SUBST> tags. This causes the requested page's header and body to be inserted in the appropriate place in the resulting page. Figure 9.10 shows the results of applying the preceding template to a simple HTML page.

Using Templates

In order to use templates, you must first define the template itself and then configure the Java Web Server to invoke the template servlet instead of simply returning the raw HTML page. Defining the template page is as easy as creating a new HTML page. You can even use your favorite HTML editor to do the job for you. Just make sure you include the needed <SUBST></SUBST> tags in the

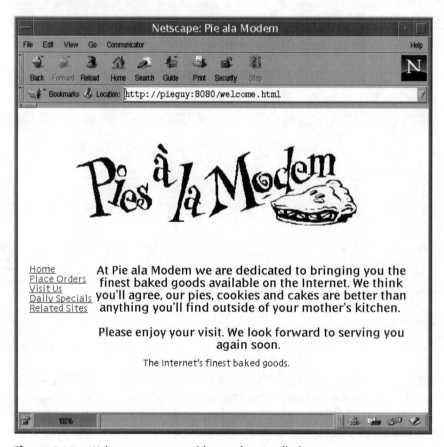

Figure 9.10 Welcome message with template applied.

appropriate places. Place the template in a file called default.template in the root of your document directory. Every page in that directory and every page in every subdirectory of that directory will automatically be merged with the default.template file. Each subdirectory may optionally contain its own default.template file. If a subdirectory contains a default.template file, that template will override any template found in a higher-level directory. This template will also be the default template for any subdirectory of that directory (until one of its subdirectories defines its own default.template, of course). This gives the Web master for a site, or that site's users, directory-by-directory control over which template is used for which file.

TIP Because your template may be applied to HTML files in subdirectories deep beneath the one in which the default.template file resides, you can't use relative path names to reference other files your template may use. For example, you can't have a <IMG SRC="../images/something.jpeg"> in your template because the ".." in the path name won't always refer to the proper directory. When referring to other files in your template, always place those files in a directory under the document root and use an absolute path name, such as <IMG SRC="/images/something.gif">. This way, the template server will always be able to find the needed files.

After defining your template file or files, use the Java Web Server admin applet to configure the server to use the template servlet. After starting the admin applet, select the Java Web Server from the list of available services and press the Manage button. This will bring up the Setup applet for the Web Server. Choose "Servlet Aliases" from the tree view on the left-hand side of the applet and add a new servlet alias. In the "alias" column you can either enter "/template" or a file name with a wildcard, such as *.html. If you enter /template, only files in or under the template directory in the Web server's document root (usually the public_html directory in the Web server's home directory) will be affected by templates. If you enter *.html, all HTML files in the site (including users' home directories) will be affected.

The default.definitions File

In addition to merging the default.template file and the requested HTML page, the template servlet also checks for the existence of a default.definitions file. You can think of this file as containing macros, or shorthand names, for blocks of HTML commonly used in your site. For example, if you include a navigation bar on each page in your site, you could define a new name "NAV" and the HTML for the navigation bar in the default.definitions file. The file uses the name/value pair syntax of a Java properties file. Having defined NAV as a valid name for the template servlet, you can now include <SUBST DATA="NAV"></SUBST> in the appropriate places in your templates. The template servlet will replace these <SUBST> tags with the HTML defined for NAV. Of course, each subdirectory can have its own default.definitions file, allowing you to write one template and essentially have its contents dynamically generated. For example, you may want to have the navigation bar in a standard location on each page in the site, but you may also want to change what links are in that bar depending on where the user is in the site. The default.definitions file allows you to accomplish this without having to define and maintain a default.template for each subdirectory.

Applying Templates to Servlets

Templates are a very compelling feature because they allow you to separate the visual design of your site from the content of each page. This feature can be doubly powerful when combined with dynamically generated content coming from servlets. In order to apply a template to your servlets, you must take advantage of *servlet chaining*. Servlet chaining allows you to pipe the output of one servlet to the input of another servlet before returning the page to the requesting Web browser.

First, go to the admin applet and select Site from the left-hand tree view. Go to the Options tab and make sure the Servlet Chains option is enabled. Now choose Servlet Aliases from the tree view. Here you will tell the Java Web Server exactly which of your servlets should be merged with the site's templates. You'll use another internal servlet called the template filter to perform the actual merging.

The next step depends on exactly which servlets you wish to use templates and how you have named the servlets on your site. In the simplest case, you want all servlets to use templates and you store all your servlets in the /servlets or /servletbeans directories, allowing the invoker servlet to find them according to its implicit naming convention. In this case, just modify the entry for the "/servlet" alias to read "invoker,templatefilter." This will chain the output of your servlet (as invoked by the invoker) through the templatefilter.

If you don't want every servlet to use templates and you have explicitly named your servlets (by using the Servlets page in the admin tool to define a servlet name or using the Servlets Alias page to map a servlet to a URL), you can define exactly which servlets are to use templates by modifying their aliases. For example, say we've defined an alias that maps our phrase servlet to the URL /phrase.html. If we want to apply our site template to this servlet we simply use the admin applet to change the alias for "/phrase.html" from "phrase" to "phrase,templatefilter."

You can also apply templates to other types of output on your system. For example, you could apply a template to dynamically compiled .jhtml files by chaining the output of the pageCompile servlet through the templateFilter

WHAT'S THE DIFFERENCE BETWEEN THE TEMPLATE AND TEMPLATEFILTER SERVLETS?

Why are there two different template servlets: template and templatefilter? Actually, templatefilter was added in Java Web Server 1.1.1 to correct a problem in earlier implementations of the template mechanism. These earlier implementations tried to use the template servlet both to serve static HTML pages and to filter the output of other servlets. It is very awkward to write a servlet that performs both roles, so rather than create and maintain a patchwork of code that handles the many special problems, and corner cases that arise for this double duty, the Java Web Server designers simply split the original template servlet into two separate, much simpler, servlets: template, which continued in its original role, and templatefilter, which took over the servlet chaining duties.

servlet. In this case, just modify the alias for *.jhtml (or for a particular .jhtml file if that's what you want) to include the chain "pageCompile,templatefilter."

You can apply servlets to almost any content on your site with the template servlet and the templatefilter. There is, however, one small problem. As of Java Web Server 1.1.2 there seems to be no way to apply a template to an implicitly named index.html file. If a user requests a URL ending in a "/" from your site, the file servlet will search for the default file name (usually index.html or index.htm) in the appropriate directory and return it to the requestor. If, on the other hand, the user requests the same URL, but with /index.html explicitly added, this will match the *.html alias and the file will be run through the template filter before being returned to the requestor. So, depending on exactly how the user requests the page, he will see either the unadorned HTML or the page in all its glory. The obvious solution would seem to be to chain the output of the file servlet, which reads the index.html from disk, through the templatefilter, which merges the file's HTML with the default.template.. However, the file servlet is used for any static file, not just an HTML file, and such a chain would cause all files on the site, *including GIFs and JPEGs*, to be run through the templatefilter. This leads to extremely poor performance and frequent out-of-memory exceptions. The workaround is to not use implicit file names on your site (this can be turned off in the admin applet) and to not use the template on the site's top-level index.html file. This means that you must make sure any changes made to the top-level default.template are also made to the index.html file. While this is annoying, it is still easier than trying to maintain every static page and the HTML generators of every servlet on the site. Hopefully, this flaw will be corrected in later versions of the Java Web Server.

Session Tracking

Often when developing Web-based applications, you must maintain some state between individual calls from a user. Since HTTP is a stateless protocol, you are responsible for keeping track of what is in a user's shopping cart, whether he has registered a unique user name with the site, what preferences he has set, and any other information that your application needs. Typically, this information has been bundled up with each dynamically generated HTML page, as hidden fields in a form or as a cookie, and passed to the user's browser only to be sent back to your application as part of the next request. This is not only inefficient and clumsy, it is also a potential security hole and often painful to program.

The Java servlet extensions provide a better way. The Java Web Server maintains a unique session object for each active user on your site. This session object can contain any information your application needs. Convenient methods in the session object allow you to retrieve information from the object and store new information into it. This provides a very easy and natural way to maintain state between HTTP requests. The session object, and the information it contains, is available to every servlet on your site, so it also provides an easy way to share that state between different servlets.

Here is an example of using session tracking. This servlet simply maintains a counter that is incremented each time the servlet is called inside that session. The servlet outputs an HTML page that reports the value of the counter.

Source Code: SessionCountServlet.java

```
import javax.servlet.*;
import javax.servlet.http.*;
import java.io.*;

public class SessionCountServlet extends HttpServlet {

  public void doGet(HttpServletRequest req, HttpServletResponse res)
    throws ServletException, IOException {

    HttpSession session = req.getSession(true);
    res.setContentType("text/html");
    PrintWriter out = null;

    try {
      out = res.getWriter();
    } catch (Exception e) {
      System.out.println(e);
    }

    Integer count = (Integer) session.getValue("test.count");
    if (count == null) {
```

```
        count = new Integer(0);
    }

    count = new Integer(count.intValue() + 1);
    session.putValue("test.count", count);

    out.println("<HTML>");
    out.println("<HEAD><TITLE>SessionServlet</TITLE></HEAD>");
    out.println("<BODY>");
    out.println("<P>I have been called " + count + " times.</P>");
    out.println("</BODY></HTML>");
    out.flush();
  }
}
```

The HttpServletRequest object req is used to retrieve the session object:

```
HttpSession session = req.getSession(true);
```

This session object works much like a hash table. We retrieve objects from it by calling the getValue method and store them with the putValue method. Any Java object can be stored in the session object. Since a primitive datatype, such as an int, can't be automatically converted to an object, in the preceding example we store an Integer and convert it to an int when needed by our code.

With just these three calls, getSession, getValue, and putValue, we can create almost any stateful protocol needed.

The obvious question is, "Where is the session information stored?" The Java Web Server actually maintains an internal table of session objects, one for each active user in the site, and includes the proper session object in the HttpServletRequest object passed to each servlet call. In order to maintain the mapping between session objects and users, the Java Web Server automatically passes a cookie containing the session ID number back to the user's Web browser at the end of each request. This cookie is then sent back with the next request so the Java Web Server can hand your servlet the proper session object. If you must support a user community whose browsers do not support cookies, either because of security and privacy concerns or because of out-of-date browsers, the Java Web Server can use a technique called URL rewriting to embed the session ID number in every URL in every page returned by the site. URL rewriting is not enabled by default; you can use the admin applet to turn it on, if needed.

Session Tracking and Security

Information in hidden fields in an HTML form or in a cookie is stored in the clear, and anyone who wishes to can read and modify that information. If you are using either of these mechanisms to create a stateful HTTP session, you are creating a frequently overlooked security hole. A malicious user can edit the information in the form or cookie and send it back to you without you being able to tell that the information has adulterated. If your application is using these mechanisms to keep track of sensitive, internally generated data, this flaw can have devastating consequences. Could a user read his account number from a hidden field, add one to it, and gain access to another user's account? Could a user change a discount rate field from 10 percent to 100 percent to get free merchandise (or to 200 percent in hopes that your backend doesn't check for sensible discounts)? Several attacks based on this flaw have already been reported, and more are sure to come.

Of course, you could always protect against this attack yourself by either encrypting any state you send back to the user or including a crypto-checksum that would allow you to detect tampering. However, session tracking offers a better way. Since stateful information is maintained on the Web server itself, it is never exposed to potentially hostile users and cannot be attacked. The only thing the user ever sees is his session ID number, and even that is resistant to attack. Instead of using a simple-minded counting scheme to assign session ID numbers (e.g., the first user is number 1, the second user is number 2) or other easily spoofed schemes, the Java Web Server constructs session ID numbers out of a hash of the user's IP address and other information. This makes it extremely unlikely that a hostile user could ever guess another user's session ID number and makes spoofing equally unlikely.

Invalidating Your Session

Session objects are not stored indefinitely. If a user enters your site, visits some servlets that set some session information, and then goes on vacation for two weeks, when she returns she'll find that the Web server no longer recognizes her. This is of great help to the Web master, since you won't have to buy huge amounts of disk to store session objects for people who may never visit your site again. The admin applet allows you to define how long sessions are live and when they should be invalidated. There is also a parameter that controls how large the cache of session objects should be. This can be used to tune performance by trading a bit of memory for faster access to the session objects.

You can also invalidate a session programmatically. The HttpSession object contains an invalidate method that marks the session object as invalid and allows the Java Web Server to discard it immediately. While you may want to invalidate a session at the end of a transaction to empty the user's shopping cart or to discard other now unneeded information, you should use this feature with great care. Invalidating the session object doesn't just destroy information your servlets have stored in the session; it destroys the session entirely. If there are other collections of servlets on your site that may have been using the session object, you may have just caused some other system some big problems.

In practice, it's best to let the Java Web Server take care of invalidating sessions. There is one practical exception to the rule. When testing servlets that use session tracking, you'll frequently end up with lots of dead wood and unused information in the session object. Rather than log in as a new user, kill and restart the Web server, or go to lunch to wait for the session to time out, it's easier to just invalidate the session and get back to work. In this case, it is convenient to have a servlet that does nothing but kill any session in which it finds itself. The InvalidateSessionServlet fulfills that function quite nicely.

Source Code: InvalidateSessionServlet.java
```
import javax.servlet.*;
import javax.servlet.http.*;
import java.io.*;

public class InvalidateSessionServlet extends HttpServlet {

  public void doGet(HttpServletRequest req, HttpServletResponse res)
   throws ServletException, IOException {

    HttpSession session = req.getSession(true);
    session.invalidate();
    res.setContentType("text/html");
    PrintWriter out = null;

    try {
      out = res.getWriter();
    } catch (Exception e) {
      System.out.println(e);
    }

    out.println("<HTML>");
    out.println("<HEAD><TITLE>Order a pie, today!</TITLE></HEAD>");
    out.println("<BODY>");
    out.println("Your session has been invalidated.");
    out.println("</BODY></HTML>");
    out.flush();
  }
}
```

Servlets and the Java Enterprise APIs

Servlets that can process forms data and other user input become much more powerful when combined with the sophisticated backend capabilities of the

Java Enterprise APIs. Servlets can use JDBC, Java RMI, or CORBA to perform actions on the user's behalf, such as placing orders, looking up account balances, and any other electronic commerce activities. These servlets, having been integrated with legacy systems and services, can allow Web users access to those services, often at a greatly reduced cost when compared to accessing the same services through 800 numbers, fax machines, and physical mail.

Here is the OrderEntry example from Chapter 6 adapted to servlets. In Chapter 6, we built the data manager infrastructure for the data tier and the OrderEntry class to encapsulate the business rules for taking orders. Here, a series of servlets allow a user to order several pies, enter address information and, using the OrderEntry class, place the order over the Internet. Notice how three-tiered design has made adding a new Internet face to the application quite easy. All the data access and logic elements created for the internal application have been reused. Only a new HTML form and a small piece of servlet code are needed to deploy the Internet version. This easy code reuse, with the associated benefit of reduced development time, is the hallmark of three-tiered design. If you compare Figure 9.11 to similar figures in Chapter 6 you will see exactly how much development has been saved by object reuse and the three-tiered design.

Here is the source code for the SelectPiesServlet:

Source Code: SelectPiesServlet.java
```java
import javax.servlet.*;
import javax.servlet.http.*;
import java.io.*;
import java.util.Hashtable;
import java.util.Enumeration;

public class SelectPiesServlet extends HttpServlet {

  // This array stores the names of all the pies we offer.
  // In real life, we'd pull a product list out of a database.
  String [] pieNames = {"Apple", "Peach", "Lemon",
                        "Blueberry", "Strawberry"};

  public void doGet(HttpServletRequest req, HttpServletResponse res)
   throws ServletException, IOException {

    HttpSession session = req.getSession(true);
    Hashtable selectedPies = (Hashtable) session.getValue("order
                                                .piesselected");

    if (selectedPies == null) {
        selectedPies = newHash(session);
    }
```

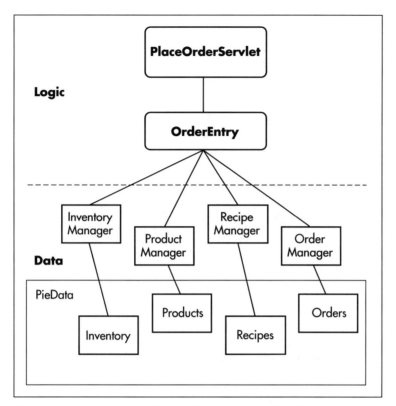

Figure 9.11   Using a servlet in a three-tiered application.

```
// Update the quantities in the Hashtable, based on which pie
// was selected in the form.
String [] pieName = req.getParameterValues("SELECTEDPIE");

if (pieName != null && pieName[0].length() != 0) {
    Integer Int = (Integer) selectedPies.get(pieName[0]);
    if (Int != null) {
        int quantity = ((Integer) selectedPies.get(pieName[0]))
                                                        .intValue();
        quantity++;
        selectedPies.put(pieName[0], new Integer(quantity));
    }
}

writeForm(selectedPies, res);
}

private Hashtable newHash(HttpSession session) {
```

```
        Hashtable hash = new Hashtable(5);

        for (int i = 0; i < pieNames.length; i++) {
            hash.put(pieNames[i], new Integer(0));
        }

        session.putValue("order.piesselected", hash);
        return hash;
    }

    private void writeForm(Hashtable h, HttpServletResponse res) {
        res.setContentType("text/html");
        PrintWriter out = null;

        try {
          out = res.getWriter();
        } catch (Exception e) {
          System.out.println(e);
        }

        out.println("<HTML>");
        out.println("<HEAD><TITLE>Order a pie, today!</TITLE></HEAD>");
        out.println("<BODY>");
        out.println("<TABLE><TR>");
        out.println("<TD ALIGN=CENTER>Pies</TD>");
        out.println("<TD ALIGN=CENTER>Quantity</TD><TD>Purchase</TD></TR>");

        Enumeration e = h.keys();
        while (e.hasMoreElements()) {
            String name = (String) e.nextElement();
            int i = ((Integer) h.get(name)).intValue();
            out.println("<TR><TD WIDTH=250 ALIGN=CENTER>");
            out.println(name + "</TD>");
            out.println("<TD ALIGN=CENTER WIDTH=100>" + i + "</TD>");
            out.println("<TD ALIGN=CENTER>");
            out.println("<A HREF=/servlet/SelectPiesServlet?SELECTEDPIE="
                        + name + ">Buy Me!</A></TD></TR>");
        }
        out.println("</TABLE><BR>");
        out.println("<CENTER><FORM METHOD=POST ACTION=/servlet/orderinfo>");
        out.print("<INPUT TYPE=SUBMIT NAME=PLACEORDER VALUE=\"Place Order\">");
        out.println("</FORM></CENTER></P>");
        out.println("</BODY></HTML>");
        out.flush();
    }
}
```

When first called, this servlet creates a session object for tracking what the user has ordered and returns an HTML page that is used to order pies. Each time the user selects one of the pie links on that page, the SelectPiesServlet is called again. It saves that selection in a hash table in the session object and returns a new HTML page showing which pies have been selected (see Figure 9.12). Eventually, the user presses the Place Order button, which calls the OrderInfoServlet via the alias orderinfo (see the CD-ROM included with this book for the source for the OrderInfoServlet). After the user presses the Place Order button, her shipping information is passed to the PlaceOrderServlet (via the alias placeorder alias). The PlaceOrderServlet retrieves the selected pies from the session object and uses the OrderEntry class from Chapter 8 to place the order.

Source Code: PlaceOrderServlet.java

```java
import javax.servlet.*;
import javax.servlet.http.*;
import java.io.*;
import java.util.Vector;
import java.util.Enumeration;
import java.util.Hashtable;
```

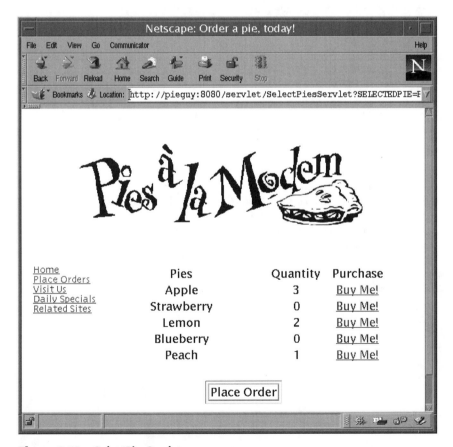

Figure 9.12   SelectPiesServlet.

```
import pie.orderentry.*;
import pie.order.OrderItem;

public class PlaceOrderServlet extends HttpServlet {

  OrderEntry oem = null;

  public void init(ServletConfig config)
  throws ServletException {

    super.init(config);

    try {
      oem = new OrderEntry();
    } catch(Exception e) {
      throw new UnavailableException(this, "Could not create OrderEntry.");
    }
  }

  public void doPost(HttpServletRequest req, HttpServletResponse res)
    throws ServletException, IOException {

    HttpSession session = req.getSession(true);
    Hashtable selectedPies = (Hashtable) session.getValue("order
                                              .piesselected");

    if (oem == null) {
        throw new UnavailableException(this, "OEM was null.");
    }

    // In a real application we'd verify the fields here. For this
    // example we'll assume the user never makes a mistake.
    String name = req.getParameterValues("NAME")[0];
    String addr1 = req.getParameterValues("ADDR1")[0];
    String addr2 = req.getParameterValues("ADDR2")[0];
    String city = req.getParameterValues("CITY")[0];
    String state = req.getParameterValues("STATE")[0];
    String zip = req.getParameterValues("ZIP")[0];
    String d = req.getParameterValues("DELIVERY")[0];

    PrintWriter out = null;
    try {
      out = res.getWriter();
    } catch (Exception e) {
      System.out.println(e);
    }

    res.setContentType("text/html");
    try {
        out.println("<HTML>");
```

```
           out.println("<HEAD><TITLE>Placing Order</TITLE></HEAD>");
           out.println("<BODY>");

           int delivery;
           if (d.equals("Standard"))
               delivery = OrderItem.STANDARD;
           else
               delivery = OrderItem.OVERNIGHT;

           Enumeration e = selectedPies.keys();
           while (e.hasMoreElements()) {
               String pie = (String) e.nextElement();
               int quantity = ((Integer) selectedPies.get(pie)).intValue();
               if (quantity > 0) {
                   oem.placeOrder(name, addr1, addr2, city, state,
                                  zip, pie, quantity, delivery);
               }
           }
           out.println("<P><CENTER><B>");
           out.println("Your order has been placed.<BR>Thank you.");
           out.println("</B></CENTER></P>");
       } catch (TooLate e) {
         out.println("We're sorry, but we can't accept overnight orders
                                                            after");
         out.println("2:00 pm EST.<BR>Try again tomorrow or change delivery");
         out.println("option to standard.");
         }
       catch (LowInventory e) {
         out.println("We're sorry but our current inventory can't fill this
                                                  order.<BR>");
         }
       catch (Exception e) {
         out.println("An unexpected error has occurred.  Please try again
                                                  later.<BR>");
         }
       finally {
         out.println("</BODY></HTML>");
         out.flush();
         out.close();
         }
   }
}
```

The combination of good three-tiered design, the Enterprise Java APIs, and servlets has allowed us to add a new Web front-end to an existing application without modifying the legacy source code or disrupting existing processes. The new application can fit naturally on top of the existing infrastructure precisely because that infrastructure was designed with these sorts of extensions and additions in mind.

Summary

The Web has grown from a simple information publishing medium to a full-fledged application distribution system. Along the way, developers have used the Java platform to add rich content to the client side of Web applications and allow for the publishing of flexible, intelligent applications. Servlets now allow the use of the Java platform on the server side of Web applications. Servlets provide a convenient way to launch and manage server-side code, avoiding the problems of daemon installation and management on heterogeneous platforms. Servlets also overcome some of the very difficult security facing those corporations wishing to adapt a Web-centric business strategy.

CHAPTER 10

Enterprise JavaBeans

Introduction

In Chapter 6 we talked about a lot of high-minded architectural goals for distributed applications. In Chapters 7, 8, and 9 we violated most of those principles. We hard-coded path names, database URLs, and JDBC drivers. We wrote single-threaded code, which assumed there would never be more than one user at a time. We coded important configuration information directly into the application instead of reading it from a properties file. Sometimes we even noted this with sly little comments like, "In real life, we'd pull this out of a database." In short, we wrote exactly the same kind of code everyone else does, without regard to scalability, maintainability, or reliability.

We could claim that we had valid pedagogical reasons for these oversights. We wanted to keep the examples short, or the main point of the example was clearer when it wasn't cluttered up with a lot of configuration code. But the simple fact is, we were lazy, just like almost every other programmer today. It is much easier to simply hard-code the path names and URLs, and if we can get the system working in the development lab, then we can throw it over the wall to the release management and QA groups with good conscience. If they have trouble getting it to work, that's their problem.

Of course, no one ever makes these mistakes deliberately. When you hard-code that path name, you know you should really be using a properties file, but right now you just want to do some testing so you take the quick-and-dirty route. You promise yourself you'll come back and fix it "as soon as I get some free time." But, of course, free time is always scarce at the end of a development cycle and you end up throwing the code, hacks, shortcuts and all, over the wall to let the release manager figure out why everything just broke.

These kinds of activities are painfully common, especially in first releases of products and internally developed systems. The result is brittle systems that break at the most unexpected times for the most bizarre reasons, applications that cannot be maintained without detailed knowledge of the oral culture of the development organization, and a flood of bug reports from the release manager (or worse, the beta customers). All of these problems end up costing the organization orders of magnitude more time than it would have taken for the developer to just do it right the first time. The programmer knows he's creating a long-term problem, but he is also goaled on whether he gets this feature working today or if he can check off this module in his weekly report. Since he has every intention of replacing the short-term work-arounds with better long-term solutions before releasing the code, he makes these mistakes with a clear conscience.

There are several solutions to this problem. The organization can institute code reviews and design walk-throughs. It can give incentive to programmers based on how well their code holds up during QA and beta testing, or it can factor the number of bugs found in that programmer's code into his performance review. Or, it can simply make it easier to do things right than it is to do them wrong.

Enterprise JavaBeans

Making it easier to do things right is one of the main goals of Enterprise Java-Beans. The designers of Enterprise JavaBeans recognized that building large distributed applications is hard and that there are many places in which even the best-intentioned programmer is tempted to cut corners and cheat on robustness, all in the name of making the next deadline. Enterprise JavaBeans helps eliminate these temptations by automating many of the most tedious tasks in distributed application design and providing a common framework and runtime that assists in deploying and running distributed business applications.

What Is Enterprise JavaBeans?

The Enterprise JavaBeans specification builds on the JavaBeans API. As you already know from Chapter 5, the JavaBeans specification allows Java classes to be self-describing and to run inside some sort of Bean Container, like a visual development tool or an application runtime. While a generic bean can be used in just about any type of application, from a GUI to a database, the Enterprise JavaBeans specification details how beans are to be used in distributed, transactional applications, and adds several specific facilities and features needed by these applications. The specification is intended to be implemented by various third parties, such as database vendors or makers of transaction processing monitors, in order to extend the Java platform into those markets. By implementing the EJB specification in their products, these vendors transform their products into Enterprise JavaBeans containers, which provide services to Java applications. Developers of classes that use the Enterprise JavaBeans specification can take advantage of services provided by these third parties, such as distributed transaction support, name space management, and persistence, without writing SQL and JDBC code by hand or tying their code to one particular RDBMS or TP vendor.

What's in a Name?

If phrases like "Developers of classes that use the Enterprise JavaBeans specification" seem awkward to you, you're not alone. The naming conventions for the JavaBeans standard and related class files, instances, and APIs are slightly confusing. However, remembering a few simple rules makes it easier to understand. First, just as JavaBeans is the name of a standard Java API, Enterprise JavaBeans is the name of an API, not of an individual class. Despite their appearance, both JavaBeans and Enterprise JavaBeans are singular nouns, so it is proper to say "JavaBeans is" and "Enterprise JavaBeans states . . ." even though such sentences don't exactly roll off the tongue. If you want to refer to an individual class file or serialized instance that implements the JavaBeans API, you should simply call it a bean. A bean that uses features of the Enterprise JavaBeans standard and is to be deployed in an EJB container can be referred to as an enterprise bean.

The Enterprise JavaBeans specification focuses on distributed, N-tiered, transactional applications. In order to support these applications, a container that implements the EJB specification provides many standard services, such as:

- Name services for locating enterprise beans on the network
- Automatic generation of the local and remote proxy classes needed to distribute the application
- Automatic persistence for an enterprise bean's state and transactional control
- Resource pooling so enterprise beans may share expensive resources like RDBMS connections
- Life-cycle management for creating new beans, stopping idle beans, and destroying unneeded beans

The Enterprise specification also defines many other useful features, like automatic multi-threading of components, security services for authenticating users, controlling what resources they can access, and configuration management. Together these features provide most of the generic services an enterprise server needs. Rather than rewriting this code for each new server, with EJBs the programmer can simply buy this infrastructure from any one of a dozen vendors and get back to work on the important part of the application, the business rules that make the application valuable to the organization.

Enterprise JavaBeans Goals

The Enterprise JavaBeans specification defines several goals for the EJB platform. These goals are consistent with the overall goals of the Java platform. They include:

- *Building a standard component architecture for distributed business applications.* This architecture will allow tools and enterprise beans from different vendors to be combined in a single, distributed application.

- *Make building distributed applications easier.* Distributed applications tend to contain a lot of common code. Code for life-cycle management, threading, transaction control, and other common tasks tends to show up over and over again, in the rough proportions of the 80/20 rule. By automating the common 80 percent of code, the Enterprise JavaBeans specification allows developers to concentrate on the valuable business logic that makes up the remaining 20 percent of code.

- *Allow expert programmers access to low-level functionality.* While the Enterprise JavaBeans specification does make it easy for a programmer to create simple applications, it does not completely hide the power of the underlying platform. Expert programmers can still access needed features to create powerful applications that do not fit into the standard framework provided within EJBs.

- *Extend the Java platform's Write Once, Run Anywhere philosophy to enterprise applications.* Enterprise beans written for one vendor's container can be moved to another vendor's product without modification.

- *Be easily implemented in existing products.* Sun worked with many industry leaders, including IBM, Informix, Oracle, Sybase, WebLogic, and others to ensure that the Enterprise JavaBeans specification could be implemented quickly and easily in existing products.

- *Provide interoperability with legacy applications not written to the Java platform and with the CORBA distributed object standard.*

Example Session Bean

A session bean is the simplest type of enterprise bean. A session bean encapsulates an application's logic and provides computational and data manipulation services to other parts of an application, but it doesn't provide any persistent storage. It doesn't use a database or other persistence mechanisms so if something goes wrong during with the application, say a network failure or a server crash, the session bean and all its state are lost. Session beans are also automatically destroyed when the user finishes her current session with the application (hence the name "session bean").

Let's take a look at a simple example of an enterprise bean. In this example, we will create a session bean that acts as a shopping basket. It knows what products we sell, accumulates orders, and can report its contents to the shopping application. We could modify the SelectPiesServlet from Chapter 9 to use this session bean simply by replacing the hash table currently used with this session bean and making the appropriate calls to the bean. We'll call this bean PieSession. (Remember the name. It becomes important a bit later.) To create a session bean we must do three things. We must define the bean's EJBHome interface, we must define the bean's EJBObject interface, and we must write a SessionBean class that implements the methods defined in the two interfaces.

The EJBHome Interface

The EJBHome interface is used by an application when it asks the enterprise bean container to create a new instance of the session bean for it. Create methods in the EJBHome interface act like the constructors for the session bean. An EJBHome interface can define as many create methods, with as many different signatures, as the application needs. Our example bean will contain a single create method that takes no arguments.

Source Code: PieSessionHome.java
```
import javax.ejb.*;
import java.rmi.*;

public interface PieSessionHome extends EJBHome {
  PieSession create() throws CreateException, RemoteException;
}
```

That's all there is to it. We import the standard extensions javax.ejb.* and java.rmi.*, extend the EJBHome interface, and list the needed create methods. Each create method must throw CreateException and RemoteException.

The name of the interface is important. Since we're creating an enterprise bean called PieSession, the interface *must* be called PieSessionHome. At deployment time and runtime, the enterprise bean container knows that any request to create a PieSession bean must go through the PieSessionHome interface. The general pattern is simple and obvious: The EJBHome interface for enterprise bean XXX must always be called XXXHome.

The EJBObject Interface

The EJBHome interface is a contract between the client and the enterprise bean container that allows the client to create a new instance of the session bean. Once the client has an instance of the bean, it needs to be able to ask the bean to do something for it. The EJBObject interface is a contract between the client and the bean itself that lets the client request the various services offered by the bean. In our example, we will define three methods in the EJBObject interface: one for getting the names of the pies we sell, one for adding a pie to the order, and one for listing the entire order. Here's the code for our EJBObject interface:

Source Code: PieSession.java
```
import javax.ejb.*;
import java.rmi.*;
import java.util.Vector;
import java.util.Hashtable;

public interface PieSession extends EJBObject {
  void increment(String pie) throws RemoteException;
  Vector getPieNames() throws RemoteException;
  Hashtable getOrder() throws RemoteException;
}
```

Again, the name of this interface is important. For our PieSession enterprise bean, the EJBObject interface must be called PieSession. The general pattern is simple and obvious. Also, note that this interface must extend EJBObject.

The SessionBean Class

Finally, we must implement the methods defined in the preceding interfaces. Following the naming patterns defined in the Enterprise JavaBeans specification, this class must be called PieSessionBean.

Source Code: PieSessionBean
```
javaimport javax.ejb.*;
import java.rmi.RemoteException;
import java.util.Enumeration;
import java.util.Hashtable;
import java.util.Vector;
```

```java
public class PieSessionBean implements SessionBean {

    protected SessionContext ctx;
    String [] pieNames  = {"Apple", "Peach", "Lemon",
                           "Blueberry", "Strawberry"};
    Hashtable selectedPies;

    public void increment(String pie) {
        System.out.println("PieSessionBean: increment called.");
        int quantity = ((Integer) selectedPies.get(pie)).intValue();
        quantity++;
        selectedPies.put(pie, new Integer(quantity));
    }

    public Vector getPieNames() {
        System.out.println("PieSessionBean: getPieNames called.");

        Vector v = new Vector();
        Enumeration e = selectedPies.keys();
        while (e.hasMoreElements())
            v.addElement(e.nextElement());
        return v;
    }

    public Hashtable getOrder() {
        System.out.println("PieSessionBean: getOrders called.");

        Hashtable order = new Hashtable(5);
        Enumeration e = selectedPies.keys();
        String s;
        Integer i;

        while (e.hasMoreElements()) {
            s = (String) e.nextElement();
            i = (Integer) selectedPies.get(s);
            if (i.intValue() > 0)
                order.put(s, i);
        }

        return order;
    }

    public void ejbCreate() {
        System.out.println("PieSessionBean: ejbCreate called.");
        selectedPies = new Hashtable(5);
        for (int i = 0; i < pieNames.length; i++) {
            selectedPies.put(pieNames[i], new Integer(0));
        }
    }
```

```
public void setSessionContext(SessionContext ctx)
    throws RemoteException {

    this.ctx = ctx;
}

public void ejbActivate() throws RemoteException {
}

public void ejbRemove() throws RemoteException {
}

public void ejbPassivate() throws RemoteException {
}
}
```

This class is a little more complicated than it may seem to be at first glance. The first three methods are simply the implementations of the methods defined in the PieSession interface. But then we see the fourth method, ejbCreate. It looks suspiciously like the create method we defined in our PieSessionHome interface, except for that strange "ejb" at the front. What is this method doing here?

Remember that the PieSessionHome interface was a contract between the client and *the enterprise bean container*, not between the client and the session bean itself. Therefore, our PieSessionBean is not responsible for implementing the create methods found in the PieSessionHome interface (at least, it doesn't directly implement those methods). When we deploy our PieSessionBean in a container, the container reflects on the PieSessionHome interface and creates, inside itself, the methods defined in the interface. When a client actually calls one of these create methods, the container uses reflection and introspection to find the corresponding ejbCreate method in our PieSessionBean class. This allows the container to do all the internal bookkeeping it needs to do to create an instance of the enterprise bean and then call our ejbCreate method so we can perform any application-specific initialization tasks, such as save local copies of any arguments passed into the create method or allocate other resources.

The general pattern is that for each create method defined in the enterprise bean's EJBHome interface, an ejbCreate method, which takes the same arguments, must be defined in the SessionBean class. Failure to include all the needed ejbCreate methods will result in an error when you try to install the bean into the container.

The final three methods in PieSessionBean come from the SessionBean interface, which all session beans must implement. These three methods, ejbActivate, ejbRemove, and ejbPassivate, are part of the Enterprise JavaBeans life-cycle management specification. Depending on how heavily used an instance of your bean is, the container may put it to sleep, wake it back up when next it is needed, or even destroy it outright. The ejbActivate, ejbRemove, and ejbPassivate methods give you an opportunity to perform any actions required when your bean is first activated and to clean up after yourself when the bean is no longer needed. In most simple applications, these methods won't be needed, but if your bean interacts with external applications it will be important to free anything you've used in order to avoid leaking memory, file descriptors, and other scarce resources.

A Simple Client Application

Finally, we need a client application to test our bean. Here we'll just use a simple stand-alone program to test the bean. You may wish to modify the three servlets from the e-commerce example in Chapter 9 to use this new bean.

Source Code: PieTest.java

```java
import java.rmi.*;
import java.util.Enumeration;
import java.util.Hashtable;

public class PieTest {

  public static void main(String[] args) throws Exception {
    PieSessionHome home =
              (PieSessionHome)Naming.lookup("//pieguy:2727/PieSession");
    PieSession pie = home.create();
    System.out.println("Got a PieSession.");

    System.out.println("We sell the following pies:");
    Enumeration e = (pie.getPieNames()).elements();
    while (e.hasMoreElements())
        System.out.println("        " + e.nextElement());

    System.out.println("Buying apple pies.");
    pie.increment("Apple");
    pie.increment("Apple");
    pie.increment("Apple");

    System.out.println("Buying a lemon pie.");
    pie.increment("Lemon");

    System.out.println("My order consists of:");
    Hashtable h = pie.getOrder();
    e = h.keys();
    String name;
    int i;

    System.out.println("Pie            Quantity");
    System.out.println("-----------------------");
    while (e.hasMoreElements()) {
```

```
         name = (String) e.nextElement();
         i = ((Integer) h.get(name)).intValue();
         System.out.println(name + "             " + i);
     }
   }
 }
```

The first thing our test program must do is make contact with the container for our enterprise bean. We could use either RMI's registry or JNDI to find the container. Exactly how we do this will depend on the container we've chosen to use to deploy the bean. Here we use RMI to get a reference to an object inside the container. This object, which was created when we deployed the bean, implements the PieSessionHome interface.

```
PieSessionHome home =
              (PieSessionHome)Naming.lookup("//pieguy:2727/PieSession");
```

We can now use home to create an instance of our PieSessionBean.

```
PieSession pie = home.create();
```

Now that we have a reference to the actual session bean, we can use it in our shopping cart. The rest of the client program simply gets the names of all the pies we sell, adds several to the shopping basket, and then prints out our order.

Why Bother?

This example doesn't really seem to add much to our e-commerce servlets from Chapter 9. All we've really done is move what should be a simple internal data structure out onto the network, a move that can't help but increase latency in the system. So, why did we bother to create a networked session bean to replace the simple local hash table used in Chapter 9?

The answer to this question lies back in Chapter 6. Remember, one of the advantages to distributed N-tiered architectures is that they give us a centralized place to manage the business logic of our applications. Even if the same business logic is to be used in several different applications, we only want to develop, modify, and maintain a single copy of that logic. The session bean plays that role in the example just shown.

Let's imagine in the future we want to add more sophisticated logic to the order tracking in our e-commerce application. For example, we may want to track the purchases someone is making and offer suggestions for other products based on patterns of user behaviors. If someone orders 4 blueberry pies, we'll want to show them a special seasonal offer for boysenberry pie. If another customer orders 10 apple pies, we'll want to promote our premium vanilla ice cream (packed in dry ice for home delivery, of course).

We could just enhance Chapter 9's SelectPiesServlet to perform these functions and still retain the local hash table. But let's say that at the same time we were adding this functionality to our Web site, we were also adding an 800-number order system. Now Session beans make perfect sense. Our Web site and our 800-number system can use the same set of enterprise beans, sharing all the logic and simplifying both systems. It is this kind of large-scale reuse for which EJBs were designed.

Choosing a Container

We've made several mentions of a container that implements the Enterprise JavaBeans specification. These containers fall into the general category of Enterprise Middleware or, as they are frequently called, Application Servers. The container can either be implemented inside another system, such as the RDBMS and TP monitors discussed earlier, or as a stand-alone system, inside a Web server or any of several other systems.

Sun Microsystems maintains a list of vendors who have endorsed the EJB specification at http://java.sun.com/products/ejb/tools1.html. One notable source for EJB containers is EJBHome (www.ejbhome.com), which offers a free reference implementation of the EJB spec. While the EJBHome container is not (at least as of this writing) fully compliant with the EJB 1.0 specification, it does offer most of the features of EJB 1.0, and as a freely available, simple, and ease-to-use reference implementation it is an invaluable learning tool for developers who are interested in EJBs.

Your choice of containers will affect many parts of your development, deployment, and maintenance cycles. While the Java code for your enterprise beans is portable between different containers, the tools used by those containers to deploy the beans and the features offered by those containers may vary widely. Please refer to your container vendor's documentation for details on tools available to build a properly formated EJB JAR file, how to install your beans, and for any tools they may provide to ease client-side development.

Under the Hood of EJBs

As you may have guessed, even in our simple example there is a lot going on under the hood. The enterprise beans container creates an object that implements the EJBHome interfaces of our enterprise beans, uses introspection and reflection to call our beans' methods on behalf of client applications, and handles resource pooling and threading for us. These are all valuable services (and are especially valuable because we didn't have to write them ourselves).

If you're writing client software that uses enterprise beans provided by someone else, you never need to know anything about how the container manages all these services. You just use the container to get handles to the beans you need and call methods on them without regard to what the container is doing. (Actually, you never even get to call methods directly on the bean. The container makes the calls for you. Client applications never touch an enterprise bean directly.)

If you're writing enterprise beans, though, it is helpful to understand how the container works and how your bean and the container interact. Exact details for these interactions can be found in Sun's Enterprise JavaBeans 1.0 specification; however, you don't need to read the entire spec to get a feel for what is going on. A basic understanding of the EJBHome and EJBObject interfaces and the SessionBean object is all it takes.

The major parts of the container and the bean are shown in Figure 10.1. The client connects to the container via the EJBHome interface and uses this interface to create a copy of the needed enterprise bean. Note that the client can simultaneously get access to multiple enterprise beans running in several containers and, of course, many, many clients can be talking to instances of a single enterprise bean simultaneously. The container maps the client's calls to create methods in the EJBHome interface to the appropriate ejbCreate methods in the SessionBean object. The container also tracks which client is associated with which instance of the bean and maps the client's calls to methods in the EJBObject interface to the method calls on the proper instance. The client never touches the bean directly. All interaction between the client and the bean is mediated by the container.

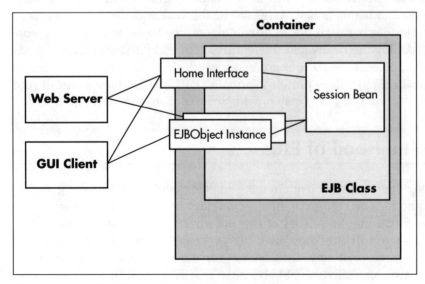

Figure 10.1 Client interaction with the container and session bean.

Example Entity Bean

The SessionBean used earlier in the chapter is the simplest type of enterprise bean. It provides computational and logical services; however, it doesn't provide any way to store data and once the bean is destroyed, its state is gone forever. Since the Enterprise JavaBeans specification is intended for transactional applications and for database applications, the SessionBean must be only part of the story.

In addition to session beans, the Enterprise JavaBeans specification defines entity beans. Entity beans are very similar to session beans, but offer the additional feature of being able to save their state automatically to some sort of permanent storage, usually an RDBMS using JDBC. Operations on entity beans are transactional in nature and will either complete or be rolled back by the server. The container takes care of generating the needed JDBC code and SQL calls. Important deployment information, such as what JDBC driver to use and the URL of the database, are not hard-coded into the bean; instead, they are specified as deployment properties when the bean is installed into the container. This separation of data storage details from business logic goes a long way to solving the problems caused by lazy or just plain overworked programmers and makes it much easier to change how an N-tiered application is architected without breaking existing clients.

TIP Entity beans are an optional part of the Enterprise JavaBeans 1.0 specification. If you plan to use entity beans, make sure the container you choose supports them. Entity beans will be a mandatory part of the 2.0 version of the Enterprise JavaBeans specification.

Like the session bean, entity beans are composed of several parts: the EJB-Home and EJBObject interfaces and the EntityBean class that implements the methods defined in these two interfaces. Entity beans must also define a primary key object, which is used to retrieve these beans from permanent storage and to search for a particular instance of the bean. Let's take a look at a simple example of an entity bean. This example is based on the Order data manager from Chapter 8.

The EJBHome Interface

First we'll define the EJBHome interface for the bean. This interface is almost identical in form to that used previously by the session bean.

Source Code: PieOrderHome.java
```
import javax.ejb.*;
import java.rmi.*;
```

```
public interface PieOrderHome extends EJBHome {

    PieOrder create(int orderno, String name, String addr1, String addr2,
                    String city, String state, String zip,
                    int productnum, int quantity, int delivery)
        throws CreateException, RemoteException;

    PieOrder findByPrimaryKey(PieOrderPK orderno)
        throws FinderException, RemoteException;
}
```

Like a session bean, an entity bean's home interface must extend EJBHome, and like a session bean, an entity bean can define one or more create methods. These create methods work just like the create methods in a session bean. They are used by the client to create a new instance of the bean and are mapped by the container to the appropriate ejbCreate method in the EntityBean classes.

An entity beans home interface must also define the findByPrimaryKey method. This method is used by a client when it wants to retrieve an existing bean, not create a new instance of the bean. The argument PieOrderPK represents the primary key for this bean. The name of this class follows the general pattern of appending PK to the name of the bean in order to define the primary key class. The primary key class simply defines a set of public variables that are used to search for the bean's state and constructor methods for creating new PK instances.

Source Code: `PieOrderPK.java`
```
public class PieOrderPK implements java.io.Serializable {
  public int orderno;

  public PieOrderPK(int orderno) {
    this.orderno = orderno;
  }

  public PieOrderPK() {
  }
}
```

Using Create and findByPrimaryKey Methods

When a client calls one of an entity bean's create methods, the container will create a new instance of the bean and make the needed calls to the underlying database to store the bean's state permanently. Usually this will involve calls to JDBC, but exactly how the container performs this action is of no concern to the client. The client should just trust that the data is now safe, somewhere, and can be recovered later. If something goes wrong with the create operation, the container will throw a CreateException to tell the client that its data is not safe.

Calling the findByPrimaryKey method does not create a new entry in the permanent data store. Instead, it creates a new instance of the bean and sets its state to the contents of an existing row in the database. Assuming the container is using a database for the permanent store, the findByPrimaryKey method generates an SQL statement based on the public variables in the primary key class. In the PieOrderPK example just shown, there is only one public variable, so the resulting SQL query would be qualified with a "where orderno = xx" clause, where xx is set to the value of orderno in the PieOrderPK used in the find-ByPrimaryKey call. Note that the names of the public variables must map to the names of columns in the database. If the container is not using a database for its store, it will take similar appropriate actions. If the container fails to find a matching entry in its date store, it will throw a FinderException.

The primary key class may contain more than one public variable. In this case, the container will treat it as a composite key and generate SQL statements with the where clauses appropriately qualified.

The Enterprise JavaBeans specification also allows for multiple finder methods. The bean developer can define methods like findLargeAccounts (double balance) to find all beans with an account balance greater than the argument, or findDelinquentAccounts() to find all accounts that are behind on their payments. Since these methods are not searching by primary key, they may find more than one match for each query. For this reason, these finder methods must return Enumeration of Entity bean references instead of a single bean reference. They must also throw FinderException if they are unable to find a bean that matches the query.

Unfortunately, there is no standard way to define how these methods behave. In most cases, the programmer will have to code his own database accesses and instantiate the beans using the ResultSet returned by the query. This requires that the bean use bean-managed persistence (discussed later in the chapter). Some container vendors, such as WebLogic (now a subsidiary of BEA Systems), provide a tool that can be used to implement these methods at deployment time. When you install the bean into WebLogic's Tengah server you can use a simple scripting language and GUI tool to define what the various find methods do. The container then automatically generates the needed SQL and implementations of the methods. You do not need to provide an implementation of these methods in your EntityBean class.

The EJBObject Interface

Like the session bean, the entity bean has EJBObject interface that lists the methods that this bean can perform. In this example, our bean will just expose two methods to get and set the name field in the bean.

Source Code: PieOrder.java

```java
import javax.ejb.*;
import java.rmi.*;

public interface PieOrder extends EJBObject {

    public String getName() throws RemoteException;
    public void setName(String s) throws RemoteException;
}
```

The EntityBean Class

The methods for the entity bean are implemented in the EntityBean class. Like session beans, naming patterns defined in the Enterprise JavaBeans specification control what this file must be called. In this case, we need to define the class PieOrderBean.

Source Code: PieOrderBean.java

```java
import javax.ejb.*;
import java.rmi.RemoteException;
import java.util.Calendar;

public class PieOrderBean implements EntityBean {

    protected EntityContext ctx;
    public int orderno;
    public String name;
    public String addr1;
    public String addr2;
    public String city;
    public String state;
    public String zipcode;
    public int productnum;
    public int quantity;
    public int delivery;

    public final static int STANDARD = 1;
    public final static int OVERNIGHT = 2;

    public void ejbCreate(int orderno, String name, String addr1,
                          String addr2, String city, String state,
                          String zipcode, int productnum, int quantity,
                          int delivery)
        throws CreateException, RemoteException {

        if (delivery == OVERNIGHT) {
            Calendar c = Calendar.getInstance();
            if (c.get(Calendar.HOUR_OF_DAY) > 13)
                throw new CreateException(
                    "Can't request overnight delivery after 2:00 PM EST.");
        }
```

```
            this.orderno = orderno;
            this.name = name;
            this.addr1 = addr1;
            this.addr2 = addr2;
            this.city = city;
            this.state = state;
            this.zipcode = zipcode;
            this.productnum = productnum;
            this.quantity = quantity;
            this.delivery = delivery;
        }

    public String getName() throws RemoteException {
        return this.name;
    }

    public void setName(String s) throws RemoteException {
        this.name = s;
    }

    public void setEntityContext(EntityContext ctx)
        throws RemoteException {

        this.ctx = ctx;
    }

    public void unsetEntityContext() throws RemoteException {

        this.ctx = null;
    }

    public void ejbActivate() throws RemoteException {
    }

    public void ejbRemove() throws RemoteException {
    }

    public void ejbLoad() throws RemoteException {
    }

    public void ejbStore() throws RemoteException {
    }

    public void ejbPassivate() throws RemoteException {
    }
}
```

Notice that we didn't have to define the findByPrimaryKey method in the file. That's because it is implemented for us by the container. Also, notice that the EntityBean interface contains several methods that the SessionBean interface does not; specifically, the ejbLoad and ejbStore methods are required by the entity bean interface. The container calls these two methods whenever it needs the bean to load its state from the database or to save itself. These methods allow you to create an entity bean that uses *bean-managed persistence*. With bean-managed persistence your bean is responsible for managing its own state. This is useful when your entity bean is wrapping a legacy system that handles the data storage. If your enterprise bean allows the EJB container to manage its persistent data (*container managed persistence*), you still need to define these extra methods in you EntityBean class, but they will never be called and can remain empty stubs.

The Entity Bean Client

Now we need a simple client. Here we'll just create a couple of orders and then retrieve one of the orders and look at its name.

Source Code: OrderTest.java

```
import java.rmi.*;

public class OrderTest {

  public static void main(String[] args) throws Exception {
    PieOrderHome home =
                 (PieOrderHome)Naming.lookup("//pieguy:2727/PieOrder");
    System.out.println("Got a PieOrderHome.");

    try {

      System.out.println("Create some standard delivery orders");
      home.create(1, "Steve", "1234 Main St.", "", "Hometown", "VA",
                  "12345", 1, 3, 1);
      home.create(2, "Dan", "4321 Market St.", "", "Hometown", "CO",
                  "54321", 2, 1, 1);
      home.create(3, "David", "1010 Maple Ave.", "", "Hometown", "NC",
                  "43210", 2, 1, 1);

      System.out.println("Find an order.");
      PieOrder order = home.findByPrimaryKey(new PieOrderPK(1));
      System.out.println("This pie was ordered by: " + order.getName());
    } catch(Exception e) {
      e.printStackTrace();
    }

    try {
      System.out.println("Now create an overnight order");
      home.create(1, "Steve", "1234 Main St.", "", "Hometown", "VA",
                  "12345", 4, 3, 2);
    } catch(Exception e) {
```

```
        e.printStackTrace();
      }
    }
  }
}
```

Just as in our session bean example, we get a reference to the EJBHome interface for the bean. This interface is implemented by the container. The implementing class is generated for us by the container when we deploy the bean.

```
PieOrderHome home = (PieOrderHome)Naming.lookup("//pieguy:2727/PieOrder");
```

After we have a reference to the PieOrderHome object in the container, we can use one of the create methods to get new instances of the entity bean. Each call to home.create results in a new row being inserted into the backing database.

```
home.create(1, "Steve", "1234 Main St.", "", "Hometown", "VA",
        "12345", 1, 3, 1);
home.create(2, "Dan", "4321 Market St.", "", "Hometown", "CO",
        "54321", 2, 1, 1);
home.create(3, "David", "1010 Maple Ave.", "", "Hometown", "NC",
        "43210", 2, 1, 1);
```

After creating the orders, we can use findByPrimaryKey to retrieve them and use the methods defined in the EJBObject interface to interact with them. (Of course, if we had bothered to save the reference to the beans returned by the home.create calls, we wouldn't have to look up the bean now. But then we wouldn't get to show the findByPrimaryKey method in action.)

```
PieOrder order = home.findByPrimaryKey(new PieOrderPK(1));
System.out.println("This pie was ordered by: " + order.getName());
```

Finally, in the second try block, we create one more order, this time requesting overnight delivery. Remember that the business logic for our order entry system says we can't take overnight delivery requests after 2:00 P.M. This rule is implemented by the create method in PieOrderBean.java. In this test program, we attempt this in a separate try block so the whole test doesn't fail if we run the test after 2:00 P.M.

Mapping between Database and Entity Bean

The container uses naming patterns to map public variables between your entity bean and the database. The names of variables that you wish the container to manage for you must correspond to the names of columns in the database. You must also tell the container which variables it should store into the database for you. This is done when you install your enterprise bean in the container. The details of this operation will vary slightly from container to container. In our example, we have 10 variables:

```
public int orderno;
public String name;
public String addr1;
public String addr2;
public String city;
public String state;
public String zipcode;
public int productnum;
public int quantity;
public int delivery;
```

These variables map to columns in the PieOrder table. The table must be called PieOrder, since the container assumes that the name of the bean corresponds to the name of the table. Our PieOrder table looks like this:

COLUMN NAME	TYPE
Orderno	int
Name	varchar
addr1	varchar
addr2	varchar
City	varchar
State	varchar
Zipcode	varchar
Productnum	int
Quantity	int
Delivery	int

TIP When the container tries to connect the variables in your bean to columns in the database table, spelling and capitalization count. Be very careful when creating the bean to follow the capitalization used in the table exactly, even if Java conventions demand that zipcode be written as zipCode and productnum as productNum.

The relations among entity beans, clients, and containers are almost identical to the relations among session beans, clients, and containers. There are only two differences: The EJBHome interface contains finder methods as well as create methods, and the container must maintain a connection to a database or other backing store to save the state of the entity beans (see Figure 10.2).

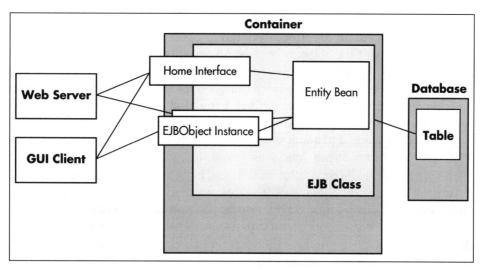

Figure 10.2 Architectural diagram of entity bean application.

EJB Architectures

Systems built around the Enterprise JavaBeans specification are suitable for several types of architectures and applications. The features provided by the EJB specification, including automatic distribution of object interfaces, multi-threaded servers, and transactional semantics, are useful whether you're processing credit card transactions, engaging in electronic commerce, or deploying internal applications for inventory control or external applications for supply chain management. Here we will examine some application designs and see how an application server that implements EJBs can be used.

Session and Entity Enterprise Beans

The first thing you must decide is whether to implement your system using entity beans, session beans, or a mixture of both. Some very simple systems may use only entity or session beans. A transactional system with an essentially two-tiered design may use only entity beans both to encapsulate what little business logic is needed and to handle updating the database. A purely computational system, such as a currency converter or other data manipulation tools, may use only session beans, since all the data needed to perform its job is passed to it with each method call and none of the data need to be permanently stored.

   More sophisticated systems, though, will probably be composed of a mixture of session and entity beans. The data managers and associated databases used in Chapter 8 are perfect examples of how these two types of beans can be used together. The data managers would be implemented as session beans that present the appropriate interfaces to higher layers of the system. Clients, be they the Web site or the 800-number system, would access the OrderEntry session bean. The OrderEntry bean, in turn, would call the various Product, Order, Recipe, and Inventory beans, just as it did in Chapter 8. These beans would also be implemented as session beans. Finally, the four lowest-level session beans would call entity beans that correspond to the database tables which, in Chapter 8, the managers had to manage using hand-coded SQL and JDBC (see Figure 10.3). By separating these functions into a hierarchy of session and entity beans, we preserve the separation of data and logic described in Chapter 6. This in turn allows the components of the system to be easily reused in new applications and gives us great flexibility in swapping out components of the system. We could add new applications on top of this infrastructure, update one of the data managers, or even replace the entire database structure with something new, all without affecting existing applications.

Deciding if a feature should be implemented as an entity bean with a little bit of logic, as we did in our PieOrder example, or as a session bean that manages collections of entity beans as proposed earlier, depends on how much logic and processing is required by the feature and how fundamental the business rules are to the type of data. In the PieOrder example, the only logic we included in the entity bean was a simple check to make sure overnight delivery orders weren't placed after 2:00 P.M. Since the fundamental limit, how long it takes to cool a pie before it can be packaged, is unlikely to change and the check must always be performed, regardless of how the order was entered, we are safe in building this logic into the entity bean itself. Other rules in the system, though, such as how we update the inventory system, how we check if we have enough flour on hand, and so on, are less tightly tied to the idea of an order and are moved up into session beans that encapsulate these rules.

Using Enterprise Beans and Legacy Applications

Application servers and enterprise beans can also be used to integrate legacy systems into the networked enterprise. As suggested earlier, a legacy data source or application could be wrapped with an enterprise bean. That bean would be responsible for formatting incoming and outgoing data and for defining a usable interface for higher levels of the system.

The question of whether to implement the wrapper as a session or entity bean again arises here. Since the legacy system is by definition not a database (otherwise, you'd just let the container do the work), you must use bean-managed persistence and do all the data loading and storing by hand. Since you have to write the data-managed code by hand, the entity bean's interface provides little added value. And, since the client sees almost no difference between

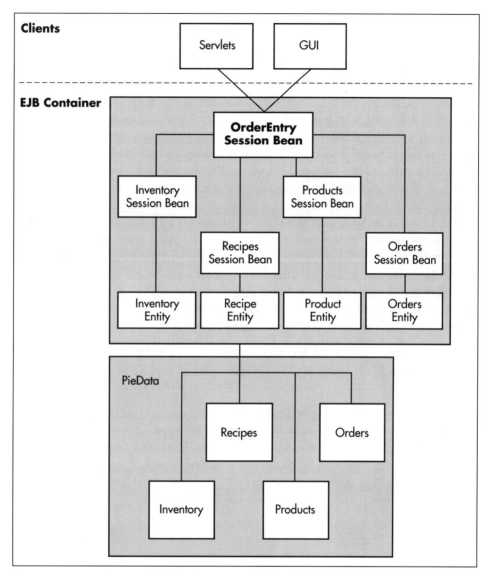

Figure 10.3   EJB interaction.

an entity and a session bean, you are free to implement the system however you see fit. Even though you still have to hand-code the data access, entity beans may be more appropriate for legacy systems that allow you to retrieve data previously stored in them. You can use the finder methods and infrastructure in the EJB specification to locate previously stored values and instantiate them as beans, saving you a little code and making the system easier to understand. A programmer familiar with using the Enterprise JavaBeans specification and finder methods will instantly feel at home with your system.

Enterprise JavaBeans and CORBA

In recent years, the Object Management Group's Common Object Request Broker Architecture (CORBA) and the Interorb Inter-Operability Protocol (IIOP) have become increasingly common frameworks for distributed applications. Web servers, transactions processors, and other systems are now shipping with built-in CORBA support, and many applications exist that depend on CORBA.

CORBA provides a basic plumbing layer for distributed objects and a set of mid-level services such as transaction processing and security. In some sense, CORBA resembles the lower third of an Enterprise JavaBeans architecture. Both share distributed objects, the need for standards on the wire protocols, and a set of common services. Recognizing this, and wanting to allow new EJB systems to coexist with and use services provided by legacy CORBA systems, the designers of the Enterprise JavaBeans specification have included a specification for allowing container vendors to implement the EJB specification on top of the IIOP wire protocol. This allows enterprise beans deployed in different vendors' containers to use each other's services. It also allows new EJB appellations to use legacy CORBA systems and new CORBA systems to take advantage of EJB applications on the same network.

Summary

The Enterprise JavaBeans specification is a good example of how the Java platform can be extended into new territory and how the power of the Java language and platform can be used in many different types of applications. With the Java platform now being included as a standard part of many TP monitors, Web servers, and database engines, expect to see the Java language become the standard for business applications over the next few years.

CHAPTER

11

Using Java Threads

Introduction

Java is multithreaded; it is not multithreaded like operating systems. Java Threads are built directly into the language, providing a simple interface on which to implement simple concurrent program behavior. The synchronization and scheduling of threads are also supported at the language level.

This chapter focuses on the multithreading features of Java and techniques for using these features. Before we jump into what Java has to offer in the way of threads, a better understanding of general threading concepts is in order.

What Are Threads?

A thread is similar to a process; it is a set of instructions that exist inside of a program that can be scheduled and executed on a given CPU. The major difference between a process and a thread is that multiple threads can exist inside a single process in the same way that multiple processes can exist inside of a single operating system. Each thread that exists inside of the process can execute a set of instructions completely independent of other threads in that same process, much like multiple processes can execute independently of each other in multitasking operating systems. Since multiple threads exist in a single process, they share the process's address space as well as other process-wide information. For example, multiple threads running in a process all share the same global variables as well as file descriptors, user IDs, and file system limits. This sharing of information makes threads share critical system resources while at the same time giving the developer the ability to create true concurrency in an application.

Threads and processes do have several features in common. Threads have stacks, stack pointers, program counters, and heap space just as processes do. This is how a thread can be scheduled in the same manner as a process. The only difference is that the thread is totally contained in the process's address space. This means that the thread can change values in the process that other threads can see.

Synchronization

Since a thread can change variables in a process that other threads can use, you can see that we need some way of communicating information between threads. Another way to look at this is a way to synchronize access to common or shared information. Thread synchronization provides a mechanism to coordinate the access of shared information from multiple threads. This prevents one thread from changing a variable that another thread may be using. Most thread synchronization is controlled through the use of function or method calls where the function uses some sort of control to prevent other threads from accessing the information. We will discuss several ways in which Java provides synchronization later in this chapter.

Scheduling

Since threads have much in common with processes, one would think that threads are scheduled in the same manner that processes are. This can be the case with some systems, but the fact is that in most cases thread scheduling is different than process scheduling. We will not go into the many different ways that threads can be scheduled here, but we do want to point out that you can't always count on the manner in which a thread gets scheduled. Another way to put this is: If your program depends on a particular style of scheduling, then that program may not behave as expected on other systems. We will discuss how Java schedules threads and some of the tips and tricks on how to develop programs that don't depend on scheduling later in this chapter.

Why Use Threads?

At this point a good question might be: Why do Java applications need to use threads? A simple answer is: Java applications that use threads are able to perform multiple tasks at the same time. For example, a Java program may need to update a graphic on the screen while at the same time accessing the network. Java threads also let you program the way humans normally think. People are constantly performing multiple tasks at any given time. Since people act in a concurrent world, it is much easier to develop programs that behave like the real world.

Threads also allow a developer to provide a high degree of interactivity with the user of the application; this usually involves the concurrent execution of multiple tasks. For example, a user may start a task using a GUI and, while that task is executing, the user may want to perform another sort of interaction with the GUI. A Web browser is an example of an application that needs to perform multiple tasks at the same time. The application must be able to display information to the screen as well as concurrently loading information from a network.

Java threads also provide an easy way to implement asynchronous behavior in applications. Synchronous actions can be performed by multiple threads while other threads are executing different tasks. When the synchronous tasks in the thread have completed, the thread can return a result to the calling application. This gives the developer the behavior of an asynchronous action without having to explicitly create asynchronous methods.

Java threads provide many different capabilities to a developer; however, Java threads are different in some ways than other thread packages. They could be considered a limited threads package when compared to other packages. For example, the POSIX threads specification, P1003.4a, is a complete threads package that can be implemented on any operating system. Java threads do not have all the capabilities of such a threads package. However, Java threads do have an advantage over such packages in their simplicity.

All of the Java libraries are thread safe. A library is thread safe if the functions or methods in that library are safe to be called from multiple threads at the same time. This means that a function can be called from multiple threads at the same time and it will not cause any problems due to the concurrency of the threads. For example, a library that uses static data to store values may not be thread safe because multiple threads that call into a function have access to the static data. If all the threads try to change the static value at the same time, unexpected results may be produced.

Not all libraries used by today's programs are thread safe. The developer that uses threads must decide what library to use and verify that it is thread safe. This is not an issue in Java because all of the Java class libraries are thread safe.

Another problem that Java threads solve in comparison to other thread packages is the use of locks. When programming with other thread packages, you are never sure what locks you have acquired and when you should release them. Java solves this problem by using a simplistic locking mechanism that is controlled by the Java runtime. This prevents the inevitable result of deadlock or data corruption that can occur when locks are not used properly.

Java's locking mechanism provides a set of primitives that let the programmer decide what needs to be protected; the Java runtime decides when to lock and unlock the designated areas. This mechanism is based on the monitor and condition variable paradigm used in Xerox's Cedar/Mesa system, which is based on the original concept from C.A.R. Hoare.

The ability to use threads from the Java language itself makes programming with threads much easier than other available threads packages. This simplicity also makes the applications that use threads easier to understand and much more robust.

Using Java Threads

We will start with the basics of Java threads, then move on to more advanced concepts. If you have worked with threads before, you still may want to read over the following sections to discover how Java utilizes threads.

Creating and Starting a Thread

There are two ways to create a thread in Java. The first way uses a class that extends (inherits) the Thread class. The subclass that is extending the Thread class acts as a thread; let's call this subclass MyThread. However, just instantiating a class, MyThread, that extends the Thread class will not make the object start executing as a thread. A call to the Thread's class start( ) method is needed to start the thread's execution. Once the start( ) method has been called, the object's run( ) method will be called. The run( ) method of the subclass is effectively the main function of the thread. This is where all of the actions that are to be performed by the thread should be placed.

For example, if you create a subclass of the Thread class, called MyThread, you need to override the Thread's class run( ) method with your own. If you don't, then your MyThread class will not do anything (see the following code example, ExtendThr.java).

In the code example you can see that the MyThread class overrides the run( ) method which simply prints a message to the terminal. When the MyThread objects, Thread_a and Thread_b, are told to start running, via the start( ) method, then the code within the run( ) method is executed by each thread.

Code example ExtendThr.java also includes a main method that defines two MyThread objects, then instantiates the two objects. When the Thread objects are instantiated, they are not running; the objects have been created but the run( ) methods have not been called. After the MyThread objects have been instantiated, the start( ) method is called for each object. The start( ) method then calls the object's run( ) method which then starts each object running as an independent thread. Note that the start method is not defined in the MyThread class. This is because the start( ) method is defined in the Thread class, which was inherited by the MyThread class.

Source Code: `EntendThr.java`

```
// This class extends the Thread class
class MyThread extends Thread {

  // Override the Thread's class run() method
  public void run() {
    System.out.println("Hello there, from " + getName());
    }
  }
public class ExtendThr {
  static public void main(String s[]) {
    MyThread Thread_a, Thread_b;  // Define the threads
    Thread_a = new MyThread();  // Create MyThread object
    Thread_b = new MyThread();  // Create another MyThread object
    Thread_a.start();  // Start the run() method in thread a
    Thread_b.start();  // Start the run() method in thread b
    }
  }
```

This method of creating a thread in Java has a drawback in that you must extend the Thread class. Since Java does not allow multiple inheritance, you can only extend one class for each subclass. This can be a problem if you need to extend other classes, for example the Applet class. Since an applet must extend the Applet class, you will not be able to extend the Thread class from this subclass.

This is why a second way of creating threads is included in Java. This second method uses a Java interface to create a thread. An interface in Java is nothing more than a definition as to what methods a class must contain if it is to implement that interface. It is like a contract between the interface and the class that implements the interface. The class that implements the interface must abide by the contract and implement all the methods that are defined in the interface. The Java interface that is used for creating threads is the Runnable interface:

```
package java.lang;
public interface Runnable {
public abstract void run();
}
```

Notice the only method the Runnable interface defines is the run( ) method.

Using this interface you can create a class that doesn't have to extend the Thread class, but can still execute as a thread. Code example RunnableThr.java shows a class, MyThread2, that implements the Runnable interface. Since this class implements the Runnable interface, the class must define all the methods in the interface. In this case, the only method that is defined in the interface is the run( ) method.

A class that implements the Runnable interface and a class that extends the Thread class are almost identical. The only real difference is the class that implements the Runnable interface does not inherit all the methods defined in the Thread class.

When a thread is created using this method, it should be given a reference to the class that implements the Runnable interface. The thread can be created by calling the Thread class or by calling a subclass of the Thread class with a target of a Runnable object. When the thread starts its execution, it will call the run() method in the Runnable target class. Code example RunnableThr.java demonstrates this by creating an object that implements the Runnable interface. The example then creates a Thread with the Runnable object as its target. When the start() method is called for the thread object, the run method in the Runnable object is executed:

Source Code: RunnableThr.java

```
// Class the implements the Runnable interface
class MyThread2 implements Runnable {
  public void run() {
    System.out.println("Hi there, from " +
                                    Thread.currentThread().getName());

  }
}


public class RunnableThr {

  static public void main(String s[]) {
    MyThread2 work2do;  // Object that has work to be done
    Thread a_thread, b_thread;  // A thread object on which to run the work

    // Create the MyThread2 object
    work2do = new MyThread2();

    // Create a thread with the MyThread2 object as its target
    a_thread = new Thread(work2do);
    b_thread = new Thread(work2do);

    // Start the thread which will call run() in the target
    a_thread.start();
    b_thread.start();
    }
  }
```

Since there are no Thread class methods available to a subclass that implements Runnable, a thread must be created with the Runnable objects as its target.

TIP If a thread is created using the Runnable interface, none of the Thread class methods are directly available inside of that class.

So what method of creating a thread should you use? The answer is not really clear. If your class only needs to override the run( ) method, then you should use the Runnable interface. If your class needs to override more than just the run( ) method, then you should extend the Thread class. A simpler answer might be: If a class needs to extend a class other than the Thread class as well as execute as a thread, then your only option is to use the Runnable interface.

Joining a Thread

Joining a thread provides a way for one thread to wait for the completion of another thread. If there is some dependency on the execution of one thread before another can continue, then a thread join should be used to wait for that thread. The join( ) method in the Thread class waits for the target thread to die before the join( ) method returns. Code example JoinThr.java demonstrates two thread objects where one thread must join the other thread before it can continue. Notice that the MyThread1 object was passed to the MyThread2 object. This allowed the MyThread2 object to join or wait for the MyThread1 thread before it could continue.

Source Code: JoinThr.java
```
// Thread class that just prints a message 5 times
class MyThread1 extends Thread {

  public void run() {
    System.out.println(getName() + " is running...");
    for (int i=0; i<5; i++) {
      try {  // Sleep a bit
        sleep(500);
        }
      catch (InterruptedException e) {}

      System.out.println("Hello there, from " + getName());
      }
    }
  }

// Thread class that waits for a target thread to exit and then
// prints a message 5 times
class MyThread2 extends Thread {

  private Thread wait4me;  // Thread to wait for

  // Constructor
  MyThread2(Thread target) {
    super();
    wait4me = target;
    }
```

```
    public void run() {
      System.out.println(getName() + " is waiting for " + wait4me.getName() +
                                                           "...");

      try {  // wait for target thread to finish
        wait4me.join();
        }
      catch (InterruptedException e) {}

      System.out.println(wait4me.getName() + " has finished...");
      // Print message 5 times
      for (int i=0; i<5; i++) {
        try {  // Sleep a bit
          sleep(500);
          }
        catch (InterruptedException e) {}
        System.out.println("Hello there, from " + getName());
        }
      }
    }

public class JoinThr {

  static public void main(String s[]) {

    MyThread1 Thread_a;  // Define a Thread
    MyThread2 Thread_b;  // Define another Thread

      Thread_a = new MyThread1(); // Create the Thread object
      Thread_b = new MyThread2(Thread_a); // Create the Thread object

    // Start the threads
    System.out.println("Starting the threads...");
    Thread_a.start();
    Thread_b.start();
    }
  }
```

The Thread's class has several implementations of the join( ) method. The only real difference in the implementations is how long the join( ) method will wait for a thread before continuing. Code example JoinThr.java used the join( ) method with no arguments; this call will wait forever for the target thread to exit. However, you can add a parameter to the join( ) method that will wait a finite amount of time. If the target thread has not joined by the specified time, then the thread calling the join( ) method will continue. Here is the output from running code example JoinThr.java:

```
Starting the threads...
Thread-4 is running...
Thread-5 is waiting for Thread-4...
```

```
Hello there, from Thread-4
Hello there, from Thread-4
Hello there, from Thread-4
Hello there, from Thread-4
Hello there, from Thread-4
Thread-4 has finished...
Hello there, from Thread-5
Hello there, from Thread-5
Hello there, from Thread-5
Hello there, from Thread-5
Hello there, from Thread-5
```

Daemon Threads

A daemon thread can be considered identical to a daemon process. The only real difference is that one is a thread and the other is a process. Daemon threads can be used in the same way that daemon processes are used—to execute background tasks. They usually provide some sort of service to other processes or threads. When the service is no longer needed, the daemon process or thread can be stopped.

Daemon threads in Java are essentially no different than other threads (non-daemon threads). The only major difference is that a daemon thread will stop its execution when all non-daemon threads have stopped in a application. For example, if a program contains two non-daemon threads and one daemon thread, then when both of the non-daemon threads have finished their execution and stop, the daemon thread will automatically be stopped and the program will exit.

This provides a convenient way to have threads run as background tasks which will go away when their service is no longer needed. If a thread that provides a background service is not created as a daemon thread, then that thread would have to be stopped explicitly before the program would stop. Since most services provided by daemons are executed in an endless loop, a thread that exits automatically, out of such a loop, can be of great use.

A thread can be made to become a daemon thread using the setDaemon( ) method. Code example DaemonThr.java creates a couple of threads and makes one of the threads a daemon thread. Both threads are started and are allowed to run for a few seconds. Then the regular, non-daemon thread stops. Since the other thread is a daemon thread, the program exits.

Source Code: DaemonThr.java
```
class normal extends Thread {

  public void run() {
    for (int i=0; i<5; i++) {
      try {  // Sleep for a bit
        sleep(500);
        }
      catch (InterruptedException e) {}
```

```
            System.out.println("I am a normal thread");
            }
        System.out.println("The normal thread is exiting");
        }
    }

class daemon extends Thread {

    public daemon() {
        setDaemon(true);
    }

    public void run() {
        for (int i=0; i<10; i++) {
            try {   // Sleep for a bit
                sleep(500);
            }
            catch (InterruptedException e) {}

            System.out.println("I am a daemon thread");
        }
    }
}

public class DaemonThr {

    static public void main(String s[]) {

        normal Thread_a;   // Define some Threads
        daemon Thread_b;

        // Create the threads
        Thread_a = new normal();
        Thread_b = new daemon();

        System.out.println("Starting the threads...");

        Thread_a.start();   // Start the Thread
        Thread_b.start();   // Start the Thread
        }
    }
```

Here is the output from code example DaemonThr.java:

```
Starting the threads...
Thread-4: I am a normal thread
Thread-5: I am a daemon thread
Thread-4: I am a normal thread
Thread-5: I am a daemon thread
Thread-4: I am a normal thread
Thread-5: I am a daemon thread
The normal thread is exiting
```

What would happen if you commented out the line that makes Thread_b a daemon thread?

Thread Groups

Thread groups allow you to collect a number of threads in a single group object. This group object can then be used by calling methods of the ThreadGroup class which will affect all the threads in that group.

Every thread created in Java belongs to a thread group. You may not be creating a group for the threads you create, but they are still added to a default group. The default group that is used when a thread is created is the main thread group. This may not be true in all cases, such as when an applet creates a thread from within a browser; that thread may be added to a browser's threads group.

Code example GroupInfo.java shows how you can list the thread group that a thread is currently in and how to list all the threads in that group. The thread group is determined by calling the getThreadGroup() method. Once the thread group is obtained, a method can be called to find out how many threads are in that group. A list of all the threads in a group can also be obtained.

Source Code: GroupInfo.java
```
// This class just keeps a thread alive
class MyThread extends Thread {

  // Constructor
  MyThread (String name) {
    super(name);
    }

  // Just spin and yield
  public void run() {
    while (true)
      if (isInterrupted())
        break;
      yield();
      }
    }

public class GroupInfo {

  static public void main(String s[]) {

    MyThread Thread_a, Thread_b, Thread_c;  // Define some Threads
    ThreadGroup this_group;
    Thread list[];

    // Get a reference to this threads group
    this_group = Thread.currentThread().getThreadGroup();
```

```
    // Print the group's name and the number of threads in the group
    System.out.println("This group's name is " + this_group.getName());
    System.out.println("There are " + this_group.activeCount() + "
                                          thread(s) in this group");

    // Create the threads
      Thread_a = new MyThread("Thread a");
      Thread_b = new MyThread("Thread b");
      Thread_c = new MyThread("Thread c");
    System.out.println("Starting three threads...");

    // Start the threads
    Thread_a.start();
    Thread_b.start();
    Thread_c.start();

    // Print the number of threads in the group now
    System.out.println("Now there are " + this_group.activeCount() + "
                                        thread(s) in this group");

    // Create an array of thread objects
    list = new Thread[this_group.activeCount()];

    // Fill the thread array with the thread objects in the group
    this_group.enumerate(list);

    // Print the names of the threads in the group
    System.out.println("Listing all the threads in this group...");
    for (int i=0; i<list.length; i++)
      System.out.println("\tThread: " + list[i].getName());

    // Interrupt the threads
    Thread_a.interrupt();
    Thread_b.interrupt();
    Thread_c.interrupt();
    }
  }
```

Here is the output from running code example GroupInfo.java:

```
This groups name is main
There are 1 thread(s) in this group
Starting three threads...
Now there are 4 thread(s) in this group
Listing all the threads in this group...
Thread: main
Thread: Thread a
Thread: Thread b
Thread: Thread c
```

When you create a thread, you have the option to add the new thread to a specific group or to just let the Java runtime decide what group your thread belongs to. You can also create a thread group within another thread group. This can provide a hierarchical way to manage a bunch of threads.

If you are not concerned with what group your thread belongs to, then just let the Java runtime system select the threads group for you. In fact, most programmers don't deal with thread groups at all. If, however, you do care what group your thread belongs to, then it is quite easy to create a thread group and add threads to that group.

Code example ThrGroup.java demonstrates how a thread group can be created and how threads can be placed in that group. Notice that you must create the thread group before you create the threads. When the threads are created, they use a Thread's class method that specifies the group name of which to join. Once all the threads have been created and placed in the group, you can manipulate all the threads in that group with just a single method call. The example interrupts all the threads in the group with just a single interrupt( ) method.

Source Code: ThrGroup.java

```
// Thread class that prints messages
class MyThread extends Thread {

  // Constructor - adds thread to target thread group
  MyThread(ThreadGroup tg, String name) {
    super(tg, name);
    }

  public void run() {
    while (true) {
      if (isInterrupted())
        break;

      System.out.println(getName() + ": is running");
      yield();
      }
    }
  }


public class ThrGroup {

  static public void main(String s[]) {

    MyThread Thread_a, Thread_b, Thread_c;  // Define some Threads
    ThreadGroup MyGroup; // Define a thread group

    MyGroup = new ThreadGroup("My Group"); //Create the thread group

    // Create the threads in the given thread group
    Thread_a = new MyThread(MyGroup, "Thread a");
    Thread_b = new MyThread(MyGroup, "Thread b");
    Thread_c = new MyThread(MyGroup, "Thread c");
```

```
// Start the threads
System.out.println("Starting the threads...");
Thread_a.start();
Thread_b.start();
Thread_c.start();

try {  // Sleep for a bit
  Thread.sleep(2000);
  }
catch (InterruptedException e) {}

// Interrupt all the threads in the group
System.out.println("Interrupting the thread group...");
MyGroup.interrupt();
}
```

Once a thread has been created, it is added to a group and cannot be moved to another group. If you want a new thread to be a member of a certain group, then make sure that you create the thread with a target group name. This can be done by using one of the many different Thread constructors that include a group parameter.

There are many ways in which to manipulate a thread group and the threads in the group by using ThreadGroup class methods. Only a few of these methods were used in the examples.

Other Methods

This chapter only covered a few of the methods needed to use Java threads in your programs. For more information about the complete list of available Thread class methods, see the Java API (java.sun.com).

Scheduling

Scheduling is the process by which a set of tasks are made to execute on a processor. Scheduling in Java is the process of taking a thread and executing the thread in the JavaVM. There are two major areas that affect how threads are scheduled in Java: thread state and thread priority.

Thread State

A thread can exist in Java in many different states, as shown in Figure 11.1. The state diagram not only shows the different states that a thread can be in, but also some of the Thread class method calls that can cause a state change. Note that this diagram does not show all the methods that can cause a state change.

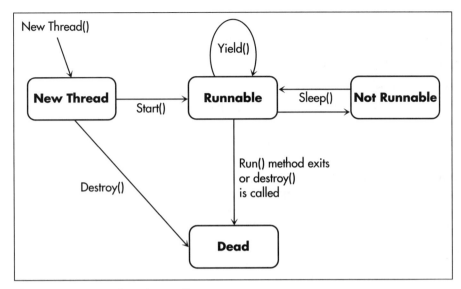

Figure 11.1   Java thread state diagram.

Runnable

When a new thread is created, a thread object exists but the thread is not running. The only thing you can do with a new thread is start it. Starting the thread will change the thread's state to a runnable state. This is why the start( ) method must be called in order for a new thread to begin executing.

When the start( ) method for a new thread has been called, the thread becomes runnable. This means that the run( ) method of thread can begin its execution. However, just because a thread is runnable does not mean that it will run. It just means that the thread can run. It is up to the JavaVM to decide which thread will run from all the threads that are in the runnable state. For example, if you create three threads, then start all three threads, all three of the threads will not run at the exact same time. The JavaVM will schedule a thread from the list of runnable threads. The JavaVM in most cases will do this quick enough that it can look as if all three threads are running at the same time. However, only one thread is executing at any given time. This is very similar to the way multitasking operating systems handle more than one process at any time. The operating system quickly switches execution between the processes.

Non-Runnable

In order for a thread to be executed it must be in a runnable state. If a thread is put in a non-runnable state, then that thread cannot be executed. A thread can be put in a non-runnable state in a number of ways:

- The sleep( ) method is called.
- The wait( ) method is called by the thread.
- The thread performs some sort of blocking call (i.e., read/write).

When any of these actions are performed, the thread is moved from a runnable state to a non-runnable state. This means that the thread cannot be scheduled for execution.

A thread in a non-runnable state can be put back in a runnable state by a method call or the completion of a blocked call. For example, a thread that has been made non-runnable by waiting for a read( ) call to finish is returned to a runnable state when the read( ) finishes.

Dead

There are two ways in which a thread can die. The first is caused when a thread drops off the end of the run( ) method. When the run( ) method has no other lines of code to execute, it just stops. This will cause the thread to stop its execution and die. For example, when the "b = c" statement in the following run( ) method finishes, there are no more lines of code to execute in the method so the thread dies:

```java
public void run() {
    a = b;
    b = c;
    }
```

A thread can also die due to a call to the stop( ) method for that thread. When the stop( ) method is called, the thread will asynchronously stop its execution and die. A thread is actually killed by the stop( ) method by receiving a Thread-Death error. When the thread receives this error, it halts its execution. Since the ThreadDeath error is an object that is subclassed from the Throwable class, you can catch the error in the thread. This can be quite handy if a thread needs to perform some sort of cleanup before it dies. Code example CatchDeath.java shows how you can catch the ThreadDeath error, then perform some actions before the thread actually dies. Notice that when the ThreadDeath error is caught, the same error is thrown again. This is very important; you must rethrow the error in order for the thread to actually die.

TIP The stop() method has been deprecated in Java 2; however, some code still uses this method to stop threads. A better method for stopping threads is to call the interrupt() method and have the target thread watch for interrupts using the isInterrupted() method.

Source Code: CatchDeath.java
```java
class MyThread extends Thread {
```

```
    MyThread(String name) { // Constructor
      super(name);
      }

    public void run() {  // override the run method
      try {
        while (true) { // sleep and print
          sleep(500);
          System.out.println(getName() + ": is running");
          }
        }
      catch (ThreadDeath ouch) { // Catch killing of this thread
        // Add any actions you want done before thread dies
        System.out.println(getName() + " is being killed");
        throw(ouch);  // rethrow the error so thread dies
        }
      catch (InterruptedException e) {}
      }
  }

public class CatchDeath {

  static public void main(String s[]) {

    MyThread Thread_a;  // Define a Thread

    // Create the thread
    Thread_a = new MyThread("Thread a");

    System.out.println("Starting the thread...");
    Thread_a.start();  // Start the thread

    // Sleep for a bit
    try {
      Thread.sleep(2000);
      }
    catch (InterruptedException e) {}

    // Stop the thread
    System.out.println("Stopping the thread...");
    Thread_a.stop();
    }
  }
```

Here is the output from running code example CatchDeath.java:

```
Starting the thread...
Thread a: is running
Thread a: is running
Thread a: is running
Stopping the thread...
Thread a is being killed
```

Determining a Thread's State

The Thread class contains an isAlive( ) method that will return a Boolean whether or not the thread is active. This method can give you some information about the state of the current thread, but it cannot tell you exactly what state the thread is in. The isAlive( ) method returns true if the thread is in a runnable or non-runnable state. This can be confusing because a thread can be sleeping in a non-runnable state, yet still be considered active. isAlive( ) will return false if the thread is dead or has not yet been started. For example, if you create a thread but have yet to start it, the thread is considered not active. There is no way to determine if an active thread is runnable or non-runnable just as there is no way to determine if a thread is dead or has not been started yet.

Thread Priority

The JavaVM uses a priority-based scheme to determine what threads are scheduled to run. Quite simply this means that a thread with the highest priority, on the runnable queue, will get scheduled for execution before a lower-priority thread is scheduled.

The JavaVM can also be preempted. This means that a lower-priority thread can be forced off of a processor in favor of a higher-priority thread. The thread is said to be forced off a processor because the thread is removed from the processor before it would have on its own.

The JavaVM supports 10 different priority levels. The lowest priority, which is defined as Thread.MIN_PRIORITY, is 1 and the highest priority, defined as Thread.MAX_PRIORITY is 10. The greater the number the higher the priority.

TIP The 10 priority levels supported in Java may not directly map to priority levels in the operating system that Java is running in. For example, Windows95 only supports seven priority levels, so some of the Java priority levels may actually be equal in the underlying operating system.

The JavaVM will schedule the highest priority runnable thread over any other lower-priority threads. If two or more threads have the same priority, then the JavaVM will schedule these threads in a round-robin manner. The only way a lower-priority thread can run over a higher priority thread is when the higher priority thread is not runnable. For example, if two threads are runnable, one with a priority of 5 and the other with a priority of 6, then the priority level 6 thread will always get scheduled first. However, if the priority level 6 thread is blocked waiting for some I/O, non-runnable, then the priority level 5 thread will get scheduled to run. A thread's priority can be set before the thread is started or while a thread is active. The priority can be set using the setPriority( ) Thread class method.

Code example Priority.java demonstrates how priorities can affect how threads are scheduled. The example creates three threads all with the same initial priority. Each thread performs some calculations, then prints a message to indicate that it is running. When all three threads have the same priority, they all get executed in a round-robin fashion. However, when the priority of one thread is increased, then only that thread is scheduled. The high-priority thread is then set to a lower priority, which causes the two other threads to be scheduled, and the lower-priority thread is not scheduled.

Source Code: Priority.java

```java
// Thread class that spins in a loop and prints a message
class MyThread extends Thread {

  // Constructor
  MyThread(String name) {
    super(name);
    }

  // Spin in a loop, print a message and then yield
  // Can't use the sleep() method because it would put the thread
   // in a non-runnable state
  public void run() {
    while (true) {
      System.out.println(getName() + ": is running");
      if (isInterrupted())
        break;
      yield();
      }
    }
  }

public class Priority {

  static public void main(String s[]) {

    MyThread Thread_a, Thread_b, Thread_c;  // Define some Threads

    // Create the threads
    Thread_a = new MyThread("Thread a");
    Thread_b = new MyThread("Thread b");
    Thread_c = new MyThread("Thread c");

    // Make sure this thread can always run
    Thread.currentThread().setPriority(Thread.MAX_PRIORITY);

    // Start the threads
    System.out.println("Starting the threads...");
    Thread_a.start();
    Thread_b.start();
    Thread_c.start();
```

```
      try {  // Sleep for a bit
        Thread.sleep(250);
        }
    catch (InterruptedException e) {}

    // Set Thread_b's priority up a bit
    System.out.println("Setting Thread b to a higher priority...");
    Thread_b.setPriority(Thread_b.getPriority() + 2);

      try {  // Sleep for a bit
        Thread.sleep(250);
        }
    catch (InterruptedException e) {}

    // Lower thread_b's priority
    System.out.println("Setting Thread b to a lower priority...");
    Thread_b.setPriority(Thread_b.getPriority() - 4);

      try {  // Sleep for a bit
        Thread.sleep(250);
        }
    catch (InterruptedException e) {}

    // Set thread_b's priority equal to the others
    System.out.println("Setting Thread b to a equal priority...");
    Thread_b.setPriority(Thread_b.getPriority() + 2);

      try {  // Sleep for a bit
        Thread.sleep(250);
        }
    catch (InterruptedException e) {}

    // Interrupt the threads
    System.out.println("Interrupting the threads...");
    Thread_a.interrupt();
    Thread_b.interrupt();
    Thread_c.interrupt();
    }
  }
```

Here is the output from running code example Priority.java:

```
Starting the threads...
Thread a: is running
Thread b: is running
Thread c: is running
Thread a: is running
Thread b: is running
Thread c: is running
Thread a: is running
Setting Thread b to a higher priority...
```

```
Thread b: is running
Thread b: is running
Thread b: is running
Thread b: is running
Thread b: is running
Thread b: is running
Thread b: is running
Setting Thread b to a lower priority…
Thread c: is running
Thread a: is running
Thread c: is running
Thread a: is running
Thread c: is running
Thread a: is running
Thread c: is running
Setting Thread b to a equal priority…
Thread c: is running
Thread a: is running
Thread b: is running
Thread c: is running
Thread a: is running
Thread b: is running
Thread c: is running
Thread a: is running
Thread b: is running
Interrupting the threads…
```

Note that the main thread in code example Priority.java was set to the highest priority. So why did the other threads run? The main thread spends a majority of its time sleeping, which causes the thread to become non-runnable. Since the thread is non-runnable, other lower-priority threads are scheduled for execution.

Time Slicing

Java threads can also be time-sliced. This means that a thread running in the JavaVM will give up its execution time slot to some other thread. The thread that was running in the JavaVM may not have finished its work, so it must be scheduled again for time in the JavaVM. Time slicing allows processes or threads to share a CPU which keeps a single thread or process from hogging the CPU.

Just because Java threads can be time-sliced does not mean that they are time-sliced. In fact, the time slicing of Java threads depends on the operating system on which the JavaVM is running on. If the operating system supports the time slicing of threads, then in most cases Java threads will be time-sliced. However, if the operating system does not support thread time slicing, then the Java threads will not be time-sliced.

There is really no easy way to determine if Java threads are time-sliced on a given system. However, you can write a program that will test to see if the environment you are working in is time-sliced. Code example Time-Sliced.java demonstrates how you might test to see if a system is time-sliced. The example creates two threads with equal priorities, then starts them. Each thread has a counter which is constantly incremented. This constant incrementing of the counter will cause one of the threads to starve the other on systems that don't support the time slicing of threads. After the threads execute for awhile, it is then an easy check to see what values the counters have for each thread. If the values are close to each other, then the system uses time slicing.

Source Code: TimeSliced.java

```java
// Thread class that adds to a count variable
class MyThread extends Thread {
  int count=0;

  // Returns the value of the count variable
  public int getCount() {
    return(count);
    }

  public void run() {
    while (true) {
      count++;
      if (isInterrupted())
        break;
      }
    }
  }

public class TimeSliced {

  static public void main(String s[]) {

    MyThread Thread_a, Thread_b;  // Define a couple of threads
    int threshold;

    // Create the threads
    Thread_a = new MyThread();
    Thread_b = new MyThread();

    // Make sure this thread can preempt the others
    Thread.currentThread().setPriority(Thread.MAX_PRIORITY);

    // Start the threads
    System.out.println("Starting the threads...");
    Thread_a.start();
    Thread_b.start();

    try {  // Sleep for a bit
      Thread.sleep(2000);
      }
    catch (InterruptedException e) {}
```

```
     // Interrupt the threads
     System.out.println("Interrupting the threads...");
     Thread_a.interrupt();
     Thread_b.interrupt();

     System.out.println("Thread a: " + Thread_a.getCount());
     System.out.println("Thread b: " + Thread_b.getCount());

     // Take the maximum counter value from each thread and
     // set the threshold value
     if (Thread_a.getCount() > Thread_b.getCount())
       threshold = (int)(Thread_a.getCount() * .2);
     else
       threshold = (int)(Thread_b.getCount() * .2);

     // If the system is time sliced, the value of the counters
     // should be close to each other.
     if (Thread_a.getCount() >= Thread_b.getCount() - threshold &&
                 Thread_a.getCount() <= Thread_b.getCount() + threshold)
       System.out.println("Your system is most likely time sliced");
     else
       System.out.println("Your system is most likely NOT time sliced");
   }
 }
```

Not all systems support time slicing. If your program depends on time slicing, then it is best that you don't count on any sort of time slicing in your program. You can do this by explicitly causing a thread to give up its time in the JavaVM by using the yield() Thread class method.

The yield() method causes the thread to be rescheduled which can allow another equal priority or higher priority thread to run. Code example Priority.java used the yield() method to ensure that the behavior of the program would be the same on both time-sliced and nontime-sliced systems. You may want to try removing the yield() call in the MyThread class in code example Priority.java and see what results you get.

Synchronization

Synchronization is critical in most multithreaded programs because most multithreaded programs involve multiple threads all of which are working with shared data and shared resources. The access to these shared resources and data must be controlled in order to guarantee correct operation of the program.

Monitors

Java threads use monitors to control access to critical sections in application code. A monitor is basically a lock that is used to protect a certain section of code. When a thread enters a critical section, it acquires a monitor. If another thread tries to enter the same critical section when another thread is already holding the monitor, then it is forced to wait until the monitor is free.

If you are familiar with mutual exclusion locks that are used by other thread packages, then you can think of monitors as a type of mutex lock. The major difference between monitors and mutex locks is that mutex locks have to be acquired and released explicitly. Explicitly locking and unlocking a mutex can lead to problems because the developer can make mistakes by releasing a lock too soon or never releasing the lock which can cause data corruption problems or deadlock conditions. Java solves this problem by controlling the locking and unlocking of the monitor for you. All you need to do is specify what you want to control access to and Java does the rest.

Every Java object and class has an associated monitor. Whenever an object is instantiated, Java adds a unique monitor to that object and its associated class. The monitor is allocated and brought to life only when it is used. This way you don't have to pay for the overhead of monitors if you are not going to use them.

A thread can acquire a monitor by entering a method that has been defined as synchronized. Just by adding the synchronized keyword in the method's definition, that object's monitor will be acquired when a thread calls into that synchronized method. When one thread holds the monitor, another thread that tries to acquire the monitor will be blocked and forced to wait until it is released.

A monitor is associated with each object that has one or more synchronized methods. A synchronized method must have the synchronized keyword in its definition:

```
public synchronized void my_method() {}
```

A monitor is also associated with each Java class. This monitor is different than the monitor that is created for each instance of the class. The class monitor is used when a call is made to a static synchronized method:

```
public static synchronized void my_static_method() {}
```

When a thread calls into a synchronized static method, then the class monitor is used to control access to the method from all instantiated objects of that class.

Figure 11.2 shows how the two different types of monitors are used. Every class has an associated monitor that controls access to static synchronized methods in that class. Every thread in an instantiated object of the class will use the class's monitor when accessing synchronized methods for that class. All instantiated objects have an associated monitor that controls the access to synchronized methods in that object. All the threads in the object will share this monitor when accessing synchronized methods in that class. Figure 11.2 shows two instantiated objects derived from class A. Each of these objects has an associated monitor. Threads in object1 will use object1's monitor to access

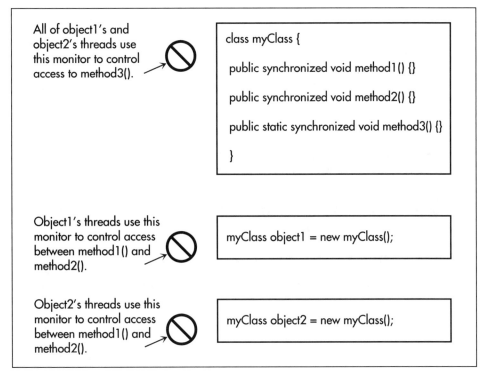

All of object1's and object2's threads use this monitor to control access to method3().

```
class myClass {

    public synchronized void method1() {}

    public synchronized void method2() {}

    public static synchronized void method3() {}

}
```

Object1's threads use this monitor to control access between method1() and method2().

```
myClass object1 = new myClass();
```

Object2's threads use this monitor to control access between method1() and method2().

```
myClass object2 = new myClass();
```

Figure 11.2   Java monitors.

object1's method1() and method2(). The same is true for object2; it will only use its associated monitor. Class A has a static synchronized method3(). Access to this method is controlled by the class's monitor. This means that object1 and object2 will share this monitor when accessing method3(). The class monitor is used when any object derived from the class calls into a static synchronized method in the class.

Code example Monitors.java uses both an object monitor and a class monitor to control access to methods from multiple threads. The example creates two different objects of class Monitors in which each creates two threads. Each of the threads calls into the Critical class, which contains a synchronized method and a static synchronized method. The Method_a method in the Critical class will use a monitor associated with each of the Critical objects. The Method_b method in the Critical class will use the Critical class monitor for all objects.

Source Code: Monitors.java
```
// This is the class that contains the synchronized methods
class Critical {
  // This method is synchronized between threads in the same object.
  public synchronized void Method_a() {
    System.out.println(Thread.currentThread().getName() + " is in
                                          Method_a");
```

```
      try {  // Sleep for a bit
        Thread.sleep((int)Math.round(Math.random() * 5000));
        }
      catch (InterruptedException e) {}

      System.out.println(Thread.currentThread().getName() + " is leaving
                                                        Method_a");
      }

   // This method is synchronized between all threads in all objects
   public static synchronized void Method_b() {
      System.out.println(Thread.currentThread().getName() + " is in
                                                        Method_b");

      try {  // Sleep for a bit
        Thread.sleep((int)Math.round(Math.random() * 5000));
        }
      catch (InterruptedException e) {}

      System.out.println(Thread.currentThread().getName() + " is leaving
                                                        Method_b");
      }
   }

// This class creates two objects of this class.  Each object creates two
// threads of which each call into the Critical class
public class Monitors implements Runnable {

   Critical CritObj;  // Reference to critical class object

   // Constructor for this class
   Monitors(String ObjName) {
     Thread Thread_a, Thread_b;

     // Create a new Critical object and two threads
     CritObj = new Critical();
     Thread_a = new Thread(this, ObjName+":Thread_a");
     Thread_b = new Thread(this, ObjName+":Thread_b");

     // Start the threads
     Thread_a.start();
     Thread_b.start();
     }

   public static void main(String args[]) {
     Monitors Mobj1, Mobj2;
     // Create two objects of this class
     Mobj1 = new Monitors("Object1");
     Mobj2 = new Monitors("Object2");
     }

   public void run() {
```

```
  // Call each method in the Critical class
  CritObj.Method_a();
  CritObj.Method_b();
    }
  }
```

Here is the output from running code example Monitors.java:

```
Object1:Thread_a is in Method_a
Object2:Thread_a is in Method_a
Object1:Thread_a is leaving Method_a
Object1:Thread_a is in Method_b
Object1:Thread_b is in Method_a
Object2:Thread_a is leaving Method_a
Object2:Thread_b is in Method_a
Object1:Thread_a is leaving Method_b
Object2:Thread_a is in Method_b
Object2:Thread_a is leaving Method_b
Object1:Thread_b is leaving Method_a
Object1:Thread_b is in Method_b
Object2:Thread_b is leaving Method_a
Object1:Thread_b is leaving Method_b
Object2:Thread_b is in Method_b
Object2:Thread_b is leaving Method_b
```

Notice that Method_a was entered by both Monitors' objects at the same time. This is because each Monitor's object has its own monitor for the Critical object. Also note that Method_b could only be entered by one thread in all of the Monitors' objects. This is due to the fact that Method_b is static, so the Critical class monitor is used.

Java monitors are also reentrant which means that a thread that has acquired a monitor can make a call back into the same method. When the thread calls back into the method, the monitor is reacquired by the thread. This feature alone can save developers many hours of frustration. When locks are programmed explicitly, developers need to be very careful that they don't make calls into functions that require a lock that is already held.

Source Code: Reentrant.java
```
// This class's MyMethod method recursively calls itself
class TestClass {

  // Keep track of how many times the method is called
  static int times = 1;

  public synchronized void MyMethod() {

    // Set a local variable and increment times
    int i = times++;

    System.out.println("MyMethod has started " + i + " time(s)");
```

```
    // Recursively call this method
    while (times < 4) MyMethod();
      System.out.println("MyMethod has exited " + i + " time(s)");
    }
  }

// This class calls a synchronized method
public class Reentrant {

  public static void main(String args[]) {

    // Create the class
    TestClass Test = new TestClass();

    // Call the class, which will call itself a few times
    Test.MyMethod();
    }
  }
```

Code example Reentrant.java demonstrates how monitors can be reentrant. The example defines a TestClass class that includes the synchronized MyMethod method. The MyMethod method simply calls itself recursively a couple of times. Here is the output from the example:

```
MyMethod has started 1 time(s)
MyMethod has started 2 time(s)
MyMethod has started 3 time(s)
MyMethod has exited 3 time(s)
MyMethod has exited 2 time(s)
MyMethod has exited 1 time(s)
```

Notice that the thread was able to call back into the MyMethod method. This demonstrates that the Java monitors are indeed reentrant.

Condition Variables

Java does not support the direct use of condition variables. However, the same effect of using condition variables can be achieved with the wait( ) and notify( ) methods. Both of these methods, in addition to the notifyAll( ) method, belong to the Java Object class.

TIP The wait( ), notify( ), and notifyAll( ) methods require a monitor to be associated with their use. Therefore, these calls can only be used in methods that have been synchronized. The Java runtime will generate an error if you try to use wait( ), notify( ), or notifyAll( ) in an unsynchronized method.

The wait( ) method behaves like a condition_wait( ) variable. The thread that calls the wait( ) method blocks and waits for a certain condition to be satisfied.

When a thread calls wait( ), the monitor that it was holding is released and the thread will block until it is signaled to wake. When the thread is signaled, it reacquires the monitor and continues execution after the wait( ) call. It is important to notice that the monitor associated with the object—that contains the synchronized method—is released when the wait( ) method is called. This will allow another synchronized method in the class to run, which may contain the code that will wake the other waiting thread.

The notify( ) method is similar to a condition_signal( ) variable. It signals a waiting thread to wake from a wait( ) method. When a thread calls the notify( ) method, it will signal the thread that called a wait( ) method to resume its execution. When the waiting thread receives the signal, it tries to reacquire the monitor. The waiting thread may block trying to reacquire the monitor because the thread that called the notify( ) method may still be using that object's monitor. Once the thread that called notify( ) has finished executing, the synchronized method will release the monitor and the waiting thread can acquire it.

The notifyAll( ) method works in the same way as the notify( ) method. The only difference is that the notifyAll( ) method will wake all the threads in the object that are blocked in a wait( ) call. All the threads that were waiting will then race to acquire the monitor. Only one thread will get the monitor, but all the others will keep trying. This call can cause some overhead in programs that have multiple threads all blocked in a wait( ) call. This is due to the fact then when all the threads are signaled to wake, they will compete and continue to compete for the monitor until all of them have had a chance to run. This is different than the notify( ) method; the notify( ) method only wakes a single thread at a time from the pool of waiting threads.

The Object class also has support for wait( ) methods that have an associated timer. If the associated timer has expired, after waiting for that period of time, the waiting thread will resume its execution. For example, a thread calls the wait method with a timer value of 30 seconds. If 30 seconds pass before the thread has been signaled to wake, then the thread will be awakened and will continue its execution regardless of whether it was signaled. This method can be quite handy if a thread has to wait on a condition that may never happen.

Code example EzSearch.java demonstrates many of the concepts that have been covered, thus far, and also demonstrates how a programmer can synchronize the execution of multiple threads using the wait( ) and notify( ) methods. The example performs a simple text search in multiple files. A thread is created for each file that is to be searched. The Search object threads send messages to a synchronized class. A thread is also created to control the program's GUI. The GUI thread receives messages from the synchronized class and displays the messages on the GUI.

The example contains a number of different classes. The Search class is used to perform the text search in the file given. The IOC class is used to implement the synchronized object that is used by the Search objects and the EzDisplay object. The Message class provides the Message object that is passed between the IOC class and the threads. The EzSearch class is used to provide the EzSearch object that acts as the main function for the program.

Notice that the ioc object is passed to each of the Search objects and to the EzDisplay object. The Search objects and the EzDisplay object use the ioc object to pass messages between the objects. This permits the EzDisplay object to read messages one at a time from the ioc object and also permits the multiple Search objects to send messages to the ioc object. The IOC class has synchronized methods which keep the multiple threads from writing over messages and from reading partial messages.

Make sure that you understand how this example works. The key concept that you should understand is how the threads in the example communicate with each other through the use of synchronized methods and the notify( ) and wait( ) methods.

Source Code: EzSearch.java

```java
import java.awt.*;
import java.awt.event.*;
import java.io.*;
import java.util.Hashtable;

// This class provides the threads that do the searching
class Search extends Thread {

   private String filename;   // File name to search in
   private String target;     // String to search for
   private IOC ioc;           // Object to pass messages to

   // Constructor for this class
   // Parameters:
   // thr_name - This threads name
   // filename - File to search in
   // target   - String to search for
   // grp      - Thread group to add this thread to
   // ioc      - object used to pass messages to
   Search(String thr_name, String filename, String target, ThreadGroup grp,
                                                            IOC ioc) {
      super(grp, thr_name);
      this.target = target;
      this.filename = filename;
      this.ioc = ioc;
      }

   // Override the run method for this thread
   public void run() {
      FileInputStream fis;
      BufferedInputStream bis;
      int chr, yield_cnt = 0, index = 0, found = 0;

      // This try block performs the I/O calls to do the reading
      // of the search file
```

```
    try {
      // Get a file stream to read from
      fis = new FileInputStream(filename);
      // Make the stream a buffered stream
      bis = new BufferedInputStream(fis);

      // Send initial message to the ioc object
      ioc.putMessage(getName()+" has found "+found+" matches in file
                               "+filename, getName(), Message.RUNNING);

      // Continue to read from the file until end of file is reached
      while ((chr = bis.read()) != -1) {
        // Is the character part of the search string
        if (target.charAt(index) == chr) index++;
        else index = 0;

        // Did we find a match?
        if (index == target.length() - 1) {
          found++;
          index = 0;
          // Send message to ioc object
          ioc.putMessage(getName()+" has found "+found+" matches in file
                                 "+filename, getName(), Message.RUNNING);
        }

        // Let another thread run...
        if (++yield_cnt % 5000 == 0) {
          yield_cnt = 0;
          yield();
        }
      }
      // Send final message to ioc object
      ioc.putMessage("EzSearch found "+found+" matches in file "+filename,
                                     getName(), Message.DONE);

      // If file was not found then send a message and exit this thread
    }
    catch (FileNotFoundException e) {
      ioc.putMessage("File "+filename+" was not found", getName(),
                                                     Message.ERROR);
    }
    catch (IOException e) {
    // If an I/O error occurs send a message and exit this thread
      ioc.putMessage(getName()+" IOException while reading file"+filename,
                                     getName(), Message.ERROR);
    }
  }
}

// This class acts as the message that is passed between the IOC class
class Message {
```

```
      public final static int RUNNING = 1;
      public final static int DONE = 2;
      public final static int ERROR = 3;

      String ID;      // Who sent the message
      String Text;    // Text of the message
      int State;      // State of the thread that sent the message
      }

// This class acts as a monitor and communication channel between
// multiple threads.  Note that the methods in this class are
// synchronized.
class IOC { // InterObject Communication
   private boolean messageWaiting = false;  // Is a message waiting
   private Message message;   // The waiting message

   // This method is used by the threads to send messages
   public synchronized void putMessage(String msg, String ID, int State) {
      // If there is a message already here then wait for the message
      // to be consumed
      while (messageWaiting == true)
        try {
          wait();
          }
        catch (InterruptedException e) {}

      // Create a new message object
      message = new Message();
      // Fill the message object
      message.Text = new String(msg);
      message.ID = new String(ID);
      message.State = State;

      // There is a new message waiting
      messageWaiting = true;

      // Notify any thread waiting for a message
      notify();
      }

   // This method is used by the display thread to get messages
   public synchronized Message getMessage() {
      // If there is not a message here then wait for one
      while (messageWaiting == false)
        try {
          wait();
          }
        catch (InterruptedException e) {}

      // There is not a message here anymore, we consumed it
      messageWaiting = false;
```

```
    // Notify any thread waiting to put a message
    notify();

    // Give the message to the thread that asked for it
    return message;
    }
  }

// This class controls the GUI for this application
// Note that this class extends the Frame class and
// implements the Runnable interface.
class EzDisplay extends Frame implements Runnable, ActionListener {

  private EzSearch ez;   // Reference to application object
  private IOC ioc;       // Object to get messages from
  private Panel CenterPanel;  // Local panel object
  // This is a hash table object used to store other objects
  private Hashtable table = new Hashtable();
  private Button quitButton;

  // Constructor for this class
  // Parameters:
  // ez  - Reference to application object
  // ioc - Object to get messages from
  EzDisplay(EzSearch ez, IOC ioc) {
    super("EzSearch");
    this.ez = ez;
    this.ioc = ioc;

    // Set a layout and a font for the GUI
    setLayout(new BorderLayout());
    Font fnt = new Font("Courier", Font.BOLD, 14);

    // Create a title label for the GUI
    Label title = new Label("Searching for \""+ez.getSearchString()+"\" in
                            "+ez.getNumFiles()+" files", Label.LEFT);
    title.setFont(fnt);
    add("North", title);

    // Create and add a quit button to the GUI
    quitButton = new Button("Quit");
    quitButton.addActionListener(this);
    add("South", quitButton);

    // Create a panel to display results
    CenterPanel = new Panel();
    CenterPanel.setLayout(new GridLayout(0, 1, 0, 10));
    // Add the panel to the GUI
    add("Center", CenterPanel);

    // Pack all the widgets together and display them
    pack();
```

```
      show();
    }

// The run method for this thread
public void run() {
  Message message;
  Color TextColor;
  Label label;

  // Give this thread an advantage over the others
  Thread.currentThread().setPriority(Thread.currentThread().getPriority()
                                                              + 1);


  // Loop forever, until quit button is pressed
  while (true) {

    // Get a message from the ioc object
    message = ioc.getMessage();

    // Set the color of the text acording to the state
    switch (message.State) {
      case Message.RUNNING :
        TextColor = Color.green;
        break;
      case Message.DONE :
        TextColor = Color.blue;
        break;
      case Message.ERROR :
        TextColor = Color.red;
        break;
      default : TextColor = Color.black;
      }

    // See if the hash table contains an object from this
    // message ID
    if (table.containsKey(message.ID) == false) {
      // Object not found in hash table, create a new one
      label = new Label(message.Text, Label.LEFT);

      // Set the foreground color for this label
      label.setForeground(TextColor);

      // Put this label in the hash table for future reference
      table.put(message.ID, label);

      // Add the label to the GUI
      CenterPanel.add(label);

      // Pack the widgets and display them
      pack();
      show();
```

```
      }

      // An object was found for the given message ID
      else   {
        // Get the object from the hash table
        label = (Label)table.get(message.ID);

        // Set the color of the label and change its text
        label.setForeground(TextColor);
        label.setText(message.Text);
        }
      }
    }

  // This method gets called when the quit button is pressed
  public void actionPerformed(ActionEvent ae) {
    setVisible(false);
    dispose();
    ez.StopSearch();
    }
  }

// This class is the main application class
public class EzSearch {

  private ThreadGroup ThrGroup;   // Thread group for search threads
  private static String SearchString; // String to search for
  private static String ListOfFiles[]; // List of files to search

  // This method returns the number of files that the application is
                                                      searching
  public int getNumFiles() { return ListOfFiles.length; }

  // This method returns the string that the application is searching for
  public String getSearchString() { return SearchString; }

  // This is the main method for this application
  public static void main(String s[]) {

    // Check to see if the application was called with the correct
    // number of arguments
    if (s.length <= 1) {
      System.out.println("Usage: EzSearch <search string> <list of
                                                      files>");
      System.exit(0);
      }

    // Set the search string and the list of files
    SearchString = new String(s[0]);
    ListOfFiles = new String[s.length - 1];
    for (int i=0; i<ListOfFiles.length; i++)
```

```
        ListOfFiles[i] = new String(s[i+1]);

    // Create an application object
    EzSearch ez = new EzSearch();

    // Create a communication object
    IOC ioc = new IOC();

    // Create the display object and start it
    EzDisplay ed = new EzDisplay(ez, ioc);
    Thread DisplayThread = new Thread(ed);
    DisplayThread.start();

    // Call the StartThreads method with the ioc object
    ez.StartThreads(ioc);
    }

// This method starts one thread for each file to be searched
public void StartThreads(IOC ioc) {
    Thread Threads[];

    // Create a thread group for the threads
    ThrGroup = new ThreadGroup("EzSearch Group");

    // Create an array of thread objects
    Threads = new Thread[ListOfFiles.length];

    // Create the thread objects, add to the group, and start the threads
    for (int i=0; i<ListOfFiles.length; i++) {
      Threads[i] = new Search("Thread"+i, ListOfFiles[i], SearchString,
                                                ThrGroup, ioc);

      Threads[i].start();
      }
    }

// This method stops the search threads and exits
public void StopSearch() {
  System.exit(0);
  }
}
```

Volatile Keyword

The Java language includes the volatile keyword which can be used in the declaration of data. It is used to force the JavaVM to perform an atomic test and set operations on the associated variable. This means that if a variable is declared with the volatile keyword, then: When the variable is read, its contents are always loaded from memory and when the variable is written, the new value is written to memory.

This may seem a bit odd considering that all variables are stored in memory. However, many times variables are stored in registers or cache on a CPU. If a thread were to set the value of a variable by storing the value in a register and another thread were to read the contents of the same variable, but reading it from another CPU, then the two threads could be setting and reading different values for the same variable.

This is what the volatile keyword protects against. It tells the JavaVM to make sure to put the stored value out to main memory so that other threads can see the new value. It also tells any threads that are reading the variable to get its value from main memory and not from a local cache or register. This keyword alone can be a big time-saver in the case where you want to make sure that a single variable is tested and set correctly by multiple threads.

The only problem with the volatile keyword is that it is not implemented in the current release of Java. This means that the only way to protect a variable that is used by multiple threads, is through the use of synchronized methods and monitors.

TIP The volatile keyword is not implemented in the current release of Java.

Java on Multiprocessor Systems

By default, some Java platforms use a user threading model called Green threads. Green threads were the original threading package that the Java virtual machine used. In most cases, Green threads have been replaced with some sort of native threading package. For example, the JavaVM on Windows95 uses the win32 threading libraries. The main difference between Green threads and a native threading package is in how the Java threads are used. Green threads only provide a user level of threading which maps all Java threads into a single thread in the native platform. JavaVMs that are based on a native threading package have the benefit of being able to map Java threads directly to native threads. This permits multiple Java threads to be executing on the native platform concurrently. Using native threading JavaVMs will allow you to write programs in Java that can be executed in parallel.

If you are using a JavaVM that does not support native threads or is using Green threads, then any Java program you write is only capable of running a single native thread. In this case the JavaVM is single-threaded; the threads that are running in a Java application are not executing in a truly concurrent manner. There is no level of parallelism.

NATIVE THREADS ON SOLARIS

Initially the JavaVM that was shipped with Solaris did not support native threads. As a result, you could not write programs that could take advantage of multiprocessor hardware. This may seem rather odd since Sun has been shipping multiprocessing hardware for quite some time and has a very mature threading model. The reason for this is quite simple. In order to keep the original JavaVM simple, Green threads were developed to be used as the default threading environment. When Java became popular and ports were underway to different environments, it was somewhat simple at that time to replace Green threads with a native threads implementation. Since Java was developed on Solaris, no port was really ever needed. So with higher priorities than native threading, the Solaris native threads port was put off. Today you can get a native threads implementation for Solaris and still use Green threads. In fact, in some cases using both threading models can be an aid in testing for thread synchronization bugs.

Thread-Safe Classes

A programmer who wishes to develop class libraries for use with other applications and classes must make the libraries thread safe. The developer can't guarantee that the methods in the library will always be called from a single-threaded program. If any methods in a class require that a single method can only be running at any given time, then that method must be protected in some way.

The previous chapters discussed ways in which to protect critical sections in Java code. Keep in mind that class libraries that are not thread safe can cause big problems if used concurrently by multiple threads.

Java Threads versus POSIX

There are quite a few differences between a standard threads package and Java threads. One common threads package that is used on many different systems is POSIX threads. POSIX threads are a complete threads package that includes many different features and synchronization methods.

Java threads is also a complete threading package; however, it does not include all the same features that other thread packages have. To counter this, Java threads are much easier to use and manage than other thread packages. Features that may be missing in Java threads could also be constructed out of other Java primitives. Java threads may not contain the level of detail that some applications require, but for most applications it satisfies any threading needs required by that application.

Table 11.1 Java Threads versus POSIX Threads Comparison

ACTION	JAVA METHOD	POSIX CALL
Thread Creation	Instantiate a thread object	pthread_create()
Thread Join	join() method	pthread_join()
Thread Exit	stop() method	pthread_exit()
Thread Yield	yield() method	sched_yield()
Get thread ID	getName() method	pthread_self()
Thread Kill	stop() method	pthread_kill()
Mutex Lock	Java Monitors	pthread_mutex_lock()
Condition Variable	wait() and notify() methods	pthread_cond_wait() and pthread_cond_signal
Semaphores	Not Available	sem_wait() and sem_post()
Attribute objects	Not Available	pthread_attr_xxx calls
Thread-specific data	Not Available	pthread_setspecific and pthread_getspecific
Thread Priorities	setPriority() method	pthread_setschedparam()
Thread Cancellation	stop() method and catch ThreadDeath	pthread_cancel()

Table 11.1 shows a comparison between Java thread methods and POSIX thread calls.

Summary

Using threads in modern programs can be difficult. Understanding the threading libraries and dealing with all the problems of creating concurrent programs is not easy. However, Java has come a long way to make the use of threads in programs much easier. Hopefully, this chapter gave you a good idea of the capabilities of threads in Java programs. Since Java is based on threads, it is almost impossible not to use them in your programs. So take advantage of Java's multithreading capabilities to make your programs more interactive and concurrent. If you are looking for more information related to multithreading, please see Appendix A.

Java Security

Introduction

Computer security used to be a reasonably straightforward concern. Before networks, desktop systems, floppy drives, and the other connectivity options we enjoy today, total system security could be enforced simply by maintaining the physical security of the computer. A machine locked within a glass room with no access from the outside world is about as secure as you can hope to get. After all, if the machine is inaccessible from outside the organization, you only have to worry about what the internal staff is doing with the system (a threat which usually greatly outweighs any threat from outside).

Unfortunately, stand-alone machines are limited in what they can do. In such systems it is very difficult to share information with co-workers, customers, or partners. Users must travel to the data, a time-consuming and sometimes expensive process, instead of the data coming to them. To overcome these limitations, we have networked our systems to other machines worldwide, a process which has enabled new applications and new ways of doing business but which has simultaneously exposed our systems to a level of threat unknown in the days of the true glass house. This balance between security and usability is one of the classic engineering trade-offs; a system which is 100 percent secure will also be 100 percent useless. We must view system security as risk management, a delicate balance between the risks we are willing to take and the cost of a break-in, between the cost of security and the need to just get the job done.

Executable Content and Security Threats

As connectivity between machines increased, the old model for security failed. While physical security is a necessary condition for security (if you can't guarantee the physical security of the system, you cannot build any kind of security), it is no longer sufficient. Viruses riding on floppy disks, network crackers, and even the occasional Internet worm all threaten our machines. These dangers present a very different type of threat, one which cannot be mitigated by the physical security of the machine. The attacks come to us, riding on the exact same communications mechanisms we depend on to make our machines useful.

Executable content on the World Wide Web is one such new threat. Executable content is in some ways more insidious than the previous generation of attacks; while a virus was typically carried into the site on a contaminated floppy, executable content is thrust upon unsuspecting users through the simple action of following a Web link. The user may not even be aware that the referenced page contains a piece of code which is now running on her desktop with full access to her files and other resources on the corporate network. Where viruses used to spread by intimate contact, that is, the unsafe sharing of floppies, executable content allows these new attacks to become invisible, airborne Trojan horses. As frightening as executable content on the Web may be, the rise of executable content in e-mail is even worse. At least on the Web the user is still an active part of importing the offending code; he must follow the link in the first place. With executable e-mail, the simple act of checking your in-box in the morning can expose you to security threats.

Java Security on the Web

But, like the network itself, executable content is too important and useful a concept for us to simply discard it as insecure. Fortunately, the designers of the Java platform were aware of this danger and designed mechanisms that can control what executable content written for the Java platform can do to the user's machine. These mechanisms allow users to download and run Java code from untrusted Web sites, RMI servers, and many other sources without undue risk to their systems. This allows users and corporations to harness the power of the network and executable content while still balancing their concerns for security.

Java Security in the Enterprise

For the first two years of the Java platform most people used it for applets in Web browsers. While these simple frontends and GUIs revolutionized application delivery on the Internet and the intranet, they did not exploit the power of Java for server-side, middleware applications. At the 1997 JavaOne conference, Sun and its partners announced a range of new APIs and initiatives intended to broaden the Java platform and make it more useful for servers, daemons, and other network services. These APIs have now been delivered in Java 2 and associated extensions. As the Java platform moves to the server side of the network, it introduces a whole range of new security-related issues. How can a Write Once, Run Anywhere service be made secure when it is deployed on a range of operating systems which might have slightly different security semantics? How can network services be built which protect themselves from abuse by clever attackers? How can the base functionality of the Java platform be extended in a secure, platform-independent manner? The new protection domain security system in Java 2 provides a way to accomplish all of these tasks.

Java Security on the Network

Once the Web client has been protected from rogue executable content and the server has been protected from attacks and misuse, the next weak link is the network itself. It does little good to bolt down the client and server if all the information passing between the two is susceptible to eavesdropping. Clear text transmitted over the network can be picked up and used by anyone with access to the network wire. This could be a sophisticated attacker intercepting traffic on the Internet or it could be a co-worker snooping the office network. In these days of laptops and portable Ethernet sniffers, it could be an attacker who simply walked in off the street and plugged into a convenient RJ-45. The Java Cryptography Extension (JCE) protects against these snooping attacks by providing a high-level API for encrypting information before storing or transmitting it. With the JCE one need never expose clear text to the network. Instead, an eavesdropping attacker will only get the much less useful cipher text for his troubles.

Java Platform Security

This chapter deals with the place of the Java Platform in an overall security plan. Keep in mind that even Java 2's security systems are no substitute for a well-planned, comprehensive security policy; X.509 certificates, digital signatures, encryption, and electronic token cards do not provide half the protection that comes from an informed user community, the members of which change their passwords frequently, remember to lock their screens when away from their desks, and don't bring floppy disks full of shareware to work each Monday morning.

Java security mechanisms do provide good solutions to some very specific problems. When used as part of an overall policy, these mechanisms can substantially increase a system's security and usability. In the remainder of this chapter we will examine Java security mechanisms from three different viewpoints: the client's, the server's, and the network's. Each of these three views has its own issues and challenges which are addressed by different aspects of the Java platform.

Java Security Fundamentals

It is surprisingly hard to build secure systems on top of typical 3GLs. The potential for dangerous bugs in code written in C, C++, or Basic makes it difficult to ensure that the system cannot be compromised by a clever, well-informed attacker. These bugs can be very subtle and exist in a deployed system for years before being found and exploited. Furthermore, while traditional operating systems may be able to distinguish individual users and protect them from the hostile actions of each other, they do not have any concept of protection based on the source of an executable; a program run by a user has all the abilities and privilege of that user. This means that executable content running in that user's browser inherits the user's identity and can steal, modify, or destroy any information that user can access. While some operating systems may provide a solution to this problem, such as the set UID bit in the UNIX operating system, these mechanisms have their own problems. Since they allow one user to masquerade as another, they are often considered a security threat themselves and their widespread use is strongly discouraged.

The Java platform has several important features that make it fundamentally more secure than other executable content systems. These safety features, which in some cases were included in the environment for reasons other than security, form the foundation of the Java security system.

Indirect Execution

Perhaps the most important difference between the Java platform and more traditional operating environments is that Java code does not run directly on the user's machine. Instead, Java code runs inside the Java Virtual Machine which then executes native CPU instructions on behalf of the Java code. This indirect execution provides the most powerful feature of the Java platform, Write Once, Run Anywhere code. It also provides an important security benefit.

As previously noted, in most desktop operating systems and even in many more powerful, server operating systems, the security system assumes that any program run by a given user should have the full authority and privilege of that user. So any executable a user runs, regardless of from where it came, can do anything that user can do to any part of the system which that user can access. The situation is even worse in the previous generation of desktop operating systems (a generation which is still very widely deployed in homes and businesses) where there is no security whatsoever. The entire machine is wide open to anything that happens to run on it.

This fundamental security assumption, that a user can trust the code she is executing, was made in the days when it was difficult to get an executable onto a system (a trip to the machine room with a half-inch tape was usually as easy as it got). So any executables on the system were presumed to be safe for any user to execute. As desktop machines, with their floppy drives and smaller tape drives, became common, this assumption became suspect. The ease with which viruses spread and the rate at which Trojan horses sneaked into the corporate PC network show how badly this assumption has held up in an environment with even limited inter-machine connectivity.

Executable Web content provides the final blow to this security model. The last thing any thinking person wants is for an untrusted (and possibly untrustworthy) piece of code from the Net to be able to do anything the user is allowed to do. But since most operating systems lack the checks and mechanisms needed to distinguish between the user and programs the user happens to be running, it is impossible to control what the program does. The best the OS (or Web browser or e-mail client, etc.) can do is offer the user the choice to run the program or not. If the user chooses to run the code, all bets are off. While some operating systems, known as *trusted* systems and usually deployed in military accounts, do distinguish between user and program, these systems are not widely used and suffer from sometimes extreme usability problems.

In order to make executable content safe, we really need a way to identify untrusted code and limit what it can do based on what the user (or more likely in a corporate environment, the administrator or security officer) determines to be safe. The indirect execution of Java code by the JVM provides just such a mechanism. Since the Java applet never has direct access to the CPU or the operating system, the JVM can limit the applet and prevent hostile actions like stealing files or implanting viruses. The applet cannot directly call OS routines to open files, make network connections, or take other risky actions. It must go through the Java core classes in order to access this type of functionality. This allows the JVM to act as a gatekeeper which prevents the untrusted applet from running amok on the user's machine. The Java security model depends on the indirect execution of code and the gatekeeping role of the JVM.

What about Just in Time Compilers and JavaChips?

If indirect execution is such a valuable security feature, without which it would be arguably impossible to secure an executable content system, where does that leave Java just-in-time (JIT) compilers which generate native machine code on-the-fly and JavaChips, in which the Java bytecode is the machine code? Do these direct execution systems compromise Java security for the sake of performance? Fortunately, the answer is no.

From the security point of view, JIT compilers are little different from interpreted Java implementations. A potential attacker is only able to send the target machine Java bytecodes. The fact that this code is then converted to machine code on the local system does not give the attacker a way to smuggle his own machine code in with the applet. All the familiar Java security mechanisms are still in place (see the Verifier discussed later). As long as you have obtained your JIT from a reputable source, an attacker will not be able to use it to pillage your machine. As long as you're not purchasing a JIT (or any other security-sensitive code) from the Chaos Computer Club or the League of Doom, you are safe.

JavaChip-based systems are similarly well protected by the JVM. The JVM sits above the chip and operating system on which it runs (see Figure 12.1). It presents the same APIs and capabilities to the applets it hosts regardless of whether the underlying chip runs the Intel, SPARC, or ARM instruction set, or even the Java bytecode instruction set. Since the underlying hardware is invisible to the untrusted Java code, the existence of a JavaChip does not impact security.

Language Safety Features

In addition to indirect execution, the Java language contains several features which make it inherently easier to secure. More importantly, the Java language also lacks many features which make it difficult to secure systems based around other 3GLs. This protection is provided by several features implemented in both the language and the runtime:

- *The Java language does not contain explicit pointers.* All memory access is by reference through object handles or primitive names which cannot be forged, pointed at sensitive parts of the security system, or otherwise abused.

- *Java Arrays are bound-checked at runtime.* Since arrays know how long they are, they can not be overstuffed in order to change memory the application should not be allowed to touch.

- *Java Strings are immutable.* Once built, a String cannot be changed. Again this prevents the all too common buffer overflow attack which plagues C and C++.

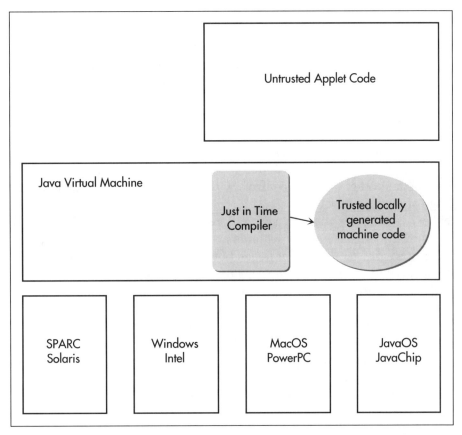

Figure 12.1   Untrusted code sits above the JVM, which protects the rest of the system from attack.

- *Java is type-safe.* Objects cannot be cast to incompatible types so nonexistent methods cannot be called on objects.

- *Java implements four levels of access protection for an object's state.* Public (available to anyone who has access to that class), protected (accessible by that class and child classes), private (accessible only by that class), and default (accessible by other classes inside this classes package).

- *Lacking an explicit initialization value, all Java primitives and objects are initialized to a well-defined default value.*

Interestingly, these features are as important for reliability as they are for security. Software metric studies have estimated that approximately 50 to 70 percent of all bugs occur in the rote, tedious, bookkeeping code needed to do pointer arithmetic, bounds check an array, or allocate and free memory. By automating these tasks the Java language removes the source of over half of all bugs, thus resulting in not only more secure but also more robust applications.

The Verifier

The limited safety features of most 3GLs are enforced by the compiler. In C and C++ illegal casts are flagged as errors during compilation (although the programmer can usually placate the compiler simply by promising it that he knows what he is doing). These languages rely on the compiler to make these checks for two simple reasons. First, without a runtime execution environment there is nowhere else to make these checks. Second, these languages were never considered an integral part of overall system security. These languages are compiled down to machine code and the operating system enforces access restrictions and other security controls without regard to the original source language of that machine code.

Neither of these restrictions or assumptions is true in the Java platform. As we saw previously, language safety features are an integral part of Java security. This means we *absolutely cannot* depend on the compiler to enforce language safety. A clever attacker could write a compiler which did not enforce all the language safety features and would generate bytecode files which did attempt to use memory pointers to attack the system or which did forge their own security-related classes. Since the compiler is not under our control, we cannot trust it or depend on it as part of the security system.

In order to overcome these difficulties, the Java platform delays these critical security checks until the code is under our control and can be examined by a JVM we trust. Instead of depending on the compiler, these checks are performed by a special class called the Verifier.

SAFETY CHECKS AND THE JAVA COMPILER

Actually, the Java compiler also performs many of these safety checks. The Verifier simply rechecks type casts and other dangerous operations. The two systems perform the same checks for two different reasons. The compiler is concerned with safety and spotting bugs early in the development cycle. The Verifier is concerned with security and preventing evil, hand-coded attacks from slipping into the system.

The Verifier is part of the JVM and is invoked by the ClassLoader every time a new class is loaded. The Verifier scans the bytecodes and ensures that the following assertions about the code are true:

- All opcodes have the proper number of arguments.
- There are no illegal casts.
- The arguments of each opcode have the proper type.

- Access to private, public, and protected classes is properly enforced.

- The JVM's registers are properly used.

By ensuring that each of these criteria is met, the Verifier enforces the language safety features previously described.

Protection Domains

The Verifier forms one half of the runtime security checks built into the Java platform. Its job is to ensure that downloaded applets contain no subtle attacks against the rest of the security system. In Java 2, the second half of the runtime security is provided by Protection Domains. Protection domains control what resources, disk files, network ports, and so on, a Java class can access once it is running inside the JVM. Protection domains operate by tracking from where each class came (for example, the local file system or an Internet host) and whether that class was signed by someone we trust. This combination of where the code came from and who has signed that code is called a CodeSource. When a class is loaded, it is placed in the protection domain appropriate for classes loaded from that code source.

For example, all class files downloaded from java.sun.com and signed by Sun could be placed in one domain. All class files from www.ibm.com and signed by IBM could be placed in another domain. Each of these two domains could be assigned a set of privileges and permissions depending on how much you trust each of these two vendors. You could define a specific directory where applets from Sun could store files and another directory for IBM's applets. Applets from either company could then read, write, and delete files in their own directory, but would be unable to look in the other's directory or at any other information on the system.

A protection domain which implements a very rigorous and restrictive policy is provided as the default domain. All unsigned classes and all those signed by someone we do not trust are placed in this protection domain so they can be safely executed without worrying about what they might try to do to the system. This provides a level of protection equivalent to the SecurityManager used in JDK 1.0 and 1.1.

How Do Protection Domains Actually Work?

A Java application can be made up of classes which have been loaded from many different sources. The privileges granted each class depend on from where that class came and who signed it. So the question is not, does this application's protection domain allow it to access a certain resource, but rather, does the protection domain in which a particular class in the application runs

WHERE DID THE SECURITYMANAGER GO?

Protection domains are a new feature of Java 2. Before Java 2 the SecurityManager was used to enforce the security policy. The SecurityManager was a special class which an application developer could, at his discretion, include in his applications. Typically, the SecurityManager would be instantiated and installed during application startup. Once a SecurityManager was installed it could not be overridden or modified, nor could it be replaced.

Whenever a class wished to access a vulnerable resource, like a file or the network, that class would have to call a method in the appropriate Java core class, that is java.io.File or java.net.Socket. When called, these methods would first check to see if a SecurityManager was installed in this runtime. If so, they would call one of the SecurityManager's methods to determine if the requested access is allowed by the security policy. java.io.File would call SecurityManager .checkRead(String file) to determine if a particular file could be read. java.net .Socket would call SecurityManager.checkConnect(String host, int port) to see if a class could connect to a certain host. If the action was allowed, the SecurityManager would silently return and the core class method would proceed. If the action was not allowed, the SecurityManager would throw a GeneralSecurityException which the core class would throw back to the calling class.

Part of the job of writing a Java application which could import and run untrusted Java classes was to include an appropriate SecurityManager in your application. The programmer would extend the base SecurityManager class and override the various check methods to implement the security policy required by the application. Thus, the authors of HotJava and Netscape Navigator included a SecurityManager in their code which protected users of those products. Someone writing a new Java application could craft a security policy appropriate for that use.

While the SecurityManager superficially looks like the protection domain architecture, it has several major flaws. First, and probably most objectionable, an application's security policy was hard-coded into a piece of Java source code. This made the security policy very inflexible. In order to change even the smallest part of the policy, a programmer had to modify the source code, recompile the application, then re-deploy the modified executable. (While in theory you could write a SecurityManager which reads its policy from a file, in practice writing this code and ensuring that the policy file was accurate and immune to tampering is so hard that most people just hard-code the policy.) Since it was so hard to modify policy, almost all organizations ended up accepting whatever policy the browser manufacturer built in. While most organizations accepted this limitation for a Web browser, they were not about to trust a third party to set security policy for other, more valuable or vulnerable, parts of their IT systems.

Another major flaw in the SecurityManager architecture was that security was built into an application, if and only if, the programmer of that application decided to include a SecurityManager. Again, this limit is acceptable for Web browsers but not for enterprise tools. What if we buy a Java tool and want to enforce a security policy on its use or on the data it can access? Unless the tools author thought to include a SecurityManager (and some way to set the policy in that SecurityManager) we're out of luck.

Finally, the SecurityManager architecture is difficult to extend. In the enterprise, Web browsers are not the only things which must be protected and the SecurityManager could not easily be extended to cover databases, handheld devices, ERP systems, or other resources.

Protection domains solve these problems. The protection domain infrastructure is built into the JVM so it is always available and can be used to secure any application, whether the programmer thought to include a SecurityManager or not. Further, Sun has provided the mechanisms needed to configure policy dynamically and to keep that policy in a file or other storage. This allows a security officer, not a programmer, to set policy for the tool and it reduces the number of people writing security-sensitive code.

The SecurityManager is actually still in Java 2. In order to be backwards-compatible with JDK 1.0 and 1.1, it had to be included. In Java 2, though, the SecurityManager is essentially just a hollowed out version of its former self that defers all security decisions to the protection domain infrastructure. Do not use the SecurityManager for new development. Its function has been completely taken over by protection domains.

---

allow that class to access the resources? This makes evaluating who is allowed to do what a fairly complicated affair.

Figure 12.2 might make this situation clearer. Here we show a Web browser that executes in several different protection domains at once: the privileged system domain, the browser's domain, a domain for trusted applets loaded from a particular Web site, and the default domain for untrusted applets.

Figure 12.3 shows two call stacks resulting from both a trusted applet and an untrusted applet trying to open a file.

The security system is able to differentiate between these two applets and the permissions they have by examining the call stack. The requirement is that when access to a system resource is attempted, every class on the call stack must be running inside a protection domain that has access to that resource. If any class on the call stack does not have access to the resource, the protection domain system throws a java.security.GeneralSecurityException or a subclass of GeneralSecurityException. In this case, the applet on the left will be allowed to access the file because it runs in a domain with the needed permission. The

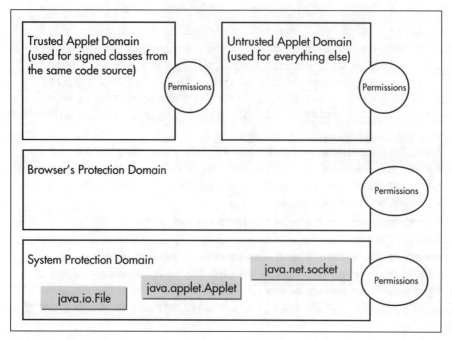

Figure 12.2 A Web browser running with four different protection domains.

applet on the right will receive an exception because, even though java.io.File is in the privileged system domain, the applet's classes are in a domain which is not allowed access to the file system.

There is one complication to this otherwise simple scheme. Some classes must be allowed to perform their jobs regardless of the protection domain of who called them. For example, we may install a class called ourclass.video .Player that must be able to open a region on the user's screen in order to play a video stream and we want any applet, trusted or untrusted, to be able to use this class. Since the previous algorithm states that all classes on the call stack must have the needed permissions in order for the runtime to grant access, this algorithm would prevent an untrusted applet from being able to use the video player.

This problem is solved by adding the concept of a privileged block of code. Any class can state that it is privileged by making the appropriate calls to the AccessController class (see later discussion). If, while descending through the call stack, the security system finds a class which has asserted privilege and has the needed privilege, the stack search will return immediately and allow the access to occur. So ourclass.video.Player could assert its privilege and allow any other class in the system to use (see Figure 12.4). We will see how to use the AccessController in the "Extending the Security Model" section.

There are two important things to note here. First, asserting privilege only allows a class to make privilege *it already has* available to other classes. It does

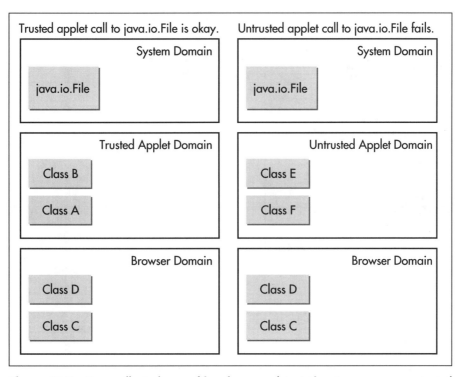

Figure 12.3 Two call stacks resulting from applets trying to access a protected resource.

not allow the class to acquire any new privileges. It would do very little good to build this elaborate protection domain runtime if all a class had to do to escape from its proper domain was to assert that it is privileged. In the previous example, ourclass.video.Player had the privilege needed to run the video player by virtue of it having been loaded from the CLASSPATH or possibly because it was signed by someone who our security policy allowed to run the player. The second thing to notice is that whenever you assert privilege inside one of your classes, you are extending the security system and possibly opening up holes or other leaks in the site's security. This is especially true if your class will run with some privilege not granted other classes on the system. It pays to be extra careful when coding part of the security system. (See the section on Writing Security-Related Code that follows.)

Defining Policy

Protection domains implement the site's security policy. The policy is defined by stating explicitly what permissions you want code running in a particular

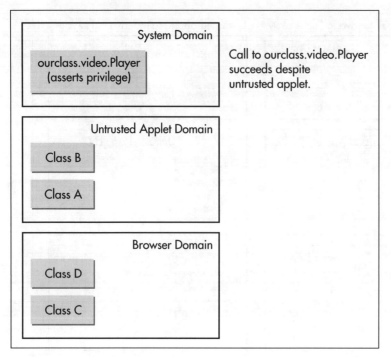

Figure 12.4 ourclass.video.Player allows other classes to use its privileges.

domain to have. Each permission in the policy is based on four pieces of information: from where the code came, who signed it, to which part of the Java platform this permission applies, and exactly what access is granted by this permission. A typical example is:

```
grant signedBy "Sun",  codeBase "http://java.sun.com" {
  permission java.io.FilePermission "/tmp/*", "read, write ";
  permission java.util.PropertyPermission "*", "read";
  permission java.net.SocketPermission "java.sun.com", "connect";
};
```

These three policy entries state that any class downloaded from java.sun.com and signed by Sun is allowed to read and write (but not execute or delete) any file in the /tmp directory, read any Property in the JVM, and open a socket connection to java.sun.com. Since, for any non-trivial policy, this policy file will become unwieldy, Java 2 provides a very conservative default policy and a policy editing tool to help properly customize the site's policy. Also, the internal representation of the policy does not depend on this syntax or file. So future releases of the Java platform or customized add-ons from other vendors can use other mechanisms, like a database or a centralized policy server, to define and maintain the site's policy.

The policy file syntax allows for wildcarding and property expansion within the file. The "*"s in

```
permission java.io.FilePermission "/tmp/*", "read, write ";
permission java.util.PropertyPermission "*", "read";
```

are examples of wildcards. Wildcards can also be used in domain names, so if we wished our SocketPermission permission to apply to any machine in the sun.com domain, we could have written

```
permission java.net.SocketPermission "*.sun.com", "connect";
```

Note, wildcards like "www.*.com" and "www.sun.*" are not legal.

Property expansion allows us to define a single policy file that will behave appropriately for many different users. For example, our policy may state that applets from a particular code source are allowed to read and write files in a special subdirectory of a user's home directory. We could explicitly list each user's home directory in our policy file.

```
permission java.io.FilePermission "/home/fritz/applet/* ", "read, write";
permission java.io.FilePermission "/home/berg/applet/* ", "read, write";
permission java.io.FilePermission "/home/smith/applet/* ", "read, write";
```

There are two problems with this. First it would be very hard to administer. Each time a user is added or removed from the system the policy file would have to change and all affected JVMs restarted. The second problem is even worse. This policy files allows applets to access files in *any user's* directory, regardless of which user is running the applet. This is probably not what we want. More likely, we want an applet to be able to access files only in the home directory of the user running it.

Property expansion solves these problems for us. Instead of explicitly listing each user in the system, we write

```
permission java.io.FilePermission "${user.home}", "read";
```

At runtime, ${user.home} is expanded to the home directory appropriate for that user. Other properties can be used in the policy file, including the file separator property ${/}. This allows you to write policy files that are appropriate for any operating system, regardless of whether it uses / or \ as the file separator. See "Default Policy Implementation and Policy File Syntax" in the JDK 1.2 documentation for complete details on how to use the policy file.

There are several different places to define a security policy. A system-wide default policy file is stored in the Java runtime's lib directory. Individual users can define their own default policy files in their home directories (if such an action is allowed by the Java runtime's security policy). If the system property java .security.policy is defined, for example by adding -Djava.security.policy=file to the command line for starting an application, the application will run under the

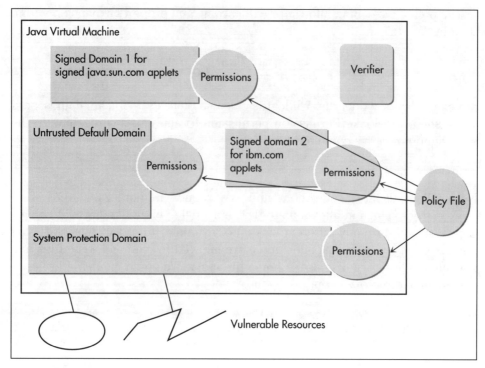

Figure 12.5 Block diagram of Java's protection domains.

policy defined in that file. In general, policy files are additive. So, if both a system default policy and a user defined policy exist, the application will run under a policy defined by the union of the permissions granted in the two files.

Putting It All Together

Figure 12.5 shows how all of these pieces fit together. The policy file defines the site's security policy. When a copy of the JVM starts, it reads that file and creates an internal representation of the policy. When a new class or JAR is loaded into the JVM, the VM examines its code source (where it came from plus who has signed it) and either assigns this class to an existing protection domain if an appropriate one exists or creates a new protection domain for that class. A protection domain carries with it a Permissions object that defines what the policy allows that domain to do. The System domain contains those Java core classes which are used to access vulnerable system resources.

Security, Applets, and Web Browsers

The original Java security mechanisms were developed to protect Web browser users from hostile applets on the Internet. These mechanisms could not rely on the traditional defense used by virus checkers which try to spot hostile applications by comparing a suspect executable to a database of known viruses. On the Internet there is just too big a risk of new attacks, against which a virus checker is helpless, spreading too quickly for the end user to reasonably be able to upgrade the checker's database.

Instead of trying to spot hostile code, the Java security mechanisms prevent attacks by stopping hostile actions. There are a wide range of actions which are forbidden to an untrusted applet. While this policy allows users to run untrusted code safely, there are some trade-offs against the functionality of an applet. To be useful applets must be allowed some access to the user's computer. An applet must at least be allowed to use the CPU and memory, display on the user's monitor, and receive input from the keyboard and mouse. Other actions, like deleting files from the user's hard drive and executing the system's shutdown command, are obviously dangerous and must be prevented. Certain actions, though, fall into a gray zone. For example, more sophisticated applets may be part of a three-tiered application and must make a connection over the Internet to a backend server in order to do their jobs. Should this action be allowed or not? Depending on the target of the connection, this could be an innocent action performed by a benign applet or a sneaky back-door attack by a malicious applet.

The Sandbox Policy

The designers of the HotJava browser, the first browser capable of downloading and running Java applets, defined which actions an applet could safely perform and which it could not. This policy was implemented in HotJava and became known as the *Sandbox*. As other browser manufacturers added Java support to their products, they followed the lead of the HotJava browser and implemented roughly the same security policy in their products.

While the details of the browser policy vary slightly from browser to browser, all commercial browsers conform to this basic policy. Applets are not allowed to:

- Read from a file system on the user's machine
- Write to a file system on the user's machine
- Get information about a file on the user's machine
- Delete a file from a file system on the user's machine
- Read any but a selected few system properties
- Connect to a network port on the client
- Connect to a network port on any machine other than the HTTP server from which it came
- Load a library or DLL
- Execute another program or script
- Cause the Java Virtual Machine to exit
- Create an unlabeled popup window

The reasons behind some of these restrictions, like the prohibition against deleting a file, are obvious. Others are a little more subtle. For example, why are applets not allowed to connect to any arbitrary machine? Why may applets only "phone home"? This restriction is in place because once an applet is downloaded to the user's machine, it is running behind any firewall that may be in place to protect the organization's computers. Once behind the firewall the applet could launch any of a number of well-known, network-based attacks against the now vulnerable computers. Similarly, the other less obvious restrictions protect against subtle attacks. For example, all pop-up windows created by applets are clearly labeled as being owned by untrusted applets. At least to the extent that users pay attention, this prevents Trojan horse applets from using popups to ask for passwords or other information which the user may not be willing to type into a Web browser.

Playing in the Sandbox

While at first glance the Sandbox policy may seem so restrictive that it prevents you from writing any interesting application as a Java applet, it is actually fairly easy to live within the Sandbox's boundaries. Companies have deployed customer management and electronic commerce systems, ground control systems for space craft, games, and many other applications, none of which require any privilege beyond those granted by the default Sandbox policy.

The guidelines for designing distributed applications (see Chapter 6) make it much easier to operate within the Sandbox's restrictions. In a three-tiered architecture, the user's machine will usually only be asked to run the GUI and possibly some of the processing of the application. All data storage and manipulation, which requires access to a disk drive, is done by a machine buried deep in the network. Not only do multitiered applications have many advantages in data distribution and reuse, maintainability, and deployment, they also fit perfectly into the Sandbox security model. If you find your application is chafing against the sides of the Sandbox, you should examine your architecture for signs of Fat Client thinking. Once these architectural flaws have been corrected, your applet will most likely fit within the Sandbox.

Of course, not all applications can be rearchitected to live within the Sandbox policy. Your applet may need to talk to a certain piece of hardware, such as an instrument controller or an A/D converter, an action absolutely forbidden by the Sandbox. And something, somewhere, has to actually save data to disk. As the Java language becomes more widely used on the back end, increasingly data storage will fall to Java classes which may be under some security restrictions.

Even in less extreme cases, where the application is a good three-tiered design, the Sandbox can impose some harsh restrictions. Remember that the three-tiered architecture is a logical one. It says nothing about where each piece of each tier should be physically deployed. Yet, the Sandbox imposes a physical limit on where certain components can reside. Since the Sandbox will only allow the applet to talk back to its own Web server, all mid-tier services the applet needs, or proxies representing those services, must also reside on that Web server. This needlessly restricts how the application can be distributed and places a potentially heavy load on the Web server. In these cases, where an applet cannot reasonably live within the Sandbox's walls, Java provides a digital signing mechanism which can be used to give an applet the needed additional privileges.

Signed Java Archive Files

The default protection domain provides a trusted execution environment for untrusted code, but it does so in a restrictive, conservative manner. No code (except that loaded from the CLASSPATH or a Java extension), regardless of how trusted its author is, can perform any action which is considered dangerous by the applet security policy. These restrictions prevent benign applets from doing many useful things for the user. Many applets writers would gladly trade away these security restrictions in return for free access to the user's machine. Fortunately few, if any, security-conscious users would agree to the trade.

Remember the motivation for the Sandbox policy: We can't establish trust in every potential applet. Instead, we'll restrict the actions of all applets in order to protect ourselves from the few bad apples. If we could make sure that a particular applet came from a trustworthy source and that it had not been tampered with while crossing the network, we could define a new policy for that applet, allowing it out of the sandbox and giving it freer access to the machine.

Signed JAR files allow us to trust an applet because they allow us to verify the source of the applet and to verify that we have received the applet intact. Once we know that the applet was sent by the person or organization which claimed to have sent it and that the bits we received are the bits the sender intended us to receive, we can make a choice: Do we trust this sender enough to allow this applet unhindered access to our computer? If the applet came from our bank, whom we already trust with our money, or our mother—who doesn't trust their mother?—the answer will probably be yes. If the applet came from a supplier with whom we do millions of dollars of business per year, or a customer who does millions of dollars of business with us each year, the answer will again be yes. If the applet came from our biggest competitor or from legionofdoom.com, the answer will be an emphatic No! Signed JARs can be used for more than just applets. JavaBeans, EJBs, and other types of code can benefit from signing.

Signing JARs

A JAR is a Java ARchive file: a collection of Java classes, HTML, GIF, and other files which together make up a Java applet or application. A JAR is essentially a ZIP file with a manifest listing every object in the JAR. When a Web browser

ARE DIGITAL SIGNATURES SECURE?

A digital signature is like a fingerprint. In the real world fingerprints allow us to identify and catch thieves after a crime has been committed. Fingerprints do not actually stop crimes. They simply make it more likely that the perpetrator will be caught and punished. Likewise, digital signatures do not prevent electronic theft. They only give us a way to trace the offending program back to its source. It is the indirect threat of being caught and punished which deters attackers. In this sense, signatures are more about *accountability* than about *security*.

Some executable content systems, like ActiveX, depend exclusively on signatures to provide security. This is a dangerous practice since the threat of prosecution has never been enough to stop criminals. After all, in the real world thieves still commit crimes despite fingerprints, security cameras, mug shots and police lineups. On the Internet, cyber-criminals could hide behind dummy companies, set up offshore sites which would be difficult to prosecute, or simply do their damage so subtly that it is not noticed until long after the user has forgotten about the offending page. Because of the difference between accountability and security, digital signatures alone actually provide very little real security.

Signatures also place a large burden on the user. He must decide who to trust, periodically review the status of each signature he does trust, and avoid the temptation to run an untrusted control "just this once" since, after all, nothing bad seemed to happen the last time he did it "just this once." Systems, like many web browsers, that allow a trusted third party to vouch for code signers solve some of these problems, but introduce their own security problems when the user gets too used to pushing the "Grant" button each time a security notice pops up.

In Java, digital signatures are only one part of the overall security system. This allows Java to deliver true security, not just the threat of catching the bad guys after the damage is done. Since many applications can be run within the Sandbox without the privilege granted by a trusted signature, the "just this once" temptation of running untrusted code is reduced. Since additional privileges are not needed by most applications, Java reduces the number of sites the user must trust, which greatly simplifies key management. Also, since Java provides very fine-grained control over what privileges are associated with which signatures, the user can limit the damage a trusted application gone bad (either through an innocent bug or through a cleverly disguise attack) can do.

encounters a page containing an applet wrapped in a JAR, the browser downloads the JAR, unpacks it locally, and then uses a Class Loader to bring in and begin running the applet, just as it would if that applet had been made up of separate class files residing on the remote machine.

JAR files may optionally be signed with a cryptographically protected message digest. It is the digital signature that provides the insurance of authenticity needed to allow the applet out of the default protection domain. Since it is the combination of the Codebase and the SignedBy attributes which specify in which protection domain a class should run, applets packaged in signed JAR files can be placed in a more privileged domain than would usually be allowed. Applets in signed JAR files can be allowed to access the file system, contact other hosts on the Internet, and perform other actions prohibited by the Sandbox policy, *if* we trust the signer of the JAR.

In Java 2, the cumbersome manual process of generating keys and signing JARs has been replaced with the keytool and jarsigners utilities. These tools are used to create and manage keys, certificates, and keystores, sign JAR files, and verify the signatures of JARs we have received from others.

Security, Applications, and the Enterprise

While the need to protect your computing assets from hostile executable content on the Web is clear, the need for such protection in Java applications and network services is less clear. After all, Java applications are fundamentally no different from applications written in other languages, so shouldn't the same OS mechanisms which protect regular applications also apply to Java applications? And, if the OS can protect regular daemons and databases, shouldn't it be able to protect services written in Java also? The answer is both yes and no.

While traditional OS security measures can protect Java applications which basically reimplement the functionality of older systems, server-side use of the Java platform brings with it several new capabilities which have profound implications on both how we write business systems and how we secure those systems. The most obvious new capability is dynamically downloaded server code. Chapter 9 showed how we could allow people outside of our organization to run services and applications on our Web server by downloading servlets, small server-side pieces of Java code which act much like CGI scripts, from remote URLs. Like applets, which can extend a Web browser on the fly, servlets can extend a Web server. But, just as we worry about hostile applets in our Web browsers, we must worry about how to protect the rest of our computing infrastructure from hostile servlets.

Fortunately, Java 2's security architecture can also be brought into service here. We can define protection domains for servlets just as we do with applets. For servlets signed by someone we trust, we can define protection domains with the appropriate permissions. These servlets will automatically be confined to those domains. This combination of dynamically downloaded services. And a protected environment in which to run them will be just as important for business-to-business application distribution as secure applets are for business to end-user applications.

Here's an example of how secure servlets could be used. Suppose we start a company which provides Internet services to small businesses. In addition to providing a connection to the Internet, disk space for their Web pages, and management services, we also provide an extensible set of business services like payment processing, order entry, and other things needed to perform electronic commerce. While many of our customers may be satisfied with our basic services, some more sophisticated customers may want to customize our systems to provide volume and seasonal discounts, track buying patterns, and perform other functions.

Of course, we need to provide these additional services in a secure manner. Our other customers would not be very happy to find out that one of their competitors is loading and running their own, unrestricted, code on a machine which also happens to contain their valuable business data. Protection domains again come to the rescue. By assigning each customer's code to its own domain, based on the digital signature of that customer, we can provide the services each needs to be competitive while maintaining the security for all our customers.

There are other places where server-side protection domains make sense. Java Remote Method Invocation (RMI) has the ability to download not just an object's state to a remote machine, but also that object's implementation. Thus, RMI provides a way to run code on someone else's machine. Again, enthusiasm for this very useful capability must be tempered with concern for security. By providing protection domains in which to run RMI classes, we can provide appropriate protection for this capability.

Protection domains for services and applications even make sense in cases where we are not importing other people's untrusted code. There are many instances where we may want to control what someone can do even with a trusted tool we provide. By setting up appropriate protection domains, we can accomplish that task also.

Extending the Security Model

Another advantage of protection domains is that they are extensible. Although the JDK, as delivered by Sun, only secures resources commonly used by the JVM—files, network connections and ports, properties and the runtime, etc.—developers can extend this system to put newly defined resources under the control of the protection domain system. For example, suppose we have a hardware random number generator attached to a machine and we wish to provide a Java class which can access that device while at the same time controlling who can use the device. We can do this through a two-step process. First, while building the Java class which accesses the device, we will define a new type of

permission to cover the device and, using several classes available in the java
.security package, build into our code the mechanisms needed to enforce these
permissions. Second, we will define a new policy to control what classes loaded
from different sources are allowed to do with the device. A default policy might
allow untrusted applets and applications to use the device to generate random
numbers. Signed and trusted applications, on the other hand, will be allowed to
reset the device, read log files, and perform other maintenance operations.

Overview of Security Classes

Our class will have to interact with several classes in the java.security package,
including java.security.Permission. This class represents permissions to access a
vulnerable resource. An abstract class, it is used to keep track of the privileges
granted within the security system. Concrete subclasses include java.io.File-
Permission, java.net.NetPermission, and java.lang.RuntimePermission.

This class defines a critical abstract method called implies. The implies method
checks that, given the permission represented by an instance of java.security
.Permission, access to a certain specific resource is allowed. For example, permission to access "/tmp/*" implies that you can access "/tmp/foo," but permission
to access "/tmp/foo" does not imply access to "/tmp/bar." It is up to each subclass
of java.security.Permission to implement its implies method properly.

There are two other related classes: java.security.PermissionCollection,
which is provided as an easy way to handle groups of related permissions, and
java.security.Permissions, which is used to contain all the permissions granted
to a particular protection domain.

For our random number generator, we will define a new subclass of Permission called fritz.random.HardwareRandomPermission by extending java
.security.BasicPermission. BasicPermission is a concrete subclass of Permission that provides a simple implementation of all the methods in Permission. It
is a handy starting place for any new Permission subclass.

```
package fritz.random
public class fritz.random.HardwareRandomPermission extends
java.security.BasicPermission
```

Once we've defined this permission and made it available to the Java runtime
by putting it on our CLASSPATH or installing the fritz.random package in the
Java extension directory, we can use it in our policy file.

```
// New permission to allow an applet to use the Java Ring's RNG.

grant codeBase "http://server:8080/~fritz/security/TRUSTED" {
      permission fritz.random.HardwareRandomPermission "Random.open";
      permission fritz.random.HardwareRandomPermission "Random.getBytes";
};
```

This permission says that any class loaded from the directory /fritz/security/ TRUSTED on Web server server will be able to use our device to generate random numbers.

The two strings in the permission file, Random.open and Random.getBytes, define *actions* our device can perform. We'll see how we can use the security system to enforce access to these actions. It is up to us, when implementing the implies method and the rest of the Permission class, to make sure the text representations of the various actions represented by this object make sense.

java.security.AccessController

Our hardware RNG is accessed through the class HardwareRandom.java. This class uses the AccessController to protect the hardware RNG from unauthorized use. The AccessController behaves much like the SecurityManager in previous versions of the JDK. It is consulted every time a security decision must be made. It is the class that actually enforces the security policy. For example, HardwareRandom.java contains the method startPolling, which checks the callers before opening a connection to the hardware. Since startPolling is called in HardwareRandom's only constructor, a calling class must have the permission "Random.open" to use the RNG. Here is the source for startPolling:

```
protected void startPolling(String nativeDevString)
    {

        // First check to see if the caller has the needed permission.
        HardwareRandomPermission perm = new
                                HardwareRandomPermission("Random.open");
        java.security.AccessController.checkPermission(perm);

        try
        {
          // Have to set a "final" copy of "this" to use in the privileged block.
          final HardwareRandom me = this;
          // ***NOTE: this is privileged code!***
          java.security.AccessController.doPrivileged(
            new java.security.PrivilegedExceptionAction() {
              public Object run() throws Exception {
                SmartCard.start();
                CardTerminalRegistry registry =
                                    CardTerminalRegistry.getRegistry();
                registry.addCTListener(me);
                return null;
              }
            }
          );
        }
        catch (Exception e)
        {
```

```
                e.printStackTrace();
        }
    }

}
```

When a class which provides access to a sensitive resource needs to make sure that the calling class file is allowed access to its resources, it calls the AccessController's checkPermission method with the appropriate subclass of java.security.Permission as an argument. So, in our random number generator class's startPolling method, we include the following calls:

```
HardwareRandomPermission perm = new
                            HardwareRandomPermission("Random.open ");
java.security.AccessController.checkPermission(perm);
```

If the caller or any other class on the call stack doesn't have Random.open permission, the call to checkPermission will throw a security exception. If the caller and all classes on the call stack do have Random.open permission, checkPermission simply returns.

Next we define our new permission type, HardwareRandomPermission. This is the class to which we referred in our policy file (see above). We could have simply used BasicPermission with the appropriate action names, such as Random.open or Random.getBytes, to control access to the RNG. But in security-related code, clarity is more valuable than compactness, so we subclass BasicPermission to create HardwareRandomPermission so that anyone reading our code or the policy file will know that we have added something new to the security system.

Source Code: HardwareRandomPermission.java
```
package fritz.random;

public class HardwareRandomPermission extends java.security.BasicPermission
{
    public HardwareRandomPermission(String s) {
        super(s);
    }

    public HardwareRandomPermission(String s, String a) {
        super(s, a);
    }
}
```

The string argument to HardwareRandomPermission's constructor is the same string we defined in the policy file. By using strings in the policy file to define actions and objects, we can easily include new actions without creating a new class for each action. For example, we could use a Random.reset permission simply by including the needed line in our java.policy file and instantiating a HardwareRandomPermission object with "Random.reset" as an argument.

Asserting Privileges

In some cases we may wish to allow untrusted classes to use resources under the control of our class. We can do this by having our class assert *privilege* to the virtual machine. The AccessController is also used when a class wishes to assert privilege. If we want to allow any class, trusted or not, to access our device we do so by writing:

```
java.security.AccessController.doPrivileged
                (PrivilegedAction action);
```

The doPrivileged method takes a class which implements the PrivilegedAction interface as its single argument. The PrivilegedAction interface defines a single method run() which takes no arguments and returns an Object. Since run is defined as returning an Object, you must return something from this method, even if your code has nothing useful to return. Otherwise your code won't compile. Of course, lacking something useful to return, you can make the compiler happy by simply returning null. You must also narrow the returned Object down to whatever real type you are returning.

Any code within the run method of the PrivilegedAction argument will be able to use its privileges regardless of whether its caller could normally access that resource or not. In this example, the class HardwareRandom is loaded from a JAR in the Java extension directory. Any class loaded from the Extension directory is treated as part of the base Java runtime and as such is not subject to the constraints of the security runtime. This allows HardwareRandom to access the serial port and perform other actions forbidden to less trusted classes. But since if HardwareRandom is being called by less trusted code, such as an untrusted applet, the Java security system will block access to the serial port. By asserting privilege, HardwareRandom temporarily loans its permissions to the untrusted class, allowing it to perform a normally forbidden operation like accessing a serial port.

The methods doPrivileged and checkPermission are usually used together to ensure that extensions to the security system do not endanger site security. The class first calls checkPermission to ensure that all calling classes have the needed permission, like HardwareRandom.open in this example, and then calls doPrivileged to allow it to do some job for the caller. It is very important that these features be used with care. See the note "Writing Security-related Code" for some cautions and suggestions.

There are several ways to call doPrivileged. Frequently you will simply define an anonymous inner class which implements PrivilegedAction, as we did in the

WHAT HAPPENED TO BEGINPRIVILEGED AND ENDPRIVILEGED?

Users of beta copies of JDK 1.2 may be scratching their heads at this point wondering, "Where did this doPrivileged thing come from?" This is because in the beta versions of 1.2 the job of doPrivileged was handled by two separate methods: beginPrivileged and endPrivileged. Any code bracketed by a begin/endPrivileged pair would be able to loan its privileges out to less trusted classes in the manner described above. Using the begin/endPrivileged pairs was much simpler than using doPrivileged and its associated interfaces. You didn't have to worry about defining new inner classes, making final copies of local variables, or casting returned values down to the proper types. From the typical developer's point of view, begin/endPrivileged worked just fine. So why change them, especially after they had been part of the API for 4 rounds of beta code?

Despite their simplicity, begin/endPrivileged had one fatal flaw. They had to be used strictly in pairs. If a programmer made a call to beginPrivileged and forgot the required endPrivileged the security system was left in an inconsistent state and could possibly be compromised (in reality the runtime would notice the inconsistency and clean up after the mistaken programmer, but why take chances?). JDK beta programmers were told always to include the call to endPrivileged in the final clause of a try block so that regardless of what may happen in the privileged block, endPrivileged would be called. Of course, since there was no way for the Java compiler to check that each begin had an end in a properly constructed final clause, you know that someone someday would have left the endPrivileged call out, creating a potential security hole.

doPrivileged trades a bit of syntactic simplicity for greater safety. Since privilege can now only be asserted in the context of a doPrivileged call, the authors of the Java security system can make sure that every assertion of privilege is properly terminated.

above method. Another common way to use the doPrivileged method is to declare that the class which needs to assert privilege implements PrivilegedAction and then call doPrivileged(this). Either way, the code in the run method will be executed with whatever privileges it has regardless of how trusted the ultimate caller is.

Using Arguments and Exceptions with doPrivileged

Assuming your run method doesn't take any arguments and doesn't throw any exceptions, doPrivileged works pretty well. Unfortunately, in order to do almost anything useful you have to violate at least one of these assumptions. Then things get a bit more complicated. Since the run method takes no arguments and throws no exceptions you have to do a little more work in order to get parameters into your privileged code and return codes back out.

If you implement the run method in an anonymous inner class, you can only access those state variables in the outer class which have been declared *final*. In the example above we save a final copy of *this* in a local variable called *me* and then use me instead of *this* in the run method.

```
// Have to set a "final" copy of "this" to use in the privileged block.
final HardwareRandom me = this;
// ***NOTE: this is privileged code!***
java.security.AccessController.doPrivileged(
  new java.security.PrivilegedExceptionAction() {
    public Object run() throws Exception {
      SmartCard.start();
      CardTerminalRegistry registry = CardTerminalRegistry.getRegistry();
      registry.addCTListener(me);
      return null;
    }
  }
);
```

If your run method may throw an exception, your class must implement the PrivilegedExceptionAction interface instead of PrivilegedAction. The run method in PrivilegedExceptionAction is declared to throw an Exception, allowing your code to report errors. We use PrivilegedExceptionAction in start-Polling because the Smart Card interfaces may throw an exception.

When Do You Lose Privileges?

Privilege is actually only granted within the context of the single thread which made the doPrivileged() call. Thus, only a single thread within the protection domain making the call gets privilege. This prevents an attacker from making a safe, privileged call in one thread, then abusing that privilege in another thread. Privilege is lost as soon as the run method returns or if that privileged block calls any piece of less-trusted code. And of course a class cannot loan out privileges it does not already have. This prevents someone from simply writing a class which asserts privilege and then plunders your machine.

The CD-ROM included with this book contains full source for the hardware random number generator, a sample policy file, and applets that use the interface class. The example assumes you have access to a Dallas Semiconductor Java iButton (like those used in the JavaRings handed out at the 1998 JavaOne

WRITING SECURITY-RELATED CODE

When you use the AccessController to allow other classes to use privileges granted to your code, you are extending Java's security system. Any bugs or unexpected side effects in your code could compromise your site's security. For this reason, you must be extremely careful about what your code does while using AccessController.doPrivileged. Fortunately, there are several common-sense guidelines for writing security-related code which help minimize the risks associated with extending your security system.

The most important guideline is to scrutinize privileged code much more closely than you would less-sensitive code. Not only should you closely examine the system's architecture and every assumption made in the implementation, these systems should be examined even more closely by a neutral third party. Human beings in general are notoriously bad at critically examining their own work (as the editor of this manuscript can attest) and programmers are no exception. Programmers, especially those not accustomed to working with security systems, often will overlook obvious attacks against their code or miss subtle holes and flaws in their architecture. Even programmers who are aware of the dangers inherent in security code and working actively to avoid these pitfalls, will sometimes overlook a possible attack against the system, as shown by the half dozen or so important security bugs found in various versions of the JDK. To guard against this threat, all privileged code must be subjected to careful, rigorous examination during its design and continual re-examination during its development, testing, and even after it has been deployed. Similarly, any new Permission classes created for a system must be carefully examined. Does the Permission really protect the intended resource against all conceivable attacks? Does the implies method grant all proper access to the resource without subtle holes that allow unauthorized use of that resource?

The next guideline is to keep security-related code, especially privileged blocks of code, as short and localized as possible. Often the privileged block will contain only one or two statements. Keeping security-related code short has two important benefits. First, it reduces the possibility that the code will contain bugs which could compromise security. The longer and more complicated a block of code is, the more likely it is that a clever attacker can find some way to misuse the code and the privilege it grants. This is especially true for code which contains many loops, if statements, and other control-flow operations. In long, complicated blocks, it is very difficult to ensure every possible combination of execution paths is free from security holes. Localizing security code also makes bug fixes easier, since there are fewer places in the code which can affect security and which must be modified to patch a bug or modify the architecture.

continues

(Continued)

The second benefit of keeping security-related code as short as possible is that it is easier to inspect and verify short, simple pieces of code. Since manual inspection is an important part of ensuring system security, you should minimize the amount of code which must be examined.

You should be very suspicious of any parameters passed into your privileged code. These parameters represent one entry which attackers could use to compromise your system. In systems built with pointer-based languages, like C and C++, parameters could be used to attack the systems by overflowing an input buffer to rewrite part of the stack or modify the values of internal system parameters. While the safety features in the Java language prevent these kinds of attacks, input parameters still represent a potential threat.

For example, your privileged code could control access to a part of the file system. Perhaps your system is to allow certain users access to files under a single directory and you expose a method that takes the file name as one parameter. Did you remember to check the inputted file name for a relative path name? Could an attacker include ".." in the file name to escape from the intended directory and run amok through the rest of the file system? This hole, and attacks based on it, has been discovered in many commercial systems. Or, suppose you are writing an administration infrastructure which provides both methods for GUI-based administration tools and platform-specific implementations of those methods. On a UNIX machine a method which allows the user to write new information into the password file could be used to attack the machine. If you allow the user to change the name field associated with his user id, do you also check to make sure the new entry does not contain a new line and a bogus new root user entry? Again, this attack was used in the real world in the infamous change finger entry attack.

Since input parameters are in some sense instructions to your code issued by untrusted persons, they must be treated with great suspicion and care. One way to avoid the danger of untrustworthy parameters is to make methods which contain privileged blocks private to the class which implements that method. Then the class can implement another wrapper method which other classes can use. This wrapper method can implement any safety checks needed on the input parameters, then make the needed privileged method invocation on behalf of the caller.

Finally, when using the classes in the java.security package, it is good practice to use the fully qualified name of the class. So, when calling the AccessController you should write:

```
java.security.AccessController.checkPermission(perm)
```

rather than:

```
import java.security;
//Lots of other code here.
AccessController.checkPermission(perm)
```

Using the fully qualified name of the classes in java.security makes it much more obvious that you are dealing with critical, security-related code. It tells other people working with and using your code to be extra careful about modifying or extending these sections, since any mistakes could have grave security consequences.

show) loaded with the Rand1 applet (see www.ibutton.com). You will have to configure the iButton software on your machine (JIBKIT .90), load the applet class files on a Web server, and use Java 2 appletviewer to run the applet. If you run the applet from a trusted source (as defined in your policy file), you'll see something like Figure 12.6. If you run it from an untrusted source, you'll see Figure 12.7.

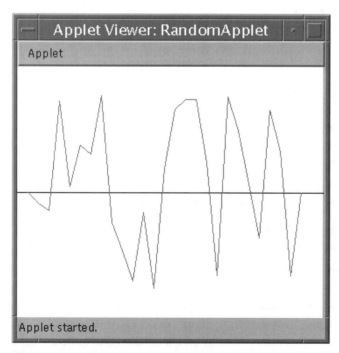

Figure 12.6 Running the test applet from a trusted codebase.

Figure 12.7 Running the test applet from an untrusted codebase.

Other Important Security Classes

In addition to the Permission and AccessController classes previously listed, there are several other security classes which, while not being as visible to application programmers, are very important for security:

- **java.security.CodeSource:** Encapsulates the URL from which a class came, along with all the signatures attached to that class.

- **java.security.ProtectionDomain:** A private class in the java.security package which implements protection domains inside the Java runtime.

- **java.security.Policy:** The runtime representation of the site's security policy.

- **java.security.SecureClassLoader:** A concrete implementation of java .lang.ClassLoader which can search for and load classes in a secure way and can create a new protection domain based on the code source of the newly loaded classes.

The implies Method

The HardwareRandomPermission used in the preceding example is very simple. It merely subclasses BasicPermission and assumes we've added the needed names as strings in our policy files. We actually could have written the entire example using BasicPermission without creating our own subclass. That said, subclassing BasicPermission or Permission is good practice because it makes the extension to the security system obvious to anyone reading your code.

Your permission class may need to support more complicated access decisions. It could allow wildcarding or other syntax that must be evaluated at runtime. In this case, you must override the implies method in your permission class and define a PermissionCollection for your permission class. Remember that the implies method is used to determine if possessing one permission, say, java.io.FilePermission "/tmp/*" "read", implies another permission, such as java.io.FilePermission "/tmp/foo" "write". In this example, the first permission does not imply the second. Your implies method must make these decisions for the security system. The PermissionCollection class allows the security runtime to test the need permission (say, you're asking for java.io.FilePermission "/tmp/foo" "read") against all the FilePermissions your class possesses.

Here is a simple example of using the implies method. We define a permission class, TestPermission, which uses five permissions: Test.a, Test.b, Test.c, Test.d, and Test.ab. None of Test.a, Test.b, Test.c, or Test.d implies any other permission. However, Test.ab implies both Test.a and Test.b. In TestPermission we override the implies method to support this behavior. We also have to define a new constructor for TestPermission so we can keep track of exactly which kind of permission we are.

Source Code: TestPermission.java

```
import java.util.Vector;
import java.util.Enumeration;

public class TestPermission extends java.security.BasicPermission
{

    private byte mask;

    public TestPermission(String s) {
        super(s);
        setMask(s);
    }

    public TestPermission(String s, String a) {
        super(s, a);
```

```
            setMask(s);
        }

    public java.security.PermissionCollection newPermissionCollection() {
        return new TestPermissionCollection();
    }

    private void setMask(String s) {
        if (s.equals("Test.a")) {
            mask = (byte) 0x8;
        } else if (s.equals("Test.b")) {
            mask = (byte) 0x4;
        } else if (s.equals("Test.c")) {
            mask = (byte) 0x2;
        } else if (s.equals("Test.d")) {
            mask = (byte) 0x1;
        } else if (s.equals("Test.ab")) {
            // 0xc = 0x8 (the value for a) & 0x4 (the value for Test.b)
            // so having permission Test.ab implies both permissions
            // Test.a and Test.b.
            mask = (byte) 0xc;

        } else {
            mask = (byte) 0;
        }
    }

    public boolean implies(java.security.Permission p) {

        if (!( p instanceof TestPermission))
            return false;

        TestPermission that = (TestPermission) p;

        return((this.mask & that.mask) != 0);
    }
}
```

The constructor sets a mask that records the permissions granted by this instance of TestPermission. The implies method simply performs a logical and of this instance and the instance passed in by the security runtime. If the result is not equal to 0, this permission implies that permission. We also have to define the newPermissionCollection method. This tells the Java runtime that we are managing our own PermissionCollection. Inside our TestPermissionCollection we call our implies method to test two permissions.

Source Code: TestPermissionCollection
```
final class TestPermissionCollection
```

```
extends java.security.PermissionCollection
{
    Vector myPermissions;

    public TestPermissionCollection() {
        super();
        myPermissions = new Vector();
    }

    public void add(java.security.Permission perm) {
        if (! (perm instanceof TestPermission))
            throw new IllegalArgumentException("invalid permission: "+
                                                perm);

        myPermissions.add(perm);
    }

    public boolean implies (java.security.Permission perm)
    {
        if (! (perm instanceof TestPermission))
            return false;

        Enumeration e = this.elements();
        while (e.hasMoreElements()) {
            TestPermission p = (TestPermission) e.nextElement();
            if (p.implies(perm))
                return true;
        }

        return false;
    }

    public Enumeration elements() {
        return myPermissions.elements();
    }
}
```

In the constructor we create a Vector to hold all the TestPermissions in our collection. When the Java runtime calls TestPermissionCollection's implies method, we compare the incoming permission with each permission in our collection, returning true if one permission implies the incoming permission and false otherwise.

Here is a simple example program that tests which permissions it has. The output of test.java is shown in Figure 12.8.

Source Code: Test.java
```
import java.applet.Applet;
```

```
import java.awt.*;
import java.io.*;

public class Test extends Applet
{
    public void paint(Graphics g) {

        int width = getSize().width;
        int height = getSize().height;
        int i;

        g.setColor(Color.white);
        g.fillRect(0, 0, width - 1, height - 1);

        String [] testPerms = {"Test.a", "Test.b", "Test.c", "Test.d"};
        String status;

        g.setColor(Color.black);
        for (i = 0; i < testPerms.length; i++) {
            try {
                TestPermission perm = new TestPermission(testPerms[i]);
                java.security.AccessController.checkPermission(perm);
                status = " ";
            } catch (Exception e) {
                status = " don't ";
            }
```

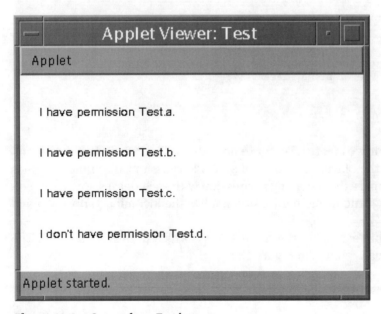

Figure 12.8   Output from Test.java.

```
        g.drawString("I" + status + "have permission " + testPerms[i]
                + ".", 20, 40 * (i+1));
    }
  }
}
```

When run under the following policy, Test finds that it has both Test.a and Test.b permissions (which are implied by Test.ab in the policy file) and Test.c permission (explicitly listed in the policy). It does not have Test.d permission.

Source Code: Test policy file
```
grant codeBase "http://server/~fritz/security/TRUSTED" {
    permission TestPermission "Test.ab";
    permission TestPermission "Test.c";
};
```

You may want to try this example under different policy files to see how they affect the output, or try modifying TestPermission to handle more complicated cases.

Protection Domains and Java Applications

Until Java 2, Java security meant protecting your computer and network from hostile actions performed by rogue applets running in your Web browser. Since a Java application only contained a SecurityManager if the designer of that application chose to include one, and since few programmers outside of Web browser authors chose to do so, most stand-alone Java applications did not include a SecurityManager. Also, since you couldn't add a SecurityManager to an existing application unless you had access to the application's source code, there was no practical way to retrofit a SecurityManager onto an existing application.

All of this changes with Java 2. Java 2 contains a secure class loader that, when enabled, allows you to define a Protection Domain for classes loaded from the file system. These classes will be treated as if they had been loaded from a trusted or untrusted network source and will be confined to the appropriate Protection Domain.

We can modify our test applet shown earlier to create a stand-alone Java application that tests its permissions.

Source Code: TestApp.java
```
import java.io.*;
```

```
public class TestApp

{

    public static void main(String [] args) {

        String [] testPerms = {"Test.a", "Test.b", "Test.c", "Test.d"};

        String status;

        for (int i = 0; i < testPerms.length; i++) {

            try {
                TestPermission perm = new TestPermission(testPerms[i]);
                java.security.AccessController.checkPermission(perm);
                status = " ";
            } catch (Exception e) {
                status = " don't ";
            }

            System.out.println("I" + status + "have permission "
                            + testPerms[i] + ".");
        }

    }
}
```

Instead of running unrestricted, as a class loaded from the file system normally would, we will place this class in the same Protection Domain in which we ran our Test applet. The results are:

```
I have permission Test.a.
I have permission Test.b.
I have permission Test.c.
I don't have permission Test.d.
```

The Java Cryptography Extension

The Java Cryptography Extension (JCE) extends the java.security package to include such basic cryptographic functions as generating keys, encrypting clear text, and decrypting cipher text. The JCE is designed to be a high-level API. It does not involve itself in the details of individual encryption algorithms nor does it actually implement any encryption algorithms itself. Instead, it specifies an interface for using a generic encryption object. A third party which wishes to implement a cryptography package, called a cryptography provider package, uses the JCE-defined interface to hide the inner workings of the algorithm it is providing. In this way a class which implements the DES algorithm can be used in the same way as one which implements the IDEA or the DES3 algorithm.

This decoupling of the cryptographic interface from its implementation has two important benefits. Many users of cryptography have established standards that define which algorithms can be used and who is authorized to provide implementations of those algorithms. The interface/provider architecture of the JCE allows these organizations to write programs using the JCE classes and interfaces and still be able to use their standard algorithms from their trusted providers. The second, even more important, benefit is that this allows Java licensees to ship the JCE in their products without subjecting those products to United States export control. Under U.S. law, any system that implements strong cryptography is classified as a munitions and requires special export licenses to ship outside of North America. By shipping the JCE without an actual implementation of the underlying cryptographic engine, Java licensees can legally export their products. In the United States and Canada, these licensees can provide a cryptography engine. Outside of North America it will be up to the end user to obtain a legal implementation of the engine. The JCE is available for java.sun.com/security. Within the United States and Canada, the download will include a simple provider package from Sun.

Using the JCE

Here is a simple application which uses the JCE. A server process accepts network connections from clients, reads the data provided by the client, and writes that data to its standard output. The client opens the connection to the server, prompts the user for the text to be sent, and sends it to the server, exiting after the text has been sent. The pair use the JCE to protect the information flowing between the two of them. Let's look at the server first.

Source Code: Server.java
```
import java.io.*;
import java.net.*;
import java.security.*;
import javax.crypto.*;
import javax.crypto.spec.*;

class Server {

  public static void main(String [] args){
```

```java
    Cipher pbeCipher = null;
    ServerSocket s = null;

    try {

        if (args.length != 1) {
            System.out.println("Usage: java Server <password>");
            System.exit(-1);
        }

        System.out.println(
                "Initializing encryption system. This takes several
                                                        seconds");
        // Salt
        byte[] salt = { (byte)0xc7, (byte)0x73, (byte)0x21,
        (byte)0x8c, (byte)0x7e, (byte)0xc8, (byte)0xee, (byte)0x99 };

        // Iteration count
        int count = 20;

        // Create PBE parameter set
        PBEParameterSpec pbeParamSpec = new PBEParameterSpec(salt, count);

        // Convert password into SecretKey object, using a PBE key
        PBEKeySpec pbeKeySpec = new PBEKeySpec(args[0]toCharArray());
        SecretKeyFactory keyFac =
                        SecretKeyFactory.getInstance("PBEWithMD5AndDES");
        SecretKey pbeKey = keyFac.generateSecret(pbeKeySpec);

        // Create PBE Cipher
        pbeCipher = Cipher.getInstance("PBEWithMD5AndDES");

        // Initialize PBE Cipher with key and parameters
        pbeCipher.init(Cipher.DECRYPT_MODE, pbeKey, pbeParamSpec);

        System.out.println("Ready...\n\n");

        // Create the ServerSocket.
        s = new ServerSocket(9000);
    } catch (Exception e) {
        System.out.println(e);
    }

    Socket incoming = null;
    InputStream in = null;

    while (true) {

        try {
            // Wait for a connection. In the real world, this code
```

```
                // should be threaded to handle several clients at once.
                incoming = s.accept();
                in = incoming.getInputStream();

                byte[] inBuf = new byte[10000];
                int len = in.read(inBuf, 0, inBuf.length);

                String clearText = new String(pbeCipher.doFinal(inBuf, 0, len));
                System.out.print(clearText);
                System.out.print("\n\n");

                System.out.flush();
                incoming.close();
            } catch (Exception e) {
                e.printStackTrace();
                System.exit(1);
            }
        }
    }
}
```

The first interesting thing the Server does is request a key from the Secret-KeyFactory. SecretKeyFactory.getInstance takes one argument that specifies the desired cryptographic algorithm. In this case, we're using password-based encryption (PBE) with MD5 and DES. This algorithm is provided in the default provider package, so at least for U.S. and Canadian residents who are not subject to U.S. munitions control laws which restrict the export of cryptographic software, it is convenient for this example. We use PBKeySpec created with our password (passed in as args[0].toCharArray( )) to generate the actual key (SecretKey pbeKey = keyFac.generateSecret(pbeKeySpec)).

Once we have the key, we create a Cipher object with the same algorithm and initialize it to encrypt using the secret key and the *salt* we previously defined. Salt is used in secret key encryption to make it harder for someone to crack our password by encrypting some plain text with likely guesses and seeing if it matches a piece of cipher text generated from some known plain text. Adding salt to the encryption algorithm forces the attacker to search a much larger space (all likely passwords × all possible salt), thereby slowing the attack and making the system more secure.

Once we have the key, we enter the while loop in which we will wait for connections. Each time we get a connection, we read the client's data, convert it to a byte array and pass it to our Cipher object. The Cipher's doFinal method decrypts the ciphertext, recovering the plain text, which we write to System.out.

```
incoming = s.accept();
in = incoming.getInputStream();
```

```
byte[] inBuf = new byte[10000];
int len = in.read(inBuf, 0, inBuf.length);

String clearText = new String(pbeCipher.doFinal(inBuf, 0, len));
System.out.print(clearText);
System.out.print("\n\n");
```

Cipher's doFinal method is used when you have all the ciphertext ready to
encrypt or decrypt at once. If you must handle a stream of text, you can use
Cipher's update method to send blocks of data to the Cipher as they become
available. At the end of the stream, use doFinal to complete the processing.

TIP After downloading the JCE, remember to install its cryptographic provider
package into your Java Runtime by editing your <JAVA_HOME>/lib/security/
java.security file to include the new provider package (see the JCE install
instructions for details). If you don't have the provider package properly
installed in the runtime, you will receive a "No such algorithm" exception when
you try to run the server.

The client is very similar. The only substantial difference is that on the client
side, we create a Cipher and initialize it to encrypt using our DES key. Here is
the full source for the client:

Source Code: Client.java
```
import java.io.*;
import java.net.*;
import java.security.*;
import javax.crypto.*;
import javax.crypto.spec.*;


// This class reads a series of lines for System.in, then
// encrypts the resulting string and sends it to a reader
// somewhere on the network.

class Client {

  public static void main(String [] args){

    String host = null;
    char[] pass = null;

    try {
      if (args.length != 2) {
        System.out.println("Usage: java Client host password");
```

```
      System.exit(-1);
    } else {
      host = args[0];
      pass = args[1].toCharArray();
    }


    Socket s = new Socket(host, 9000);
    OutputStream out = s.getOutputStream();


    StringBuffer strB = new StringBuffer();
    boolean done = false;
    BufferedReader in = new BufferedReader(new
                                        InputStreamReader(System.in));


    // Read System.in until we encounter a null string.
    while (!done) {
System.out.print("> ");
      System.out.flush();
      String str = in.readLine();

      if (str == null) {
        done = true;
        } else {
        strB.append(str);
        strB.append("\n");
      }
    }


    System.out.println("\nEncrypting data.  This takes several
                                              seconds.");


    String cleartext= new String(strB);

    // Salt
    byte[] salt = { (byte)0xc7, (byte)0x73, (byte)0x21,
    (byte)0x8c, (byte)0x7e, (byte)0xc8, (byte)0xee, (byte)0x99 };

    // Iteration count
    int count = 20;

    // Create PBE parameter set
    PBEParameterSpec pbeParamSpec = new PBEParameterSpec(salt, count);

    // Convert password into SecretKey object, using a PBE key
    PBEKeySpec pbeKeySpec = new PBEKeySpec(pass);
    SecretKeyFactory keyFac =
                    SecretKeyFactory.getInstance("PBEWithMD5AndDES");
    SecretKey pbeKey = keyFac.generateSecret(pbeKeySpec);
```

```
    // Create PBE Cipher
    Cipher pbeCipher = Cipher.getInstance("PBEWithMD5AndDES");

    // Initialize PBE Cipher with key and parameters
    pbeCipher.init(Cipher.ENCRYPT_MODE, pbeKey, pbeParamSpec);

    byte [] ciphertext = pbeCipher.doFinal(cleartext.getBytes());

    out.write(ciphertext, 0, ciphertext.length);
    out.close();

    System.out.println("Done.");

  } catch (Exception e) {
    System.out.println(e);
  }
 }
}
```

TIP Cryptography is hard, much harder than it appears to be at first glance.
While the preceding code shows you the proper way to use the various JCE
APIs, it does not claim to be a bullet-proof crypto protocol. Unless your are very
sure you know what you are doing, you are probably better off buying a crypto
package from a reputable supplier than you are trying to write one yourself.
Even very large companies, that should have known better, have been caught
using what crypto-guru Bruce Schneier calls "kindergarten cryptography," and
their products have suffered as a result.

Security-Related Bugs

While the fundamental security model previously described has held up well,
there have been several important bugs found in various implementations of
the model. In February 1996, Felton, Dean, and Wallach of Princeton's Safe
Internet Programming group announced the first of a series of bugs found in
various versions of the JDK 1.0. This bug allowed an applet to get around one of
the important security restrictions by spoofing an IP address. During the next
four months, six more security bugs were found in the JDK. These included
flaws in the Verifier, DNS name resolution, ways to cast an object of one class
to another class and curcumventing the Java type safety mechanisms, and
others. The details of these attacks can be found in McGraw and Felton's *Java
Security* (John Wiley and Sons, 1997).

In late 1996, Sun released the public beta of the JDK 1.1. This release was quickly followed by a flurry of reports of new security bugs, including several problems with the new code-signing mechanisms. More recently, researchers at the University of Washington have reported several weaknesses in the Verifier that could possibly be used to subvert the Java security system.

These bugs raised serious questions about Java security. While Java's security design is strong, it doesn't really matter if the implementation of that design is not equally as strong. An attack that exploits a bug in an implementation detail can cause just as much damage as one that exploits a flaw in the design of the system.

Sun, recognizing that Java's security is an important part of the platform, tried to increase the level of confidence people could have in its protection. First, it released full specifications and a source reference implementation for the entire Java platform and invited researchers from all over the Internet to investigate the Java security system. The fact these bugs were found very quickly by reputable researchers at places like Princeton, Cambridge, and other universities, shows that this strategy had some merit. The overall security of the Java platform was strengthened by the efforts of these researchers. Security holes, instead of festering hidden while the system became more and more widely deployed only to be discovered and exploited years later, were found, reported, and fixed before any attacks based on them were found in the wild.

Coping with Bugs

As new releases of the Java platform become available and as more features are added to the Java platform, it is likely that new security bugs will be found. It is an unfortunate fact of life that all large systems contain bugs and that bugs often can be used to compromise security. While the Java language's inherent safety can reduce the number and impact of bugs, it cannot change this fundamental fact.

Of course, the danger of new bugs in Java is no different than the danger of new bugs in any other system. Over the years, the security community has developed some common-sense guidelines for dealing with the ever-present threat of new attacks, bugs, and break-in techniques. These guidelines can be applied to Java systems just as they have been applied to traditional operating systems, e-mail systems, and other parts of our computing infrastructure.

You must realize that security is not a state; it is a process. You cannot build a secure system, then sit back comfortably believing that it cannot be compromised. Instead, you must build a security process that assumes that new bugs will appear, new assaults will be developed, and that the next generation of attackers will be better connected, better equipped, and better informed than the current crop. Your process must include provisions for keeping current with new security information; identifying compromised systems; obtaining, qualifying, and deploying patches; and returning to a state of watchfulness after each attack.

There are several Java resources that will help you in these efforts. First, Sun maintains two Web sites that contain up-to-date information on Java security. The first, java.sun.com/security, contains white papers, specifications, details on new security directions, and other information. The second, java.sun.com/sfaq (security frequently asked questions), contains more topical data on recent attacks, patch levels, and timely information. You should make it a habit to visit these two sites frequently.

The Princeton Safe Internet Programming group also maintains a valuable Web site at www.cs.princeton.edu/sip/. This site tracks a wide range of Internet security threats, including new developments in Java security. Finally, the CERT Coordination Center at the Software Engineering Institute of Carnegie Mellon University maintains an excellent security Web site at www.cert.org/ and also publishes CERT Advisories to alert you about newly found and emerging threats.

Summary

Computer and network security is a widely misunderstood and underappreciated field. Even today, with reports of thousands of credit card numbers stolen over the Net and serious security flaws being found in the major browsers and e-mail readers, too many people disregard security or trade it away for a negligible increase in usability.

The Java security system addresses this problem by allowing both browser and applications vendors to build security into the very roots of their products in a way which is transparent to the user, scalable, and adaptable to the various requirements of a wide range of applications. By enabling a security system which is neither overly restrictive in cases where there is very little danger (like when running applets within the Sandbox policy) nor so lax that it provides little protection against dangerous situations (as is the case when trusting in digital signatures alone), the Java platform achieves a high level of security without compromising usability. The user is not tempted to turn off or go around security mechanisms just to get the job done, a common problem which has led to break-ins and security failures at many sites.

Java 2's protection domains are well suited for an untrusted environment like the Web and are extensible enough to cover the many issues which will arise as the Java platform moves to the mid-tier and data tier of sophisticated enterprise applications. The Java Cryptography Extension provides a solid base on which to build e-commerce systems and other secure transports. Together, protection domains and the cryptography extension provide a consistent, extensible, cross-platform security architecture with capabilities rarely seen in a general-purpose, commercial system.

CHAPTER

13

Using the Java Native Method Interface

Introduction

This chapter introduces the new Java Native Interface (JNI) and discusses its use. The JNI is a set of libraries that provide a native method interface for Java. It allows Java programs to interoperate with non-Java programs. For example, the JNI permits you to call a C program from within a Java program. The reverse is true as well; you can call a Java program from within a C program. C is not the only language that Java can interoperate with; almost any language is capable of interoperating with Java programs. Why would you want to write native methods for use in Java programs? Here are some easy answers:

- The Java class libraries may not have a feature that your application needs, but the underlying operating system provides such a feature.

- You may have existing or legacy code that you would like to access from a Java program.

- You may need the performance of native code that is not available in Java.

There are more reasons for using native methods in Java, but for the most part native methods provide the ability to do something in another language that Java can't do. As Java matures and more class packages are added, the need for native methods will be decreased. All three of the justifications for native methods previously given will soon go away as Java matures.

The JNI

The JNI differs from earlier versions of Java native method interfaces. It has no restrictions on how the Java Virtual Machine (JavaVM) is implemented. This allows different suppliers of the JavaVM to use the JNI interface and not have it depend on their implementation of the virtual machine. Programmers also have the advantage in that only one set of APIs is needed to interact with native code. This makes it possible to write one common native library that will interact with all Java Virtual Machines. However, this does not mean that you can write a native library and have the library work on all systems. It simply means that if you write a native library for a given operating system and architecture, that same library will interoperate with different Java Virtual Machines running on the same platform. For example, if you create a native library on Solaris/SPARC, that library will work with different virtual machines running on a Solaris/SPARC platform. You might ask why one platform would have different virtual machines. Well, quite simply, a single platform can have a Netscape JavaVM, JDK JavaVM, HotJava JavaVM, and so forth. All of these Java Virtual Machines could use the same JNI to interoperate with your native library.

A native method is a procedure or function of some sort that is implemented in a language other than Java and must have the ability to communicate with Java in some manner. This includes Java calling into the native method as well as the native method calling into Java (Figure 13.1). The methods and functions that perform much of this communication are included in the JNI. It is really just a set of methods that are accessible from the native method.

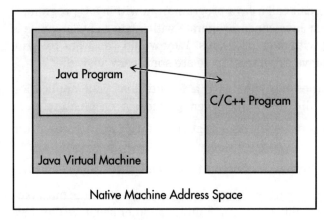

Figure 13.1   Java native method.

There are two ways the JNI package can be used: Java calling a native method and a native method or program invoking the Java Virtual Machine. We will investigate both of these.

Java Calling a Native Method

All of the JNI functions are available to a native method through the use of an interface pointer. This is really just a fancy name for a pointer to an array of function pointers. C++ programmers commonly refer to such a pointer as a virtual function table (see Figure 13.2).

The interface pointer is always passed as a parameter when Java calls into a native method. The native method can then dereference this pointer to gain access to a table of methods (functions) which can be used to gain access to information needed from Java. It is also important to note that this interface pointer is only valid in the thread from which it was called. Knowing this, you should never pass the interface pointer to other threads, since each thread should have its own pointer. Because each thread has its own interface pointer, you are guaranteed that the pointer will be the same when called from the same thread. This means that the native method will always see the same interface pointer if it is being called from the same Java thread. Also keep in mind that native methods can be called from any number of Java threads and therefore can see many different interface pointers from each Java thread.

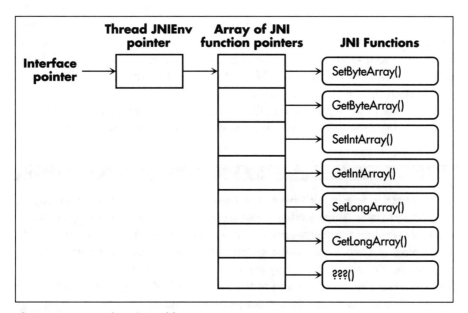

Figure 13.2   JNI function table.

So now you know the real story—Java does have pointers! Well, you can't use pointers from within Java, but now you know that you can get a pointer to Java.

Let's take a look at how it all works. Example Simple.java shows a very simple example of a Java program calling a native method. There are four parts involved in making a call from Java to a native method: the Java code, the native method code, the native method header file, and the native method library. First let's take a look at the Java code:

Source Code: Simple.java
```
public class Simple {
  native String getMessage();
  static {
    System.loadLibrary("simpleJNI");
  }

  public static void main(String srgs[]) {
    System.out.println(getMessage());
  }
}
```

There are only two things that may look a bit different with this code than you would find with all Java implementation. First, the getMessage() method was defined as being native. This tells Java that the implementation of this method is provided through the use of a native method. That is all that is needed to declare a method as being native. The second piece of code that you may have noticed is the static initialization block. It is executed left to right and top to bottom before any other code in the class is executed. So, by placing the call to System.loadLibrary() in the static block, we can be sure that the native method library is loaded before any calls are made to any of its functions. The loadLibrary() method loads a given library from the underlying system. This is a library that is not part of the JavaVM. In this case, the "simpleJNI" library will be loaded when the Java code is executed.

The Java code in the example can then be compiled using javac. When it has been compiled successfully, then you must run javah on the resulting .class file.

NATIVE METHOD NAMING

The name used to specify a native method library in Java does not map directly to the library's name. The JavaVM follows a standard for the name mapping, but the actual mapping is platform-specific. For example, the Solaris operating system converts a Java library name of "my_stuf" into a native library name of libmy_stuf.so. This same Java library would be converted to my_stuff.dll on a Win32-based system. It is up to you as the native method's implementor to correctly name the library on the system you are using.

The javah program will read a given set of .class files and produce native method header files. For the example, we ran the following command:

```
Javah -jni Simple
```

This produced a Simple.h file. The -jni option used with the javah command specified that we wanted to use the JNI mapping for native method calls. For more info about javac or javah, see your JDK (Java 2) command documentation.

Source Code: Simple.h
```
*/#include <jni.h>
/* Header for class Simple */

#ifndef _Included_Simple
#define _Included_Simple
#ifdef __cplusplus
extern "C" {
#endif
/*
 * Class:     Simple
 * Method:    getMessage
 * Signature: ()Ljava/lang/String;
 */
JNIEXPORT jstring JNICALL Java_Simple_getMessage
  (JNIEnv *, jclass);

#ifdef __cplusplus
}
#endif
#endif
```

At this point we have the Java source file, the Java class file, and the native method header file. We need to create the native method code as well as the native method library. Let's take a look at the native method code:

Source Code: GETMESSA.C
```
#include <jni.h>
#include "Simple.h"

JNIEXPORT jstring JNICALL Java_Simple_getMessage(JNIEnv *env, jclass
                                                        jClass) {
  char *str = "Hello World!";
  return((*env)->NewStringUTF(env, str, strlen(str)));
  }
```

This native method used C as its implementation language. There are several things to note in this sample code. First, notice the signature of the C function; it may look a bit complicated. If you were to inspect the header file that was generated from the javah command, you would notice that it contains a function prototype for the native method. We will discuss the mapping of Java methods to native methods a bit later; for now just assume that the name of the C function is Java_Simple_getMessage().

Even though our definition of the getMessage() method in Java took no arguments, the C function takes two arguments. The first argument is a JNIEnv pointer. The JNIEnv pointer is the interface pointer that we discussed earlier which pointed to an array of function pointers. We will soon see how this pointer is used. The second argument is a jclass variable, which can be used to reference the calling Java class. Also notice that theJava_Simple_getMessage() function returns a jstring. The jstring return type is a Java String; this is *not* the same as a char * string in C.

The implementation of the function is quite simple. First we created a regular C string, then used that C string to create a Java string. Notice that we used the JNIEnv pointer to access the NewStringUTF() function in the JavaVM. The NewStringUTF() function takes a C string and converts it into a Java String. The Java String that is created is then returned to the calling Java program.

When the getMessage() method returns, the Java program simply prints its value. In this case it prints "Hello World!"

Now that we have the basics of how Java JNI and native methods are called, we will dive into more details.

Method Naming

The function used in the previous example C program was named Java_Simple _getMessage(). This name may not appear very intuitive compared to the name we gave the method in the Java program. There is a formula for mapping Java names into their native method names. Concatenating the following creates the native method name:

- All method names start with a prefix of "Java_".
- Then a mangled, fully qualified class name is used followed by an underscore "_".
- Then a mangled method name follows.
- If the method has multiple signatures (overloaded), two underscores "__" are added which are followed by a mangled argument signature.

Using our simple example, you can see where the Java_Simple_getMessage() name was derived. The JavaVM uses the native method name to locate the proper function in the native library. The virtual machine also uses a set of rules for locating native methods. It first looks for the simple name, Java _ClassName_MethodName. If that name can't be found because the native method is overloaded, the virtual machine looks for a long function name, Java_ClassName_MethodName__Signature.

Java mangles the names of classes, methods, and signatures to guarantee that the Java names will translate into valid C function names. The following rules are used to mangle the Java names:

- "_" (Underscore) is used to replace a slash "/" in fully qualified class names.

- "_0xxxx" is used to replace the Unicode character xxxx.

- "_1" is used to replace an underscore "_" in any Java names.

- "_2" is used to replace a semicolon ";" in method signatures.

- "_3" is used to replace a bracket "[" in method signatures.

That's it. Now you should be able to construct a native method function name from any given Java method name using these rules.

Parameter Naming

Now that we know how a Java method name is translated into a native method name, we need to know how Java method parameter types and return types are translated into native types. As in the previous simple example, the first parameter passed to a native method is the interface pointer. This pointer is of type JNIEnv and is always passed as the first parameter of a native method. The second parameter passed to all native methods is either a reference to an object or a class. When the Java declaration for the method is static, then the second parameter, of type jclass, is a reference to the class in which the method is declared static. When the Java declaration for the static method is nonstatic, then the second parameter is a reference to a Java object. This parameter is of the type jobject, which refers to the calling Java object of the native method. Since the type of this parameter is jobject, which maps into the Java Object class, it can refer to any object that can be defined in Java.

The remaining parameters in the native method refer to the parameter types passed from the Java method. This is also true for the return value. All Java types can be translated in some manner to suitable types for native definitions. Table 13.1 shows the mapping between Java types and native C types.

Since Java uses a method's signature to differentiate between overloaded methods, a way of mapping a Java method signature into a native representation is needed. Table 13.2 shows what native representations are used to express a Java method signature.

Using this table you should be able to map any Java signature into its native equivalent. The following example shows how a Java method signature is

Table 13.1 Mapping between Java Types and Native Types

JAVA TYPE	NATIVE TYPE	DESCRIPTION
boolean	jboolean	unsigned 8 bits
byte	jbyte	signed 8 bits
char	jchar	unsigned 16 bits
short	jshort	signed 16 bits
int	jint	signed 32 bits
long	jlong	signed 64 bits
float	jfloat	32 bits
double	jdouble	64 bits
void	void	N/A

mapped into a native equivalent using the signature mapping table:

```
Java Signature:    double[] calculate(int, String, short, float[]);
Maps to:           (ILjava/lang/String;S[F)[D
```

The JNI also uses some other mappings to represent certain Java types. Table 13.3 shows the definitions of JNI types that can be used in implementing native methods.

Table 13.2 Native Representations Expressing Java Method Signature

TYPE SIGNATURE	JAVA TYPE
Z	Boolean
B	byte
C	char
S	short
I	int
J	long
F	float
D	double
L fully_qualified_class;	fully qualified Java class
[type	type[]
(args_types) return_type	method type

Table 13.3   Other Useful JNI Definitions

TYPE	VALUE
JNI_FALSE	0
JNI_TRUE	1
jsize	size of a native pointer
jref	void *
jobject	jref
jclass	jref
jstring	jref
jarray	jref
jfieldID	void *
jmethodID	void *
jvalue	typedef union jvalue {
	jboolean z;
	jbyte b;
	jchar c;
	jshort s;
	jint i;
	jlong j;
	jfloat f;
	jdouble d;
	jref l;

Referencing Data from a Native Method

When a Java program calls into a native method, most likely some amount of data is passed to the native method and some data is expected back from the native method. So how does a native method access data that is stored in the JavaVM? Well the answer can be simple or rather complex. Let's answer the simple part first. If simple scalar types are being passed from Java into the native method, then the scalar values are simply copied into the native code. Scalar types include integers, characters, shorts, floats, and so forth.

However, if any Java object is passed into the native method, then only a reference to that object is passed. This may seem somewhat logical, as copying large Java objects between the virtual machine and the native code can create a large overhead. The references are passed to the native method using one of the types listed in Table 13.1; however, it is not as simple as just passing the reference. The JavaVM must keep track of all Java objects that are passed into a native method. This is done to keep the Java garbage collector from collecting Java objects that may be used in the native method. You can imagine what could happen if your program was in the middle of some operation and the JavaVM garbage collected an object that you were referencing. Since the JavaVM keeps track of objects that are referenced in native code, it would also be convenient for the native code to notify the JavaVM that an object is no longer needed. This capability does exist in the JNI and really acts as a free( ) or delete( ) function for Java objects. The act of notifying the JavaVM that an object reference is no longer needed does not guarantee that the object will be garbage-collected immediately; it just tells the JavaVM that it no longer has to keep a live reference of the given object.

Reference Types

Now that we can pass a Java object to a native method, the next question is: What is the scope of a Java object reference? As with most languages, the object reference can be either local or global. By default, all Java object references are passed to the native method as local references. A local reference is only valid for the duration of the native call. Once the native method returns, all local references are freed for you. You can decide to free your own local references as you like but, if you choose not to, the references will automatically be freed when the native code returns. To ensure that you can free a local object reference and the JavaVM can garbage-collect it, the JNI does not permit you to create any extra local object references. If you were allowed to create copies of local object references, the JavaVM could not determine if the object was needed or if it could be garbage-collected.

On the other hand, global object references are valid until they are explicitly freed. This means that a global object reference will remain valid between calls to multiple native methods. So which one do you choose? Well, you may not have to make up your mind just yet. The JNI permits you to create global references from any local reference. This makes it quite easy to delay a scope decision. In fact, you could even make the decision to make a reference global at runtime. The native method interface does not care if you pass or return a local reference or a global reference; it treats them the same.

Since Java objects are represented by object references in native code, we must have a way to access the data associated with the Java object. The JNI provides a set of functions that access the data represented by Java objects. The JNI accessor functions allow access to local and global data through the use of the opaque object references. The JNI accessor functions provide a common interface to allow native methods to access data in the JavaVM. This common interface allows you to develop native methods that can access data on different JavaVM implementations.

Of course, accessing all data using JNI functions can generate quite a bit of overhead. You should take this into consideration when you are designing where Java code stops and the native code starts. In most cases, native methods should perform a set of tasks that either can't be done in Java or can be implemented better in a native language. In this case, the overhead of using JNI functions is not of great concern. In other cases, the overhead of using JNI functions is not acceptable. For example, let's say that you have a large integer array defined in Java and you pass this array to a native method. You would not want to loop through this array and access each member of the array using a JNI function. For this reason the JNI API provides a set of functions that copy a set of data elements between the JavaVM and some sort of native buffer. This permits access to a chunk of data from within the JavaVM without having to call a JNI function to access each data element.

Accessing Java Fields and Methods

Just as the JNI permits access to Java object data, it also permits access to Java fields and methods. A native method can gain access to Java class fields and methods using a symbolic name and a type signature for the particular field or method. This is done in much the same way that introspection works. A JNI function is used to locate a field or method and, if the requested field or method exists, a valid ID is returned. Once a field or method ID is obtained, the native method can use the ID in subsequent JNI calls. Let's take a look at how this works. If a native method is trying to locate a method that has a Java definition such as

```
public int myMethod(long, float, String);
```

then a JNI call is required to locate the method ID for this Java method. Let's assume that we are looking for this method in the myClass class. That call would look like this:

```
    jmethodID jmid =
(*env)->GetMethodID(myClass, "myMethod", "(JFLjava/lang/String;)I");
```

Notice that the class name, method name, and method signature are needed. The method signature was constructed using the rules previously discussed. Once a valid jmethodID is obtained, any number of calls can be made from the native method to the Java method. This can be done using yet another JNI call:

```
jint retValue = (*env)->CallIntMethod(obj, jmid, 19, 4.56, str);
```

In this case a valid object of the myClass type is needed as well as the jmethodID. Notice that the parameters needed to match the method signature are also required in the call. Several calls to the same method can be made without having to obtain the method ID over and over again. However, having a valid field ID or method ID does not protect against the JavaVM from unloading the class that one of the IDs is referencing. When the JavaVM unloads a class, any field or method IDs referencing that class become invalid. It is up to you as a good programmer to make sure that you always have valid field or method IDs. If you plan to use a field or method ID for an extended amount of time, make sure that the native method keeps a live reference to the class that the ID refers to. Another way around this problem, but less efficient, is to revalidate the field or method ID before any calls are made using the ID.

There are several JNI functions that perform all of the actions we have discussed up to this point. It is not our intention to go over each call and describe what function it performs. That is what good API manuals are for. However, Table 13.4 shows the major types of JNI functions that are available. For more information about all of the supported JNI functions see java.sun.com.

Table 13.4   JNI Functions

FUNCTION TYPE	DESCRIPTION
Version Information	Provides information about JNI version
Class Operations	Define, create, and compare classes
Exceptions	Create and throw exceptions
Global and Local References	Create and delete object references
Object Operations	Allocate and create objects
Accessing Fields of Objects	Get and set object field values
Calling Instance Methods	Calling instance methods
Accessing Static Fields	Get and set static field values
Calling Static Methods	Calling static methods
String Operations	Create, convert, and more, String functions
Array Operations	Create arrays and retrieve elements
Registering Native Methods	Register native methods
Monitor Operations	Monitor enter and exit functions
JavaVM Interface	JavaVM creation and operation functions

Error Handling from Native Methods

At this point you know how to move data back and forth between Java and native code. You also know how to gain access to Java fields and methods, but what if an error occurs in your native code? What should you do with the error? Once again the answer is simple and complex at the same time. Since the JNI can pass objects back to Java and exceptions in Java are simply Java objects, then it is possible to pass an Exception object back to Java from the native method. Any native code can raise any type of Java exception, then decide to handle the exception in the native code or pass the exception back to the JavaVM. This all seems quite simple, so where is the complex part? Well, since native code is not restricted in the same way that Java code is, certain errors can occur in the native code but the native code can continue to execute. For example, let's say a certain call is made in the native code that produces an error. The error code is returned from the call and it is then up to the programmer to either check for such an error or ignore the error and continue on with the next native instruction. In this case, an error has occurred but nothing was done to correct the problem. This can't happen in Java. When an exception is thrown in Java, the code is forced to deal with the exception or the code will terminate.

For this reason, only a limited number of exceptions are actually thrown when an error occurs in a program that uses the JNI functions. It is up to you as a programmer to decide how you will handle native errors and possible exceptions. In some cases, you may ignore certain errors in a native program; in doing so, the native code could create an invalid state which can cause the JavaVM to crash. The best bet is to use common sense and decide what calls will require some amount of error checking. If an error is detected, you must also decide whether to throw an exception back to the JavaVM or deal with the error condition in the native code.

Invoking Java from Native Code

We have talked about how Java programs can call out to native code, but up to this point we have not talked about how a native program can invoke the JavaVM to execute some Java code. For example, you may have an existing C program that would like to call a Java class to perform some sort of operation. It is possible for this C program to start a JavaVM, load a requested Java class file, and execute the class file. This allows you to build applications that are Java-enabled without having to link your existing native code in with the JavaVM. Let's take a look at how this works.

Source Code: Cmain.c

```c
#include <jni.h>

void main(int argc, char **argv) {
  jclass javaClass;
  jmethodID javaMethod;
  jstring str;
  jobject Array mainArgs;
  JavaVM *jvm;
  JNIEnv *env;
  JDK1_1InitArgs jvmArgs;

  /* Get the default VM args and create Java VM */
  JNI_GetDefaultJavaVMInitArgs(&jvmArgs);
  jvmArgs.classpath = "/opt2/Java/java/lib/classes.zip:.";
  JNI_CreateJavaVM(&jvm, &env, &jvmArgs);

  /* Find the Java Window Class*/
  javaClass = (*env)->FindClass(env, "Java Window");

  /* Find the main method */
  javaMethod = (*env)->GetStatic MethodID(env, javaClass, "main",
                                          "([Ljava/lang/String;)V");

  /*create a simple Java string */
  str = (*env)->NewStringUTF(env, "A string argument");
  /* put the Java string into an array of strings */
  mainArgs = (*env)->NewObjectArray(env, 1, (*env)->FindClass(env,
                                          "java/lang/String"), str);

  /*Call the main method with the array of strings */
  (*env)->CallStaticVoidMethod(env, JavaClass, javaMethod, mainArgs);

  /* Destroy the VM */
  (*jvm)->DestroyJavaVM(jvm);
}
```

The Cmain.c program invokes a JavaVM and calls the main( ) method in the ColorView.java program found in Chapter 2. This effectively starts the Java application running which then brings up a Java window. This is a very simple example, but it shows how you can start a JavaVM, find a Java class, then invoke a method in the class.

There are five major steps involved in invoking a JavaVM, then executing a method in a given class:

1. Create an instance of a JavaVM.

2. Find and load a given class into the JavaVM.

3. Obtain a valid method ID for a given method.

4. Invoke the given method.

5. Destroy the JavaVM.

Let's take a closer look at these operations. The JNI_CreateJavaVM( ) function is used to load and initialize an instance of a JavaVM. This function returns a valid JavaVM reference and JNIEnv interface pointer. The native thread that calls this function is considered the main thread of the JavaVM. Since the JNIEnv interface pointer is only valid in the thread that obtained the pointer, another function is required to attach other native threads to the same instance of the JavaVM. This can be done using the AttachCurrentThread( ) JNI call. This will attach the current native thread to an existing JavaVM as well as returning a valid JNIEnv interface pointer for the thread. Once this has been done the native thread will act just like any other thread that is executing in the JavaVM. The thread that called the attach function will remain attached to the JavaVM until it specifically detaches itself using the DetachCurrent-Thread( ) function.

Finding and loading the Java class as well as invoking a Java method have been previously discussed. There is nothing different in the way you would access fields, methods, and data from what we have discussed in previous sections.

When the Java class has finished its execution and the native program no longer needs access to the JavaVM, the JavaVM must be unloaded and detached from the main thread. This cannot be done in the same way an arbitrary thread can detach itself from the JavaVM. Only the main thread can unload the JavaVM and the main thread must be the only thread running in the JavaVM when it is unloaded. The main thread simply makes a call to the DestroyJavaVM( ) function in order to unload and detach the JavaVM. Again, the main thread, the one that called the JNI_CreateJavaVM( ) function, must be the only thread running. This includes all Java threads that we created as part of the execution of a called method as well as any native threads that were attached to the JavaVM. This restriction forces you to make sure that all resources are freed before the JavaVM is destroyed. This enforces that resources, locks, and such are not in use and that the JavaVM can exit cleanly.

You may have noticed in the example that we used a call to retrieve a set of JavaVM initialization arguments. This was done because different JavaVM implementations may require a certain set of initialization structures in order to operate correctly. The initialization values that are required can differ between JavaVM implementations, and thus require the native application to set certain values. The JNI includes a JavaVMInitArgs structure that can be modified to contain required values for the particular JavaVM implementation. You will notice that in our example we just requested the default set of initialization values.

Summary

This chapter has covered most of what you should need to know in order to exchange data and functionality between Java and native programs. Again, we did not cover all the calls available in the JNI, but hopefully have discussed the issues and some of the capabilities of the JNI libraries.

CHAPTER

14

Understanding
Network Computers

Introduction

For too long many parts of the IT industry have, like Goldilocks, been faced with a choice between extremes. Unfortunately, while Goldilocks had three bears from which to choose, IT has only had two: *too big* and *too small*. This problem is caused by the huge gap between the power and flexibility of PCs and workstations on one hand and the low purchase price and administration costs of character-based terminals on the other. Client/server systems in the late 1980s and mid-1990s made many claims of huge cost savings to be had by replacing expensive, centralized mainframes with inexpensive servers and powerful desktops. While the initial purchase price of these new systems was many times smaller than the older mainframe systems, the early cost estimates used to justify these new systems tended to ignore or underestimate the long-term cost of administering and maintaining the large number of individual desktop machines needed to make client/server computing work.

After years of struggling with administration problems, IT shops have now begun to realize what it costs per year to keep a typical desktop PC up and running. Estimates of the PC's total cost of ownership made by independent research organizations range from $8,000 to $14,000 per year for equipment depreciation, administration costs, employee downtime, and *futzing*, a generic term intended to measure the cost of productivity lost to such activities as figuring out which of 200 different alert beeps is the most pleasing or whether the cursor should turn into a wasp or a dinosaur when the user is idle. For even moderately sized PC installations, these annual costs quickly overcome any initial cost savings the system provided. A site with 1,000 PCs, which was at the low end of the industry average for total cost of ownership, would still be spending $8,000,000 per year just to keep the PCs running. Compared to this kind of ongoing cost, a $20,000,000 mainframe surrounded by 3270 terminals costing $0 per year seems like a bargain.

The Network Computer splits the difference between the powerful and flexible, but costly, PC or workstation and the profoundly limited, but profoundly inexpensive, dumb tube. The Network Computer strives to provide the best of both worlds: the graphical display, local processing power, and scalability of desktop clients, and the low total cost of ownership and maintainability of character-based terminals. Network computers achieve this goal by reducing the typical desktop machine to its core, essential components and by removing much of the needless complexity which has accumulated around desktop operating systems over the last decade. The result is a small, powerful device which allows users to accomplish their tasks without requiring constant nursing and futzing.

By splitting the difference between the *too big* desktop computer and the *too small* dumb tube, the Network Computer provides IT with the long-sought *just right* computer.

What Is a Network Computer?

The Network Computer is defined by the Network Computer Reference Profile (NCRP) which was jointly developed by Apple, IBM, Netscape, Oracle, and Sun Microsystems. The Reference Profile, now controlled by The Open Group, defines the Network Computer in terms of minimum hardware and network capabilities, media formats, and Internet standards support. These standards are:

HARDWARE:

- Minimum screen resolution of 640 × 480 pixels
- Pointing device, such as a mouse, track ball, or other device
- Text input capability, such as a keyboard or other device
- Audio output
- Persistent local storage not required
- Optional support for SmartCards (ISO 7816) and other digital token cards

NETWORK:

- Internet Protocol (IP)
- Transmission Control Protocol (TCP)
- File Transfer Protocol (FTP)
- Telnet
- Network File System (NFS): Note that NCs which do not provide distributed file services need not implement NFS
- User Datagram Protocol (UDP)
- Simple Network Management Protocol (SNMP)
- Dynamic Host Configuration Protocol (DHCP)
- Bootp

MEDIA FORMATS:

- JPEG
- GIF
- WAV
- AU

INTERNET STANDARDS:

- HyperText Markup Language (HTML)
- HyperText Transfer Protocol (HTTP)
- Java application environment, including the Java Virtual Machine and Java class libraries

INTERNET MAIL STANDARDS:

- Simple Mail Transfer Protocol (SMTP)
- Internet Message Access Protocol Version 4 (IMAP4)
- Post Office Protocol Version 3 (POP3)

A Standards-Based Platform

Traditional desktop environments define a computing platform in terms of products from certain vendors; a platform uses this CPU and runs this operating system. In contrast, the Network Computer Reference Profile only specifies open, widely accepted standards which must be supported, without saying how those standards are to be implemented. Because it uses universally accepted standards, like HTML and TCP/IP, and the platform-independent Java environment, the NC Reference Profile can be implemented on top of any CPU, with any operating system, including micro and nano kernel systems, using any bus or card architecture and any packaging.

This standards-based approach to defining the platform grants vendors an unprecedented degree of freedom in how they implement Network Computers. Various manufacturers can optimize their boxes for a wide range of price-points and functionality and, as long as they all meet the standards previously listed, each of these boxes will qualify as a true Network Computer. One vendor may build a very small, low-cost, low-power, low-heat device for kiosks and other embedded, single-application environments. Another vendor may build a desktop device with a large enough CPU and enough memory to support several applications, including typical office applications like word processing and spreadsheets, simultaneously. Applications designed for Network Computers will work on any of these devices without porting, modification, or different versions for each box.

NC Implementations

Several different styles of NC are already on the market. Each of these styles represents a solution to the trade-offs of time to market, cost, complexity, and starting point of its maker (see Table 14.1). The three main styles now available are: X-terminal displaying a Java-enabled browser, X-terminal-like devices with integral browser and Java capabilities, and the pure NC. All of these styles of devices may be equipped with optional FlashRAM to speed to booting process and dial-up or serial line network support.

The first style is little more than a traditional X-terminal with a backend server which runs the Web browser and any Java applications. This device provides nothing that the traditional X-terminal did not, and suffers from all the bandwidth and backend processor bottlenecks which prevented the X-terminal from becoming widely popular. This implementation was strongly driven by time to market; it takes little more than a new nameplate and an ad campaign to

Table 14.1   NC Implementations

STYLE	BROWSER	JAVA	X	WINDOWS	BAND-WIDTH	WAN-SUITABLE
X-terminal	Server	Server	Yes	Emulation	High	No
X-terminal w/native Java Browser	Native	Native	Yes	Emulation	Medium to High	Yes
Pure NC	Native	Native	Emulation	Emulation	Medium to High	Yes

turn a vendor's existing X-terminal into a more marketable Network Computer. In the long run, though, this solution has little to offer and it will probably fade away as the vendors who chose this strategy move to one of the other two solutions or, failing to make this move, go out of business. Interestingly, there are also some recent entries to this market which use Windows emulation instead of X emulation for the window system. These have the advantage of being able to access legacy Windows applications but still suffer from the disadvantages of the X-terminal.

Most X-terminal manufacturers will probably settle on the second style of NC. By implementing a browser and a Java Virtual Machine in the boot package for the X-terminal, these vendors get the benefits of a pure NC implementation and very good performance for legacy X applications with only a slight increase in time to market. Since some applications and processing can be moved to the NC in the form of Java applets, they also reduce the large bandwidth needs which prevented X-terminals from operating on a low-bandwidth wide area network and also overcome some of the server scalability issues which have plagued X-terminals. Versions of this style of NC which use Windows emulation technology instead of X are also available.

The pure NC represents a different approach to the NC trade-offs. Instead of retrofitting an existing X-terminal with a browser, the pure NC is designed and optimized for the new network-based Java application environment. It implements natively only those features required by the NC Reference Profile. All other functions, including legacy X and Windows applications, and other applications are delivered to the NC by the network. As Java-based X and Windows emulators become faster, and as the X-terminal market further optimizes its devices for the NC profile, most practical differences between these two styles of NC will disappear.

Is a PC an NC?

The Network Computer Reference Profile could easily be implemented on top of a typical desktop machine, like a Windows PC, an Apple Macintosh, or a UNIX workstation. Most commercial desktop machines today already meet or exceed the hardware, networking, and media format specifications. Adding a Web browser and appropriate mail client (two applications which are increasingly likely to be bundled with the base OS) makes the platform fully compliant with the Reference Profile. Does this mean that a PC is really a Network Computer?

In a strictly technical sense, the answer is yes; a PC or other desktop machine is a Network Computer. This is a very important feature because it allows organizations who are building applications for NCs to deploy those applications to their existing desktop machines without costly upgrades or reinvestment in those platforms. This compatibility provides an easy migration path from today's desktop-centric computing to true network computing. Organizations who wish to make this move can start today by deploying their first network applications without disrupting their current environments.

In a broader sense, though, PCs and NCs are very different beasts. The Network Computer has been designed from the ground up to meet three goals which are not explicitly listed in the NC specification previously listed and which set the NC apart from the PC:

- Maintain architectural neutrality
- Lower total cost of ownership
- Enable a greater level of system security

Architectural neutrality allows vendors to design Network Computers for a wide range of price-points, environments, and task loads. Architectural neutrality also prevents the vendor lock-in which is so common in computing systems. Since no one company owns the underlying processor or operating system, the Network Computer gives users vendor-neutral systems without sacrificing compatibility.

While the Reference Profile does not say how vendors should build their Network Computers, those devices already on the market show several common features intended to lower total cost of ownership. NCs typically lack user-managed local storage, boot over the network, get all data and applications from the network, and have much simpler user interfaces. These features work together to reduce administration time, eliminate backups of individual desktops, and lower user *futz* time.

Network Computers are also more secure than PCs and other desktops. They help control the flow of information both into and out of the corporation. Because the typical NC lacks a CD-ROM, floppy, or other removable medium device, end users are unable to import viruses, Trojan horses, and other hostile executables. Any untrustworthy executable which the user could encounter will be Java applets, which are subject to the security constraints of the Java security model (see Chapter 12). Also, because the NC doesn't have any local storage, it is easier to prevent the introduction of viruses into the network and to eradicate viruses if they ever do take hold. One needs only to protect the central application repository, instead of thousands of individual hard drives which could serve as reservoirs for the virus. Security officers must also worry about theft of information from the inside. It does little good to have a strong firewall monitoring outgoing traffic if an industrial spy can simply copy sensitive information onto a floppy and walk out with it at the end of the day. The lack of removable media makes it easier to prevent this kind of theft.

YOU MEAN I CAN'T HAVE A DISK?

Although today's typical Network Computer lacks a disk, there is nothing in the Reference Profile, goals of the NC, or in the security considerations, which forbids incorporating a disk in an NC. The problem is not so much having a disk, as having to manage the disk and the information stored on it. So, local disks make perfect sense in Network Computers, as long as that disk is treated as a non-volatile cache, not as user or application storage space. A caching disk would store frequently used applets and information and automatically synchronize itself with the central, *gold* copy, either through standard browser caching techniques or through one of the *application push* systems, like Marimba's Castanet, which are now available. All user data, and the attendant backup and management burden, would remain on a centralized server, which can be more easily and less expensively managed.

A local caching disk would reduce network bandwidth requirements, reduce latency experienced when switching between applications, and allow the NC to operate on larger data sets than would be possible if it relied only on physical memory. These advantages would allow the NC to fit into a wider range of markets than it currently can. For a remote embedded device like a kiosk connected to the rest of the network by a 28.8 modem, being able to keep a local copy of a 300-MB video file would be a big advantage.

Network Computer Advantages

Reduced total cost of ownership is the most frequently cited and probably the most tangible benefit of Network Computers. However, for corporations considering deploying NCs, cost of ownership is not the only or even the primary concern. A recent Yankee Group survey, "Making a Business Case for the Network Computer," February 1997, found that CIOs ranked cost of ownership fifth, behind single point of control, unified software platform, central storage, and low initial cost, on their list of reasons to buy NCs. While all four of the higher-rated concerns are actually aspects of the total cost of ownership, it is interesting that CIOs are considering these concerns separately. While it is possible that these CIOs have not realized that total cost of ownership encompasses all of these factors, it is more likely that they are struggling with these issues across their entire IT infrastructure, not just on the desktop, and that they see the NC as one more tool for getting these costs under control.

There is also the issue of how much benefit the company reaps from owning the device. A device which costs $20,000 a year to own, but directly or indirectly generates $100,000 per year of revenue, is more valuable than a device which costs $1,000 a year to own but only generates $1,100 per year in revenue. Two of the top five reasons to be interested in NCs, unified software platform and central storage, directly translate into higher individual productivity and greater return on the desktop investment. A unified software platform allows the IT organization to develop internal applications like benefits management, time cards, and workflow tools once, and deploy those tools to all users, regardless of what type of desktop they have. The alternatives are either to port the applications to each platform, an expensive proposition, or to mandate a single hardware platform across the enterprise. The latter forces either a least common denominator approach which hobbles the power users or a greatest common denominator approach which puts inappropriately large machines on too many desktops. Both of these approaches reduce the benefit/cost ratio of desktop machines.

The low initial and long-term costs of the NC have another advantage. They allow desktop devices to be deployed to users who never had any sort of computer before. This could mean Human Resources (HR) kiosks in shared areas of a factory, NCs on the loading and receiving docks of a warehouse, and other previously disconnected areas of the corporation. With the NCs in place, these employees can enjoy the benefits of online information, like accessing corporate data via a Web browser, e-mail, and groupware. When treated as an information appliance, not as a general-purpose computer, the NC allows these isolated areas of the company to be connected. This may even benefit some developers. In a surprising number of development houses, especially large contractors who must squeeze every dollar out of a contract, the developers themselves don't have desktop machines or access to even something as simple as e-mail. While this may be hard to believe, there are still development houses which are working on sophisticated network systems for their customers, yet still run their own business with paper memos. The NC can help these organizations finally practice what they preach.

A single point of control and a unified software platform have another advantage. They allow all users to generate and manipulate information with the same tools and prevent unapproved tools from entering the enterprise. It is much easier to prevent the introduction of unauthorized software when the desktop devices lack floppy drives. At first glance this centralized control might look like a return to the IT tyranny of the late 1970s and early 1980s. If the corporate standard for word processing is FrameMaker, a user could argue that he already knows Word and uses it at home, so he is more productive with that tool. What right does the IT shop have to take away his favorite software? It was the revolt against this tyranny which fueled the PC revolution in the first place.

While this user may have a point, that he is more familiar with and therefore more productive in Word, he is missing the bigger picture. The whole point of producing information is to have it used by other people. His personal productivity might be higher when using his favorite tools, but as other people struggle to import his nonstandard formats into the standard tools, the overall productivity of the organization drops dramatically. This problem becomes even worse when you consider the number of different applications and tools which a typical knowledgeable worker may use. If left to itself, the profusion of different formats and tools could result in an information logjam, as people struggle to bring data into the one tool that makes them "more productive." It can also result in information fiefdoms, as a single department becomes sole master of some critical data because it is the only one that can use the tools needed to create and manage that data. Unfortunately, this describes too many organizations today all too well.

These islands of information may have sprung up for another reason. In the past, there were several distinct realms of computing, with very little overlap. The tools that ran on low-end PCs did not run on high-end workstations and dumb terminal users were stuck with text-based tools which weren't compatible with either of them. By providing an inexpensive-to-own but powerful desktop for even those users who once were stuck with dumb tubes, the NC enables standard tools which can be used across the whole enterprise.

IT organizations that wish to reassert this central control of applications must be careful not to go too far. In the 1970s and 1980s IT shops often were unresponsive to user needs and too expensive for many departments. Users are still justifiably suspicious of attempts to centralize information and applications. The previous scenario only works if it is a true partnership between IT and the user community. Users must realize that the goal is to increase productivity of the corporation as a whole, a goal which may require them to give up some of their favorite tools (and, hopefully, in the process give up hours of frustration trying to import information into those tools). IT must also realize that strict compliance with the corporate tool standards is not always possible or even desirable. For example, the art department will require much more powerful and sophisticated publishing and drawing tools than are needed by the average user. Also, because the art department must interface with outside vendors, like service bureaus and printers, it might need to generate information in nonstandard formats. The IT organization must realize that these cases will arise and must work with the users to make sure that the disjunction between standard tools and user needs does not result in the isolation of those users.

Network Computer Longevity

A long and productive life is another important, anticipated advantage of the Network Computer. NCs promise to break the vicious circle of software upgrade requires hardware upgrade, which enables software upgrade, which requires hardware upgrade, ad nauseam; a trap into which many PC users have fallen. This vicious circle dramatically shortens the useful life of a PC and has led some companies to such extreme steps as to no longer treat PCs as capital equipment. Instead PCs are treated as disposable cost items. The problem is also demonstrated by popular office suites which now consume more than 500 MB of disk or Web browsers which require more than 50 MB just to install. NCs, by their very nature, spread the computational, storage, and management load across the network. This allows NCs to age more gracefully than fat-client PCs can. A well-planned upgrade in network infrastructure, like faster mid-tier servers or a new, more powerful network application, can simultaneously upgrade every NC on the network. New investments can be moved from the desktop to the network where they can be better managed and leveraged across the organization.

No NC has been in service long enough to prove these claims; the oldest NCs have only been deployed for a few months. Although lacking the years needed to demonstrate their potential longevity, there are good reasons to think that NCs will meet this challenge. Historically, thin clients, like 3270s and other dumb tubes or PCs being used for a single application, have had very long service lives. It is not unusual to find a 3270 terminal which is decades old and still ticking. This is because these devices are not general-purpose computers and are not expected to keep up with every new trend in computer science. Instead these information appliances are expected to do their job well without a lot of bells and whistles. As a result, these devices can give years of useful service without being made obsolete by new window systems, upgraded word processors, and other packages of dubious value.

Of course, in any organization, 3270s and character terminals should be the first candidates for upgrade to NCs. The new emphasis on information and collaborative workflow in modern enterprises, combined with new applications which must be deployed to every user in order to be maximally useful, have finally made the dumb tube obsolete. The challenge for IT architects and application designers is to replace these devices with NCs, without perpetuating the vicious upgrade cycle which consumes PCs today. By focusing on the network, not the desktop, as the application platform, application designers should be able to avoid the traps into which fat-client users have fallen. The remainder of this chapter contains some hints and guidelines for building applications which will age gracefully.

The Network Computer Market

When compared with traditional PCs, the Network Computer trades some degree of functionality and flexibility for simplicity and lower total cost of ownership. When compared with character-based terminals, the NC makes the exact opposite trade-off. It trades some of the dumb tube's "plug it in and forget it forever" simplicity for better user interfaces, a broader application base, and more powerful, local computing resources. These trade-offs, and the fact that the NC market is still maturing, determine where it is appropriate to deploy NCs today.

The Network Computer is not intended to replace every PC or workstation, nor will it necessarily eliminate all character-based devices. It is intended to be, in those environments where a dumb tube is *too small* and a PC is *too big*, the *just right* computer which provides the needed level of power and functionality without introducing an unaffordable level of complexity and maintenance.

Diversity versus Intensity

Application environments can be characterized by two variables: diversity, the number of different applications required to do a job, and intensity, the computing power required by those applications. Figure 14.1 shows the NC market based on these variables.

The lower left quadrant is the least demanding environment. Here the users only need one or two fairly undemanding applications in order to do their jobs. Data entry, customer management, reservation and check-in counters fall into the low-diversity/low-intensity category. Typically, these applications are deployed on character-based terminals, low-powered PCs, or even high-powered PCs running nothing but a 3270 emulator. Clearly, Network Computers are a perfect fit for these environments.

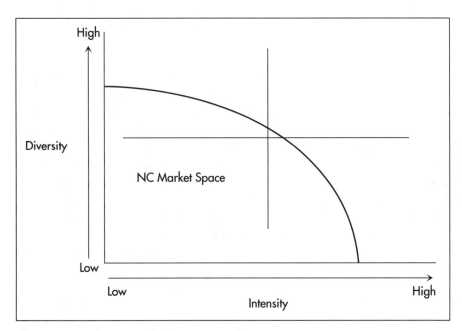

Figure 14.1   The Network Computer market.

The lower right quadrant contains high-intensity but low-diversity applications, environments in which users require a small number of demanding applications. This category includes kiosks whose main function is to run a gift registry, but which also runs promotional videos when it is idle. Process control applications and other dedicated devices also fall into the high-intensity/low-diversity category, as do those applications which require a large number of specialized or dedicated peripherals. Today, these applications typically are deployed on either PCs or Unix workstations. While Network Computers are inappropriate for the high end of this category, the NC can be used in the mid-range. This is especially true of applications which are pushed into the high intensity range by large processing demands. Since the typical NC's CPU is as powerful as those found in mid-range PCs, a JIT-enabled NC is able to compete effectively in this application space.

In the low-intensity/high-diversity world the users spend most of their time switching between a variety of low-powered applications. For example, a typical office suite might include a word processor, Web browser, spreadsheet, e-mail client, and several tools specific to that particular office. While each tool may be very powerful and offer many features, the typical user takes advantage of only a handful of the available functions. As in the high-intensity/low-diversity category, the Network Computer can compete in the low and mid-range of this market. Here the limit is not the speed of the CPU, it is the speed of the network. If the user is constantly switching between applications and must wait for each application to download every time it is needed, the NC will not be appropriate. But for those environments in which applications small enough so that several can be cached locally, allowing for much faster switching between applications, the NC is a good fit. Since Java applications designed for NCs are typically much smaller than similar applications designed for fat clients, the NC is actually appropriate for a larger portion of this market than one might think. For example, commercial Java word processors can begin running with as little as several hundred KB to a MB of code, compared to several tens of MB for a fat client word processor. Larger memory on the NC, or a small caching disk, will extend the NC even further into this space.

Finally, we are left with the most demanding environments: the high-intensity/high-diversity applications of the upper right quadrant. These applications include the MCAD or ECAD engineering workstations, where the user needs basic office tools like e-mail, browser, and spreadsheet, along with several very demanding applications like CAD packages, simulators, and finite element analyses tools. A software developer who uses several edit-compile-debug tools, maintains a test database, and handles the bug tracking and release control functions also requires at least a PC-class machine or maybe even a powerful Unix workstation. This environment also includes content creators, like graphic artists and art directors who have several drawing, desktop publishing, and image manipulation tools, and who *actually use* all the features those tools provide. Today, these markets are dominated by high-end PCs and workstations. The NC is not appropriate for this market now or in the foreseeable future. Instead, these users' current desktops can be *side-graded* by installing a Java-capable browser and Java runtime OS extensions. Then these true power users will be able to use both their existing tools and any Web-oriented, Java tools which the IT organization deploys.

It is somewhat surprising to map these four categories of application mix to users in a corporation. We typically find that NCs are appropriate for a much wider range of users and that those users span a wider range of job titles and salaries than you might expect. In many organizations, only a relatively small number of engineers, artists, and others require the power and flexibility of a PC or workstation. Other users, on both sides of the engineers' pay scale, are perfectly suited for an NC (see Figure 14.2).

Unfortunately, the terms we use to describe the various types of work previously described here tend to overemphasize the importance of those users who require workstations and to downplay the importance of the NC's target market. After all, given the choice, who wouldn't rather be a knowledge producer than a knowledge consumer or a content creator than a process worker? But this split in value of the worker is false. Looking at the chart in Figure 14.2, and comparing it to the four categories of application type, we see that the senior executive who uses her desktop for e-mail, reading reports, and getting news feeds is just as much a candidate for an NC as the order entry clerk at the left-hand side of the drawing. Assigning someone an NC is not a judgment of his value to the organization. It is simply an attempt to use the right tool for the job.

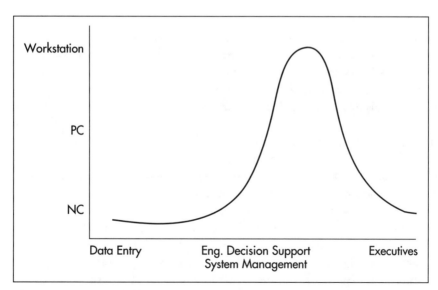

Figure 14.2 Potential NC users can be found in all levels of an organization.

Network Computer Competitors

Many vendors in different market spaces share the goal of reducing overall cost of ownership. The March 17, 1997 issue of *Information Week* listed three possible competitors to the Network Computer: the traditional PC, new lower-cost PCs targeted at under $1,000, and the NetPC. It is interesting to see how these three stack up against the Network Computer.

Network Computers do not really compete against the traditional PC. They only compete in those applications where the traditional PC is *too big*. There is a fairly clear line between those environments where the power and flexibility of a PC or other desktop is required and those environments where a PC was deployed because the only other choice was a dumb tube. This is the market for the NC. As the NC matures and more applications move to the network-centric architecture, and as the PC responds to competitive pressures from NCs, this line is likely to blur. But for today, the PC and NC compete in separate spaces.

SUPPORTING LEGACY APPLICATIONS

At first glance, the NetPC seems to have one advantage over the NC: It can run existing PC applications. Since NC runs only Java and Web-based applications, this provides the NetPC with a short-term advantage. As more native Java versions of a wider variety of applications become available, this advantage will diminish. In the meantime, there is a way to run legacy applications on Network Computers.

Java window servers, for both X and Windows, are available today (see Figure 14.3). With these, a Network Computer can at least display the GUI portion of a desktop application. The application itself will be running on a backend compute server. The NC will only be acting as the display engine. This situation is very familiar to people accustomed to the X environment. It is the traditional X-terminal. It is less familiar in the Windows space, where the ability to remotely display an application running on a network server is relatively new.

Using remote display technology also extends the NC into applications areas where it may not have initially been a good fit. Think of a user who fits into the lower left quadrant of the application space graph (refer to Figure 14.1) most of the time, but occasionally requires desktop applications not available yet in Java. For example, a nurse may use a Java-based health care information system for seven and one half hours per day, but at the end of his shift need to use Word or a legacy X application to update a daily report. In this case, remote display technology allows the NC to fulfill that user's needs. Of course, if a user requires more frequent access to power-user desktop tools, that user is not an appropriate candidate for either an NC or a NetPC.

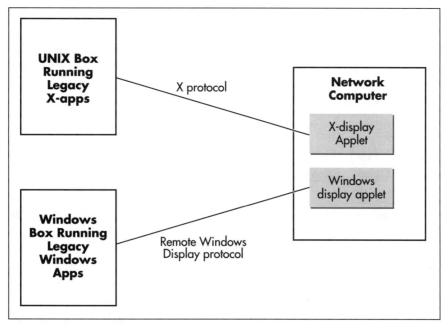

Figure 14.3 Application servers and display emulation technology allow NCs to run legacy X and Windows applications.

The same argument holds true for new low-cost PCs. While their initial purchase price may be lower, they share the same support and administration problems which make their larger, more expensive cousins inappropriate for the NC market space. Since the NC's value proposition is in its reduction of *long-term* support costs, not its initial purchase price, a sub-$1,000 PC which still costs $8,000 to $14,000 to run, would not fair well against an NC.

The NetPC is a different story. The NetPC is a stripped-down, low-cost PC, with a sealed case and a lighter version of the Windows operating system. In many important respects the NetPC is an NC or at least as close to a true NC as a PC can get. It gets its applications over the network; it has no local, user-managed storage; and it has many of the same remote management features as the NC. The NetPC does not have several important features, the lack of which prevents it from claiming true NC status. First, it is not architecturally neutral. The NetPC is based on particular products from particular vendors, not on open, universally accepted standards like the NC. Second, the NetPC is still prey for all the viruses and other nasties that plague the PC world. Finally, the NetPC is still mostly a paper device. Actual implementations of the NetPC are only now nearing availability. Time will tell if the NetPC can exist in a market niche between their full-powered cousins and the Network Computer, or if they will be squeezed out by the maturing NC and advances in the traditional PC.

Regardless of whether the NC, the NetPC, or both survive, the IT organization and the end user have already won. By calling attention to the great costs associated with owning a traditional PC, the NC has forced desktop vendors in both camps to find ways to reduce the total cost of ownership for their devices and to consider cost of ownership to be an important design criterion for future products. This change will be of enduring value to desktop customers.

Designing Applications for Network Computers

Applications designed for typical desktop machines are usually quite fat. In keeping with the desktop-centric attitudes of the PC world, these applications are likely to be monolithic, doing all processing locally, storing all data locally, and storing the entire program in one stovepipe executable. If they use the network at all, it is probably only for network file services or for access to a remote database. While these monolithic or, at best, two-tiered designs worked moderately well in the desktop-centric world, such designs are clearly not suitable for Network Computers. NC applications should exploit network resources to their fullest and reduce IT cost of ownership by moving expensive administrative tasks, like data backups and OS maintenance, from the desktop, where this cost must be paid once for each of the thousands of machines deployed, to the network, where dedicated servers maintained by a smaller staff of competent professionals can be administered much more cost effectively.

We have already dedicated an entire chapter to the three-tiered software architecture. These principles are the basis of NC applications. The three-tiered design, with its dependence on the network, is perfectly suited for the NC environment. The GUI, and possibly some or all of the logic tiers, run locally on the NC and provide the sophisticated user interface, predictable response times, and inexpensive scalability users have come to expect from desktop machines. The data tier, and possibly some of the logic, are deep within the network, providing greater control over mission-critical systems, allowing for both the exploitation of data by several applications simultaneously and centralized management.

The Universal Java Platform

Since we have already discussed in great detail the philosophy and implications of the three-tiered design the remainder of this section will deal with issues which specifically affect Network Computers. While these principles are a must for applications intended for NCs, widespread use of these principles will guarantee that applications will be truly Write Once, Run Anywhere. When possible, the following guidelines should be employed even for applications which are intended to be deployed on PCs or workstations.

One of the greatest benefits of the Java platform is that it is a single universal computing platform. As previously mentioned, this allows organizations that wish to move to network computing to begin deploying Java applications on their existing hardware. New applications which are eventually intended to be deployed on Network Computers will run today on the organization's desktops, with only the minimal new investment of a Web browser.

This investment protection is a very attractive feature for most organizations and provides a sensible evolutionary path for moving from desktop-centric to network-centric computing. New business functionality can be written for NCs and deployed on existing desktops. Over time, through simple attrition, some of these desktops may be replaced with Network Computers, which may be introduced into areas which never had desktop machines. At this point those users who require the power and flexibility of a traditional desktop machine can continue to use their PCs and workstations while still enjoying the benefits of the new network-centric applications. The IT organization is not stuck with developing and maintaining two versions of the application, one for the power users and one for the NC users. Likewise, the power users are not hobbled by difficult-to-use applications designed to run on the dumb tubes which the NCs have replaced.

Avoiding Native Methods

Reviewing the "What Is a Network Computer?" section gives us an idea of some of the design principles NC applications must follow. The Network Computer Reference Profile states that a true NC can browse HTML pages using HTTP and can run the Java applications it finds on those pages. While a particular NC may have other capabilities, such as running other executable content schemes or local applications, the NC profile does not mandate any other capabilities; NC application designers should not assume that they will be available.

This restriction means that NC applications must be written exclusively for the Java platform or for HTML. Since an NC application can never know what, if any, OS will underlay the JVM on which it finds itself, NC applications cannot use inherently OS-dependent native methods, dynamic libraries, or processor-specific native code. Nor should an NC application employ other non-portable executable content schemes like ActiveX, plug-ins, or helper applications. Using any of these extensions will destroy the Write Once, Run Anywhere property which allows NCs and traditional desktops to co-exist on the network and to share applications between them.

Fortunately, this restriction is not as onerous as it may first sound. Since JDK 1.1, many features which once could only be accessed by reaching over the sides of the Java platform to the native OS below have become part of the Java standard. With Java 2 and the addition of many new and powerful features, like the Java Media APIs, there is little remaining temptation to leave the Java platform. Since the NC Reference Profile also specifies other basic OS functionality like network protocols, mail handlers, and media types, NC application developers should be able to live comfortably within this restriction.

The 100% Pure Java Initiative

When doing your own custom development, you have full control over which features you use and you can avoid anything which would limit how your application may be deployed. But what guarantee do you have that applications you purchase will be able to run seamlessly on your NCs, PCs, and workstations?

Recognizing that business users need assurance that their purchased applications play by the same rules that their internally developed applications do, Sun Microsystems and over 100 other software vendors have banded together to create the 100% Pure Java Initiative. Announced in February of 1997, the 100% Pure Java Initiative created a branding program for applications which meet a few simple guidelines. Applications which pass the 100% Pure Java certification test suite are entitled to use the exclusive 100% Pure Java logo (see Figure 14.4). To date over 400 applications ranging from development toolkits to mainframe connectivity services and home finance have been certified as 100% Pure. The 100% Pure Java brand has also been expanded to include Java-Beans and other development building blocks.

The 100% Pure Java Initiative places several restrictions on applications:

- Written in 100% Pure Java

- No native method calls

- Confirms to the Core Java API specification

- Bundles all needed classes or uses only classes included in the Java Reference Implementation

- Passes the independent certification test suite

Figure 14.4 The 100% Pure logo.

The independent testing for 100% Pure Java compliance is done by Key Labs for a modest certification fee. Vendors wishing to certify their applications can obtain a copy of the test suite, allowing them to pretest their applications before submitting to Key Labs. It is a good practice for development shops to use the 100% Pure Java test suite to guide their development efforts. Testing earlier can reveal design flaws and other problems which could cause difficulties later in the development effort.

Since these restrictions are essentially the same as those listed in the design principles for NC applications, 100% Pure Java applications will run well on Network Computers. With the rapidly growing number of commercially available JavaBeans and the rising popularity of componentware development, the 100% Pure Java Initiative also provides several benefits to application developers at large. Without a strong branding program, developers may inadvertently purchase a component which introduces nonportable elements into the application. For example, a component may have unexpected hooks into ActiveX. If the development shop happens to be working exclusively on ActiveX-capable machines, these hooks might not be found until the application is deployed to the user community on the company's Intranet or, more embarrassingly, to the world at large on the Internet. Developers can protect themselves from these faux pas by purchasing only 100% Pure Java componentware, and by thoroughly testing their applications and applets on a variety of platforms and browsers before releasing them.

Java Compatible Branding

For organizations committed to Write Once, Run Anywhere and to Network Computers, building and buying 100% Pure Java applications is only half of the battle. These corporations also need a guarantee that the Java Virtual Machines embedded in their operating systems, Web browsers, and other devices are 100 percent compliant with the Java specification and will run all their 100% Pure Java applications. Since many of the early virtual machine implementations suffered from subtle incompatibilities, bugs, and other differences which limited compatibility, many people are justifiably suspicious of how far Write Once, Run Anywhere actually goes.

In order to combat these differences and ensure that every Java Virtual Machine is compatible with all other virtual machines, Sun Microsystems has created the Java Compatibility Kit (JCK). The JCK is an automated suite of specification and implementation tests which covers the Java language, the virtual machine, and the Java APIs. All licensees who wish to use the Java brand name with their product must pass the JCK's test suite. Those vendors who do pass this test suite are entitled to display the Java Compatible logo (see Figure 14.5).

While vendors have always been required to pass a validation test suite before calling their products Java, previous versions of the test suite have not

Figure 14.5 The Java Compatible logo assures that a vendor's Java Virtual Machines properly implement the Java specification.

been as extensive or rigorous as those available today. For example, when the alpha version of the JDK 1.0 was released, there were only about 300 individual tests in the JCK. Over time more and more tests have been added to the JCK, so by the release of JDK 1.0.2 there were over 3,400 tests. For JDK 1.2 (Java 2) the compatibility test suite had grown to almost 11,000 tests. This rapid growth in the number of compatibility tests, along with the increasing rigor of the Java language, VM and API specs themselves, provides a much greater assurance of compatibility among Java implementations than was available with JDK 1.0.2. The 100% Pure Java application branding program and the Java Compatible Virtual Machine branding program work together to ensure Java users that, once written, their Java applications will run anywhere.

Network Computer User Interfaces

The NC is much simpler than a traditional desktop and is, at least today, intended for a very different class of users than today's power users. Consequently, the user interface for Network Computers is much simpler than that found in a typical desktop OS like Windows or the Macintosh. In many NCs the browser itself may be the entire user interface. The NC will provide a login screen to authenticate users, the browser, and possibly a simple pull-down menu to allow users to log off or lock the screen. All applications are delivered through the browser. Some applications, like internally developed HR tools, may be Java applets which are embedded in a page. Other applications, like an e-mail or USENET news client, may be built into the browser. In either case, the browser is the entire desktop, applications are accessed via HTML hyperlinks, and no application, other than the browser, can run on the NC.

For the users and applications targeted by the NC, this scheme works well. Since the NC is not intended to replace the power user's desktop, where four or five applications may be needed simultaneously, NC user interfaces do not need to deal with sophisticated window management, configuration options and their associated popup menus, and other features. The simple browser interface, with which many people are already familiar, is more than adequate for the needs of the target user group and can substantially reduce training and futzing. The goal is to provide, in an easy-to-use, intuitive fashion, the 20 percent of windowing functionality required by the 80 percent of less-than-power-users.

When Is My Client Too Big?

Most Network Computers today support at least 64 MB of RAM, and possibly some non-volatile storage like FlashRAM, for storing a local copy of their operating system. Since most NCs will not have access to swap disks or virtual memory, these 64 MB represent a hard limit on how large client-side applications can be. For cost reasons, many NCs may be deployed with only 32 MB or less memory.

NC application designers must account for and deal with this limit. For HTML-based applications, like simple document publishing, the browser will usually take care of memory management for you, caching pages as they are visited and discarding pages as memory becomes tight. Memory limits are usually only a problem when dealing with graphics-intense pages, where a single page could possibly fill all available memory. Of course, if users switch frequently between several pages, inadequate memory can still be a problem. The needed pages will not be cached and the resulting increase in latency, caused by having to download the page each time it is needed, will be very frustrating. Since memory is reasonably inexpensive, NCs in most application areas should be configured with enough memory to provide a large cache for the browser.

For larger applications, like office productivity tools, memory management is a bigger problem. Today, a fat-client word processor may take several dozen MB of memory. Such applications will not be very useful on a thin client. Even with a thin application, no NC will have enough memory to hold a 500-page book or schematics for a jumbo jet. An NC application which tried to manipulate this much data would have to perform very sophisticated operations, like network swapping and page mapping, which are usually left to the operating system. In this case, the resulting size and complexity will likely make the application so large and cumbersome that it should not be deployed on an NC to begin with. In these cases, both the user and the IT department would be better off if a workstation or PC were deployed for this application.

However, for the large number of applications which can fit comfortably on an NC, the question remains, "How do I fit the most functionality into the limits of an NC?" There are several tricks for minimizing the memory footprint of an NC application:

- **Use HTML where possible:** If your application has a browser-based component, use HTML and the browser for text display, tabular data, and other simple, noninteractive display tasks. The browser's classes have to be loaded with the rest of the application, so why not use them for simple display tasks? HTML is relatively compact, so even if some pages are flushed from the cache, downloading them when needed again won't introduce unacceptable latency.

- **Java bytecodes:** While 32 or even 64 MB of memory might not sound like a lot by today's standards, it can be adequate for a large number of Java applications. The Java bytecode represents a very compact instruction set, with most instructions being only one byte long and with the average bytecode replacing four or five machine instructions from a traditional CPU. This makes Java class files several times smaller, for the same functionality, than traditionally compiled code, and allows more powerful and sophisticated applications to run with a smaller memory footprint.

- **Use core classes and standard extension:** The Java core classes and the standard extensions will already be resident in the NC's memory. Using these classes, instead of custom classes with similar functionality, will reduce the memory footprint of your application and reduce download times. For example, RMI is built into the JDK, while in JDK 1.0 and 1.1 CORBA ORB connections were not. All things being equal, an application intended to be deployed on a wide range of clients, including older Web browsers, should use RMI instead of CORBA in order to conserve memory.

- **Use the network:** Remember, these are Network Computers; not all of your application has to run on the client. An overly large client might be a sign that you have not properly divided the three tiers in this application. Take advantage of services deployed on the network so that processing load and memory usage are transferred to the network, where large servers with potentially gigabytes of memory are available. This is one of the goals of the three-tiered architecture and is commonly used in large commercially available Java applications. For example, few office productivity tool vendors would even consider putting their entire document processor on an NC. Instead, significant portions are moved to a mid-tier machine. A page server gives the NC just a few pages at a time. A server-based spell check engine allows for spell checking without requiring that each page of the document, along with the word dictionary and the actual spell checker code, be downloaded to the client.

Use these guidelines to extend the functionality of your NCs and to make sure you are getting the most out of your network.

Deploying and Managing Network Computers

This section examines some of the new issues the NC brings to the network and discusses how to deploy NCs across various types of networks and geographical distributions. An organization which already manages a large distributed network of servers and desktop machines probably already has the infrastructure and expertise needed to deploy Network Computers. In many ways the Network Computer is easier to manage than the fatter desktop systems it is intended to replace. That, after all, is the whole value proposition for the NC: It will reduce the cost of owning and operating desktop computers.

Network Requirements

Network Computers, of course, require network connections and, having grown up in the age of the Internet, most NCs expect that network to look a lot like the Internet itself. The network must run TCP/IP, use DNS, and have NFS, HTTP, and IMAP servers. While some NCs, especially those designed for the 3270 replacement market, may support other network interfaces like Token Ring, the typical NC uses Ethernet. These networking requirements are basically the same as those already in place in many desktop-centric enterprises and those shops that are not already using these standards should be adopting them for other reasons.

Bandwidth requirements are another concern. Testing at early adopter sites has shown that, excluding boot traffic which will be discussed later, Network Computers do not require significantly more network bandwidth than PCs running similar applications do. This should not be surprising, since from a software architecture and network design view, NCs running at least the GUI layer of a three-tiered application are not much different from a PC running the client side of a traditional client/server application. Any organization which is already familiar with operating an Ethernet network will find little changes when NCs are introduced. Rules of thumb, like limiting each subnet to approximately 30 to 50 machines to avoid collisions and using switched Ethernet, still apply.

If the NCs are replacing character terminals instead of PCs, the situation changes quite a bit. Terminal applications usually have a much different load pattern than GUI-based applications. Where a GUI might generate relatively infrequent bursts of relatively large packets, terminals generate a steady stream of low-volume traffic whenever the user is busy. This is because the terminal has no local processing and must talk back to the host after each key stroke in order to get its job done. 3270 terminals, with their limited local storage and processing, can more closely resemble bursty PCs in their network traffic patterns. In either case, a company replacing terminals with NCs should carefully evaluate its network to ensure that network bottlenecks do not hinder application performance.

Boot Servers

Boot servers are the one new network device required by the NC. When the NC is first turned on, it broadcasts its presence to the network and asks for a boot server to provide it with an IP address and operating system. This process can be fairly complicated and require several different protocols like RARP, bootp, DHCP, and NFS. The boot server must handle all these protocols and have enough capacity to support the booting of many NCs simultaneously. When booting, the typical NC will generate about 4 MB of traffic over the course of roughly one minute. This is not too great a load for even a fairly small server. In most cases, the network itself will be the limiting factor that determines how many NCs can be supported per subnet.

Since some of the protocols used to boot an NC are often not routed by network hardware, each subnet may require its own boot server. This does not mean that each boot server can only support one subnet. For a shared Ethernet, 30 to 40 simultaneously booting NCs will saturate the network before a small boot server, like an entry-level Netra J from Sun Microsystems or a small Pentium server, breaks a sweat. In situations where many NCs must be frequently booted simultaneously, keep the number of machines per subnet below 40 and configure each boot server with more than one network interface so it can serve several subnets. In cases where users reboot less frequently and simultaneous boots will be rare, a single, small boot server can handle many times more NCs (see Figure 14.6). In this case, the number of NCs per subnet/boot server will be dominated by the network traffic generated by the application, not by the boot traffic. This application-specific load will vary according to the type of application and the split between the client and the server parts of the application. For a Web-based application which relies on browsers and HTML, network traffic will be minimal and many NCs can be supported per Ethernet segment. For terminal emulation packages or office productivity applications,

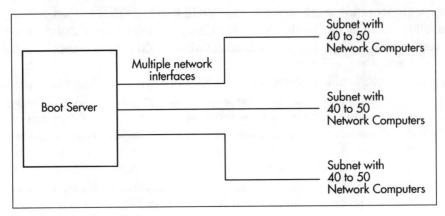

Figure 14.6   A single boot server can support multiple subnets.

network traffic will be much higher, forcing the number of NCs per segment down to 40 or so NCs per subnet.

An NC boots only rarely. Even in cases where the NC is rebooted during shift changes, this is only three times per day. Therefore, most boot servers will be idle almost all the time. These machines can easily do double duty as HTTP or application servers. Doubling up the functions on the boot server keeps it busy during the long periods when there are no boot requests at all and makes better utilization of the investment in that server.

FlashRAM

The previous discussion assumed that all the NCs were on a local high-speed LAN. But the low administrative overhead and field-replaceable unit status of the NC makes it perfect for remote deployment over a WAN to small field offices or remote work sites. In this case, the network link to the nearest boot server might be as small as a 28.8 modem or an ISDN line. Booting over these slow networks is not an attractive option. In order to overcome this limitation, most NCs support some optional non-volatile storage, either as FlashRAM or a small disk which stores a local copy of the OS. When equipped with non-volatile storage, an NC can be booted over the network once, to load the non-volatile storage, after which each subsequent boot will take place from FlashRAM, reducing the bandwidth requirements to those remote sites and greatly cutting the frustrating boot times.

Even if all NCs on the network are equipped with FlashRAM, there still must be a boot server somewhere on the net. Although this server won't be used every day, periodically an OS upgrade will become available. When this happens, the new boot software is loaded on the boot server. The next time the NC boots it contacts the boot server, notices the new software, and stores the new system software in its non-volatile storage.

The use of FlashRAM makes the NC much more appropriate for remote deployment. But there is a small cost. FlashRAM is more expensive than volatile RAM, so it increases the cost of each NC by roughly $100 to $200. If the NC is locally deployed on a fast LAN and is only booted infrequently, the added cost of FlashRAM may not be justified.

Deployment Situations

The number of NCs per site, geographical distribution of sites, and the speed of the wide area network all affect how NCs are best deployed and managed within an organization. In the simplest case, all the NCs are on a high-speed LAN. In this situation the NC adds little extra complexity to the network design. The boot servers are the only really new device on the networks and in most cases the boot server will double as an HTTP server or application server which would have had to have been in place even if every desktop in the organization was a traditional PC.

Things get more interesting when we consider geographically dispersed deployments with either single NCs in a remote office or small clusters of NCs in satellite offices. In both scenarios, the WAN deployment, combined with the need to reduce or eliminate any remote administration of boot, proxy, and application servers, makes the NC deployment more challenging. If the price we pay for $0 administration desktops is an administration-intensive server in every three- or four-person office, we have gained very little over a traditional PC deployment.

If there are only one or two people in a remote office, there is little choice but to use FlashRAM in the NCs, attach them to the WAN, and begin work (see Figure 14.7). Regional servers at the larger network hubs provide the boot services occasionally needed by the NCs. In this setup the remote devices are as close to $0 administration as you can get. The only administration that has to be performed locally is turning the machine off and on. Everything else, from OS upgrades and software distribution to user administration, is done on the back-end of the network.

If network bandwidth is not a problem this model of distribution can scale to fairly large remote deployments. Unfortunately, WAN bandwidth is often a scarce resource. For a small trade-off in complexity, we can make some interesting optimizations of bandwidth. By adding a remotely managed boot server to these smaller offices, we can cache frequently used applications and pages, avoid the use of FlashRAM by booting off the local office Ethernet, and provide local application processing and transaction capabilities.

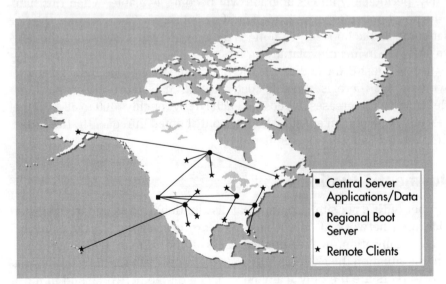

Figure 14.7 Small remote offices will FlashRAM in their NCs and regional boot/upgrade servers.

Using the local boot server may make sense even if you opt to put FlashRAM in the NCs (see Figure 14.8). By acting as a caching proxy, the server reduces both bandwidth and latency. For example, say there are five people in a remote office, attached to a 56-Kb line, and that these people frequently switch back and forth between four fairly large applications. Without a local caching proxy, every user will have to pull a copy of each application across the 56-Kb line. Even if a user's neighbor has just fetched the exact same application and a perfectly good copy of the bytecodes for that application is sitting no more than six feet from the user, without a local caching proxy that user will have to execute a lengthy and annoying download to get the app. With a local server, only the first user to access the application will have to pull it down over the net.

If these users frequently switch back and forth between applications, the local caching proxy becomes even more important. Without the proxy, the organization would either have to put enough physical RAM in each NC to hold all the applications used in a day, or the users would experience a long latency each time they switched applications and had to wait for the application to download once again. The caching proxy solves this problem by making each application switch as fast as a local download.

TIP The drawings in Figures 14.7 and 14.8 should look pretty familiar by now. They're just the three-tiered architecture we saw back in Chapter 6, right?

Not quite. The three-tiered architecture is strictly a logical architecture which separates parts of a system based on function, reusability, and need for centralized access and control. Where those parts are deployed—on desktops, regional

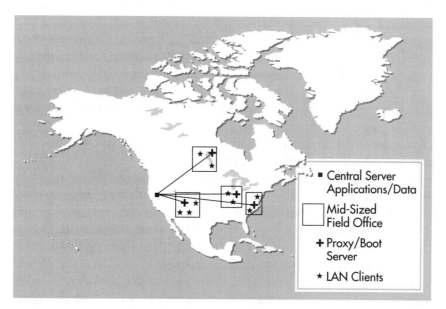

Figure 14.8 For larger offices, a local boot/proxy/upgrade server saves network bandwidth without adding an unacceptable cost or administration burden.

servers, or data centers—is an implementation detail which should not concern the designer of the software. The questions being answered during the design phase, such as:

- **What are the problems we are trying to solve?**
- **What data sources are required?**
- **What are the business rules?**
- **Where might these pieces be used again in the enterprise?**
- **What interfaces between layers best describe the functionality?**

are not affected by such details as whether a part of the logic layer will run in California or New York.

These hardware details are not all that important during the software design phase. It is much easier to optimize a well-designed, reusable system for a particular hardware layout than it is to introduce good design into a prematurely optimized system. And, of course, trying to reuse a system, which has been tightly coupled to a particular hardware implementation, is next to impossible.

A Fallacy of Cost and Benefits

At first glance the previously discussed items may seem like a lot of very expensive infrastructure to support a $500 Network Computer. What happened to my fabulous cost savings?

The savings are still there, just not quite where you might have expected them. Remember that Network Computers don't promise to reduce the initial purchase price of the systems or even promise that initial purchase price plus setup costs will be all that much lower than for PCs. Instead, the promise is to reduce your long-term, overall cost of ownership. This means reducing management costs, application distribution costs, and the cost of lost productivity due to downtime and futzing. Building a strong network infrastructure is all part of achieving these goals. NCs are attractive because of these long-term benefits, not because of a reduced initial purchase price.

Market researchers, like Gartner Group and Forrester, have estimated that the average cost of owning a desktop PC or workstation is $8,000 to $15,000 per year. These same surveys have found that for those desktops which can take advantage of a strong, well-managed network, the cost of ownership can be as low as $5,000 to $7,000 per year. When the PCs on that well-run network are replaced with Network Computers, early experience shows that the cost of ownership should be roughly halved to $2,500 to $3,500 per year. While the cost of building and maintaining the network infrastructure is still there, the savings from the NCs will substantially offset the network's cost of ownership. Besides, you probably had to have the network in place anyway. Very few businesses will find value in 5,000 stand-alone PCs. In fact, for most enterprises these PCs would be next to useless. These days, in order to benefit the enterprise, all desktop computers must be networked; this network must include backend services like file servers, print servers, databases, mail systems, and HTTP servers. Since you have to pay for the network whether you're using PCs or NCs, you might as well make sure the network itself is well run and cost effective. Then, since the infrastructure previously listed for Network Computers maps quite well to what is already found in the well-networked enterprise, the move to NCs will be reasonably painless.

Of course, if cost of ownership was the only consideration, the NC would not be a viable alternative to the 3270 or VT220 terminal. For absolute bare-bones cost of ownership, nothing beats the zero-state, totally field-replaceable, plug-it-in-and-forget-it-forever dumb tube. But as more enterprises use the network as both a communication channel to their employees and a medium for delivering internal applications, those users stuck on character-based terminals become increasingly isolated. In a networked enterprise, the cost of communicating with these employees—paper copies of the new Web-based employee handbook, accounts payable departments to handle paper copies of forms which everyone else submits electronically, and so forth—soon outweighs the savings of the character terminals. For these situations, the NC represents an opportunity to plug these isolated employees into the network without the expense of fat-client PCs. Eventually, we may even see this type of enterprise connectivity pushed out to the factory floor and other areas where users have traditionally had no connectivity whatsoever. An information kiosk built around an NC would be rugged enough and inexpensive enough for wide deployment to all levels of the enterprise.

Java Application Environments

Various versions of the Java platform have now been licensed by the makers of many nontraditional computing devices, such as embedded systems, Smart-Cards, and home Web access devices like television-based browsers. These devices have display, memory, and I/O device limitations which greatly limit the size of any runtime system and the appropriateness of some functionality, like high-end graphics or sound.

In order to support these systems, three new Java Application Environments have been defined: JavaCard, EmbeddedJava, and PersonalJava APIs. Each of these environments includes the Java Virtual Machine and some subset of the Java core classes. Which classes are included in which environments is determined by whether those classes make sense on that platform, memory limitations, and other considerations.

The JavaCard API includes the JavaVM, the JavaCard classes, and some device-specific ISO support classes. Since a SmartCard does not have a display or I/O, it has no need for graphics, AWT, sound, or other classes found in the

Java Development Kit. This JavaCard API can be used to program stored-value cards, authentication systems, and other SmartCard functionality.

The EmbeddedJava API includes the JavaVM, required Java Classes for utility functions, and the Java I/O classes. The EmbeddedJava API is designed to fit in 500 KB of memory. This API can be used in print engines, cellular phones, PDAs, and almost any other device which contains a CPU.

The PersonalJava API is designed for devices with at least 2 MB of memory and some sort of display and input devices. It is intended for devices, like set-top boxes, portables, and other NC-like devices, which do not need the full Java distribution. These devices typically will be used to display the GUI and possibly run some of the logic of a well-segmented three-tiered application. As such, they will not talk directly to the database and won't need JDBC. Other functionality typically used on the enterprise side of the network connection is also left out of PersonalJava. Instead, a PersonalJava application will depend on a backend network system for this functionality. PersonalJava includes the JavaVM, required Java classes, Beans, Java I/O, Java Applet, networking, and a light version of AWT.

Summary

The Network Computer simplifies client/server computing through a low-cost, easy-to-administer, maintainable desktop system. For a broad class of users, it is the most appropriate information appliance available. The NC will reduce an IT organization's total cost of ownership by reducing downtime, eliminating software upgrades, and getting rid of per-desktop backups, security management, and other administrative tasks.

The NC will never replace every PC and workstation, and in fact is not intended to replace every PC. It is a valuable new option for organizations looking to control desktop costs while simultaneously bringing a new level of service and connectivity to every user, both in the company and with its customers and suppliers.

CHAPTER

15

Understanding JavaOS and JavaStation Details

Introduction

Whenever a concept is being introduced, it helps to have a sample implementation to examine in detail. This is why sample programs are listed and dissected in books such as this. The previous chapter provided a conceptual overview of the Network Computer (NC) model and effectively set the stage for us to focus on an example implementation of an NC. In this chapter, we will examine Sun's family of NCs, known as the JavaStation family. We will also provide an overview of JavaOS and HotJava—the two main software components used by the JavaStation family. Finally, we will discuss some limitations of the current JavaStation product line and explore some possibilities for future implementations of Sun's NC offerings.

Overview of Sun's JavaStation Family

Sun's JavaStation family has been designed with one main goal: to provide a very low-cost Network Computer platform which supports *100% Pure Java*. (For information on the 100% Pure Java Initiative, see java.sun.com.)

In order to keep costs as low as possible, Sun designed the JavaStation systems using as many commodity off-the-shelf PC components as possible. These components are usually targeted for the very high-volume PC market and as a result their prices are very low. In addition to providing a cost savings, the usage of commodity hardware components allowed Sun to leverage existing hardware designs instead of having to reinvent the wheel and thereby incur additional development costs. Also, customers can recycle some of their existing PC hardware components (keyboards, mice, RAM, video monitors, etc.) for use with the JavaStation systems. These considerations are very important, since one of the main goals of the Network Computing model is to reduce the overall costs associated with an end-user system.

The JavaStation product line has been designed from the beginning to consist of *Pure NC* systems (see Chapter 14); as a result there is no implementation of any sort of native windowing system (such as X-Windows) other than what the core Java platform provides. All members of the JavaStation family run JavaOS and use either HotJava or a custom Java application as the "main" user application. Administrators can easily change which application is run, and since any *100% Pure Java* application can be configured to automatically run on the JavaStation, great flexibility is afforded to users and administrators..

Since the software environment is basically the same across the entire family of JavaStations, most of the differences between the various systems are hidden from end users and application developers. Since all the JavaStations conform to the Network Computer Reference Profile (NCRP) (see Chapter 14), any applications developed to that specification will run on a JavaStation. Architecturally, the JavaStation family shares many similarities, but just what does a JavaStation look like "under the hood"? We will answer that question by examining the current members of Sun's Network Computer product line.

JavaStation "Brick"

The first member of the JavaStation family was the JavaStation "brick" model. This product was driven mainly by time-to-market issues. Sun wanted to quickly create an NC implementation which would enable customers to participate in *proof-of-concept* pilot programs for NC applications. Since timing was critical (there were no other NC devices on the market yet), Sun used its already completed SPARCstation-4 workstation design as the base architecture for the JavaStation "brick" and modified the design as necessary for an NC class appliance. As a result, the *internal* architecture of this JavaStation greatly resembles a SPARCstation-4 system. (See *SPARCstation-4 Architecture White Paper*, Sun Microsystems.)

Note that while the JavaStation "brick" is based on a Sun workstation design, *Solaris will not run on the JavaStation "brick."* The main modifications made to the SPARCstation-4 design were:

- No support for external Sbus devices
- No support for SCSI
- No support for a floppy drive
- Integrated audio hardware—for audio output only (optional on SPARC-station-4)
- No parallel port
- A single serial port
- Support for commodity PC components (keyboard, mouse, RAM, etc.)

Figure 15.1 shows a block diagram of the internal structure of the JavaStation "brick."

Although the JavaStation "brick" uses the Sbus as its internal bus, there are no provisions for adding Sbus cards to extend the functionality of this system. As time was the critical factor in the development cycle for the original Java-Station, the system was packaged using Sun's standard workstation peripheral cabinet called a *Unipack*, which is usually used to package external worksta-

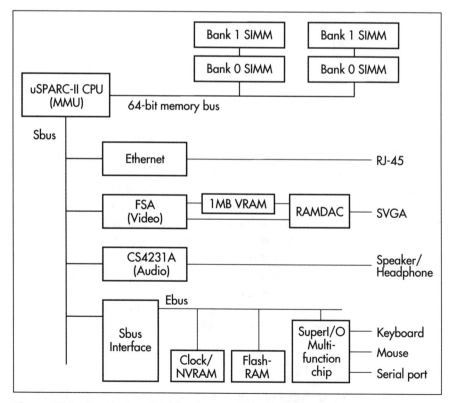

Figure 15.1   JavaStation "brick" architecture block diagram.

tion devices such as disk or tape drives. This brick box may not look as sporty as the newer JavaStation "tower" model, but it does provide the user with the ability to stack the JavaStation with other desktop items. In the following sections we will examine the components shown in Figure 15.1 in greater detail.

The Motherboard and CPU

As shown in Figure 15.1, the JavaStation "brick" motherboard uses Sun's Sbus as the internal interconnect bus. At the heart of the JavaStation "brick" is a 110-MHz microSPARC-II CPU; this is the same CPU used in Sun's entry-level workstation products such as the SPARCstation-4 and SPARCstation-5. This CPU was designed to be flexible in supporting uniprocessor embedded systems and as a result has a number of integrated features that helped simplify the design of the original JavaStation. For example, in addition to implementing the actual SPARC processor, the microSPARC-II chip has built-in logic to support:

- A SPARC Reference Memory Management Unit (SRMMU)
- 16 K of instruction cache; 8 K of data cache
- Integrated Dynamic RAM (DRAM) controller
- Integrated Sbus controller
- Power management

The design goals of the microSPARC-II CPU included the ability to provide a low-cost, high-performance, low-power CPU for uniprocessor applications which made it a perfect fit for the JavaStation. (See *The microSPARC-II Processor, Technology White Paper*, Sun Microsystems Computer Corporation, 1995.)

Most components, including the CPU, are soldered onto the motherboard. In fact, about the only components that can be swapped are the single inline memory modules (SIMMs). This is about as close as one can get to the field-replaceable unit or FRU model; if *anything* in the hardware breaks, you must replace the entire unit. This may sound restrictive at first, but there are benefits to this model—if there is only *one* solution to a whole bunch of problems, the answer to the question "How do I solve this problem?" becomes fairly simple. This feature addresses the total cost of ownership (TCO) issue as described in the previous chapter. Now, before you get depressed by thinking about hardware failures, remember that this JavaStation has no moving parts (well, except for the cooling fan). As a result, the probability that a unit will fail is *much* lower than with other desktop computing devices.

Memory

There are several different types of memory in the JavaStation family and it's important to understand the purpose and functionality of each different type.

When most people think of memory, they think of a system's random access memory (RAM) or the memory used to store application programs and data. Obviously, the JavaStation must contain this type of memory. However, the JavaStation may also include two other types of memory: *FlashRAM* and *NVRAM*. In the following sections, we will examine each of these different types of memory and how the JavaStation uses them.

Random Access Memory

Dynamic-RAM or "DRAM" is used to implement the JavaStation's main memory system. This is the memory that is used for applications, data, and the running operating system. The JavaStation "brick" uses industry-standard PC-type memory modules called single inline memory modules (SIMMs) for this memory. Although there are many different types of SIMM modules in the computing market, the type of SIMMs used in most PC systems is usually the least expensive. To take advantage of these lower-cost components, the JavaStation "brick" uses PC-standard 72-pin, 60-ns, non-parity DRAM SIMMs. Each individual SIMM may be either a 4-MB or 16-MB single-sided SIMM; single-sided means that memory chips are installed on only *one* side of the SIMM.

The JavaStation "brick" contains four slots for SIMM modules. DRAM on this JavaStation is configured as two *banks*, with each bank composed of two SIMM slots. Each bank of memory must either have zero or two SIMMs installed in it. As a result, whenever you add memory to a JavaStation "brick," you *must* add SIMMs in groups of two. Each bank can support different capacity SIMMs, but both SIMMs within a given bank must be the same capacity. Table 15.1 illustrates the possible SIMM configurations for the JavaStation "brick."

FlashRAM

As described in the last section, DRAM is used to implement the JavaStation's main memory system. DRAM has some disadvantages, however, that necessitate the usage of other types of memory in a computer system. For example,

Table 15.1 JavaStation "Brick" SIMM Configurations

| BANK 0 | | BANK 1 | | |
SLOT 0	SLOT 1	SLOT 2	SLOT 3	TOTAL RAM
4MB	4MB	—	—	8MB
4MB	4MB	4MB	4MB	16MB
16MB	16MB	—	—	32MB
16MB	16MB	4MB	4MB	40MB
16MB	16MB	16MB	16MB	64MB

DRAM loses the ability to store data when power is lost. When a computer is first turned on, DRAM is empty; so how does the computer start itself up? Usually read-only memory (ROM) is used to solve this problem. ROM is a type of memory that always stores data, regardless of whether power is applied. The problem with ROM is that you can't change the data once it's written (hence the read-only name). As a result, ROM is used mainly to store programs and data that don't change—such as the code necessary to start the computer when power is first applied. PCs call their ROM data the BIOS, and Sun systems call their ROM data the OpenBoot PROM (OBP). (PROM stands for programmable read-only memory, and is essentially the same thing as ROM for the purposes of our discussion.) ROM works well for this application, but its functionality is limited by the fact that you cannot change the contents of the ROM. If you wish to change the contents of the ROM (e.g., for newer software, bug fixes, etc.), you have to physically replace the chip that implements the ROM.

FlashRAM is a special type of memory that combines some of the properties of both DRAM and ROM. FlashRAM can store data even after power is removed from the chip and its contents can be updated when necessary (e.g., it can be written to). This allows a computer vendor to store the computer's startup program permanently, yet offers the flexibility to upgrade the contents of the FlashRAM to take advantage of bug fixes, new functionality, and so forth. PC vendors have begun to replace the older ROM technology with FlashRAM to implement their BIOS; Sun's newer systems also incorporate FlashRAM technology.

At this point you're probably thinking, "Hey, if FlashRAM does everything that DRAM and ROM do, why don't systems replace DRAM with FlashRAM?" The answer to this question boils down to two items: cost and speed. At the time this book was written, FlashRAM chips cost approximately twice what DRAM chips did (for the same capacity). This ratio is likely to fluctuate wildly as hardware technology advances and in the future cost may no longer be an issue. Speed, however, is likely to remain an issue. FlashRAM is very slow compared to DRAM—so slow, in fact, that some systems actually copy the data from FlashRAM to DRAM when they start up, then execute the program from DRAM (this operation is often called *shadowing*).

FlashRAM may be used to store two different items (separately) in the Java-Station: the OBP and JavaOS. The following sections will examine how the JavaStation uses each of these items, and how it uses FlashRAM to enhance its operation.

The OpenBoot PROM (OBP)

In the JavaStation, the role of the OBP is to:

- Run some tests to ensure the JavaStation is capable of starting up.
- Load and run JavaOS.
- Provide some hardware support for JavaOS.

If you've ever powered-up a Sun system and been presented with the infamous OK prompt, you've interacted with the OBP; the OBP is what issues the OK prompt and responds to user input. By default, the JavaStation never issues the OK prompt; it automatically tries to load JavaOS without user intervention. It *is* possible to interact with the OBP on the JavaStation, but the process of doing so is convoluted and beyond the scope of this book. For the most part, you'll never even know that the OBP exists within the JavaStation.

The OBP may be stored in FlashRAM or ROM on the JavaStation (depending on the model). The advantages of using FlashRAM to store the OBP should be obvious by now—any upgrades to the OBP software (say, to support a new network-booting protocol) can be easily installed with software. The use of FlashRAM to support the OBP doesn't have nearly the same impact as using FlashRAM to store JavaOS, but it's important to understand that when discussing the JavaStation (or any other NC for that matter), FlashRAM may be used for *several* purposes—not just to store JavaOS.

JavaOS

Whenever an NC starts up, it must load its operating system. Since most NC systems do not include a disk drive, the network is usually used to download the operating system. If you have a handful of JavaStations connected to a LAN such as Ethernet, downloading the operating system over the network is hardly an issue. However, if you have a single boot server that serves several thousand JavaStations, having every system try to boot simultaneously may swamp the network or boot server. Also, if you have a JavaStation in a remote location, connected to the corporate network by a slow serial line (e.g., 28.8-Kbps modem), latency becomes a serious issue. For example, let's assume that the JavaStation needs to download 5 MB of stuff in order to boot. Using a 28.8-Kbps modem, which has a sustained bandwidth of approximately 2.5 KB/sec, it would take roughly *30 minutes* just to download the operating system! Clearly, this is unacceptable. The solution is to store JavaOS in FlashRAM.

Storing JavaOS in FlashRAM means the JavaStation can effectively start running *immediately*. JavaOS only has to be downloaded *once* and it is then stored in FlashRAM. Obviously, upgrades to JavaOS require another download, but this download can be scheduled and prepared for in advance, without unnecessary disruption to end users. FlashRAM provides obvious benefits to remote JavaStation users connected by slow serial links, but it has advantages even for systems connected to a high-speed LAN; load on the network and boot server is decreased. As discussed in the last chapter, this allows a single network segment and/or boot server to service a larger number of NC clients, which improves the overall scalability of the NC model.

Since the development of the JavaStation "brick" had severe time constraints, the capability to load JavaOS into FlashRAM was *not* included in the design. However, newer members (e.g., the "JavaStation Tower") of the JavaStation family *are* equipped with FlashRAM for JavaOS. Although we are focusing on the JavaStation "brick" as our current example from the JavaStation family, the advantages of FlashRAM technology warranted its discussion here.

NVRAM

NVRAM, or non-volatile RAM, is similar in functionality to FlashRAM; it is capable of retaining memory contents even when power to the JavaStation is removed. Unlike FlashRAM, however, NVRAM requires a power source to retain its contents. This power source is usually implemented in the form of a small battery embedded into the NVRAM chip itself. This battery has a long lifetime—usually measured in *years*—but finite nonetheless. PC users often refer to NVRAM as CMOS data or BIOS memory, although these definitions are based more on the NVRAM's contents than the component itself. Traditionally, Sun systems has used NVRAM to store OBP configuration data such as the HostID and Ethernet address of the system. Since the JavaStation "brick" was based on the SPARCstation-4 architecture, NVRAM was included in its design. Newer members of the JavaStation family store the configuration data in other locations and as a result do not include NVRAM.

Again, the most important thing to understand is the distinction between what the JavaStation uses the various types of memory for: DRAM is used for JavaOS, applications and data; FlashRAM may be used to store the OBP and/or the boot image of JavaOS; NVRAM is used to store system-configuration data such as the Ethernet address of the system. Application developers and end users will not *need* to know these issues, but understanding such issues can help them architect better business solutions as well as resolve problems.

Video

Video on the JavaStation "brick" is a hybrid design; the SPARCstation-4 Fast Sbus Video (FSV) accelerated frame buffer is coupled with an S-VGA style monitor interface (15-pin high-density connector). Once again we see Sun taking advantage of commodity hardware by allowing the use of any S-VGA monitor with the JavaStation. The monitor interface supports the DDC1/DDC2B protocol, which allows the JavaStation to automatically determine the best screen resolution to use for the display.

Unfortunately, not all display monitors are DDC-compliant, which can lead to problems on the JavaStation. Although the hardware will drive any S-VGA style monitor, JavaOS currently *assumes* the monitor is capable of 1024×768 resolution at a 60-Hz refresh rate if it cannot use the DDC protocol to identify the monitor. This default configuration was not chosen arbitrarily; 1024×768 @ 60 Hz is usually supported by even the smallest, least-expensive PC monitors. By setting this as the default video configuration, the JavaStation supports *most* monitors automatically. However, if you connect older PC monitors to a Java-

WHAT EXACTLY IS THE DDC PROTOCOL?

One of the problems that has plagued computer users for quite some time has been configuring the video display subsystem of a computer. Originally, specific video cards were matched to specific display monitors. If you tried to plug in a display monitor that wasn't configured to synchronize itself with the video card, either the display showed garbage or, sometimes, the display monitor literally fried itself. Something had to be done to simplify the situation. One solution came in the form of so-called multi-sync monitors; these were display monitors that had some smarts in them so they could usually figure out how the video card was sending data and automatically sync up with it. This helped address the problem, but provided only for a single-ended solution; the display monitor could figure out what the video card was doing, but the video card never knew what sort of capabilities the monitor supported. To address this issue, the Video Electronics Standards Association (VESA) created a specification that allowed a monitor and a video card to actually communicate with each other. Known as the display data channel (DDC), this protocol allows the display monitor to tell the video card what resolutions and so forth that it is capable of displaying, so the video card can adjust its output accordingly. To the end users, this greatly simplifies things—all they have to do is plug in a DDC-compliant display monitor to a DDC-compliant video interface, and their video works!

Station, you may have to manually reset the screen resolution through the user interface (e.g., HotJava). Although this is not a difficult task, it must be done manually (or through a special application). How do you avoid this? Only connect monitors to the JavaStation that are capable of at *least* 1024 × 768 resolution or use DDC-compliant display monitors. You shouldn't have any problems with monitors that are sold with the JavaStation, obviously. Of course, as more monitors become DDC-compliant, this issue becomes moot.

The FSV frame buffer supports 8-bit indexed color and has some simple acceleration hardware to support a variety of common windowing tasks, such as displaying text, polygon fill, stipple, and scrolling. There is 1 MB of Video RAM (VRAM) installed on the JavaStation "brick" motherboard; this is *not* expandable. These components allow this JavaStation to support 256 different colors simultaneously with a default screen resolution of 1024 × 768 (S-VGA standard). Different monitors will support different video configurations, but the recommended default settings are:

14″ monitor; 800 × 600 resolution, 75-Hz refresh

17″ monitor; 1024 × 768 resolution, 60-Hz refresh

There are several adapter cables available that allow you to use non–S-VGA monitors with the JavaStation; for example, Sun has adapter cables that allow you to connect Sun workstation monitors that use the standard 13W3 connector to a JavaStation. If you've got a relatively new monitor that's capable of 1024 × 768 resolution, chances are good that you can connect it to a JavaStation—as long as you get the appropriate adapter cable.

Regardless of what video resolution the JavaStation defaults to, the JavaStation "brick" offers the user several choices for video resolution, including:

1024 × 768 @ 60 Hz (recommended for 17-inch or larger monitors)

800 × 600 @ 75 Hz (recommended for 14-inch monitors)

640 × 480 @ 75 Hz

640 × 480 @ 60 Hz

. . .

HotJava provides a GUI-based mechanism for users to choose their video configuration, or custom applications can be designed to configure the video system appropriately.

Networking

The JavaStation "brick" offers two forms of network media: 10-megabit twisted-pair Ethernet (10BASET) and an RS-232 serial port. Most JavaStations will no doubt use the Ethernet port as their network interface. Note that twisted-pair Ethernet is the *only* form of Ethernet supported on the JavaStation; thinwire (10BASE2) and thickwire (10BASE5) Ethernets will require a media adapter to connect to a JavaStation. 100-megabit Ethernet (100BASE-TX) is supported on the JavaStation "tower," and ISDN and/or IBM's Token Ring network are likely candidates for future members of the JavaStation family. More advanced networking technologies, such as ATM or Gigabit Ethernet, are unlikely to be supported in the JavaStation, mainly due to cost-related issues. These types of networks are high-bandwidth and high-cost, and applications that require the bandwidth these networks provide are outside of the market segment that NC systems address.

The serial interface is driven by a PC type 16550A–compatible chip, and the JavaStation "brick" has a standard 9-pin DB-9M connector which is used to connect to a serial device. This interface supports a full-duplex data rate of up to 115 Kbps (bits per second). In early versions of JavaOS the serial port was officially unsupported, but it was used for JavaOS console I/O functions, including accessing the OBP. Newer versions of JavaOS support networking through the serial port via the Point-to-Point Protocol (PPP), although this is *not* supported on the JavaStation "brick" (since the "brick" doesn't support loading JavaOS into FlashRAM, an Ethernet connection is *required*; therefore, a PPP connection would be redundant). Although a modem enables a JavaStation to communicate with a remote network, the serial port has many other uses. For example, when used in a kiosk-type application, auxiliary input devices (other than the standard keyboard and mouse) such as a touch-screen can be attached to a JavaStation. JavaStations used in point-of-sale (POS) applications may attach a barcode scanner device to the serial port. Or, the serial port can be used as an output device. The most obvious application is to support a local printer. Going back to our kiosk-type application, the serial port may be used to control a VCR or video-disc player. As you can see, the possibilities are endless. In fact, a single serial port is likely to prove a limitation; future NC applications will no doubt require *several* serial ports.

Audio

The JavaStation "brick" supports audio *output* only. There is a built-in monaural speaker inside the JavaStation "brick," as well as a 1/8 stereo headphone jack on the back panel. Newer members of the JavaStation family support audio *input* as well as output. The hardware chip, which is called a CODEC, in the JavaStation "brick" supports the following stereo-audio sampling rates:

16-bit 48-kHz digital audio tape (DAT) standard

16-bit 44.1-kHz compact disc (CD) standard

16-bit 16-kHz medium-quality audio

8-bit 8-kHz voice-grade telephony standard

Although the hardware supports the sampling rates just listed, JavaOS has software restrictions. Currently, JavaOS supports only 8-bit u-law format audio content (Sun's .au format), which enables telephone-grade audio content to be played on the JavaStation.

Other Peripheral Interfaces

The remaining peripheral devices that can be attached to the JavaStation "brick" are simply the keyboard and mouse. Here we see the final example of using commodity PC-style components in the JavaStation. Sun chose to use the PC PS/2–style keyboard and mouse interface to the JavaStation instead of the costlier Sun standard keyboard and mouse. This allows cost savings both initially and long-term; PS/2 keyboards and mice are extremely plentiful and inexpensive. These components are connected to the JavaStation through the standard 6-pin DIN PS/2–style connectors on the back panel; there are separate connectors for the keyboard and mouse.

As illustrated in Figure 15.1, the JavaStation "brick" uses the National Semiconductor Super I/O chip to control the keyboard, mouse, and serial port. This is the same chip that many PC systems use. The use of this chip in the JavaStation "brick" helps ensure compatibility with PC market components and takes advantage of the cost savings associated with such a high-volume, highly-integrated chip. Actually, the JavaStation uses only a fraction of this chip's total functionality; future JavaStations may take advantage of the additional capabilities of the Super I/O chip. (See the *PC87xxx SuperI/O Data Sheet*, National Semiconductor Corporation.)

JavaStation "Tower"

The newest member of the JavaStation family is the JavaStation "tower" model. Although strikingly different from the "brick" model in outward appearance, system functionality is very similar. However, since the JavaStation "tower" was the first Sun NC to be designed from "the ground up" as a Network Computer (recall that the JavaStation "brick" used the SPARCstation-4 architecture as a baseline), it contains many enhancements over the original JavaStation "brick." The following sections will highlight the differences between the two JavaStation models.

Enclosure

First and foremost, the JavaStation "tower" model is packaged quite differently than the "brick" model. In addition to "looking cool," the form of the JavaStation "tower" has a function as well; it was designed so the internal components could be cooled *without* the use of a cooling fan. As a result, the JavaStation "tower" is both quieter and less prone to failure than the "brick" model. The downside, of course, is that you cannot stack components on top of the "tower" model. The power supply on the JavaStation "tower" is external (as opposed to the internal power supply on the "brick" model), which eases the servicing of the unit as well.

The Motherboard and CPU

The JavaStation "tower" uses a completely new internal architecture, which was specifically designed for use in NC applications. Figure 15.2 depicts the architecture of the JavaStation "tower." At the heart of the new design is the new microSPARC-IIep processor. Sun designed this CPU to be used in embedded uniprocessor applications, and it has similar functionality to the microSPARC-II processor used in the JavaStation "brick" system. However, this CPU is much newer than the microSPARC-II, and as a result takes advantage of numerous improvements in technology. Similar to the older microSPARC-II chip, the microSPARC-IIep includes several integrated components designed to simplify the design of systems incorporating this processor:

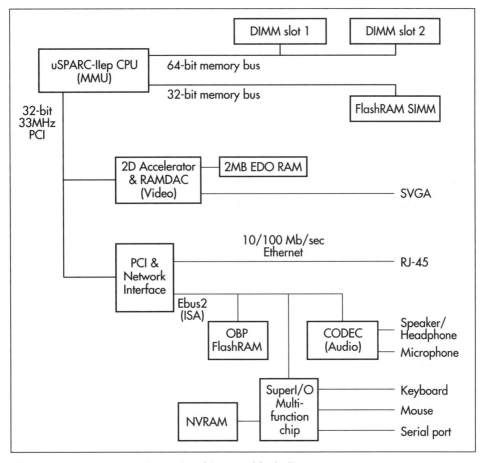

Figure 15.2 JavaStation "tower" architecture block diagram.

- A SPARC Reference Memory Management Unit (SRMMU)
- Internal Instruction and Data (I&D) cache memory and controller
- Dynamic RAM (DRAM)/FlashRAM controller
- Peripheral Component Interconnect (PCI) controller
- Power management

The "ep" in "microSPARC-IIep" stands for "Embedded" and "PCI," and gives us a clue to one of the main differences to the older "microSPARC-II" design—the use of the PCI bus instead of SBus. The JavaStation "tower" uses a 33-MHz PCI bus as the main system bus instead of the slower SBus used in the JavaStation "brick." The newer CPU and PCI bus used in the JavaStation "tower" helps give this JavaStation model better performance than the older "brick" model. Although the PCI bus is used internally, there are *no* PCI expansion slots available on the JavaStation "tower."

Memory

Random Access Memory

Similar to the "brick" model, the "tower" model uses DRAM to implement its main system memory. However, instead of using SIMMs, the JavaStation "tower" uses "Dual In-line Memory Modules," or "DIMMs." DIMMs are simply a new "form factor" (168 pins instead of 72 pins for SIMMs) for memory systems, and most newer PC systems now use DIMMs instead of the older SIMM-style of memory. The primary advantage of DIMMs over SIMMs is memory density—more physical memory can be installed in a physically smaller space with DIMMs than with SIMMs. As a result of the increased memory density, fewer DIMM slots are required to implement the same amount of RAM. Therefore, while the "brick" model has four (4) SIMM slots, the "tower" model only requires two (2) DIMM slots. Memory can be configured by using either one or two DIMMs, and you can use two different-capacity DIMMs if necessary (e.g., one 32-MB and one 16-MB DIMM). This simplifies the rules for memory configurations on the JavaStation "tower." Physical memory in the JavaStation "tower" is limited to the same amount as the JavaStation "brick"—64 MB total.

FlashRAM

One of the biggest advantages the JavaStation "tower" has over the JavaStation "brick" is the ability to use FlashRAM to store JavaOS. We discussed the benefits of FlashRAM in the JavaStation "brick" section of this chapter, but also mentioned that the "brick" model couldn't use FlashRAM to store JavaOS (it uses FlashRAM only for the OBP). The JavaStation "tower" supports up to 8 MB of FlashRAM via a single 80-pin FlashRAM SIMM, and fully supports booting JavaOS directly from FlashRAM. The "main" Java application can also optionally be stored in FlashRAM, which enables faster booting even when using a low-bandwidth network interface (e.g., PPP over a modem). By supporting FlashRAM, the JavaStation "tower" is much better suited to "remote" NC applications, such as branch office support. The JavaStation "tower" also uses a separate FlashRAM (*not* the FlashRAM SIMM mentioned earlier) to store the OBP, which allows administrators to easily upgrade the system's firmware as newer versions become available.

NVRAM

The JavaStation "tower" does contain a small (2-kilobit) Electrically Erasable PROM (EEPROM) that is used to store hardware configuration data such as the systems hostid and Ethernet address. This NVRAM is different from the "brick" model's NVRAM, however, in that a much cheaper/simpler memory chip is used to reduce costs.

Video

Although the general graphics capabilities of both JavaStation models are similar, the JavaStation "tower" does have slightly upgraded features. Specifically, the "tower" has doubled the amount of graphics RAM from 1 MB to 2 MB, and uses a 64-bit interface to Extended Data Output (EDO)–type RAM for the video RAM (VRAM). Using the 64-bit interface improves the performance of the graphics subsystem, and the added RAM allows the JavaStation "tower" to support higher screen resolutions—up to 1280×1024 pixels as opposed to the JavaStation "brick's" limitation of 1024×768 pixels. The JavaStation "tower" includes a higher-performance 2D graphics accelerator as well, which improves the performance of basic windowing operations (e.g., scrolling, moving, etc.). Any PC-style monitor may be used, including DDC1/DDC2B-compliant monitors, and the standard PC "HD-15"–type video connector is identical to the one used on the JavaStation "brick." Similar to the "brick" model, the JavaStation "tower" supports several 8-bit indexed color resolutions, as listed in Table 15.2.

Networking

Networking is another area in which the JavaStation "tower" greatly improves upon the capabilities of the JavaStation "brick." The largest improvement is the support of 10/100BASE-TX "auto-sensed" Ethernet. "Auto-sensed" means that the JavaStation "tower" not only supports the faster 100-megabit Ethernet, but the system will automatically switch between 10-megabit and 100-megabit Ethernet, depending on what the capabilities of the network are. There is literally *no* configuration procedures to switch between 10- and/or 100-megabit networks—just plug the JavaStation "tower" in and turn it on. However, note that we *have* experienced a problem when connecting to an auto-sensing "Gigabit Ethernet" network—you may have to disable the "auto-negotiating" feature *on the Ethernet switch (not the JavaStation)* when connecting to a switch that supports "gigabit Ethernet." Future versions of the OBP or Ethernet switch firmware should alleviate this issue, but keep this in mind when using the

Table 15.2   JavaStation "Tower" Supported Graphics Resolutions

RESOLUTION	REFRESH RATE
800×600	75Hz
1024×768	60Hz
1024×768	75Hz
1280×1024	60Hz
1280×1024	66Hz

JavaStation "tower" on a "Gigabit Ethernet" network. The greater performance and capacity of 100-megabit Ethernet can greatly improve the performance of an NC application, especially when combined with the FlashRAM feature used for storing JavaOS and the "main" application.

Another enhancement to the "tower" model is the support of PPP over a serial modem connection. Since JavaOS can be stored in the FlashRAM, very little network traffic is necessary to boot up a JavaStation "tower." As a result, some applications may perform acceptably over a simple modem/PPP connection. In this case, the JavaStation "tower" stores configuration information in the NVRAM regarding network connection data, such as the phone number to dial, the user/password used to establish the PPP connection, and so forth. When JavaOS starts up from the FlashRAM, the PPP connection will be established automatically and, from that point forward, the operation of the JavaStation is the same as it is with an Ethernet connection (albeit with slower network performance). As popular as Ethernet has become, it's not nearly as ubiquitous as telephone lines—telephone lines are available just about *anywhere*, so PPP support allows much greater flexibility in the distribution of NC applications.

Audio

Audio functionality for the JavaStation "tower" is pretty much identical to that found in the JavaStation "brick"; the only difference is that the "tower" supports audio input as well as output. The "tower" has a "microphone input" connector on the back of the system to facilitate this capability.

OBP and DHCP

The JavaStation "tower" includes a feature-enhanced OpenBoot PROM (OBP). In addition to supporting the newer hardware, the OBP has been modified to support the Dynamic Host Configuration Protocol (DHCP) (see the section on JavaOS and DHCP later in the chapter). DHCP is used to automatically obtain host configuration parameters, including IP address and network parameters as well as JavaOS boot parameters. Actually, JavaOS has always used DHCP to determine its configuration, but the OBP hadn't supported it until the JavaStation "tower" product was released. Recall from earlier in the chapter that the OBP is the software that is executed when the system is first started. Traditional Sun workstations use the OBP to load the operating system from a disk, and the system's configuration data is stored on the disk. Since the JavaStation "brick" was designed using the SPARCstation-4 as a baseline, the OBP was almost identical to the OBP on a SPARCstation-4, and as such had no provisions for DHCP. Sun workstations *do* however support "diskless booting," which means they require some mechanism for automatically obtaining network configuration information. Traditionally, Sun workstations used the Reverse Address Resolution Protocol (RARP) and Boot Parameters (BOOTPARAM) protocol for this purpose. DHCP was designed to replace these two protocols with a single protocol, and to enhance and extend their overall functionality as well. Historically, as disk prices plummeted, fewer and fewer systems required "diskless" operation; that is, until the Network Computing paradigm was created. The "diskless" operation of NCs required a mechanism for automated client configuration. Since RARP and BOOTPARAM were already included in the OBP, they were used in the JavaStation "brick" (remember, time to market was critical for that system). As a result, the JavaStation "brick" model actually configures itself *twice* when booting: First, the OBP uses RARP and BOOTPARAM to download JavaOS over the network, then JavaOS uses DHCP to obtain its configuration information. This means that administrators must ensure that the RARP/BOOT-PARAM configuration matches the DHCP configuration, or confusion is sure to ensue. Also, DHCP supports features that aren't present in RARP/BOOTPARAM, which makes it difficult to manage the two protocol sets simultaneously. DHCP supports advanced capabilities such as booting across subnets (RARP requires a server to exist on *every* subnet, while DHCP can route boot requests from numerous subnets to a single server) and dynamic IP address assignment (RARP requires IP addresses to be statically assigned to systems), which can greatly ease the administration of client systems. The solution, obviously, was to implement DHCP in the OBP, which obviates the need for RARP/BOOTPARAM.

Once DHCP support was added to the OBP, an updated version of the OBP for the JavaStation "brick" was created as well. Therefore, the JavaStation "brick" OBP can be upgraded to support DHCP, which helps maintain consistency within a "heterogeneous" JavaStation environment. The upgrading of the OBP software can be automated as part of the boot process, which is a perfect example of how the NC paradigm can ease administrative overhead—imagine having to upgrade the BIOS on 10,000 PCs!

Summary

We've spent the last couple sections discussing Sun's current JavaStation products, but as we've seen, the differences between them mostly address administrative issues—although the actual *implementations* have changed, the overall *functionality* of the platform itself hasn't. A Java application will run unchanged on either JavaStation model. This is a good example of how eliminating platform dependencies can benefit an IT organization—the features of the newer JavaStation "tower" help enhance the administration, performance, and distribution of NC applications without regard to the application itself. The NCRP defines a consistent platform for Java applications, which ensures NC applications will run on *any* NC. We will now determine if Sun's JavaStation products comply with the NCRP.

The JavaStation and the Network Computer Reference Profile

Recall the hardware components of the Network Computer Reference Profile (NCRP) as discussed in the previous chapter. Does the JavaStation qualify as a Network Computer, according to the specifications of the NCRP? Here are the hardware requirements of the Network Computer Reference Profile (NCRP):

- Lower cost than personal computers.
- Enable security.
- Minimum screen resolution of 640 × 480 (VGA).
- Pointing device.
- Text input device (keyboard).
- Audio output.
- Persistent local storage *not required*.

Although cutthroat competition within the PC industry has driven initial purchase costs of PC hardware down drastically, TCO issues for PCs continue to plague IT organizations. Experience has demonstrated that NCs are *not* a good replacement for general-purpose PCs. However, NCs *are* proving to be a more cost-effective solution in specific areas, such as point-of-sale (POS) and kiosk applications. So-called "single-function terminals" are also a good fit for NC applications, such as IBM 327x "green screen" terminal replacement projects. Sun has narrowed the focus of JavaStation applications to these areas, where significant cost savings over PC-based solutions can be realized. The hardware aspect of security with the JavaStation is addressed by its lack of removable media; there is no floppy drive. All the hardware resource requirements (video resolution, input devices, and others) are at *least* minimally met. Although local persistent storage (e.g., disk) is an option defined in the NCRP, the JavaStation family currently has no capabilities to support it.

When viewing the NCRP, it becomes clear that most of the specifications deal with the software environment as opposed to the hardware environment. So far, so good; JavaStations have the hardware resources necessary to support the NCRP specification. In the next two sections we will look at the software components of the JavaStation family, JavaOS and HotJava. Only after examining all of these components can we complete our example of a Network Computer implementation.

JavaOS

The main purpose of the Network Computer model is to reduce the overall costs associated with end-user desktop computing appliances. Two components of this cost are:

1. The initial purchase cost of desktop systems.

2. The administration and maintenance costs of desktop systems.

The Network Computer Reference Profile (NCRP) was created to allow vendors to create low-cost, standards-based desktop appliances. As discussed in the previous chapter, most networked PC systems or UNIX workstations sold today can be equipped with a Java Virtual Machine (JavaVM), which essentially turns that system into an NCRP-compliant device. However, this solution doesn't address either of the previously stated costs. In the last section we provided an overview of the JavaStation, a system that can be less expensive to purchase than a PC or workstation. However, of the two costs just listed, administration costs usually outweigh the purchase costs of desktop systems. How does the JavaStation family address the second cost item listed—the administration and maintenance of the desktop system? Creating less expensive hardware platforms that run Windows or UNIX would *not* address this issue. In order for the NC model to prove useful a *new* software environment was required. Enter JavaOS.

Overview

JavaOS is a small, portable, and efficient operating environment specifically designed to support Java applications directly on low-cost hardware platforms— without requiring a host operating system. The sole purpose of JavaOS is to support the Java Virtual Machine (JavaVM) and the core Java APIs. Traditional operating systems such as Windows or UNIX must provide a diverse operating environment to support the entire gamut of applications necessary in today's computing market. As a result, these operating systems are not only complex, but they require significant hardware resources. Many of these resources are not necessary to support NC-type applications, yet they are still required to support such general-purpose operating systems. Since JavaOS has only a single purpose—support the JVM—not only is it capable of running on systems with more limited hardware resources, it's also much simpler. The simplicity of JavaOS makes it *much* easier to administer and as a result reduces the overall cost of maintaining desktop systems.

JavaOS was designed to be as portable as possible, and to minimize the hardware requirements necessary to support itself. Since it was designed to support *only* Java applications, JavaOS can take advantage of many of the features the Java language provides. For example, since the security model of Java is well-defined (no pointers, etc.), JavaOS does not require a CPU to provide multiple modes of execution (e.g., supervisor/kernel mode and user mode) to support system security and integrity. As a result, JavaOS can support just about *any* processor on the market, including very low-cost embedded processors. By limiting the hardware required to support JavaOS as much as possible, many new types of devices can be built that utilize the Java platform and take advantage of Java's strengths. The following sections provide specifics of JavaOS and illustrate many of its strengths.

Architecture

Traditional operating systems such as Windows and UNIX usually implement the Java platform in one of two ways:

1. Embedding the JavaVM and foundation classes into an application, such as a Web browser.

2. Implementing the JavaVM as an application.

Both of these methods require a host operating system, such as Windows or UNIX. Note the dotted line at the top of Figure 15.3; this represents the Java API. Anything above this line is platform-independent—this is the level where all Java applications run. The Java Application Programmer is concerned only with this API; anything below the dotted line is magic. Every vendor that wishes to support the Java platform must implement the items *below* the dotted line.

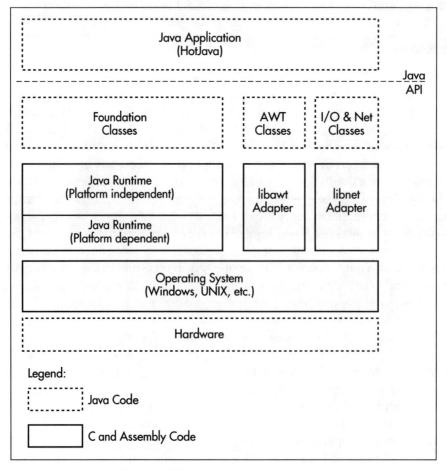

Figure 15.3 Host OS Java architecture.

Fortunately, several of the items below the dotted line are actually written in Java, which simplifies the tasks associated with implementing the Java platform on a given platform. Notice that each of the Java API packages available to the applications programmer has a corresponding box under the dotted line. These boxes represent the glue that ties the Java API to the platform-independent and platform-dependent boxes, which implement the actual functionality of the Java API. The Java runtime box, which is the heart of the JVM, includes the bytecode interpreter, class loader/verifier, and garbage collector/memory manager. This box is usually implemented using (relatively) platform-independent C code, but most JavaVMs actually implement at least the bytecode interpreter in assembly language for better performance. Each of the Java API packages has a library associated with it, which again is usually implemented in C code. Although some of the functionality of the Java API may be implemented within these libraries, most of the Java API is implemented by calling native platform-dependent library routines and system calls. The layer which maps the Java API calls into platform-dependent calls is called the *adapter* layer; this layer is usually written in C or assembly language.

Underneath the adapter layer is the actual operating system. The benefit of this design is that the vendor is free to use whatever services the operating system provides to implement the Java platform in the most efficient manner. For example, if the operating system supports native threads, Java threads can be mapped directly to native OS threads to take advantage of the associated performance benefits. Other platform-specific features may be utilized as well, as long as they support Java applications *transparently;* Java applications should never be written to platform-specific APIs, since doing so would cripple the Write Once, Run Anywhere philosophy.

Notice that the Java API makes certain assumptions about the services offered by the host operating system; for example, the OS must support TCP/IP networking, windowing/graphics primitives, and input devices such as a keyboard and mouse. In fact, the tasks associated with supporting the Java platform on a given operating system are comprised largely of mapping the functionality required by the Java API into the appropriate operating system service. In order to support the Java platform, *JavaOS must directly implement all functionality required by the Java API, since there are no operating system services to be relied upon.* This may sound daunting at first, but remember that JavaOS does *not* have to implement the functionality of an *entire* general-purpose operating system; it need only implement the functionality required by the Java platform.

Figure 15.4 illustrates the architecture of JavaOS. At the top of this diagram is the same dotted line that was in Figure 15.3; anything above this line is platform-independent Java code and will run on any Java-enabled system. However, comparing Figure 15.3 with Figure 15.4 illustrates the differences between JavaOS and Java runtime implemented using a host operating system. It is

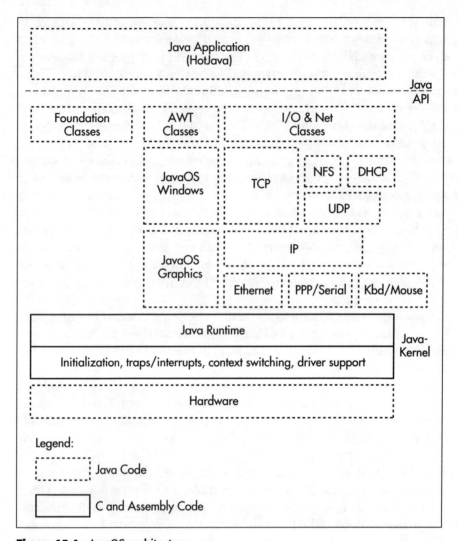

Figure 15.4 JavaOS architecture.

important to note that from a Java application's point of view, *the API provided by JavaOS is exactly identical to the API provided by a Java runtime implemented on a host operating system.*

We've already shown that JavaOS is responsible for implementing the functionality required by the Java Platform. This functionality includes support for:

- Booting and initialization of all hardware and software resources
- Interrupt handling
- Thread scheduling
- Device drivers

- Foundation class functionality
- AWT/Windowing
- Networking and I/O

Obviously, all the other components of the Java runtime must be implemented as well, such as the bytecode interpreter/verifier, garbage collector/memory manager, and class loader.

Recall that one of the goals of JavaOS was portability. Traditionally, stand-alone (*stand-alone* in this context refers to software that is written to run directly on hardware, *without* an operating system) software is extremely platform-specific; since the software is interacting directly with the hardware in a given platform, this is understandable. JavaOS by its very definition is stand-alone software and the traditional platform-dependency of such software may seem poised as a threat to the portability of JavaOS. Fear not, Grasshopper! Pretty much everything about the Java phenomenon challenges traditional thought. As you may have already noticed, most of the components of JavaOS are actually *written in Java!* If this seems bizarre, don't worry—it is.

When Sun began designing JavaOS, they wanted to make it as portable as possible. One of the most useful tools they had to support portability was—you guessed it—Java! Obviously, writing JavaOS entirely in Java would be impossible—in order to interact with hardware you *must* be able to perform certain operations that the Java language doesn't allow, such as accessing specific memory locations by address. However, it turned out to be fairly easy to encapsulate many such operations into native methods within Java. Two special classes were written: one to support memory access (by address) and another to handle hardware-interrupt fielding operations. (These special classes are *not* accessible by Java applications, for (hopefully obvious) security reasons.) As a result, *everything* that can possibly be implemented in the Java language *is* written in Java—including device drivers! C and assembly language were used only when the use of Java would've forced severely convoluted (disgusting) code, when performance was critical or when hardware-related issues required it.

Why write device drivers in Java? Aren't devices inherently platform-specific? It is true that device drivers are usually considered platform-dependent. However, many common hardware components are used to implement devices, regardless of the vendor. For example, the standard 16550A serial I/O chip is ubiquitous in the PC and embedded hardware markets. Although the interconnects or buses that various systems use to interface to this chip may differ, programming the 16550A hardware requires the same steps regardless of what platform the chip is used in. By separating the software that controls the system bus from the device driver, the portability of JavaOS is once again enhanced. The software necessary to control the system bus (called a *bus* or *nexus* driver) is likely to remain platform-dependent code, due to the complexity and variety of such interfaces.

Obviously, it makes the most sense to write the lowest-level code in C or assembly language. As indicated in Figure 15.4, the parts of JavaOS that deal with hardware traps, interrupts, context switching, and booting/initialization are implemented in C or assembly language. Whenever possible, this platform-dependent code performs only the steps necessary to allow *platform-independent* code to handle the bulk of the work. For example, the platform-specific, interrupt-handling code usually just queues an event to an interrupt service routine (ISR), which is implemented as a Java thread and returns. For performance, the Java runtime is implemented in C and assembly, just as in the host operating system–based Java runtime.

By limiting the use of non-Java code, the portability of JavaOS is enhanced considerably. But what about the performance of JavaOS? As it turns out, since JavaOS eliminates much of the overhead of the traditional operating system, performance, while still not exactly something to write home about, is much better than what might be expected. As the Java runtime is further developed and tuned, JavaOS' overall performance will increase. JavaOS now supports a Just-In-Time (JIT) compiler on some platforms (including the JavaStation "tower"), which greatly enhances performance. When systems equipped with the picoJava CPU become available, the performance of JavaOS will increase significantly—in fact, JavaStations equipped with picoJava processors may very well exceed the performance of even the most powerful PC and workstation systems running a hosted Java platform. (Obviously, this refers to the performance of Java applications.)

Notice that there is another implicit benefit from using Java to implement components of JavaOS; any improvements made to the Java runtime automatically benefit *both* Java applications and JavaOS! As the performance of systems increases, portability issues play a larger role. In this respect, JavaOS is already ahead of the game.

The Java-Kernel

Modern operating systems try to modularize their functionality as much as possible, and sometimes separate the core resource management logic into a layer of software known as the *micro-kernel* (see Figure 15.5). All other components of the operating system interact with the micro-kernel to perform their tasks. An application relies on the operating system (sometimes the operating system is referred to as the *kernel*) to provide certain services, and in turn the operating system relies on the micro-kernel to provide certain services. This architecture not only enhances the portability of an operating system, but it also provides extraordinary flexibility for implementing new features.

Since the JavaOS runtime executes operating system code (e.g., handles exceptions and interrupts) as well as user applications, it can be thought of as performing a similar function as a micro-kernel. This Java-kernel is responsible

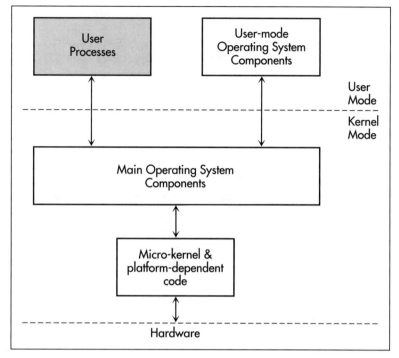

Figure 15.5   Basic micro-kernel architecture.

for implementing the low-level functions that are required by the JavaVM. Specifically, the Java-kernel must provide routines that:

- Handle memory management
- Manage concurrent thread execution
- Service hardware traps and interrupts

When JavaOS is booted, the Java-kernel executes its bootstrap code. This code allocates and initializes several memory regions, including the Java heap, the Object Handle heap, device direct memory access (DMA) buffers, and device I/O registers. (For details on the internals of the JVM, see *The Java Virtual Machine Specification* [Addison-Wesley, 1997].) In order to allocate the memory necessary to support devices, the bootstrap code must also identify any installed devices and bind the appropriate device driver to the corresponding memory areas.

JavaOS does *not* require a memory management unit (MMU), since JavaOS and all threads are run in a single address space. This is possible due to the protection provided by the Java language itself (e.g., no pointers). However, if an MMU is present, JavaOS may use it to make uncontiguous segments of physical memory appear contiguous, which can greatly simplify the memory allocation routines within JavaOS. An MMU may also be used to remap device I/O areas,

WHAT IS DMA?

To a CPU, even the fastest devices are extremely slow. Even when using the fastest disk drives available today, an I/O operation to a disk takes several months from the point of view of the CPU. If a CPU had to manually perform every I/O operation that a device requested, an extraordinary amount of time would be wasted while the CPU performed each I/O transaction. DMA is a scheme where the CPU can put some data in a buffer in memory, then tell some device to perform an I/O operation to that data buffer. The device directly accesses the memory, without any CPU involvement, to complete its task, then notifies the CPU when the job is done. While the device is performing the I/O, the CPU is free to perform more useful work. For example, if JavaOS has to transmit some data over the network, it creates a data buffer, then tells the Ethernet device to transmit the data. While the device is working on transmitting the data, the CPU is free to execute other threads; the Ethernet hardware accesses memory directly to perform its task. When the data has been transmitted, the Ethernet hardware will interrupt the CPU, so the data buffer may be freed up for another I/O transaction. The use of DMA greatly enhances the performance of a system.

which may simplify device-driver logic. Once JavaOS finishes executing the bootstrap code, however, the MMU is never modified. After all the memory regions and devices are initialized, the bootstrap code passes control to JavaOS.

While JavaOS is running, many Java threads will need to be serviced by the CPU. The Java-kernel supports this by enabling the JavaVM to *context switch* between threads as necessary. As we've already shown, JavaOS runs in a single address space and uses only a single execution mode of a processor (JavaOS always runs in the supervisor mode of the CPU, even when executing Java applications). Traditional operating systems use separate address spaces for each application. By using only a single address space, the Java-kernel's context-switching code is simplified and is capable of higher performance than in traditional operating systems. Running exclusively in the supervisor mode of a CPU allows JavaOS to be simpler and more efficient than traditional operating systems.

During normal execution, JavaOS needs to service processor traps and interrupts. The Java-kernel supports this by incorporating *glue* logic which distributes these exceptions to the appropriate Java device driver or exception handler. Most of these routines post an event to the appropriate driver then simply return; the goal is to handle as much work as possible in the Java code.

Now that we've provided an overview of the architecture of JavaOS, the following sections will focus on specific subsystems within JavaOS.

Filesystem

JavaOS is designed for use in network appliances that are not capable of supporting local disks. As a result, JavaOS doesn't support local disks. However, JavaOS *does* provide some filesystem functionality in the form of Sun's Network File System (NFS) and a ROM-based file system.

Network File System

JavaOS includes an NFS (version 2) client. This is primarily intended for Java applications to be able to access user-specific data files, such as HotJava's per-user customization data. (Most Java applications refer to such data as *properties*.)

This is *not* intended to be used as a mechanism to load class files; there is no provision for a CLASSPATH variable when using JavaOS. When a user logs into JavaOS, his or her home directory is mounted automatically via NFS. JavaOS uses several mechanisms to determine what directory should be mounted: a boot argument to JavaOS, the NIS automount maps, or the home directory as specified in the user's NIS passwd map entry. For further information on NIS or the automount service, consult Sun's Solaris documentation. (JavaOS has several parameters that may be specified at boot time. For further information on JavaOS boot parameters, contact Sun.)

ROM-based Filesystem

Newer versions of JavaOS support a special type of filesystem that is embedded in ROM. This is intended for use in embedded devices, where a network connection may not exist. At the time of this writing, the ROM-based filesystem was still a new concept undergoing development. (For updated information, please contact Sun.)

Processor Scheduling and Threads

JavaOS is a *single-user, multitasking* operating system. Multiple tasks are implemented through the use of multiple Java threads. Recall that JavaOS uses the Java-kernel to enable support for context switching between multiple concurrent threads. Also, recall that JavaOS implements several operating system functions as threads, such as interrupt service routines (ISRs). In order to manage all these threads effectively, JavaOS splits threads into two separate categories: user threads and system threads.

User Threads

User threads are threads created by a Java applet or application—these are the threads that most people think about when discussing Java. JavaOS schedules these threads using a priority-based mechanism similar to other JVMs (see [Lind97]).

As with other JavaVM implementations, multiple user threads may be grouped into thread groups for security and control, and thread groups can be nested to build thread hierarchies.

System Threads

System threads are used to implement operating system functions within JavaOS. ISRs, exception handlers, and JavaOS debugging threads are implemented as system threads. System threads are essentially just like user threads, except they are allowed some special privileges. For example, an interrupt must be serviced as soon as possible, so the thread that implements the ISR must have a higher-than-normal priority. Most system threads have a higher priority than user threads, so only JavaOS itself is allowed to create system threads. A special system thread—the idle thread—has a priority that's lower than any other thread in the entire system. As a result, whenever there aren't any threads waiting for the CPU, JavaOS schedules the idle thread. The use of a special thread to handle the case when the CPU has nothing to do simplifies the design of JavaOS' thread scheduler, and will make it easier to port JavaOS to multiprocessor platforms should the need arise.

System threads also allow specific memory requirements to be specified, unlike user threads. An operating system function may require more stack space than is provided to a thread by default. Finally, JavaOS considers system threads to be special. For example, you cannot stop or destroy a system thread. Without the distinction between system and user threads, JavaOS would be significantly less robust and efficient, since it would be possible for an application thread to affect the operation of operating system functions.

Monitors and Thread Synchronization

JavaOS manages several data structures that allow thread synchronization. Java programmers use the synchronized keyword when declaring methods which must access data that other threads may also be accessing simultaneously. This keyword tells the JavaVM to synchronize the execution of multiple threads to avoid conflicts and makes it very easy for the developer to utilize threads.

JavaOS uses monitors to implement thread synchronization. A monitor is a special data structure which can be thought of as a token that allows a method to execute. Only a single thread can hold a monitor at any given instant; if another thread requests the monitor, that thread will be stopped until the thread that currently holds the monitor releases it. Whenever a thread executes a method that was declared with the synchronized keyword, JavaOS attempts to assign the appropriate monitor to the thread *before* executing the method. If another thread already has the monitor, JavaOS suspends the requesting thread until the other thread releases it. Several threads may be awaiting a monitor at any given instant. When a thread releases a monitor, JavaOS picks a suspended thread, assigns the monitor to it, and starts it running. Monitors are released when the synchronized method returns.

Although a given monitor can only be assigned to a single thread at a time, a thread may hold multiple monitors simultaneously. This may occur if a synchronized method calls another synchronized method. JavaOS does not guarantee that deadlocks will be detected or avoided; the application developer must utilize good design techniques and algorithms to avoid such situations (see Chapter 11).

Virtual Memory

JavaOS was designed to run on platforms with minimal hardware requirements. Virtual memory implementations traditionally require significant hardware resources. As a result, *JavaOS does not provide virtual memory.* The application developer must remain keenly aware of the application's memory footprint when developing Java applications. In a fully configured JavaStation (64 MB of RAM), the application should have roughly 60 MB of RAM (JavaOS uses about 4 MB) available to applications. However, this memory must be shared by *all* currently running applications. Applications should be designed to intelligently use memory. For example, classes should be loaded only as necessary. JavaOS supports some mechanisms to notify an application when memory starvation is occurring, but there is no substitute for good application architecture and implementation.

When running a single application on JavaOS, low memory situations should not present any issues. Nonetheless, developers must be aware that their application may be executed simultaneously with other applications and they should allow graceful execution in tight memory situations.

Device Drivers

Although device drivers in JavaOS are written in Java, they currently must be statically linked with the JavaOS image. This requires the driver writer to have the complete source code and build environment for JavaOS. Although this is currently a restriction, not many NCs are capable of supporting expansion slots yet, and the vendor of a particular NC will provide the drivers necessary for any embedded devices supported by its platform. As a result, this restriction shouldn't prove too limiting. Sun is actively working on a set of APIs to allow third-party device drivers to interface with JavaOS; these APIs will be included in a future release of JavaOS. In addition to easing the task of creating device-driver software, these APIs will allow JavaOS to dynamically load drivers *only when necessary;* this eliminates the need to statically link drivers with the JavaOS binary and doesn't require the driver writer to have JavaOS source code.

The most critical issue with regard to device drivers currently involves access to the serial port. We've already discussed some of the possible applications for a serial port, but only recently has JavaOS provided a general mechanism for accessing the serial port. In the original versions of JavaOS, developers were forced to statically link any serial-port drivers into the JavaOS image, as the previous paragraph describes. This is extremely inflexible; you had to have separate JavaOS binaries to support *every* different serial device you wished to use. For example, several different versions of JavaOS were created to support various models of touch-screens (for use in kiosk-type applications). Not only was this a nightmare to administer, but also you had to have full source code to JavaOS, just to support a serial device!

Newer versions of JavaOS have included an API that allows applications to access peripheral ports (e.g., serial, parallel, etc.). This allows an application to support *any* device capable of being connected to the serial port, without having to modify JavaOS. Obviously, this is a major improvement. Known as the Java Communications Port API, this interface offers applications standardized access to serial, parallel, and (in the future) Universal Serial Bus (USB) devices. Instead of having to statically link a driver to the JavaOS binary, "drivelets" (driver applets) can be created to interface with serial devices via the Java Communications Port API. This interface is merely the first step towards the full device-driver API that will appear in future versions of JavaOS, as even this architecture has its limitations. For example, these drivelets must currently be packaged with the application (via a JAR file, for example), and there is currently no mechanism for maintaining persistent device-object state or configuration information. Future JavaOS APIs will include mechanisms for automating the downloading and installation of drivers as well as maintaining persistent device and/or platform-specific configuration data.

Sun is also working on market-specific APIs for controlling devices under JavaOS. For example, the "Java Point-Of-Sale" (JavaPOS) APIs will define a standardized interface to point-of-sale devices. Such devices may include magnetic (e.g., credit) card readers, UPC scanners, keypads, cash drawers, and SmartCard readers. These APIs will be layered (automatically) on top of other device APIs (such as the Java Communications Port API), which will simplify the development of POS applications. As JavaOS technology expands and more appropriate applications are identified, other APIs will be defined to further leverage the benefits of Java and JavaOS.

Networking and Protocols

JavaOS must implement all the networking protocols necessary to support the Java networking APIs. In addition, JavaOS requires some networking protocols to support themselves as networked appliances, such as software to allow interaction with network-management devices. As a result, a significant part of JavaOS is dedicated to the implementation of network protocols.

JavaOS includes a large suite of network protocols, partially illustrated by Figure 15.4. The main Internet protocols used to implement the basic transport and routing mechanisms in JavaOS are IP, TCP, UDP, and ICMP. JavaOS implements these protocols over Ethernet (10 and 100 Megabit) as well as PPP (e.g., serial modem), depending on hardware support for specific networks. JavaOS includes several other networking protocols as well, including those shown in Table 15.3.

Of the protocols listed in the table, one of the most important is DHCP, the Dynamic Host Configuration Protocol. When JavaOS is first booted, it has no way of knowing how to configure the IP stack, which is critical to the operation of any NC. DHCP is a protocol used to automatically configure many parameters within JavaOS, including the IP stack. Upon booting, JavaOS broadcasts a message to the network, requesting a DHCP server. When a DHCP server hears this request, it sends client-specific data back to the system that made the request. JavaOS uses this data to configure itself. Obviously, a network must include a DHCP server to support JavaOS. Usually the same system that acts as a boot server for NCs also provides the DHCP service, but this is not required as long as *some* system on the network is configured to provide the DHCP service.

Windowing and Graphics

Next to networking, the largest component—in terms of memory usage—of JavaOS is the windowing and graphics subsystem. JavaOS uses the Tiny AWT library to implement the functionality required by the Java graphical APIs. ("Tiny" refers to the fact that it places fewer requirements on the underlying window system; it doesn't mean that it's smaller than other AWT implementations.) The graphics code in JavaOS is capable of most standard graphics operations, including:

Table 15.3 JavaOS Networking Protocols

PROTOCOL	FUNCTION
ARP	Maps Ethernet addresses to IP addresses
DHCP	Configures JavaOS network parameters at startup
DNS	Hostname to IP address resolution
LPD/LPR	Printing to remote networked printers
NIS	User account information lookup
NFS	Networked file sharing
PPP	IP networking through serial-port
RDATE	Sets local system's time from remote server
SNMP	Network Management of JavaStations

- Managing overlapped windows
- Rendering bitmapped fonts
- Scrolling operations
- Graphics rendering ops, such as drawing lines, arcs, and polygons
- Fill operations

As shown in Figure 15.4, the entire JavaOS windowing system is written in Java. This system uses the services provided by the underlying graphics system, which is mostly written in Java; at the very lowest level the graphics code must interact with the framebuffer hardware, so this code is implemented as native methods. The device driver for the framebuffer is capable of overriding any graphics-primitive methods in the generic graphics code, to take advantage of hardware graphics accelerators. This architecture is quite elegant and allows JavaOS to easily support a myriad of graphics devices.

Graphics implementations are traditionally memory hogs. Due to the limited hardware resources of an NC-class device, coupled with JavaOS' lack of virtual memory, efficiency in the graphics subsystem of JavaOS was deemed a critical design goal. As future versions of JavaOS are released, this subsystem is likely to become even more efficient.

Printing

JavaOS has traditionally supported printing over the network to a print server using the "Berkeley LPR/LPD" network printing protocol. Newer versions of JavaOS also support printing to a "local" (e.g., device connected to a serial port) printer that is capable of printing either HP PCL5 or PostScript print jobs.

Platforms Supporting JavaOS

When it was first announced, JavaOS was running on both SPARC and Intel x86-based platforms. Since that time, platforms based on the several other processors have been added to the list. An extraordinary amount of interest in JavaOS has fueled projects to support many new platforms. Our discussion has focused on one specific implementation—Sun's SPARC-based JavaStation. Given the simplicity and portability of JavaOS—and the unprecedented amount of interest in it—it is very likely that JavaOS will be ported to a huge variety of platforms.

JavaOS will never be a replacement for general-purpose operating systems such as Windows or UNIX, nor was it ever intended to be. One of its strengths is that it allows a Java runtime environment to exist on hardware systems that may not be capable of running a general-purpose OS. This capability greatly expands the scalability of the Java platform to include the low end of the spectrum of hardware platforms available. *This is the area of the computing market that JavaOS will prove most beneficial.*

Is JavaOS Really an Operating System?

The classic textbook *Operating System Concepts* (see the References section at the end of this book) defines an operating system as "a program which acts as an interface between a user of a computer and the computer hardware." Obviously, by this definition JavaOS *is* an operating system. However, this issue can be argued many ways, depending on one's perspective. Compared to more traditional operating systems, JavaOS is different in that it *does not:*

- Need a filesystem
- Need separate address spaces
- Define a unique set of system services
- Support many programming languages
- Support virtual memory
- Define the user interface

However, JavaOS also has similarities to those same operating systems, in that it *does:*

- Require booting
- Support a well-defined API
- Support a windowing system
- Support password-protected logins
- Support multitasking
- Support device drivers
- Support networking

Perhaps instead of arguing over whether JavaOS is an operating system or not, the following question should be asked: "Why does it matter?" JavaOS is a tool that is applicable to certain tasks; it is no more and no less.

The "Main" Application (HotJava?)

JavaOS by itself is not very useful; after all, its only function is to provide an environment for a Java application to run in. This application is what the user interacts with, and what defines the overall utility of the NC. Early versions of JavaOS came with HotJava embedded as the one and only application that could be run. This environment was soon recognized as being too restrictive, since only Java applets (*not* applications) could be executed within it. A mechanism was therefore defined that allowed custom Java applications to be run *instead* of HotJava when JavaOS is started. This affords the NC developer with much greater flexibility. HotJava is still the default "main" application, but a "custom main" application can also be defined and even stored in FlashRAM (on hardware platforms that support it) to eliminate downloading the application at JavaOS startup. Such an application *must* be *100% Pure Java*, and must use *only* the APIs supported directly by JavaOS (i.e., no native methods for *any* platform). This application may either be a third-party "shrink-wrapped" application or a custom proprietary solution—*any 100% Pure Java* application will work. The procedures for creating a customized "main" application are beyond the scope of this chapter, so we will focus on HotJava as the "main" application. (For further information on custom "main" applications under JavaOS, contact Sun.)

HotJava is the name of Sun's 100% Pure Java Web browser. This browser was actually one of the very first proof-of-concept applications written in Java, meant to demonstrate the viability of developing applications in Java. As time progressed, and the popularity of Java exploded, HotJava grew into a fully supported application. JavaOS provides a stand-alone implementation of the Java platform, but it does not provide a user interface (UI) to that platform. It didn't take much effort to realize that JavaOS and HotJava would work well together.

JavaOS uses HotJava as the UI to the JavaStation. The combination of JavaOS and HotJava provides a complete, multitasking, graphical UI–based operating environment. HotJava effectively manages the desktop metaphor, acting as a window manager. HotJava can support multiple independent windows, each of which may browse HTML documents and/or run one or more Java applets. Although newer versions of JavaOS are capable of running "main" applications other than HotJava, HotJava provides a decent framework for developing Web-based applications.

Overview

Traditional Web browsers are monolithic applications, with extensibility provided only through plug-ins. These browsers may have a JavaVM embedded into them, but the JavaVM is only used to support Java applets within the context of Web-based content. Changes in the overall functionality of the browser often require a new version of the browser software; even plug-ins are usually limited to merely extending the types of data the browser can display.

HotJava presents a much more modular approach and is actually more of an application framework than a Web browser. First and foremost, HotJava is a Java *application*, which means it runs *inside* a JavaVM instead of embedding a JavaVM within itself. As a result, HotJava utilizes all the advantages of the Java language (dynamic binding, platform independence, etc.). HotJava is also highly modular; instead of hard-coding browser functionality, HotJava is architected as a core framework which interacts with several modular subsystems (see Figure 15.6).

For example, traditional browsers are hard-coded for the various URL protocols (e.g., HTTP, FTP, gopher, etc.) they support. If a new protocol comes along, the browser binary would have to be upgraded to support it. As illustrated in Figure 15.6, HotJava has a separate component, called a *protocol handler*, for each of these protocols. HotJava's core framework doesn't even understand the HTTP protocol; it just knows how to invoke the HTTP protocol handler, which does all the actual work. This allows for great flexibility—a new protocol simply needs a new protocol handler for HotJava to utilize it.

Since HotJava is written in Java, it can use Java's normal mechanisms for loading classes to incorporate new functionality into itself. For example, suppose a Web document specified that a document be loaded with the URL video:toaster.avi. The author of this Web document could write the Java code to implement the video protocol handler and include the appropriate class file(s) on the Web server. When HotJava sees the video URL, it can download the class file(s) necessary to support the video protocol, then actually use the downloaded protocol handler to transfer the video:toaster.avi URL automatically. Obviously, there are security issues associated with this sort of example; however, it illustrates the modular architecture of HotJava.

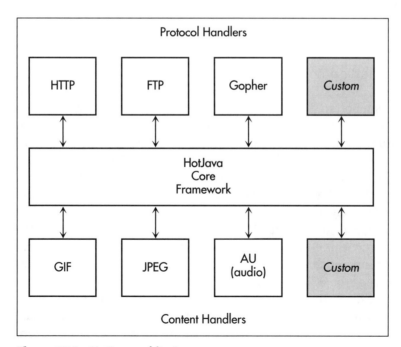

Figure 15.6 HotJava architecture.

In addition to supporting extensible protocol handlers, HotJava also supports *content handlers*. A content handler performs the same function as plug-ins do in other Web browsers—it extends the types of data a browser is capable of displaying. As illustrated by Figure 15.6, content handlers are implemented as modules that interact with the HotJava framework. As in our example dealing with protocol handlers, content handlers can be downloaded dynamically to support new media formats. And unlike plug-ins from other browsers, content handlers can take advantage of the platform-independence that Java enables.

HotJava was designed to be easily configured and supports numerous customizations through an ASCII-based properties file that is loaded on startup. The browser supports a number of built-in configuration pages that can be used to update the properties file or it can be edited directly. Properties are simple property-value type assignments and can be used to control most aspects of HotJava's operation, including screen layout, controls, and menu configurations. Applets can also access and/or change many HotJava properties dynamically, through a special API. This flexibility, combined with the extensibility offered through protocol and content handlers, allows developers to utilize the HotJava environment as an effective framework for application development.

Although the HotJava environment may not be well suited to more sophisticated or customized applications, it does provide the GUI functionality necessary for most applications that fit the NC model.

HTML

HotJava implements the official HTML 3.2 standard, with extensions to support tables, frames, and the OBJECT tag. Many popular extensions to the HTML 3.2 standard are *not* supported, however, such as the BLINK tag (Sun has actually received many suggestions to not include this tag!) and many extended attributes of standard tags. Sun will continue to enhance HotJava to support more features, especially as they are added to future official HTML specifications. For now, however, you should make a concerted effort to develop content using *only* the HTML 3.2 standard; try to avoid vendor-specific extensions to the HTML standard. This may seem restrictive at first, especially if you are used to using such non-standard extensions. However, remember the benefits of the Write Once, Run Anywhere model—the same concept applies to HTML. All modern browsers support the HTML 3.2 standard, so you should be safe if you develop content using the official HTML specification as your guideline.

Sun has also packaged the HTML parser from HotJava as a JavaBean component called the "HotJava HTML Component." This allows a developer to easily embed an HTML parser into a custom application (for further information, see http://java.sun.com).

TIP HotJava has one unique feature that helps developers debug their HTML! The HTML parser can enable a special browser button whenever it detects invalid or unofficial HTML statements. (This button has an exclamation mark in a yellow diamond shape, similar to a traffic warning sign.) If the user hits this button, HotJava displays a list of errors and the location of the invalid statements in the source HTML file. Each error listed is a hyperlink, which can be selected to bring up the actual HTML source. This feature can be a major benefit to Web content and application developers that are concerned with verifying their HTML code.

Security

Networks are great for enhancing the capabilities of a computing system, but everything has its price. More and more emphasis is being placed on security, especially when dealing with networks. HotJava supports many security-related features to help address the need for security in a networked environment. (Older developer versions of JavaOS which support the version 1.02 of JDK may not include all of these features.) This support includes:

- Signed applets for access control and authentication
- Secure sockets layer (SSL) version 3.0
- HTTPS (secured HTTP) protocol
- Certificate-based authentication
- SOCKS protocol

By default, HotJava prevents applets from accessing any local files. When running on a general-purpose OS, HotJava can be configured to allow various types of local file access, depending on the needs of the application. Since the focus of our discussion is the JavaStation and JavaOS, there aren't any local files to interact with, so obviously this isn't an issue. Applications developed for Network Computers should not rely on any sort of local storage.

Supported Protocols

JavaOS provides the core network protocols necessary for a system to communicate on the network, but many application-level protocols are necessary to support NC and Web-based applications. The Network Computer Reference Profile (NCRP) specifies the set of protocols a Network Computer must support. HotJava supports the following protocols, which build on the set of protocols supported directly by JavaOS:

- HTTP 1.0, plus some HTTP 1.1 features including cookies and keep alive
- HTTPS (Secured HTTP, as discussed in the Security section)

- SOCKS (an older secured network protocol)
- File Transfer Protocol (FTP)
- Gopher
- Simple Mail Transfer Protocol (SMTP)
- MIME e-mail encapsulation
- WebNFS

Protocol handlers can easily be developed to support new protocols within HotJava as well. Notice that HotJava does not support e-mail client protocols such as POP or IMAP. These protocols would be implemented by an e-mail client application or applet instead. The reason for this distinction is that Hot-Java by itself has no provisions for managing a user's mailbox. Many Web documents have hyperlinks to send an e-mail message (usually using the mailto: URL protocol), however, so a browser must be capable of *sending* e-mail. Implementing a full e-mail client application can be quite complex, so such functionality was deferred to another application.

Supported Media Formats

HotJava is equipped with several content handlers to support the more common media file formats. Among the media types supported are:

- GIF images (including animated GIF files)
- JPEG images
- AU audio files
- Java Archive (JAR) files

Many vendors are working on Java-based content handlers for other media formats, but it will take some time before the majority of other popular media formats are supported. Some vendors offer applets—which effectively perform the same functionality as content handlers—that support various media formats as well. For now, however, developers using HotJava are restricted to the previous list of media formats, unless they develop their own content handlers.

HotJava/JavaOS and the Network Computer Reference Profile

Now that we've provided an overview of the software environment of Sun's JavaStation family, we can complete our analysis of how the JavaStation measures up to the Network Computer Reference Profile (NCRP) specification. Recall the software requirements of the NCRP:

- Supports IP networking protocol (including TCP, UDP, etc.)
- Supports secure connections via SSL (optional)
- Supports FTP (optional)
- Supports Telnet (optional)
- Supports NFS (optional)
- Supports SNMP
- Supports DHCP or Bootp
- Supports HTML
- Supports HTTP
- Supports the Java Application Environment
- Supports SMTP
- Supports POP/IMAP
- Supports common media file formats: JPEG/GIF/AU/WAV

Obviously, HotJava and/or JavaOS support the majority of this list, including most of the optional features. Even Telnet is supported under HotJava, by an applet that connects to a Telnet server. This server software (and applet) comes bundled with Sun's Netra j server line. The Netra j product line is preconfigured to serve all aspects of the JavaStation family. The JavaStation doesn't require a Sun server, since all aspects of the Network Computer are based on open industry standards. Obviously, however, each vendor will make its server systems as attractive as possible to support NC devices.

NFS is implemented by JavaOS, but it is not intended to be used directly by users; its main purpose is to provide a mechanism for applications to access per-user configuration files. Finally, the POP/IMAP protocols are not directly supported by HotJava, but third-party e-mail client solutions are available. The only real issue is the current lack of support for WAV format audio files. These files are the PC standard audio file format and they are very popular on the Internet. Since the AU format audio files are supported, the JavaStation qualifies as an official NC according to the NCRP, but with the popularity of this type of media format it would be beneficial for the JavaStation to support it in the future.

JavaStation Software Bundle (Netra j)

The Java APIs, JavaOS, and HotJava are all developed in different engineering groups at Sun. As a result, there are many different version-control schemes used, which results in a plethora of potentially confusing version numbers. To help minimize such confusion (you be the judge on how well this works), Sun bundles all the required software to support the JavaStation in a server software package known as Netra j. Netra j is an unbundled Solaris software package that can be added to any Solaris/SPARC system. Netra j includes a Web-based administrative interface, which is designed to make the administration of JavaStations extraordinarily simple. Unlike older versions of JavaStation software, you *must* acquire the Netra j software package to receive the latest versions of JavaOS.

The Netra j package includes several software components, including the following:

- JavaOS
- HotJava
- Several third-party software products to enable JavaStation end-user functionality, including support for display X-windows output, a telnet and SNA terminal client, and NC application development tools

Older distributions of JavaStation software were known as Java Software Environment (JSE) distributions. It is important to note that releases of the JSE prior to version 2.0 were considered developers' releases, meaning that production environments should be running at least the JSE version 2.0 or, better yet, Netra j release 2.0 or above.

Future Directions

The whole Network Computer industry, although still in its infancy, is moving forward at a breakneck pace. It is extremely difficult to accurately forecast the future products of this market, but we can examine some directions that are currently being taken, and attempt to project where these directions will lead. Remember, the following sections are speculation based on activities current at the time this book was written, so caveat emptor.

JavaStation

The NC hardware market is just beginning to heat up. Initial NC appliances have very little (if any) expansion options and are targeted at very specific markets. As the market matures and product lines become increasingly competitive, many changes are likely. Support for SmartCards—intelligent security access cards—will likely surface within the next year or so. Expansion slots may appear in some JavaStation models, to allow some limited expansion. Remember, however, that the NC was not meant to replace PC or UNIX-based desktops; applications requiring large amounts of expansion options are not good candidates for NC desktops. Support for built-in modems seems natural.

Infrared serial devices are gaining popularity in the PC market; it's not hard to imagine them becoming popular with NC systems as well. In fact, with the myriad of serial devices available in the computer market, support for multiple serial ports will likely become crucial for future JavaStations. A wider variety of networking interfaces will probably become available, possibly including ATM, Token Ring, Gigabit Ethernet, and so forth. The most exciting possibilities, however, lie with Sun's picoJava CPU family. Executing Java bytecodes as the processor's native instruction set promises to dramatically increase the performance of the JavaStation line.

In a report Sun published in the fall of 1996, test runs of the picoJava chip performed as fast as *five times* the speed of a system using an Intel Pentium processor (at the same clock speed) with a JIT compiler! (*Sun Microelectronics' picoJava-I Posts Outstanding Performance*, Sun Microsystems, November 1996.) Obviously, comparisons of this kind are tricky at best, but such a dramatic performance boost is compelling. Not only does performance look extremely promising, but the picoJava CPUs should use significantly less power and cost a fraction of what the CPUs in PC and UNIX systems cost. All this adds up to incredible performance boosts with lowered costs. There is little doubt that if the forecasted capabilities of picoJava are realized, the future success of the JavaStation family is ensured.

JavaOS

As its popularity continues to increase, JavaOS is likely to be ported to many new platforms. However, new platform support isn't the only interesting activity involving JavaOS. Currently, perhaps the most exciting thing happening with JavaOS is the device-driver API that Sun is working on. This API will allow third-party products to become more readily available, which will enhance the expandability of NC platforms. As more and more devices are supported by JavaOS, more applications for NC appliances will be discovered. This API will also enhance the portability of JavaOS, by further separating machine-dependent code from machine-independent code. Another possible enhancement includes support for a local disk, which would likely support a document cache, virtual memory, or both. Virtual memory would remove memory usage restrictions from application developers, but the cost of implementing virtual memory may outweigh its benefits (such applications are likely better suited for a PC or UNIX desktop). Performance enhancements such as improving JIT compiler technology are likely to play a major role in future versions of JavaOS. And finally, Sun's acquisition of Chorus Systems will likely affect JavaOS. Chorus Systems is a company that builds a highly modular embedded operating system called "ChorusOS." This OS is has a micro-kernel-based architecture, and can run in as little as 10 KB (yes, that number is correct!). What does this have to do with JavaOS? Well, ChorusOS already runs on several platforms and has an architecture that makes porting to new platforms relatively simple. JavaOS could benefit from ChorusOS' architecture, and leave all the low-level, platform-specific code to the micro-kernel. Such an implementation would still further separate machine-dependent code from machine-independent code, and allow JavaOS to take advantage of features that it currently isn't capable of (support for multiprocessor machines, real-time threads, new classes of devices, etc.). All of this is good news for the Java developer.

In addition to these enhancements, JavaOS will continue to evolve to support newer versions of the Java APIs. As the functionality of these APIs increases, JavaOS must address their needs. JavaOS will also adapt to the requirements of new classes of consumer devices. "Embedded Java" and "Personal Java" products will help shape future implementations of JavaOS as new classes of Java-capable devices become available. Sun's recent JINI initiative is designed to turn pretty much *any* electronic device into a participant in a truly global distributed computing environment. These are just the *technical* factors affecting JavaOS' market demands, and customer requirements will also play a big part in the future.

HotJava

As the default user interface to both JavaOS and the JavaStation, HotJava is where the most visible changes are likely to occur. Enhancements to the GUI components will improve the look and feel of HotJava, as well as any applications that use HotJava as a framework. Changes to the HTML specification will be incorporated into HotJava as well. Obviously, more media formats will be supported through content handlers. Real-time streaming data is likely to be supported, so video media can be played within the context of HotJava. And finally, support for some sort of scripting language, such as TCL and/or JavaScript, would be very beneficial to developers.

Summary

Throughout the course of this chapter, we've examined Sun's JavaStation as an example implementation of a Network Computer. This initial NC offering from Sun was driven more by time-to-market issues than any other consideration and used the basic architecture of Sun's SPARCstation-4 workstation as a design base. Newer members of the JavaStation family support additional hardware such as faster networking and FlashRAM, which can ease network utilization as well as enable remote JavaStation operation.

All JavaStations run JavaOS, which is a small and efficient single-user, multitasking operating system designed to support the Java runtime environment and full Java API on platforms with limited hardware resources. JavaOS requires fewer hardware resources than traditional general-purpose operating systems such as Windows or UNIX, which helps lower the cost of NC appliance hardware. By focusing on one very specific purpose—supporting the Java runtime environment—JavaOS eliminates much of the complexity of other general-purpose operating systems. JavaOS itself is implemented in Java as much as possible, which helps to ease the porting effort necessary to support JavaOS on a new platform. JavaOS includes networking support for both the Java networking API as well as the network management of JavaOS-based clients. The two largest software components of JavaOS are the networking protocols and the windowing/graphics subsystem.

HotJava, Sun's 100% Pure Java Web browser, is the default "main" application and is used to manage the desktop metaphor on JavaOS. HotJava acts as an effective window manager, allowing multiple unrelated windows to each display HTML data as well as run Java applets. HotJava provides a very flexible, extensible framework for developers to implement NC applications—it's more than just a Web browser.

The NC market is still being formulated and many things are changing rapidly. As the market matures, so will NC products; increased functionality and expandability are two key growth areas for the JavaStation, JavaOS, and HotJava product lines. It's hard to predict exactly what the future holds for Sun's NC offerings, and only one thing is certain: Things will change.

CHAPTER

16

The Future of Java

Introduction

If fabled *Internet time* is really equivalent to dog years, then when it comes to the Java platform a typical analyst's three- to five-year forecast is only good for five to nine months. This makes predicting the future of the platform a dangerous business. There are simply too many new ideas fighting for viability, too many small startups striving for a foothold in the market, and too many promising, but as yet untested, approaches to problems, both old and new, to say for certain what will be developed over the next three to five years.

Instead, in this chapter we will concentrate on the next year or two. Within this time frame several industry trends and new technologies have become well enough established that we can begin to see how they will play out. Some of these trends, like the move to distributed architectures and the rise of a componentware market for the Java platform, are already having a huge impact on the industry and have been discussed at length elsewhere in this book. Here we will look at the most promising of the remaining trends.

The Java Revolution

Sometime in the mid-1980s marketers discovered a powerful new phrase: *Paradigm Shift*. From a marketing perspective, this was an almost magical phrase. After all, who wants to be stuck in an obsolete paradigm? What CIO would buy a competitor's product when that product was more than just out of date; its entire paradigm was dead? Suddenly every new product represented a new paradigm. If version 3.2 of a word processor fixed half the bugs left over from version 3.1, it was a paradigm shift. If a new GUI came out with rounder buttons, it represented the death of the old square button paradigm.

Unfortunately, for advertising copywriters, but fortunately for the rest of us, users soon realized that *paradigm shift* was too often just another way to say *costly upgrade* and began to tune out all the spectacular claims made by paradigm pushers. So it was with great surprise that this jaded generation found itself in the middle of the Java revolution, the first genuine paradigm shift in the hardware and systems industry in almost 15 years.

How Paradigms Shift

A paradigm, as defined by historian of science, the late Thomas S. Kuhn, in his book, *The Structure of Scientific Revolutions* (University of Chicago Press, 1970), is a framework of agreed-upon concepts and methods which control how a group solves problems and, more importantly, what problems the group considers worth solving. The paradigm is the dominant mind set, world view, or gestalt of the group. Under the geocentric paradigm astronomers assumed that the Earth was at the center of the universe. For them the interesting question was how to reconcile the wandering motion of the planets with the circular motion of the stars. This led to elaborate systems of *epicycles* in which the planets moved around circles, which moved around larger circles, which moved around larger circles, and so on down to the largest circle which moved around the Earth. When viewed from a heliocentric paradigm, this theory sounds unwieldy, cumbersome, and obviously wrong, so it is surprising to find out how well it actually worked. Geocentric astronomers could account for almost all the motion they saw in the heavens and predict the location of the stars and planets well enough to allow sailors and explorers to navigate the globe. Getting rid of the small remaining anomalies seemed to be just a matter of adding another epicycle here or taking one away there.

This state is quite common for a mature paradigm. Everyone accepts the tenets of the world view. The major problems have been solved and useful work is being done within the confines of the paradigm. Rival theories, if there are any, lack the power and richness of the dominant paradigm. There is usually a feeling that "This time we've got it right" and confident predictions that systems built on this world view will stand forever.

In the computing industry we have seen this state of affairs several times. Roughly every 10 to 15 years we settle into a new paradigm with the hope that "This time we've got it right." The current desktop-centric paradigm has ruled the roost since the mid-1980s. It freed users from the constraints of "tyrannical" IT shops and created a new market of productivity tools like the office suite with its spreadsheet, word processor, and calendar. Desktop-centric operating systems run over 80 percent of the computers in the world and, with the addition of some small work group servers and better management software, these desktop-centric systems could, just possibly, stand forever.

If the dominant paradigm is so successful, why does it eventually fall? Usually, it is because the small remaining problems, which were supposed to be solved by a simple mopping up action, prove to be much more difficult than anyone imagined. In the case of geocentric astronomy, it became harder and harder to fix an anomaly in one area without breaking something somewhere else. Astronomers could push these last remaining little problems around within the framework of geocentrism but could never actually eliminate them. This, combined with new discoveries like the moons of Jupiter, led to the growing realization among (mostly) younger astronomers that something was fundamentally wrong with their discipline. This discontent opened the door for the heliocentrism of the Copernican revolution.

The desktop-centric world began to show similar cracks in the early and mid-1990s. Companies began to realize how much typical desktop computers cost to own and operate. Client/server systems which had promised to solve the interconnection and data-hostage problems which were plaguing corporate IT shops had failed to deliver on these promises (see Chapters 6 and 14). Upgrades to new desktop operating systems, which were to have corrected the last little anomalies left in the desktop world view, arrived with much fanfare but had little effect on the problems. Against this background the Java revolution fermented.

Asking the Right Questions

The dominant paradigm's most important effect is not its ability to shape how questions are answered. Its most important effect is its ability to control what questions are asked. This effect is most easily seen during a paradigm shift. When faced with an anomalous movement of a planet, Copernican astronomers did not simply find a better, faster way to add new epicycles to the heavens. They boldly declared that they were done with epicycles all together. They had found better questions to investigate. Even though they did not as yet have the answers to those questions, they were not going to waste any more time on the problems of the old world view.

As any paradigm shift must, Java computing also raises a new set of questions to challenge the industry. We no longer search for better ways to manage thousands of fat clients. We look for ways to move complexity off the desktop and back to more centralized servers where it can be effectively managed. Instead of trying to find a single word processor that will satisfy every user, we look for a common format, like HTML, or self-describing documents, like XML, which will allow any user to view and modify information regardless of what tool was used to create it. Where we once built bloated pieces of client-side code which talked to databases at the other end of the network, we now spread the processing load evenly across several tiers of processes and machines. The Java platform has changed how we think about software distribution, network management, development cycles, and other fundamentals of IT.

It is worth noting that a new paradigm can triumph over an existing one even if the newcomer is not, at least at first, as accurate or complete as its predecessor. The Copernicans were rightly criticized for not being able to match the accuracy of geocentric astronomers. Since the geocentric astronomers had thousands of years to perfect their epicycles, it shouldn't be surprising that it took the Copernicans another 150 years before their calculations were as accurate as their geocentric counterparts. Heliocentric astronomy won the day, not because it was quantitatively better than geocentrism, but because where geocentrism offered only a set of problems with which astronomers had wrestled for generations, heliocentrism offered new questions and the opportunity for real advancement.

Similarly, computing with the Java platform offers a fresh, exciting challenge to today's developers and entrepreneurs. This can be seen in the numerous small startups and new developers being attracted to Java development. The opportunity to get in on the ground floor of the next major revolution and to shape its outcome is too exciting for many people to pass up. We can glimpse the future of the Java platform by looking at some of what this talented group is creating today.

Vertical Market APIs

New market-specific APIs are one of the most exciting growth areas in Java APIs. In vertical markets ranging from financial services to network management, traditional rivals are working together to develop standard, Java interfaces and infrastructure for their industries. Tired of the cost and poor supportability of proprietary systems, these companies see a common Java infrastructure as a way to level the playing field, increase competition, and deliver a new generation of customer service without each company having to pay to develop a system from the ground up. These include:

- **Java Commerce:** Java Commerce, which includes the Commerce Java-Beans, the Java Wallet, and the JavaCard, provides a comprehensive set of APIs and services for building financial applications. These include open, flexible payment schemes, secure transactions systems, and network-based purchasing services.

- **Java Dynamic Management Kit:** JDMK provides a set of open, extensible classes and a supporting framework for managing individual systems, network hardware (like routers, hubs, and switches), and network services and applications. JDMK enables seamless administration of the entire networked enterprise from any browser.

- **Java Telephony API:** JTAPI is a core set of classes which provide simple call management services, such as placing, answering, and hanging up on telephone calls. With JTAPI, developers can add basic telephone services to Web pages and other Java applications. JTAPI also includes a set of standard extensions which add more complex services like mobile phone support and call center management.

This is just a small sample of the many new vertical and horizontal APIs being added to the base Java platform.

With customers expecting new services to be delivered on Internet time, cooperating rivals have neither the time nor resources to develop these new services alone nor the stomach to fight the inevitable, unproductive standards wars which result from two industry giants each promoting its own proprietary version of a technology. In this climate, the Java platform is seen as a vendor-neutral, unifying force. Even in cases where competing systems have already been announced or deployed, Java APIs can prevent the splintering of an industry. For example, much as JavaBeans allows a developer to write a component which can be deployed on any of several rival architectures, like Active X and Netscape's ONE, Java Commerce's Wallet gives financial developers a standard way to handle any of the proprietary money and payment mechanisms already available.

These industries are also eager to exploit the raft of new Java developers coming onto the market. Especially in industries which must support esoteric programming APIs and system services, like in smart cards and telephony, the reduced training costs and increase in the available developer pool is very exciting. Where before it might take years of experience for a developer to become productive in a specific industry, a competent Java programmer, working with a well-designed industry API that encapsulates the complexity of the underlying systems, could become productive with just a short introduction to the needed industry-specific concepts. Also since the years of hard work required to learn a particular industry usually do not transfer to other industries, these market-specific APIs help individual developers by making their skills more marketable.

Maintaining Simplicity

One of the Java platform's greatest strengths is its inherent simplicity. The Java language expresses the algorithmic portion of an application, and the Java core and standard extensions provide access to system services through classes which share a common, object-oriented programming model. Java developers do not have to remember one set of concepts for programming the user interface, another for accessing the database, and a third for an RPC mechanism. Every portion of the system looks like Java objects, acts like Java objects, and programs like Java objects. This simplicity is valued both by corporations that have found it makes developers more productive and by over 200 universities that are now teaching Java in their programming classes (hopefully putting an end to the stream of business majors whose only coding experience has been in BASIC).

But as more and more new APIs, some very market-specific, are placed under the umbrella of Java, will we eventually reach a day when the Java platform has become as Byzantine and incomprehensible as some of today's desktop operating systems? Hopefully not. The Java platform has several things going for it which may prevent this fate.

First, almost all of the parties involved in building these extensions recognize the importance of preserving the unity and integrity of the Java brand. This will prevent the platform from being splintered into multiple, incompatible versions as Unix was during the 1970s. Java compatibility branding and the 100% Pure Java program will protect the Write Once, Run Anywhere attribute from dilution by vendors wishing to hijack the Java platform. More importantly though, the modular design of the Java APIs provide a natural, easy extensibility not found in many systems (see Figure 16.1). A programmer may first learn the Java language, the core classes, and the standard extensions. This broad base will allow the newly trained programmer to address many different types of applications. There is no need to learn the entire edifice of the platform in order to use this base. Later when the need for other facilities, such as database access and distributed interfaces, arises, the programmer need only learn those additional classes. There is never a need to absorb everything at once.

When a programmer must learn a new set of classes, the object-oriented nature of the Java language flattens the required learning curve. Since everything in the system, from remote network services to telephone switch programming to a serial port, is accessed through an opaque interface, the neophyte programmer need not learn all the complexity hidden inside these black boxes. The pure object-oriented Java language prevents the kinds of spaghetti code jumbles which make so many older systems incomprehensible. The language also benefits from a well-designed set of programming themes which are used throughout the platform. Common design patterns make sure

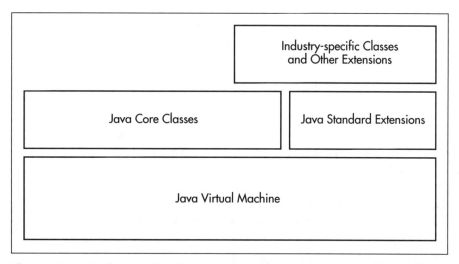

Figure 16.1 Market-specific APIs may be added to the Java platform without violating the overall simplicity or "feel" of the environment.

that a new set of classes will act and behave like more familiar ones. These repeated design patterns make it very easy to learn new Java classes and APIs.

With these three factors, backing from industry partners committed to maintaining a simple, standard Java core, a modular design which allows for incremental growth, and an object-oriented nature which hides the complexity of new systems, the Java platform provides a stable base for new development and new industries for the foreseeable future.

Hegemony of the Java Platform

With the Java platform being used in almost every segment of the computing industry and with a generation of developers whose first and maybe only programming experience will be with the Java language, will we ever reach a day when the Java platform has eliminated every other language and platform? Probably not.

Systems-Level Programming

There are several areas in which the Java platform is currently not usable and in which it will probably remain inappropriate. For example, as a reference-based language, it is impossible in Java to address directly a particular piece of memory. All memory accesses are by name, through an abstract reference. This makes it impossible to write device drivers and other systems which must directly manipulate individual bytes and bits of memory. For these systems we

NOT ALL EXTENSIONS ARE A GOOD IDEA

There is a tremendous temptation to extend the Java platform in directions it should not go. In some cases this temptation results from a natural tendency to overcome some of its current limitations by taking advantage of similar functionality that exists in the underlying operating system. In other cases, the temptation may come from a vendor wishing to gain a proprietary lock-in, which would compromise the Write Once, Run Anywhere capability. In both cases, these extensions should be approached with extreme caution. Two examples of this tendency are static Java compilers and Microsoft's J/Direct system.

Static compilers overcome any remaining performance concerns by compiling the Java source code to native machine code instead of the usual byte-codes. Assuming the static compiler does a good job of optimizing the resulting machine code, this allows a programmer to gain the productivity advantages of coding in the Java language without the potential performance penalty. But in the trade-off the programmer also loses some important features. Obviously, Write Once, Run Anywhere is out the window. Less obviously, the programmer has also traded away the Java security mechanisms. Native machine code is not contained by indirect execution and can do anything it wants on the machine. Statically compiled Java code presents the same dangers as those found in any compiled code, including viruses and uncontrollable Trojan horses.

With the release of HotSpot execution technology, static compilers lose most of their appeal. HotSpot-powered Java Virtual Machines are nearly as fast as compiled code, but do not sacrifice the other benefits of the Java platform.

In the case of J/Direct, the temptation is to tie code directly to the Windows platform in order to take advantage of the extremely large number of controls, third-party components, and DLLs that exist for the PC. While this may be appropriate in some cases, programmers who chose this route are again throwing away Write Once, Run Anywhere and security. As more and more of the tempting functionality is implemented for the Java platform, the temptation of "going native" will decrease. Programmers considering going native should carefully examine what they will gain from the native code and what they will be losing. Before indulging in native code, look for a 100% Java Pure alternative. If one is available, using it will preserve Write Once, Run Anywhere and the Java security model, and allow the code to take advantage of the wide range of nontraditional computing devices coming onto the market.

need a lower-level language, like C, C++, or even assembler, to provide memory management and hardware access. In fact, this is the case today in JavaOS. Even though more than 80 percent of JavaOS is written in Java, the lowest-level modules are written in C++. These modules provide device drivers written in the Java language the ability to access the hardware control registers they must use to manipulate their associated peripherals. While widespread use of this sort of low-level language extension would negate the Write Once, Run Anywhere ability, for some limited applications these native methods are required. For operating systems, imbedded runtimes and similar applications, we should expect to see the continued mixing of pure Java code and lower-level languages. Developers must be careful to evaluate this mix and weigh the benefits of the machine-specific code against the need to port and maintain that code on potentially many different platforms. As the Java platform matures more and more, system-level functionality will be encapsulated by Java APIs. As this happens, the need for most applications to use native methods should disappear.

Application Programming

Operating systems development represents one end of the development scale. At the other end of the scale live content developers who lack the skills needed to use a 3GL like the Java language. This group includes Web site designers, financial analysts, and other persons whose main responsibilities do not include programming, but who still do some simple development. Today, these developers are probably using a scripting language like TCL, a spreadsheet's formula language, or a visual development tool. For these developers, the combination of Java objects developed by computer science professionals and an application-specific language will allow them to build very sophisticated applications.

The sheer size of this group makes it an important market for Java components. The developer market can be viewed as an upside-down pyramid, with a small number of highly trained, very low-level developers building supporting infrastructure, like operating systems and databases, on the lowest levels and a larger number of increasingly less sophisticated developers on each of the higher levels. One goal of the Java platform, JavaBeans, scripting languages, and the three-tiered architecture is to allow each higher level of developer to exploit fully the work of those developers on the levels below. In this way businesses can reduce development costs, increase code reuse throughout the organization, and allow problem specialists who may lack computer science training a greater role in building problem solutions. The goal is to allow developers at each level to apply their unique skills to a problem set and to create value for developers in the next higher tier (see Figure 16.2).

For the large number of developers in the top one or two tiers, expect a combination of simple scripting languages and visual development environments

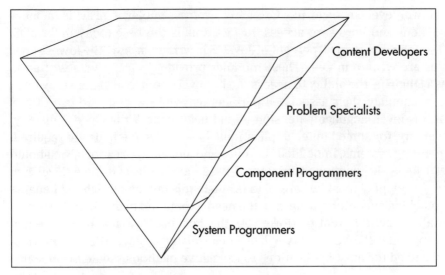

Figure 16.2 Careful design makes the work of computer specialists available to other IT professionals.

which can leverage pre-existing Java code to be the tools of choice. Especially as the number of commercial off-the-shelf JavaBean components increases, this group will become an increasingly important segment of the developers' market.

New Application Architectures

In Chapters 6 through 10 we discussed distributed applications and relevant APIs such as Java RMI, JavaIDL, Enterprise JavaBeans, servlets, and JDBC. These APIs and the applications built with them share a common architecture; they are based on the request and reply model of distributed computing. While the request and reply model is useful in many types of applications, it is not the only way to distribute an application. For systems handling data which is of interest to many different higher-level systems, systems which connect to the network only intermittently and must do work while disconnected, and for systems which must coordinate the activity of many different people simultaneously, other application architectures are more appropriate.

Messaging Architectures

In messaging architectures, system components are divided into two groups: message producers and message consumers. Producers do not need to know who is subscribing to them and consumers do not need to know the details of who is producing information or how that information is produced. New consumers can be attached to a producer and existing consumers can be removed without affecting the producer or any other consumer. All communication between producers and consumers is through well-defined messages passed over an information bus. This architecture is especially well-suited to asynchronous applications. Messaging systems are very similar to the JavaBeans event model, only now the events are distributed over the network.

Messaging architectures are typically implemented as either publish and subscribe systems or as queuing systems. Although very similar to one another, publish and subscribe systems tend to stress the broadcast nature of their event distribution model. Queuing systems tend to use a more point-to-point topology. The new Java Message Service API allows Java developers to take advantage of both types of architectures.

This sort of very loosely coupled system is useful when a single data source must be able to update a large, constantly changing set of consumers. A typical example would be a point of sales (POS) device. When an item, for example a sweater or pair of pants, is purchased, the POS device must notify the inventory system so that it can accurately track inventory levels. Later the company may decide that this sales information is useful to the marketing department so it can track the effectiveness of weekly promotions and to the sales department for calculating commissions for the sales clerks.

It would be difficult to build this system using the request and reply principles described in Chapter 6. The inventory, marketing, and sales systems would have to constantly poll each POS device for new sales, or the POS devices would have to keep a list of each interested system and call a method in each system every time a sale is rung up. The difficulty in maintaining all these different asynchronous connections would force the developers to build their own custom messaging system.

Messaging architectures enable these systems by providing a formal mechanism for implementing the second option just presented (see Figure 16.3). Instead of forcing each system to keep track of all other systems interested in its data, messaging systems, especially publish and subscribe systems, provide a subscription tracking broker which allows a system to express an interest in a particular type of event, such as a sale, return, or inventory shortage. The subscription broker then takes care of forwarding events from data producers onto all interested consumers without the producers knowing where the data is going or the consumers worrying about from where it came. In the previous example, the inventory system would receive sales events from all the POS devices. If later, the store added a mail order or Internet sales outlet, the subscription broker would forward sales events from these new systems without the inventory system needing to know about the new sales outlets. The sales commission system, on the other hand, would have subscribed only to sales events generated by POS devices in the stores. The subscription broker would make sure that the commission system did not receive the mail order and e-commerce events.

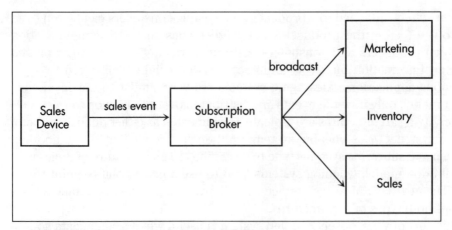

Figure 16.3 Other data distribution mechanisms.

Several companies, including Active Software, Open Horizon, and Tibco, have built enterprise-wide publish and subscribe systems for Java. Others, notably IBM with its MQSeries, have concentrated on queuing systems. These commercial implementations include a subscription broker and information bus which is scalable across many client systems on different subnets. They also add application monitoring and management tools, interfaces to legacy data sources, like relational databases, and security tools to control which systems can subscribe to which events. For asynchronous applications in which developers may have little idea who will eventually be interested in the data their systems produce, messaging systems can be the epitome of agile software.

Disconnected Computing

Network computers, Internet applications, and distributed applications all assume one thing: a continuous, reliable, high-speed connection to the network. Unfortunately, this assumption depends on the three lies of network computing: Bandwidth is infinite, latency is 0, and the net never goes down. Many applications, like personal productivity tools, can live with the slight possibility of a network failure. Developers of mission-critical applications, on the other hand, must explicitly recognize that eventually there will be a network outage and design a system which can recover from these failures. Some applications, like an e-mail reader for a laptop, might be intended to be removed from the network for extended periods with the expectation that they will sync up with network servers when next they are reattached.

For transactional, mission-critical applications this problem has been, for the most part, solved. Highly available servers, transaction monitors, two-phase database commits, and industrial strength systems and network management reduce downtime and allow for graceful recovery after a failure. Next-generation distributed application architectures, like CORBA and the messaging architecture, include reliable networking, guaranteed event delivery, and some limited fail-over mechanisms.

The picture is less rosy for the deliberately disconnected applications. Laptop use has now become common enough that people routinely carry their work out of the office, away from a reliable network connection. Today, the most common disconnected protocol for a nomadic PC is a floppy disk shuffled back and forth between the laptop and desktop. As in the days of the Sneaker-Net, information is lost as it is copied back and forth between devices. Versions begin to skew as changes are made to one copy of a file and not propagated to other copies. Worst of all, two users cannot effectively modify the same information simultaneously.

With smaller laptops, palmtops, and personal digital assistants becoming common, and with high-speed wireless metro networks on the horizon, we can see a new generation of applications for which this SneakerNet approach to disconnected computing will not work. Real estate agents and insurance adjusters will want to be able to download listings and case records to a hand-held and carry them to the site, without locking co-workers out of the database. When they return to the office, they'll want the database to be automatically updated with notes made on site. This same scenario works for many applications where data must be gathered in the field and then stored centrally; for building contractors, overnight delivery drivers, and meter readers an automatic mechanism for keeping copies of data stored centrally and on disconnected devices in sync would be a great boon.

While there is no general, standard mechanism for synchronizing these data, some existent application-specific protocols show what is possible. The IMAP4 protocol allows a disconnected user to download e-mail to a laptop, read it later, view attachments, and respond to messages, all on the road. When next the device is connected to the network, the IMAP4 protocol automatically syncs up the server copy of the mailbox, sends the outgoing e-mail messages, and downloads new mail. A similar calendaring protocol called ICAP is being developed.

Working groups for the Mobile Network Computer Reference Profile are currently addressing these needs. These working groups are defining services for data replication and synchronization and other needed mobile service, like power management and the ability to switch seamlessly between high-speed LANs and low-speed WAN, dial-up, and wireless connections.

Collaborative Environments

Today's networking conference tools are little more than network-based telephones. Even with (low-quality) video and shared white boards, they are only a little more functional than the much simpler telephone conference. Two major problems prevent network conference tools from allowing true distributed collaboration over the network. First, they are too session-oriented. In order to hold a network conference, the organizer must pick a time, notify participants, adjust schedules to accommodate last-minute changes, and make sure that all participants are running compatible conference tools. This process is much more akin to setting up a large meeting than it is to ad hoc collaboration. It lacks the spontaneity of a simple phone call and cannot approach the kind of interaction available to groups who share a physical location. Dropping by someone's office and running into someone in the hall remain the two best ways to interact with another person. Today's network conferencing tools cannot duplicate these natural interactions.

The second problem is that these conference tools lack a model of persistent objects in the virtual space. In the real world, we can carry a stack of magazine clippings into a meeting and pass them around. We can write on the white board, mark it with a large, red "Do Not Erase," and expect our notes to be there after lunch. We can bump into someone in the hallway and duck into the mail room to make a quick copy of the article we are reading. Without support for these ordinary transactions, network conferencing tools remain a pale imitation of face-to-face meetings.

Commercial vendors are taking these ideas and building collaborative persistent virtual spaces. These spaces, which may exist on the network and be accessed through a special tool or a simple Web page, allow people to "wander the halls" of cyberspace, carrying their personal effects with them and running into other inhabitants. In a typical example, a distributive engineering team may have a project Web page. A set of Java applets on that page form a virtual break room for members of that project. Simply by leaving their Web browsers open to that page, team members can be "in" the break room. The applet tells them who else is in the room, notifies them when people enter or leave, and allows them to talk with and share files, e-mails, and other types of information. This facilitates the kind of impromptu meetings which are so productive in the real world. When a team member needs to be alone to concentrate on some work, simply closing the Web browser shuts out the distractions of the break room.

In the same way, individual offices and smaller conference rooms can be created for private meetings on the Web. The usual set of network conferencing tools, like video, audio, and shared white boards, are also available. One of the leaders in the collaborative persistent virtual space market is PlaceWare, a spin-off of Xerox's Palo Alto Research Center (PARC). PlaceWare was created by the same researchers who, a decade ago, created the textual MUDs and MOOs found all over the Internet. Now these concepts have been applied to Java and Internet technologies with great success. Researchers at the University of Wisconsin, the NCSC, and Virginia Tech are applying similar ideas to scientific, mathematical, and educational systems written in Java.

Jini

No discussion of future Java technologies would be complete without mentioning Jini. Jini, which has been under development in Sun for many years and is intimately related to the Java platform, is the infrastructure for large scale distributed enterprise systems, ubiquitous portable devices, home automation, and other information appliances. Industry pundits predict that soon we will all wear 5 to 10 IP-addressable devices on our persons. Jini is the system which will allow these devices to discover each other's services, share information, and come and go from the network without creating a world in which we are forced to spend 5 hours a week *futzing* with our belt PCs. These devices will exist as loosely coupled, self-managing *federations*, without any centralized control.

Jini is based on several simple ideas. First, the Java platform allows us to consider every device as a Java Virtual Machine. This simplification solves many very hard problems in distributed computing. A cell phone can carry with it a GUI which will display on any PC, workstation, or Mac, without needing 20 MB of EEPROM to hold the three different ports of the application. Code can be passed from service to service in a secure fashion due to the Java platform's strong, built-in security mechanisms. Objects on one machine can address objects on another system in a type safe manner, bring the safety of the Java language to the network.

Second, Jini makes no distinction between hardware and software. Everything on the network is represented as a Java object and treated as a service provider. Users of a service neither know nor care if that service is implemented by a dedicated piece of hardware or by a process running on a desktop computer.

Third, Jini services are self-discovering. There is no need to preconfigure two devices or services to talk to each other. Instead, when a new service joins a Jini federation it can advertise itself to any interested party in the federation and find out what services are already available in the federation. If my new cell phone has a nice GUI for programming its speed dial numbers and other features, it can discover the application services offered by my desktop automatically. Assuming a wireless network, like Blue Tooth, the simple act of bringing the cell phone near the desktop machine will allow the phone to download and run its GUI on the PC.

Fourth, no resource in a Jini network is permanently dedicated to any service, device, or application. All connections, resource allocations, and services are *leased* in a Jini federation. This makes the federation able to deal with intermittently connected devices, unreliable networks, and other hazards of the real world without slowly leaking memory, sockets, and IP ports. When I grab my cell phone and run from the office, the Jini federation takes care of cleaning up the mess of open sockets, running applications, and locked memory I've left. As soon as the lease on the cell phone's resources expires, the self-healing Jini federation clean ups the mess, with no human intervention.

Finally, Jini includes a very powerful, flexible distributed programming model which can be used for many types of applications. The JavaSpaces API allows applications to share data and objects, pass messages, and distribute computing loads and pass messages in a way which is very well suited for the dynamic nature of a Jini federation. Based on the Linda distributed computing model developed at Yale, JavaSpaces is a distributed tuple space for Java objects. Applications can write objects into the space, search the space for object of interest, read those objects from the space, and ask to be notified whenever an interesting object is written into the space.

The Jini system and devices built around it will be available in 1999. It has profound implications for both portable information appliances and traditional enterprise systems.

Summary

In March of 1998, the Java platform turned three years old. In just three short years, it has spawned a brand new type of desktop computer and accumulated an estimated 800,000 serious developers. It has been adopted as the platform of choice for projects in over 80 percent of Fortune 1000 companies and the teaching language of choice for over 200 universities. According to the Business Research group, there are more Java developers working on Internet applications than C, C++, and Visual Basic developers combined. It has become the *lingua franca* of the Internet and has united industries as diverse as manufacturing, finance, and systems management.

With its elegant, simple language, extensible modular design, and inherent security, the Java platform has proven to be the answer to some of the most pressing and difficult questions facing the computer industry today. Perhaps this time we've finally gotten it right and these systems will stand forever.

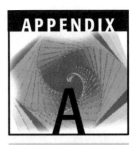

Further Reading

Many chapters in this book have referred to or cited some other reading material. This appendix lists many different sources for more information.

"A Note on Distributed Computing" by Jim Waldo, Geoff Wyant, Ann Wollrath, and Sam Kendall. Sun Microsystems Laboratories technical report SMLI TR-94-29, November 1994. www.sunlabs.com/technical-reports/1994/abstract-29.html.

"Remote Method Invocation Specification," JavaSoft, Sun Microsystems. java.sun.com/products/jdk/1.1/docs/guide/rmi/spec/rmiTOC.doc.html.

"Object Serialization Specification," JavaSoft, Sun Microsystems. chatsubo.javasoft.com/current/doc/serial-spec/serialTOC.doc.html.

"Effective Three-tiered Engineering," Balick, Fritzinger, and Siegel. Sun Microsystems, 1996.

Reengineering the Corporation, Hammer and Champy. HarperBusiness, 1993.

Managing the Software Process, Humphrey. Addison-Wesley, 1989.

Peopleware: Productive Projects and Teams, DeMarco and Lister. Dorset House, 1987.

"Software's Chronic Crisis," Gibbs. *Scientific American*, September 1994.

"Tips for Transforming an IS Development Staff," Gill. *UniForum Monthly*, October 1994.

The Java Virtual Machine Specification, Lindholm, Tim, and Frank Yellin. Addison-Wesley, 1997.

Java Virtual Machine, Meyer, Jon, and Troy Downing. O'Reilly & Associates, 1997.

Operating System Concepts, Peterson, James L., and Abraham Silberschatz. Addison-Wesley, 1985.

TCP/IP Illustrated, Volume 1, Stevens, W. Richard. Addison-Wesley, 1994.

Computer Networks, Tanenbaum, Andrew S. Prentice-Hall, 1981.

DNS and BIND, Albitz, Paul, and Cricket Liu. O'Reilly & Associates, 1992.

Managing NFS and NIS, Stern, Hal. O'Reilly & Associates, 1991.

Configuration and Capacity Planning for Solaris Servers, Wong, Brian. Sun Microsystems Press, 1997.

SPARCstation-4 Architecture White Paper. Sun Microsystems.

The microSPARC-II Processor, Technology White Paper. Sun Microsystems.

Web Site Programming w/ Java, Harms, Fiske, Rice. McGraw-Hill, 1996.

The Java Media Framework User's Guide. Sun Microsystems, copyright 1997.

The Java 2d API. Sun Microsystems, copyright 1997.

The Java 3d API. Sun Microsystems, copyright 1997.

Fundamentals of Interactive 3d Computer Graphics, 2d ed., Foley, vanDam, Feiner, and Hughes. Addison-Wesley, 1989.

The Java Virtual Machine Specification, Lindholm, Tim, and Frank Yellin. Sun Microsystems Press, 1997; Addison-Wesley, 1997.

Java Virtual Machine, Meyer, Jon, and Troy Downing. O'Reilly & Associates, 1997.

Operating System Concepts, 2d ed., Peterson, James L., and Abraham Silberschatz., ed. Addison-Wesley, 1985.

TCP/IP Illustrated, Volume 1, Stevens, W. Richard. Addison-Wesley, 1994.

Computer Networks. Tanenbaum, Andrew S. Prentice-Hall, 1981.

DNS and BIND. Albitz, Paul, and Cricket Liu. O'Reilly & Associates, 1992.

Managing NFS and NIS. Stern, Hal. O'Reilly & Associates, 1991.

Configuration and Capacity Planning for Solaris Servers. Wong, Brian. Sun Microsystems Press, 1997.

SPARCstation-4 Architecture White Paper. Sun Microsystems.

The microSPARC-II Processor, Technology White Paper. Sun Microsystems.

The microSPARC-IIep Processor, Technology White Paper. Sun Microsystems.

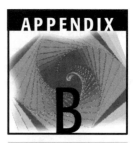

APPENDIX B

Authors on the Net

This appendix gives you more information about the authors as well as e-mail addresses where they can be reached.

Daniel J. Berg

Daniel J. Berg, currently with Sun Microsystems, is a Distinguished Engineer and the Chief Technologist for Sun's U.S. Reseller Channel. Mr. Berg has spoken at several national and international conferences and symposiums on the topic of Java technology as well as other leading Sun technologies. He has also published several books and papers covering and detailing Sun technologies. Mr. Berg has previously acted as an independent consultant and has held positions at IBM, Honeywell, and the University of Minnesota. Daniel can be reached at daniel.berg@Sun.COM.

J. Steven Fritzinger

J. Steven Fritzinger is a Java Technologist for Sun Microsystems and specializes in software development technologies, distributed architectures, and Java security issues. He is a member of Sun's NAFO Java Team and of the Board of Governors for the Java ACES, Sun's worldwide Java field organization. Steve has worked on several Java and Internet projects, including white papers and education on Java security, CSX's TWSNet electronic commerce system, and PBS:Online's Life On The Internet Web site and the Web site for the 1997 U.S. Open. Steve can be reached at steve.fritzinger@Sun.COM.

Barton Fiske, Contributor of Chapter 3

Barton Fiske is a Java author and Sun employee, specializing in 3d graphics, multimedia networks, and of course Java. A graduate of the Rochester Institute of Technology, Barton has been working in the industry for over ten years, the last five of which have been with Sun. Barton can be reached at barton.fiske @Sun.COM.

David Simmons, Contributor of Chapter 4

David Simmons is a Java architect and Technology Manager for Sun Microsystems. Specializing in JavaStation installations, JavaServers, and application architecture, David has worked with many of the earliest adopters of Java. David graduated from Columbia University in New York City, and worked at Los Alamos National Laboratory designing network monitoring software prior to joining Sun. David can be reached at david.simmons@Sun.COM.

Doug Sutherland, Contributor of Chapter 7

Doug Sutherland is a System Architect at the JavaSoft division of Sun Microsystems in Cupertino, California (home of the Java programming language). He's responsible for helping corporate enterprise developers deploy Java applications by assisting with architecture and resolving technical issues. He's also an evangelist of Java technology, touring around to speak at various conferences, trade shows, and other events. He specializes in distributed object-oriented systems and enterprise computing with Java. Prior to joining JavaSoft, he worked in the trenches of application development in the financial services sector, where his prior experience included software engineering, systems analysis, technical architecture, and project management. Doug can be reached at doug.sutherland@Sun.COM.

Geordie Klueber, Contributor of Chapter 15

Geordie Klueber is a Tactical Engineer at Sun Microsystems, where his technical adventures have brought him into close contact with JavaOS and the JavaStation product line. In addition to Sun's Network Computer product line, his areas of interest include performance tuning, systems programming, and networking. Geordie has been working with UNIX since 1985, and his experience runs the gamut from applications programming to systems administration to kernel hacking. During his tenure at Sun, Geordie has worn many hats, including Course Instructor and Professional Services Consultant.

Geordie is a member of the minority group that actually *enjoys* living in Rochester, New York ("The Imaging Center of the World!"). His education (both technical and social) at the Rochester Institute of Technology (RIT) has been significantly augmented by RIT's Computer Science House (CSH), a student organization that thrives on achieving the impossible. In his spare time, Geordie is trying really hard to become a musician and to get a life. Geordie can be reached at geordie.klueber@Sun.COM.

Index

A

Abstract windowing toolkit (AWT), 13–51
   data transfer, 36–37
   event model, 15–24
   mouseless operation, 33–36
Access checks, 108
AccessController, 354–364
   writing code for, 357–359
Access methods, of properties, 103–104
Activation, 153
   framework, 112–113
adapter\CountAdapter.java example, 23
adapter\CountTest.java example, 22–23
Adapter layer, 445
add() method, 35
Administration costs of computing, 443
Aliases, for servlets, 229–230, 232, 233
Anti-aliasing, 58
APIs:
   communication of, 5
   core, 57
   licensing, 57
   market-specific, 472–473
   servlet, 176–179
Applets:
   cgi-like functionality of, 86
   communication between, 77–78
   cool, 66

   player, 67–68
   running of, 69–70
   security of, 239–240
   sending to a URL, 87
   servlets, communication with, 176–179
   for servlet installation, 230–231
   versus servlets, 239–242
   and signed JAR files, 349–351
   untrusted, 335, 346–347
Application(s):
   database services in, *see* Java Database Connectivity (JDBC)
   financial, 473
   five-tiered, 123
   for Network Computers, 410–415
   N-tiered, 123
   100% Pure Java, 412–413. *See also* 100% Pure Java Initiative
   protection domains for, 352
   terminal, 417
   three-tiered, 120–136. *See also* Three-tiered application architecture
Application architectures, 116–123, 478–483
   collaborative environments, 481–483
   disconnected computing, 480–481
   distributed computing, 115–144
   messaging architectures, 478–480
Application builders, 101–102

Application environments, *see* Application architectures
   diversity versus intensity, 405–407
Application programming, 477–478
Architectural neutrality, 400
Arguments, objects as, 168–171
Arjuna, 151
Array class, 105, 107
Arrays, 336
   design patterns for, 104
Asynchronous action, 293
Atoms, 39
Audio:
   clips, retrieval of, 6
   of JavaStation "brick" model, 435
   of JavaStation "tower" model, 440
   of Java 2, 6
   synchronization of, 64
Audio synthesis interfaces, 60
AWT (abstract windowing toolkit), 13–51

B
Background tasks, daemons for, 299–301
Bandwidth:
   considerations of, 128–130
   for Network Computers, 417
BasicServer.java example, 79
Batch updates, 217, 219–220
BeanBox, 102
Bean event objects, 16
BeanInfo class, 110
Beans, *see* JavaBeans
Behavior, 59
Berkeley P-System, 2
Binary large objects (BLOBs), 205–207,
   216, 217
BLINK tag, 460
Blocks, code, 342
Boolean types, property design patterns
   for, 104
Boot servers, 418–419
Bound properties, 105
Bridges, between beans and existing
   components, 100
Browsers, *see* Web browsers
Buffer overflow attacks, 336

BufferedReaders, 95
BufferedWriters, 95
Bugs:
   coping with, 376–377
   security-related, 376–377
Bus architecture, 126
Bus drivers, 447
Business logic:
   access to, in client/server systems,
      119–120
   access to, in three-tiered architectures,
      120–121
   security of, 241
Bytecode, 150, 416

C
C, 2
C++, 2
CallableStatement, 204–205
Callbacks, from server to client, 164–168
Call Level Interface (CLI, X/Open),
   186–187
Canvas class, 43
Casting, 154
CatchDeath.java example, 306–307
CERT Coordination Center, security Web
   site of, 377
Chaos Computer Club, 336
checkMemberAccess( ), 108
Circles, with Java2D, 58
Class class, 106
Classes:
   core, 416
   monitors for, 314–318
   native method access to, 389–390
   privileges of, 342–343
   security of, 353–365
   thread-safe, 328
CLASSPATH, 228, 359
Client(s), 74–75
   multiple, and callbacks, 164–168
   for network communication, 81–82
   remote, 159–163. *See also* Java RMI
   service requests of, 75
   size of, and Network Computers,
      415–416

stub/skeleton layer and, 152–153
    tracking, with vectors, 166–168
Client.java example, 81
Client/server systems, 118–120
    debugging, 124–125
    interconnection strategies, 125–126
    management of, 127
Client updates, 127
Clipboard, 14, 40–43
clipTest.java example, 41–42
Clouds, 151
Cmain.c example, 392
Code, privileged, 357–359
CODEC, 435
Code reuse, 135, 260
Collaborative environments, 481–483
Collection API, 5
Color management, with Java 2D, 58
Color objects, 25
Color scheme, for user interface, 24–27.
    See also Desktop color
ColorView, java example, 25, 27
    with printing capabilities, 28–30
    with scrolling capabilities, 30–32
Columns, reading of, 195, 196–197, 207
Common gateway interface (CGI),
    222–224
Common Object Request Broker Archi-
    tecture, *see* CORBA
Communication:
    between objects, 77–78
    two-way, 84–86
Compatibility branding, 413–414, 474
Compilers, for security, 338
Component classes, 43
Component librarian, 135
Components, 100–101
    and application builders, 101–102
    availability, 124
    as integral parts, 118–120
    lightweight, 43–46
    stand-alone, 122
Compositing, 58
Concurrency, 148
    with threads, 292, 293
Condition variables, 318–326

Connection interface, 192–193
Connection object, 187
Connection pooling, 217
Constrained properties, 105
Constructor classes, 105–106
Containers:
    choosing, 277
    for components, 100
    extending, 43–44
Content:
    dynamically generated, 221
    executable, 332, 334–335
Content developers, 477
Content handlers, 69, 460
Controller, 47–48
CORBA (Common Object Request Bro-
    ker), 139–140
    and Enterprise JavaBeans, 290
    interfacing with, 116
    versus RMI, 149–151
CORBAServices, RMI integration with,
    183
Corporations, Java use by, 3
CountAdapter.java example, 107
CounterChangeListener.java example, 18
CounterEvent.java example, 20
Counter.java example, 19
CounterTest.java example, 20–21
Cryptography, 370–375
Culture of reuse, 135, 260
Cursor, moving in ResultSet, 193–194
Customization:
    of beans, 111–112
    of components, 101, 102
Customizer class, 112
Cut and paste, 14, 36–37

D

Daemons, 79
Daemon threads, 299–301
DaemonThr.java example, 299–301
Data:
    availability of, 126
    centralizing, 128–129
    declaration of, 326–327
    management of, with JDBC, 141

Data *(Continued)*:
　sharing, 60–62
　storage of, 10
　storage of, and the Sandbox policy, 348
　storage of, in three-tiered architecture, 121
DatabaseBean.java example, 244–247
Database drivers, 185–186
Database managers, off-the-shelf, 118
DatabaseMetaData, 197
Databases:
　connecting to, 192
　connection interface, 192–193
　connections, closing, 197–198
　location of, 207–209
　URL for, 192
Data buses, 131
　building, 139–140
　legacy system interface with, 136–139
Data flavors, 37–40
Data managers, for building applications, 210–216
Data service layer, 208–216
Data streams, 88
Data transfer, 14, 36–43
Data types:
　BLOBs, 205–207
　mappings of, 195–198
Data-typing specification, 112
dateTrans.java example, 39–40
DCOM system, 140, 151
DDC (display data channel) protocol, 433
Deadlock conditions, preventing, 18
Decision support systems (DSSs), 126–127
Default behavior of JavaBeans, 100
Default HTTP port, 83
default.template example, 251
Delegation event model, 13, 15–24
Demilitarized zone (DMZ), 240
Design, with Java Media, 54–57
Design patterns, 108–109
Desktop color, 14, 24–27
Desktop PCs:
　costs of, annual, 395–396
　as Network Computers, 400
　paradigm shift in, 471
Device drivers, 447–448, 453–454, 465
Digital signatures, 350
Direct memory access (DMA), 449, 450
Direct3d, 59
Disconnected computing, 480–481
Disks, and Network Computers, 401
Distributed applications:
　design of, 115–144
　and JavaSpaces, 10
Distributed interaction, 60–61
Distributed objects, 140, 141, 145
Distributed systems, 147
　comparison/contrast of, 149–151
　management of, 127
Distributed transactions, 217
Diversity of applications environment, 405–407
doXXX methods, 226–227, 234
Drag and Drop, 14, 36–37, 50–51
Drag sources, 50–51
DriverManager, 187–189, 191
Drivers:
　connecting to database, 192
　device, 447–448, 453–454, 465
　installation of, 191
　for JDBC, 187–189
Drop targets, 50–51
Dynamic Host Configuration Protocol (DHCP), 440–441
Dynamic-RAM (DRAM), 429

E

EJBHome interface, 271–272, 277–278, 279–280
EJBObject interface, 272, 281–282
Electronic commerce, 10
E-mail:
　executable content in, 332
　in HotJava, 462
EmbeddedJava, 7, 9, 423–424, 466
Emerald, 151
Endpoints, 153
Enterprise APIs, *see* Java Enterprise APIs

Enterprise JavaBeans, 116, 142–143,
     267–290
   architectures, 287–290
   choosing a container, 277
   entity bean, 279–286, 287–288
   goals, 270
   and off-the-shelf products, 124
   session bean, 271–277, 287–288
EntityBean class, 282–284
e.printStackTrace( ), 89
Error handling, from native methods,
     391
Error messages, 88
Ethernet, 434
Event(s):
   called by components, 101
   identification of, 108–109
   multicast, 17, 21
   registration of, 17–18
   sources of, 18–22
   types of, 101
   unicast, 21
Event adapters, 22–24
   example code for, 22–23
   and security, 24
Event control, with components, 101
Event exceptions, 21
Event filters, 24
Event handlers, for remote transactions,
     162–163
Event listeners, 16–17
   creation of, example, 18–21
   registration of, 17–18
Event management services, 59
Event mechanisms, see Delegation event
     model
Event models, for beans, 103
Event objects, 15–16
   creating, 18–21
   naming conventions, 15–16
Exception handling, 84
   and partial failures, 150
Exceptions:
   creating new types, 16
   getter and setter reporting, 104
   printing message to user, 88–89
executeQuery(String), 193

execute(String), 193
executeUpdate(String), 193
Execution, indirect, 334–335
Extensions to Java, 476
EzSearch.java example, 320–326

F

Failures, partial, 147, 148, 150
Felton, Dean, and Wallach, 376
Field class, 105–106
File(s):
   printing, 91
   reading, 91–95
   type, determination of, 89
   writing, 91–95
File I/O:
   fundamental checks for, 90–91
   permissions for, 91
File objects, 89–95
FilePath.java example, 90
FileReader.java example, 91–92
Filesystem, 451
   ROM-based, 451
File Transfer Protocol (FTP), 74
FileWriter.java example, 93–94
Filters, 24, 58, 138
finalize( ) methods, 197
Financial applications, 473
Firewalls, 240–241
First Person Inc., 146–147
Five-tiered architectures, 121, 208. See
     also Three-tiered application
     architecture
Flags, filter, 138–139
FlashRAM, 419, 429–430, 438
Focus traversal, 34–35
Font handling, 58, 70
Fonts, availability of, 70
For loops, 202
FormServlet.java example, 236–237
Futzing, 395–396

G

Garbage collection, 146
   distributed, 154
   in Java 2, 7
   and native methods, 388

Geometric primitives, 58
Geometric transformations, 71
getAsciiStream() method, 207
getBinaryStream() method, 207
getDocumentBase() method, 83
Get methods, 194
getObject methods, 197
getOutputStream(), 227
getParameterValues, 238–239
Getter methods, 103–104
getUnicodeStream() method, 207
getWriter(), 227
getXXX() methods, 194–197, 207
Glasgow specification, 112–113
Gosling, James, 2, 147
GoTo.java example, 87
Graphics capabilities, 51, 455–456
Graphics context, 28
Green threads, 327–328
GroupInfo.java example, 301–302
GUI builders, 102
GUIs:
    for bean customization, 112
    and event adapters, 22
    look and feel of, 49–50

H
Handheld devices, Java use of, 4
Heaps, storage of, 6–7
HotJava, 457–460
    future of, 466
    HTML standard in, 460
    and media formats, 462
    NCRP support, 462–463
    protocol support, 461–462
    security of, 461
HotJava browser, 9
    launching, 69
HotJava Views, 9–10
HotSpot execution technology, 476
HTML:
    for display tags, 416
    generate HTML page, 224–225
    in HotJava, 460–461
    for multimedia use, 67
    page building with, 227–228

HTML forms, user input from, 236–238
HTML layout tags, 67
HTTP (HyperText Transfer Protocol), 74,
    115
    anatomy of a servlet, 225–228
    servlets, dispatching, 176
HTTP servers:
    portability of, 10
    sending information of, 222
HTTPServlet, 226
HTTP sites, security of, 224
HyperLinks, implementing, 87

I
Idle thread, 452
IETF, and ports, 75
IIOP protocol, and CORBA-RMI integra-
    tion, 183
Image copy, 58
Image display, 58
Image processing, 63
Immersion, 64
Implementation details, 148
Implies method, 365–369
Indexed properties, 104
Indexing, of ResultSet, 194–195
Init parameters, 242–244
Input and output (I/O), 87–97
Input arguments, 156
Input parameters, security of, 358
InputStream, 206–207
instanceof operator, 154
Intel Corp., and Java Animation API, 57
Intellectual property, protecting, 241
Intensity of application environments,
    405–407
Interactive development environments,
    102
Interconnections, 125–127
Interface(s):
    Connection, 192–193
    EJBHome, 271–272, 277–278, 279–280
    EJBObject, 272, 281–282
    between Java and RDBMSs, 185–186
    Java Native Interface, 379–394
    look and feel of, 14

ResultSet, 193–194
Statement, 193
for thread creation, 295
Interface Definition Language (IDL):
in CORBA, 149
mapping to, 116
Interface layers, in three-tiered architectures, 123
Interface pointers, 381–382
Internationalization support, 4
Internet:
file I/O and, 95
networking principles of, 74, 76
placing orders, 260
Internet Engineering Task Force (IETF), 74
Internet Shopping Cart, 95
Interrupt service routines (ISRs), 451
Introspection, 101, 105, 108–110
InvalidateSessionServlet.java example, 259
IP address 127.0.0.1, 82
isAlive( ) method, 308
isDirectory( ) method, 89
ISO, and Java, 9
IT stovepipe, 116–117

J
Java:
and application programming, 477–478
corporate intranet use of, 3–4
design goals of, 2–3
input and output, 87–97
language safety features of, 336–337
and networking principle, 76
paradigm shift to, 470–471
RDBMSs, interfaces with, 185
as server platform, 222
simplicity of, 474–475
and systems-level programming, 475, 477
universality of, 410–411
Java Advanced Imaging, 63
Java Animation API, 57, 62
Java APIs, 444–446
licensing of, 55–56

Java Application Environment, 423–424
JavaArchive (JAR) files, 349–351
java.awt.datatransfer.Clipboard class, 40
java.awt.MenuShortcut, 35
java.awt.Toolkit.getSystemClipboard( )
method, 41
JavaBeans, 6, 99–113. *See also* Enterprise JavaBeans
as aggregates, 113
component model, 100–101
customization of, 111–112
design goal of, 99
event mechanism, 103
Glasgow specification, 112–113
integration of, 14
Java RMI of, 62
and JDBC 2.0, 217
manipulation of, 101–102
platforms, 124
properties of, 103–105
serialization methods, 112
servlet beans, 244–247
and Swing set components, 47
javac, 382–383
JavaCard, 9, 423–424
JavaChips, 336
Java City, 53–54
building recipe for, 66–70
implementation of, 63–66
Venn diagram of, 65
Java Commerce, 473
Java Compatibility Kit (JCK), 413–414
Java Core Refraction API, 105
Java Cryptography Extension (JCE), 333, 370–375
example code, 371–375
Java Database Connectivity (JDBC), 116, 141–142, 185–220
Java Developer's Kit (JDK) 1.0, 4, 414, 416
and security, 339, 341, 376
Java Developer's Kit 1.1, 4, 6, 13
AWT specification, 38–39
core classes, 416
data transfer, 37, 50
lightweight user interface, 43

Java Developer's Kit 1.1 (*Continued*):
  and native OS, 411
  printing, 14, 27–28
  reflection, 105
  RMI, 183
  scrolling, 30
  and security, 339, 341, 376
Java Dynamic Management Kit (JDMK), 473
Java Electronic Commerce Framework (JECF), 10
Java Enterprise APIs, 116
  and servlets, 259–265
  use of, 139–143
Java foundation classes (JFCs), 6, 14
javah program, 382–383
JAVA IDL, 116, 139–140
java.io hierarchies, 76
Java just-in-time (JIT) compilers, 336, 448
Java-Kernel, 448–450
java.lang.reflect package, 105
Java Media, 53–57
  design, 54–57
  implementation of, 63–66
  overview of, 57–63
  usability of, 55–56
Java Media Framework (JMF), 59–60
  package hierarchy, 61
Java method signatures, 385
Java naming and directory interface (JNDI), 11, 217, 276
Java Native Interface (JNI), 140, 151, 379–394
  error handling, 391
  Java calling native methods, 381–384
  Java class fields and methods access, 389–390
  Java object data access, 387–389
  native methods invoking Java, 391–393
java.net hierarchies, 76
JavaOS, 10, 425, 442–457
  architecture, 444–448
  audio support of, 435
  device drivers, 453–454
  filesystem functionality of, 451
  future of, 465–466

and the JavaVM, 443
monitors, 452
NCRP support of, 462–463
networking protocols of, 454–455
as an operating system, 457
and other platforms, 456–457
performance, 448
portability of, 445–448
printing, 456
processor scheduling, 451–453
serial port of, 434
storage of, in FlashRAM, 431–432
thread management, 451–452
and virtual memory, 453
windowing and graphics subsystem, 455–456
Java platform, 4–9, 57
JavaPOS APIs, 454
Java RMI (Remote Method Invocation), 62, 116, 139–141, 145–149
  callbacks and, 164–168
  client/server example, 155–164
  versus CORBA, 149–151
  CORBAservices, integration with, 183
  design goals, 151–152
  distributed programming with, 154–155
  in the future, 183–184
  garbage collection of, 154
  objects as arguments, 168–171
  and Object Serialization, 179–183
  polymorphism, 171–176
  security of, 352
  and servlet API, 176–179
  and system architecture, 152–154
Java runtime box, 445
Java runtime environment (JRE), 5, 7, 8. *See also* Runtime environment
Java security, 331–378. *See also* Security
java.security.AccessController, 354–355
java.security.CodeSource, 364
java.security.Permission class, 353
java.security.Policy, 364
java.security.ProtectionDomain, 364
java.security.SecureClassLoader, 364–365

JavaServer, 10
Java Share, 60–62
Java Sound Engine, 60
JavaSpaces, 10, 145–146, 184
Java Speech, 62–63
JavaStation, 425–442
    future of, 464–465
    goal of, 425–426
    and Network Computer Reference
        Profile, 442
JavaStation "brick" model, 426–436
    audio output of, 435
    CPU, 428
    memory, 428–432
    motherboard, 428
    networking of, 434–435
    peripheral devices of, 435–436
    video in, 432–434
JavaStation "tower" model, 436–441
    audio, 440
    CPU, 436–437
    DHCP, 440–441
    enclosure, 436
    memory, 438
    motherboard, 436–437
    networking, 439–440
    OBP, 440–441
    video, 439
Java Telephony API, 62, 473
Java Threads, *see* Threads
Java 2, 4–7
    and compatible branding, 414
    defining policy, 344
    Drag-and-Drop, 37, 50
    Java Sound libraries, 68–69
    Java 2D class hierarchy, 58
    Keytool and jarsigners, 351
    and native methods, 411
    performance improvements, 6–7
    and security, 333, 339, 340–341, 351,
        369, 378
    stopping threads, 306
Java 2D, 14, 51, 58
    class hierarchy, 58
    features of, 70–71
    for multimedia productions, 70

Java 3D, 58–59
    for multimedia productions, 71
Java types, 195–198, 204, 386
JavaVM (Java Virtual Machine):
    compatibility branding of, 413–414,
        474
    gatekeeping role of, 335
    and JavaOS, 443
    and name mapping, 382, 384
Java Web Server, 228, 233–235
    performance of, 235
    thread safety, 233–234
Jcomponent class, 47
JDBC (Java Database Connectivity), 116,
        141–142, 185–220
    architecture of, 187–189
    features of, 191–204
    use of, 189, 189–191
JDBC 2.0, 216–220
JDK, *see* Java Developer's Kits; Java 2
JFCs, *see* Java foundation classes
Jini, 11, 483–484
JoinThr.java, 297–299

K

Kernels, 448
Keyboard accelerators, 47
Keyboard equivalents, 35–36

L

Latency, 148
Legacy systems:
    data bus interface with, 136–139
    and Enterprise JavaBeans, 270,
        288–289
    integration of, 136–139
    Network Computer support of, 408
Legacy wrappers, 151
Libraries, 293
    Java Native Interface, 7, 379–394
    thread-safe, 328
Licensing Java APIs, 55–56
Listener methods, 18, 21
Live content, 87
Locks, 293–294
    versus monitors, 314

Logic, application:
  in client/server systems, 118
  for failure recovery, 147
  in three-tiered systems, 121
LONGVARBINARY, 204, 205, 207
LONGVARCHAR, 204, 205, 207
Look and feel, choosing, 49–50

M

MacOS, 56
MalformedURLException, 82, 83
Management, role in move to three-
    tiered architecture, 134–135
Media content factories and handlers,
    60
Media objects, synchronization of,
    58–59
Media players, 69–70
  construction and control, 60
Media types, HotJava support of, 462
Memory management, and Network
    Computers, 415–416
Memory management unit (MMU),
    449–450
Menus:
  accelerators, 35–36
  popup, 32–33
  shortcuts, 35–36
messaging architectures, 478–480
Method(s):
  event, 16
  getter and setter, 103–104
  names of, 156
  native methods access to, 389–390
Method class, 105–106
Micro-kernel, 448
microSPARC-II chip, 428
MIME (Multipurpose Internet Mail
    Extension) notation, 38, 39
M x N interconnections, 125–126
Model, 47
Model-view-controller (MVC) concept,
    47–49
Modifier class, 105, 107
Modifier keys, 35–36
Modula-3 Network Objects system, 151

Monitors, 313–318
  JavaOS use of, 452–453
Monitors.java example, 315–317
Monoliths, 116–117
  data availability of, 126
  tightly coupled, 118–119
Mouseless operation, 14, 33–36
MPEG sequences, 64–65
Multicast invocation, 153
Multichannel rendering, 60
Multimedia operations:
  portability of, 56
  reusability of, 56–57
  usability of, 55–56
MultiThreaded Server.java example, 80
Multithreading, 146. *See also* Threads
Multitiered applications, *see* Five-tiered
    architectures; N-tiered architec-
    tures; Three-tiered application
    architecture
  and Sandbox policy, 348
MyBeanBeanInfo.java example, 110

N

Native environment, services of, 112
Native methods, 380
  avoiding, 411–412
  calls to JavaVM, 387–389
  code for, 383–384
  error handling from, 391
  invoking Java from, 391–393
  Java calls to, 381–384
  naming, 382, 384–385
  parameters of, 385–386
Navigation, mouseless, 33–36
Net components, for remote clients,
    159
NetPCs, 408–410
  legacy application support, 408
Netra j, 463–464
Network(s):
  clients, 74–75
  security of, 333
Network Computer(s), 395–424
  advantages of, 401–404
  application design for, 410–415

architectural neutrality of, 400
and boot servers, 418–419
and client size, 415–416
competitors of, 408–410
costs of, 399–400, 422–424
deployment of, 419–422
and FlashRAM, 419
implementations of, 398–399
in JavaStation, 426
and legacy applications, 408
longevity of, 403–404
management of, 417–422
market for, 404–407
native methods, avoiding, 411–412
network requirements of, 417
and the 100% Pure Java Initiative,
    412–413
security of, 400
standards-based platform, 397–398
standards of, 396–397
user interface, 414–415
Network Computer Reference Profile
    (NCRP), 396, 399
and JavaStation, 426, 442
software requirements of, 462–463
Network connections, closing, 79
Network extensible Window System
    (NeWS), 2
Network failures, 480–481
Network File System (NFS), 451
Networking, 73–97
general principles, 74–76
JavaOS support of, 454–455
and JavaStation "brick" model,
    434–435
and JavaStation "tower" model,
    439–440
Network limitations, and servlets,
    241–242
Network protocols, 77–78
NewProtocol.java example, 77–78
Nexus drivers, 447
notifyAll() method, 318–320
notify() method, 318–320
Novocaine method, 84
N-tiered architectures, 123, 209

NullPointerException, 21
NULL value, 195
NVRAM (non-volatile RAM), 432, 438

O
Oak, 147
Object(s):
collections of, 5
communication between, 77–78
distributed, 145
local versus remote, 154–155
location of, see Java RMI
as method arguments, 168–171
monitors for, 314–318
passing to native methods, 387–389
persistence of, 95
reference types, 388–389
serializing, 95–96
state of, 47
storage of, persistent, 179–180
transportation of, 181–183
Object aggregation, 112, 113
Object Delegation model, 112, 113
Object identifiers, 153
ObjectInputStream, 96
Object Management Group (OMG), map-
    ping to, 116
Object-oriented systems, 2. See also Java
    RMI
and polymorphism, 171–172
ObjectOutputStream, 96
Object registry specification, 112
Object Request Broker (ORB), 150
interfacing with, 116
Object serialization, 152, 179–183
OBP, 430–431, 440–441
ODBC (Microsoft), 186
100% Pure Java defined, 46
100% Pure Java Initiative, 412–413, 474
OpenBoot PROM, 430–431
OpenGL, 59, 71
Operating systems, 445–447. See also
    JavaOS
OrderEntry, 213–215
as a servlet, 260–265
OrderTest.java example, 284–285

OUT parameters, 205
Output Stream, 93

P

Package objects, 5
Page compilation, 248–250
Panel class, 43
Paradigm shift in computing industry,
    470–472
Parameters:
  input, security of, 358
  naming of, 385–386
paramtst.html example, 238
Paths, specifying, 89
pathSeparator, 89
PCs, desktop:
  costs of, annual, 395–396
  low-cost, 408–409
  as Network Computers, 400
Peer applications, for mouseless opera-
    tions, 34
Performance, 6–7
  of JavaServer, 235
  and native peers, 43
  and page compile, 249–250
Permission class, 353–354
Persistence:
  of bean properties, 103
  of components, 101
Personal Java, 7, 423–424, 466
phrase.jhtml example, 248–249
PhraseServlet2.java init() example,
    242–243
picoJava, 448, 465
PieOrderBean.java example, 282–283
PieOrderHome.java example, 279–280
PieOrderPK.java example, 280
PieSessionBean example, 272–274
PieSessionHome.java example, 271
PieTest.java example, 275–276
PlaceOrderServlet.java example, 263–265
Player applet, 67–68
  initiating, 69–70
  playback and response control, 70
Pluggable look and feel, 14, 47–50

Pointers, interface, 381–382, 385
Point of sales (POS) devices, 479
Point-to-point method invocation, *see*
    Java RMI
Policy file, for site security, 345–346
Polymorphism, remote, 171–176
popUp.java example, 32–33
Popup menus, 14, 32–33
Portability of multimedia, 56
Ports, 75–76
POSIX threads, 328–329
Precomputer-generated digital video
    sequences, 64–66
Prepared statements, 202–204
Primitive shapes, 70
Princeton's Safe Internet Programming
    Group, 376, 377
Printing, 14, 27–30, 456
PrintJob class, 28
Priority.java example, 309–311
Processing, local versus distributed,
    145–146
Process methods, 168
ProductManager, 210–212
Properties, 47, 103, 451, 460
  access to, 103
  of beans, 103–105
  bound, 105
  of components, 101
  constrained, 105
  design platform of, 103–104
  indexed, 104
PropertyChange event, 111
Property editors, 111–112
protection domains, 339–343
  extensibility of, 352–369
  in Java 2, 340–341, 369–370
  security policy for, 343–345
  for servlets, 351–352
Protocol handlers, 77, 457
Proxies, 152

Q

Query, 193–194
QuickTime VR, 64

R

Random access memory (RAM):
  of JavaStation "brick" model, 429
  of JavaStation "tower" model, 438
Readers, 95
ReadFile() method, 91
Reading data, *see* Input and output (I/O)
readObject() method, 97
Reentrant.java example, 317–318
Reference counters, 154
reflectInfo.java example, 106
Reflection, 101, 105–108, 109
  security of, 108
Registry, 157, 158
Relational database management system
      (RDBMS), 185
  adding value to, 207–216
  and Enterprise JavaBeans, 116, 143
  and URL, 192
Relational databases, interfacing with,
      116
Remote clients:
  connecting to, 81–82
  creating, 159–163
Remote interface, defining, 156
Remote memory management, 148
Remote method calls, 159
Remote Method Invocation, *see* Java RMI
Remote reference layer, 152, 153
Remote server, creating, 156–159
Replication strategies, 153
RepresentationClass classes, 38–39
Repurposed software, 56–57
req, 226
res, 226
ResultSet interface, 193–194, 217,
      218–219
ResultSetMetaData, 197
Return types, 156
Reusability, of multimedia applications,
      56–57
RMI, *see* Java RMI
RMI libraries, network support of, 76
RMI SecurityManager, 157
rmic, 152, 158–159

Rotation, 58
RowSets class, 217
Rows of data, 195
RPC (Remote Procedure Call), 148
RS-232 serial ports, 434
run() method, 141, 306
Runnable interface, 295–296
RunnableThr.java example, 296
Runtime containment, 112
Runtime environment, 345
  property editors in, 111
  setup of, 68–69

S

Sandbox policy, 347–349
Sbus, 427
Scalability, of distributed systems, 58,
      147
Scalar types, 387
Scene graphs, 58–59, 71
Scheduling, 292, 304–313
  processor, 451–453
  thread priority, 308–311
  and thread state, 304–307
Screen scraper, 136
Scrolling, 30–32, 47, 218–219
ScrollPane, 14
  container, 30–32
SecretKeyFactory, 373
Security:
  of applets, 239–240
  bugs in, 376–377
  of CGIs, 224
  and clipboards, 41
  and cryptography, 370–375
  and digital signatures, 350
  and event adapters, 24
  of executable content, 332
  of HotJava, 461
  of intellectual property, 241
  of JavaChips and Java JITs, 336
  of Java on the Web, 332
  of Java 2, 6, 340–341
  with language safety features, 336–337
  of Network Computers, 400

Security *(Continued)*:
  for networked environments, 146
  of OS, 351
  physical, 331
  with protection domains, 339–343,
    369–370
  of reflection classes, 108
  of RMI, 183
  and serializing objects, 181
  of servers, 240–241
  of servlets, 234–235
  and session tracking, 257–258
  Sun Web sites for, 377
  with the Verifier, 338–339
  of Web servers, 87
Security classes, 353–365
SecurityManager, 340–341
SelectPiesServlet.java example,
  261–262
Self-discovery of components, 101
Serial devices, connection of, 434–435
Serializable objects, 95–96
Serialization API, 5, 179–183
Server process, 78–79
Servers, 74–75
  callbacks from, 164–168
  multithreaded, 80–81
  naming, 157, 158, 160
  security of, 240–241
  stub/skeleton layer and, 152–153, 159
Server-side environments:
  object-oriented, 176–179
  security of, 351–352
Server-side includes, 236
Services:
  to network clients, 74–75
  protection domains for, 352
  protocol, 112
Servlet directory, 228
ServletRequest, 226–227
ServletResponse, 226–227
Servlets, 176–179, 221–266
  advantages of, 222–224
  aliases for, 229–230, 232, 233
  versus applets, 239–242
  beans, 244–247

  business logic, protection of, 241
  core, 236
  download times of, 241–242
  ease of development, 241
  Enterprise APIs, 259–265
  extensions, 235
  for HTML pages, 224–225
  an HTTP servlet, 225–228
  init parameters, 242–244
  installation of, 228–232
  page compilation, 248–250
  protection domain of, 351–352
  as proxies, 240, 241
  security of, 234–235
  servlet beans, 244–247
  session tracking, 256–259
  templates, 250–255
  for user input, 236–242
SessionCountServlet.java example,
  256–257
Session tracking, 256–259
SetChoiceList.java example, 85
Set objects, 5
Setter methods, 103–104
Settop boxes, 4
setXXX() methods, 204
Shadowing, 430
shortCut.java example, 36
Signed JAR files, 349–351
Simple.java example, 382
Single inline memory modules (SIMMs),
  428, 429
Sites, dynamically generated, 221
Skeletons, 152–153, 158–159
sleep() method, 306
SmartCards, 464
  and JavaCard API, 9
SMTP (Simple Mail Transfer Protocol),
  75
Sockets, 75–76
  network, 76
Software:
  agile, 124–125
  race conditions, 17, 18
  reuse of, 56–57, 135, 260
  stand-alone, 447

Solaris, 464
    native threads on, 328
Sound capabilities, *see* Audio
SPARCstation-4 systems, 426
Speech recognition, 62–63
Splines:
    with Java 2D, 58
    paths of, 71
SQL (Structured Query Language),
        186–187
    and mapping between Java types,
        195–197, 204
    writing the SQL, 198–201
SQL92 Entry Level, 186–187
Starbase, 59
Statement interface, 193
Statements:
    callable, 204–205
    prepared, 202–204
Static compilers, 476
stop( ) method, 306
Streams, reading and writing to, 95–97
String constants, 6
String messages, 168
Strings, 336
    and getParameterValues, 238–239
    for native method calls, 384
Structured Query Language, *see* SQL
Stubs, 152–153, 158–159
    downloading, 151
    and polymorphism, 176
Stub/Skeleton layer, 152
Sun Labs, RMI development at, 147
Swing set, 14, 46–50
    components of, 47, 48
    and JavaBeans integration, 47
    pluggable look and feel, 47–50
Synchronization, 59, 292, 313–327
SystemColor class, 25
System.out.print( ) method, 93
Systems-level programming, 475, 477

T
Tab key, 34
Table objects, 5
TCP/IP, 74

Telephone services, API for, 62, 473
Telnet, and HotJava, 463
Templates, 250–255
10baseT, 434
Terminal applications, 417
Test policy file example, 369
Test.java example, 367–368
TestPermissionCollection example,
        366–367
TestPermission.java example, 365–366
texasButton.java example, 44–45
texasTest.java example, 46
Text search, 319–326
Threads, 291–329
    acceptor, 233–234
    and condition variables, 318–326
    creating, 294–297
    daemon, 299–301
    dead, 306–307
    Green, 327–328
    groups of, 301–304
    handler, 233–234
    for incoming connections, 80
    interface pointers of, 381
    joining, 297–299
    monitors for, 313–318
    native, 328
    non-runnable, 305–306
    POSIX, 328–329
    priority of, 308–311
    runnable, 305
    scheduling of, 292, 304–313
    starting, 294–297
    state of, 304–307
    synchronization of, 292, 313–327,
        452–453
    system, 452
    and time slicing, 311–313
    user, 451–452
    and the volatile keyword, 326–327
3D APIs, 58–59
3D objects, 71
Three-tiered application architecture,
        120–123, 208. *See also* Network
        Computers
    building, 209–216

Three-tiered application architecture
(*Continued*):
change to, 133–135
client updates, 127
data availability of, 126–127
deployment of, 128–130
distribution of, 127
interconnection strategies, 125–127
legacy problems and, 132
legacy systems, integration of,
136–139
limits of, 130–133
maintenance of, 124–125
and the Sandbox policy, 348–349
updating, 124–125
3270 applications, 136
ThrGroup.java example, 303–304
Time management services, 59
TimeSliced.java example, 312–313
Time slicing, 311–313
Tiny AWT library, 455
Tooltips, 47
TooManyListenersException, 21
Training, for three-tiered systems, 133
Transaction process monitor (TPM), 116,
142–143
Transactions, 201–202
distributed, 217
Transferable interface, 37
Transient keyword, 96, 97
Translation, 58
Transport layer, 153
Trojan horses, 348, 476
Trusted systems, 335

U
UIFactory, 50
Unicast application example, 155–164
Unicast method invocation, *see* Java RMI
Unicast registration, 21
UnicastRemoteObject class, 155
Uniform resource locators, *see* URLs
Unipack, 427–428
UNIX, 56
Java implementation of, 444
URLConnection object, 86–87

URLs, 82–87, 192
constructing, 82–84
reading from, 84–87
servlets, loading from, 228–229
valid versus invalid, 83
Usability, of multimedia, 55–56
Users:
input from, 236–242
interface framework for, 43–46
interface for remote methods,
161–162
presentation to, 121
sending to other sites, 87

V
Validation, of property changes, 105
VARBINARY, 204
VARCHAR, 204
Variables, and volatile keyword, 326–327
Vectors, 166–168
Verifier, 338–339
security bugs in, 376
Versioning, 5
Version skew, 125
Vertical markets, APIs for, 472–473
Video:
in JavaStation "brick" model, 432–434
in JavaStation "tower" model, 439
synchronization of, 64
View, 47
Virtual function table, 381
Virtual memory, 453
Virtual worlds, 64
Virus checkers, 346–347
Viruses, 332
Void pointers, 186
Volatile keyword, 326–327
VRML (Virtual Reality Modeling Language), 71

W
wasNull() method, 195
Wave table synthesis, 60
Web browsers, 54, 64, 458–460
launching, 69–70
Web page builders, 102

Web servers, 75
   extensions for, 235
While loops, 195, 202
Wild cards, 345
Windowing, in JavaOS, 455–456
Windows, Java implementation of, 444
Windows95, desktop color selection, 24
Wizards, 112
Workstation Java platform, 4–7. *See also*
   Java 2
World Wide Web (WWW), 221
   and CGIs, 222–224
   executable content on, 332
Wrappers:
   legacy, 151
   for security, 358
Write capability, of applets, 86

write( ) method, 93
Write Once, Run Anywhere, 3, 222, 334,
   476
   and Enterprise JavaBeans, 270
   security of, 333
Writers, 95
WriteServer.java example, 86
Writing data, *see* Input and output (I/O)

X

XGL, 59
X/Open SQL Call Level Interface (CLI)
   standard, 116
X-terminals, 398–399

Y

yield( ) method, 313

Sun Microsystems, Inc.
Binary Code License Agreement

READ THE TERMS OF THIS AGREEMENT AND ANY PROVIDED SUPPLEMENTAL LICENSE TERMS (COLLECTIVELY "AGREEMENT") CAREFULLY BEFORE OPENING THE SOFTWARE MEDIA PACKAGE. BY OPENING THE SOFTWARE MEDIA PACKAGE, YOU AGREE TO THE TERMS OF THIS AGREEMENT. IF YOU ARE ACCESSING THE SOFTWARE ELECTRONICALLY, INDICATE YOUR ACCEPTANCE OF THESE TERMS BY SELECTING THE "ACCEPT" BUTTON AT THE END OF THIS AGREEMENT. IF YOU DO NOT AGREE TO ALL THESE TERMS, PROMPTLY RETURN THE UNUSED SOFTWARE TO YOUR PLACE OF PURCHASE FOR A REFUND OR, IF THE SOFTWARE IS ACCESSED ELECTRONICALLY, SELECT THE "DECLINE" BUTTON AT THE END OF THIS AGREEMENT.

1. **License to Use.** Sun grants you a non-exclusive and non-transferable license for the internal use only of the accompanying software and documentation and any error corrections provided by Sun (collectively "Software"), by the number of users and the class of computer hardware for which the corresponding fee has been paid.

2. **Restrictions.** Software is confidential and copyrighted. Title to Software and all associated intellectual property rights is retained by Sun and/or its licensors. Except as specifically authorized in any Supplemental License Terms, you may not make copies of Software, other than a single copy of Software for archival purposes. Unless enforcement is prohibited by applicable law, you may not modify, decompile, reverse engineer Software. Software is not designed or licensed for use in on-line control of aircraft, air traffic, aircraft navigation or aircraft communications; or in the design, construction, operation or maintenance of any nuclear facility. You warrant that you will not use Software for these purposes. You may not publish or provide the results of any benchmark or comparison tests run on Software to any third party without the prior written consent of Sun. No right, title or interest in or to any trademark, service mark, logo or trade name of Sun or its licensors is granted under this Agreement.

3. **Limited Warranty.** Sun warrants to you that for a period of ninety (90) days from the date of purchase, as evidenced by a copy of the receipt, the media on which Software is furnished (if any) will be free of defects in materials and workmanship under normal use. Except for the foregoing, Software is provided "AS IS". Your exclusive remedy and Sun's entire liability under this limited warranty will be at Sun's option to replace Software media or refund the fee paid for Software.

4. **Disclaimer of Warranty.** UNLESS SPECIFIED IN THIS AGREEMENT, ALL EXPRESS OR IMPLIED CONDITIONS, REPRESENTATIONS AND WARRANTIES, INCLUDING ANY IMPLIED WARRANTY OF MERCHANTABILITY, FITNESS FOR A PARTICULAR PURPOSE, OR NON-INFRINGEMENT, ARE DISCLAIMED, EXCEPT TO THE EXTENT THAT THESE DISCLAIMERS ARE HELD TO BE LEGALLY INVALID.

5. **Limitation of Liability.** TO THE EXTENT NOT PROHIBITED BY LAW, IN NO EVENT WILL SUN OR ITS LICENSORS BE LIABLE FOR ANY LOST REVENUE, PROFIT OR DATA, OR FOR SPECIAL, INDIRECT, CONSEQUENTIAL, INCIDEN-TAL OR PUNITIVE DAMAGES, HOWEVER CAUSED REGARDLESS OF THE THEORY OF LIABILITY, ARISING OUT OF OR RELATED TO THE USE OF OR INABILITY TO USE SOFTWARE, EVEN IF SUN HAS BEEN ADVISED OF THE POSSIBILITY OF SUCH DAMAGES. In no event will Sun's liability to you, whether in contract, tort (including negligence), or otherwise, exceed the amount paid by you for Software under this Agreement. The foregoing limitations will apply even if the above stated warranty fails of its essential purpose.

6. **Termination.** This Agreement is effective until terminated. You may terminate this Agreement at any time by destroying all copies of Software. This Agreement will terminate immediately without notice from Sun if you fail to comply with any provision of this Agreement. Upon Termination, you must destroy all copies of Software.

7. **Export Regulations.** All Software and technical data delivered under this Agreement are subject to US export control laws and may be subject to export or import regulations in other countries. You agree to comply strictly with all such laws and regulations and acknowledge that you have the responsibility to obtain such licenses to export, re-export, or import as may be required after delivery to you.

8. **U.S. Government Restricted Rights**. Use, duplication, or disclosure by the U.S. Government is subject to restrictions set forth in this Agreement and as pro-vided in DFARS 227.7202-1 (a) and 227.7202-3(a) (1995), DFARS 252.227-7013 (c)(1)(ii)(Oct 1988), FAR 12.212 (a) (1995), FAR 52.227-19 (June 1987), or FAR 52.227-14(ALT III) (June 1987), as applicable.

9. **Governing Law.** Any action related to this Agreement will be governed by Cali-fornia law and controlling U.S. federal law. No choice of law rules of any jurisdic-tion will apply.

10. **Severability.** If any provision of this Agreement is held to be unenforceable, this Agreement will remain in effect with the provision omitted, unless omission would frustrate the intent of the parties, in which case this Agreement will imme-diately terminate.

11. **Integration.** This Agreement is the entire agreement between you and Sun relat-ing to its subject matter. It supersedes all prior or contemporaneous oral or writ-ten communications, proposals, representations and warranties and prevails over any conflicting or additional terms of any quote, order, acknowledgment, or other communication between the parties relating to its subject matter during the term of this Agreement. No modification of this Agreement will be binding, unless in writing and signed by an authorized representative of each party.

For inquiries please contact: Sun Microsystems, Inc. 901 San Antonio Road, Palo Alto, California 94303

Java™ Development Kit Version 1.2 Supplemental License Terms

These supplemental terms ("Supplement") add to the terms of the Binary Code License Agreement ("Agreement"). Capitalized terms not defined herein shall have the same meanings ascribed to them in the Agreement. The Supplement terms shall supersede any inconsistent or conflicting terms in the Agreement.

1. **Limited License Grant.** Sun grants to you a non-exclusive, non-transferable limited license to use the Software without fee for evaluation of the Software and for development of Java™ applets and applications provided that you: (i) may not re-distribute the Software in whole or in part, either separately or included with a product. (ii) may not create, or authorize your licensees to create additional classes, interfaces, or subpackages that are contained in the "java" or "sun" packages or similar as specified by Sun in any class file naming convention; and (iii) agree to the extent Programs are developed which utilize the Windows 95/98 style graphical user interface or components contained therein, such applets or applications may only be developed to run on a Windows 95/98 or Windows NT platform. Refer to the Java Runtime Environment Version 1.2 binary code license (http://java.sun.com/products/JDK/1.2/index.html) for the availability of runtime code which may be distributed with Java applets and applications.

2. **Java Platform Interface.** In the event that Licensee creates an additional API(s) which: (i) extends the functionality of a Java Environment; and, (ii) is exposed to third party software developers for the purpose of developing additional software which invokes such additional API, Licensee must promptly publish broadly an accurate specification for such API for free use by all developers.

3. **Trademarks and Logos.** This Agreement does not authorize Licensee to use any Sun name, trademark or logo. Licensee acknowledges as between it and Sun that Sun owns the Java trademark and all Java-related trademarks, logos and icons including the Coffee Cup and Duke ("Java Marks") and agrees to comply with the Java Trademark Guidelines at http://java.sun.com/trademarks.html.

4. **High Risk Activities.** Notwithstanding Section 2, with respect to high risk activities, the following language shall apply: the Software is not designed or intended for use in on-line control of aircraft, air traffic, aircraft navigation or aircraft communications; or in the design, construction, operation or maintenance of any nuclear facility. Sun disclaims any express or implied warranty of fitness for such uses.

What's on the CD-ROM?

Java City Demo   Java City is a Java Media–based demonstration. This example uses many parts of the Java Media framework to show how multimedia can be used in Java programs.

Example source code from book   All of the examples used in the book are included on the CD-ROM.

Java™ 2   The long-awaited major release of Sun's Java™ Software Development Kit is here. With the Java™ 2 platform, Sun clearly defines what constitutes the core Java technology platform for the enterprise.

Java resources Web page   A convenient Web page is presented for ease in finding critical Java information found on the Web.

Hardware Requirements

The CD-ROM will work on any system that understands the Rock Ridge format.

Using the Software

All of the packages contained on the CD-ROM have a README file associated with their use.

User Assistance and Information

The software accompanying this book is being provided as is without warranty or support of any kind. Should you require basic installation assistance, or if your media is defective, please call our product support number at (212) 850-6194 weekdays between 9 AM and 4 PM Eastern Standard Time. Or, we can be reached via e-mail at: wprtusw@wiley.com.

To place additional orders or to request information about other Wiley products, please call (800) 879-4539.

Java 2

Copyright 1998 Sun Microsystems, Inc., 901 San Antonio Road, Palo Alto, CA 94303-4900 USA. All rights reserved. Java, JavaBeans, JDK and other Java-related marks are trademarks or registered trademarks of Sun Microsystems, Inc. in the U.S. and other countries.

Use of this software is subject to the Binary Code License terms and conditions found in this book and on the CD-ROM. Read the license carefully. By opening this package, you are agreeing to be bound by the terms and conditions of this license from Sun Microsystems, Inc.

Restricted Rights:

Use, duplication or disclosure by the United States Government is subject to the restrictions as set forth in the Rights in Technical Data and Computer Software Clauses in DFARS 252.227-7013(c) (1) (ii) and FAR 52.227-19 (c) (2) as applicable.